Preparing Today's Students
for Tomorrow's Jobs in
Metropolitan America

THE CITY IN THE TWENTY-FIRST CENTURY
Eugenie L. Birch and Susan M. Wachter, Series Editors

A complete list of books in the series is available
from the publisher.

Preparing Today's Students for Tomorrow's Jobs in Metropolitan America

Edited by

Laura W. Perna

PENN

UNIVERSITY OF PENNSYLVANIA PRESS

PHILADELPHIA

Published by
University of Pennsylvania Press
Philadelphia, Pennsylvania 19104-4112
www.upenn.edu/pennpress

Printed in the United States of America on acid-free paper

10 9 8 7 6 5 4 3 2 1

Library of Congress Cataloging-in-Publication Data

Preparing today's students for tomorrow's jobs in metropolitan America /
edited by Laura W. Perna. — 1st ed.
    p. cm. — (The city in the twenty-first century)
    Includes bibliographical references and index.
    ISBN 978-0-8122-4453-3 (hardcover : alk. paper)
1. College graduates—Employment—United States.   2. Vocational
guidance—United States.   I. Perna, Laura W.   II. Series: City in the
twenty-first century book series.
HD6278.U5P74 2013
331.11'4450973—dc23

                                                    2012018383

CONTENTS

Introduction
Laura W. Perna   1

I. DEFINING SUCCESS IN PREPARING
INDIVIDUALS FOR WORK

Chapter 1. Tinker, Tailor, Soldier, Sailor . . . A Public Policy Agenda
on Today's Students and Tomorrow's Jobs
Alan Ruby   19
Chapter 2. Assessing and Measuring Workforce Readiness: A Discussion
toward the Development of a Universal and Valid Measure
Katherine M. Barghaus, Eric T. Bradlow,
Jennifer McMaken, and Samuel H. Rikoon   37
Chapter 3. Work-Based Learning: Initiatives and Impact
Bridget N. O'Connor   57

II. THE ROLE OF DIFFERENT EDUCATIONAL PROVIDERS
IN PREPARING STUDENTS FOR WORK

Chapter 4. Improving Career and Technical Education
in the United States
Nancy Hoffman   75
Chapter 5. Postsecondary Education and Economic Opportunity
Anthony P. Carnevale, Nicole Smith, and Jeff Strohl   93
Chapter 6. Community College Occupational Degrees:
Are They Worth It?
Thomas Bailey and Clive R. Belfield   121

Chapter 7. The Conundrum of Profit-Making Institutions
in Higher Education
    William G. Tierney   149

III. IMPLICATIONS FOR INSTITUTIONAL
PRACTICE AND PUBLIC POLICY

Chapter 8. Strengthening the Education and Workforce Connection:
What Types of Research Are Required to Determine How Well Career
Pathways Programs Prepare Students for College and Careers?
    Lashawn Richburg-Hayes, Michael Armijo, and Lisa Merrill   177
Chapter 9. Conceiving Regional Pathways to Prosperity Systems
    Ronald F. Ferguson   203
Chapter 10. Aligning Secondary and Postsecondary
Credentialization with Economic Development Strategy,
or "If Low Educational Attainment = Poor Metropolitan
Competitiveness, What Can Be Done about It?"
    Laura Wolf-Powers and Stuart Andreason   224
Chapter 11. Creating Effective Education and Workforce Policies
for Metropolitan Labor Markets in the United States
    Harry J. Holzer   245

Conclusion
    Laura W. Perna   260

Notes   275
List of References   287
List of Contributors   315
Index   321
Acknowledgments   333

Introduction

Laura W. Perna

Although disagreeing about how much of an increase is required, most scholars agree that the United States must raise the educational attainment of its population in order to meet the knowledge requirements of future jobs (see Zumeta 2010 for a discussion of this debate). In *Help Wanted: Projections of Jobs and Education Requirements through 2018*, Anthony Carnevale, Nicole Smith, and Jeff Strohl (2010) attempt to quantify this need. They project that, by 2018, about two-thirds (63 percent) of all jobs (including both new and replacement jobs) will require at least some postsecondary education or training, up from 59 percent in 2008 and just 28 percent in 1973 (Carnevale, Smith, and Strohl 2010). Their projections further suggest that "most job openings for people with a high school education or less will be low-wage jobs, and many of these will be part-time or transition jobs" (Carnevale 2010: vii). Carnevale, Smith, and Strohl demonstrate in their chapter in this volume that workers with postsecondary education will have access to a wide range of occupations, whereas workers with no more than a high school diploma will be concentrated in blue collar, sales and office support, and food and personal services occupations.

Rather than focusing on the magnitude of the required increase in college degrees, other reports call for better "alignment" between education and workforce needs, emphasizing the need for greater attention to the correspondence between what workers know and can do and the knowledge and skills required to perform available jobs. In *Degrees for What Jobs?*, the National Governors Association (2011) concludes from its review of survey and other data that "businesses and states are not getting the talent they want—and students and job seekers are not getting the jobs they want" (p. 8). The report recommends that state leaders take "steps to strengthen universities and colleges as agents of workforce preparation and sources of more [economic] opportunity, more growth, and more competitive advantage" (p. 3).

Along the same lines, in its December 2009 report, the Springboard Project, a Business Roundtable Commission, stresses the need to improve education and skills, stating, "The American workforce has reached a critical juncture; even when the unemployment rate declines, new jobs will require higher levels of education and skills than many of the jobs of the past. Our workforce increasingly finds itself lacking the skills and education demanded by the growing needs and challenges of today's global marketplace" (p. 5). Nearly two-thirds (61 percent) of employers responding to a survey by the Springboard Project agreed that finding "qualified workers to fill vacancies at their companies" is difficult (p. 5). Similarly, the Society for Human Resource Management (2008) questions the preparation of U.S. workers for the highly skilled jobs that are characteristic of an increasingly competitive global workforce.

Drawing from its work with leaders of education, business, government, and philanthropy, the Business-Higher Education Forum (2011) also identifies the lack of alignment between the interests, education, and training of workers and employer needs, stating, "Critical disjunctions exist between what is taught and learned in postsecondary education and the skills that are in high demand in the workplace. Another mismatch exists between student interest in high-growth jobs and employer demands for workers who can fill those jobs. Moreover, even in fields where student interest is in equilibrium with workforce demands, students may be underprepared for jobs in those fields" (p. 4).

As measured by degree completion, the mismatch between the educational qualifications of the population and the educational requirements of current and future jobs is particularly dramatic in many of our nation's metropolitan areas. As one example, Figure I.1 shows that in Philadelphia, the share of the population that is educationally qualified for unskilled jobs substantially exceeds the share of unskilled jobs (jobs that require no more than a high school education, 53 percent versus 38 percent). In contrast, the share of the population that is educationally qualified for professional jobs (jobs that require at least a bachelor's degree) is lower than the share of pro-

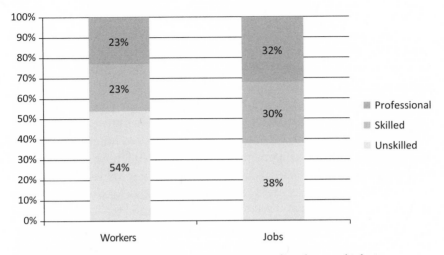

Figure I.1. Mismatch of educational requirements of workers and jobs in Philadelphia. *Source:* Shorr 2011. Data from: 2007–9 American Community Survey Public Use Microdata Set; Economic Modeling Specialists, Inc.: Complete Employment—4th Quarter 2010.

fessional jobs available (24 percent versus 32 percent). Only 24 percent of Philadelphia's population is educationally qualified for skilled jobs (jobs that require some postsecondary education but less than a bachelor's degree), even though skilled jobs represent 30 percent of all jobs.

Philadelphia is not the only metropolitan area that is experiencing this type of mismatch. The Brookings Institution's (2010) *The State of Metropolitan America* report offers a "demographic typology" to categorize the 100 largest metropolitan areas based not on region but on measures of population growth, population diversity, and educational attainment. The seven categories are: diverse giant (n = 9), skilled anchor (n = 19), next frontier (n = 9), new heartland (n = 19), industrial core (n = 18), border growth (n = 11), and mid-sized magnet (n = 16). The education and employment challenges vary across and within these groupings. For instance, most of the "skilled anchors" (seventeen of the nineteen) metro areas are located in the Northeast and Midwest and "have made the difficult transition to service-based economies" from manufacturing and shipping (p. 32). These skilled anchors are also characterized by large numbers of medical and higher education institutions as well as less racial/ethnic diversity than other large metropolitan areas. Although one might expect these skilled anchors to be characterized by the availability of more and higher paying jobs in the service sector, skilled anchor cities like Philadelphia, Baltimore, Boston, and Rochester face high urban unemployment.

In metropolitan America, unemployment rates are especially high for young adults and people of color. In 2009 in a number of cities nationwide, the unemployment rate for individuals age sixteen to nineteen was more than twice as high as the citywide average. Illustrating this pattern, in the city of Cleveland the unemployment rate for youth (age sixteen to nineteen), at 32.4 percent, was substantially higher than the city average (18.8 percent) (Bureau of Labor Statistics 2009a). In Dallas the unemployment rate for youth (35.2 percent) was more than three times as high as the citywide average (10.7 percent). Unemployment rates are also typically higher for Blacks than for others. For instance, in the city of Charlotte, the average annual unemployment rate in 2009 was 17.2 percent for Blacks compared with an overall rate of 12.4 percent. Similarly, in the city of Indianapolis, the average annual unemployment rate was 22 percent for Blacks but 11.4 percent overall (Bureau of Labor Statistics 2009a).

"Before the worst of the recession set in," employment rates for college-educated workers were fairly uniform across the 100 largest metropolitan areas, but varied considerably across metro areas for workers with lower levels of education (Brookings Institution Metropolitan Policy Program 2010: 112). In five of the nation's largest metropolitan areas, fewer than 60 percent of adults who had no more than a high school diploma were employed (Stockton, Calif.; McAllen, Tex.; Fresno, Calif.; Detroit-Warren, Mich.; Bakersfield, Calif.). Higher levels of education also provided some cushion from the impact of the Great Recession on unemployment. Between December 2007 and 2009 unemployment rates nationwide increased from 2.0 percent to 4.7 percent for college graduates, but from 4.7 percent to 10.6 percent for high school graduates (Brookings Institution Metropolitan Policy Program 2010). This pattern plays out in individual metropolitan areas. The inverse relationship between educational attainment and unemployment is especially dramatic in such cities as Detroit. In Detroit the average annual unemployment rate in 2009 for adults age twenty-five and older ranged from 6.2 percent for those with at least a bachelor's degree, to 18.1 percent for those with some college, to 26.7 percent for those with a high school diploma, to 38.8 percent for those without a high school diploma (Bureau of Labor Statistics 2009b). Similarly, in Baltimore average annual unemployment rates ranged from 4.9 percent for those with at least a bachelor's degree, to 6.8 percent for those with some college, to 14 percent for those with a high school diploma, to 26.2 percent for those without a high school diploma (Bureau of Labor Statistics 2009b).

Beyond employment rates, raising the level of educational attainment is associated with a number of economic and non-economic benefits for individual workers and urban areas more generally (Baum, Ma, and Payea 2010). In 2008 median earnings for full-time workers nationwide age twenty-five and older were considerably higher for those whose highest degree was a bachelor's degree ($55,700) or associate's degree ($42,000) than for those whose highest degree was a high school diploma ($33,800) (Baum, Ma, and Payea 2010). The national pattern is evident in individual metropolitan areas. As one example, in Philadelphia median earnings increase with the level of educational attainment, rising from $28,200 for those who have no more than a high school education, to $36,662 for those with some postsecondary education but less than a bachelor's degree, to $50,919 for those with at least a bachelor's degree (Shorr 2011).

Increased levels of educational attainment are also associated with greater job satisfaction, lower rates of poverty, better working conditions, improved health, and other individual benefits (Baum, Ma, and Payea 2010). As Carnevale, Smith, and Strohl illustrate in their chapter in this volume, postsecondary education has also become increasingly important to attaining a middle-class income. Society benefits from higher levels of educational attainment through increases in taxes paid, lower rates of dependence on social welfare programs, and greater civic and community engagement (Baum, Ma, and Payea 2010).

In February 2009, President Barack Obama alluded to the societal benefits of postsecondary education when he articulated the goal of having the United States "once again" lead the world in the educational attainment of its population:

> I ask every American to commit to at least one year or more of higher education or career training. This can be community college or a four-year school; vocational training or an apprenticeship. But whatever the training may be, every American will need to get more than a high

school diploma. And dropping out of high school is no longer an option. It's not just quitting on yourself, it's quitting on your country—and this country needs and values the talents of every American.

The importance of addressing the mismatch between the educational attainment of individuals and the educational requirements of jobs in metropolitan America is underscored by the size of these areas and the challenges that these areas are experiencing. The nation's 100 largest metropolitan areas are not only home to about two-thirds of the nation's population but also are growing at a faster rate than the rest of the nation (Brookings Institution Metropolitan Policy Program 2010). These large metropolitan areas are also on the front lines of several other national trends, including the racial/ethnic diversification of the population and gaps in educational attainment across groups (Brookings Institution Metropolitan Policy Program 2010).

In part because of immigration, the racial/ethnic diversity of the population of the United States has been increasing. In 2008, non-Whites represented one-third of the total U.S. population but half of children under the age of eighteen in the 100 largest metropolitan areas (Brookings Institution Metropolitan Policy Program 2010). The majority of the nation's multiracial population (68 percent), Blacks (74 percent), Hispanics (80 percent), and Asians (88 percent) reside in the nation's 100 largest metropolitan areas (Brookings Institution Metropolitan Policy Program 2010).

Attention to the racial/ethnic diversity of the population is particularly important given differences in educational attainment across groups. Educational attainment is lower for Blacks and Hispanics than for Whites and Asians, especially in the nation's large metropolitan areas (Brookings Institution Metropolitan Policy Program 2010). In 2008, the bachelor's degree attainment rate was 21 percentage points lower for Blacks and Hispanics in large metropolitan areas than for Whites and Asians (Brookings Institution Metropolitan Policy Program 2010).

The Challenges of Better Preparing Today's Students for Tomorrow's Jobs

Addressing the national mismatch between educational qualifications of workers and jobs is complicated by persistent low levels of educational attainment in many metropolitan areas. The definition and measurement of high school graduation rates are widely debated. Nonetheless, "a growing consensus has emerged that only about seven in 10 students are actually successfully finishing high school," considerably fewer than the commonly accepted 85 percent graduation rate (Swanson 2008). Moreover, average high school graduation rates mask the markedly lower rates for racial/ethnic minorities than for Whites, for boys than for girls, and for students from lower income families than for students from higher income families. High school graduation rates also tend to be lower for students attending urban schools than for those in rural and suburban high schools; on average, high school graduation rates are 15 percentage points lower in urban schools than in suburban high schools (Swanson 2008). High school graduation rates are more than 25 percentage points lower in the urban segments than in the suburban segments of twelve of the fifty largest metropolitan areas (Swanson 2008).

High school graduation rates are even lower in the nation's largest urban centers (Swanson 2008).[1] Using the Cumulative Promotion Index (CPI) to calculate graduation rates,[2] the Editorial Projects in Education Research Center found that only 52 percent of students attending public schools in the fifty largest U.S. cities graduated on schedule (Swanson 2008). In all but six of the fifty largest cities, 2003–4 high school graduation rates were below the national average rate of 70 percent. High school graduation rates were shockingly low in Detroit (25 percent), Indianapolis (31 percent), Cleveland (34 percent), and Baltimore (35 percent). Together, the public school districts in the fifty largest cities account for 14 percent of the nation's ninth graders but 23 percent of the nation's non-graduates (Swanson 2008).

Moreover, as described in other chapters in this volume (Alan Ruby; Harry Holzer), even those students who graduate from high school in many large metropolitan areas face substantial hurdles to meaningful employment with the opportunity for career progression, in part because today's workforce requires additional skills beyond a high school education to compete in an advanced service economy. Thus, individuals with no more than a high school education may obtain an entry-level position, but, without further education, face considerable challenges in climbing the rungs of the career ladder. The changing nature of employment means that, increasingly, jobs require workers with complex communication and expert thinking skills, rather than routine manual or cognitive skills (National Governors Association 2011).

Ironically, metropolitan youth have relatively low levels of formal education even when an abundance of educational opportunities are seemingly available. As one example, the economic development marketing organization Select Greater Philadelphia (2011) reports that the Philadelphia metropolitan area is home to more than 100 colleges and universities. Yet even with the apparent availability of higher education institutions, college enrollment and completion rates are lower for Philadelphia youth than the national average. Of 100 students who started ninth grade in Philadelphia in 1999, only 48 graduated from high school on time (compared with 69 nationwide), 23 entered college directly after high school (compared with 42 nationwide), and 10 graduated from college within six years (compared with 20 nationwide) (Center for Collaborative Learning 2010).

Other data document the persisting stratification of educational attainment by family income and race/ethnicity. Summarizing analyses conducted by Tom Mortenson, the Pell Institute for the Study of Opportunity in Higher Education (2011) reports that, between 1977 and 2007, bachelor's degree attainment rates increased by 45 percent and 17 percent among dependent eighteen- to twenty-four-year-olds in the top and second family income quartiles, respectively, but by only 7 percent for those in the second-lowest family income quartile, and 2 percent for those in the lowest family income quartile. Bachelor's degree attainment rates by the age of twenty-four were 46.8 percentage points higher in 2009 for dependent students in the top half of the family income distribution than for dependent students in the lower half of the distribution (Pell Institute for the Study of Opportunity in Higher Education 2011). Although the share of the U.S. population with at least a bachelor's degree has increased over time, degree completion rates also remain substantially lower for African Americans and Hispanics than for Whites (Baum, Ma, and Payea 2010).

Stratification occurs not only in terms of who earns what types of educational credentials but also in terms of who attends what types of postsecondary educational institutions. Individuals with low incomes and racial/ethnic minorities disproportionately attend less-selective four-year colleges, community colleges, and for-profit institutions (Baum, Ma, and Payea 2010; National Center for Education Statistics 2011b). As William Tierney discusses in his chapter in this volume, both the number of for-profit institutions and the number of students enrolling at these institutions have grown tremendously over the past two decades (National Center for Education Statistics 2011b). The concentration of low-income students, Black students, and Hispanic students in for-profit institutions and community colleges, as well as less-selective and minority-serving four-year colleges and universities, when coupled with other characteristics of these institutions (such as rising cost of attendance, relatively high student loan default rates, and low completion rates, National Center for Education Statistics 2011a), raises questions about how well participation in particular educational programs provides individuals with the knowledge and skills that are required to meet employers' needs.

Moreover, as William Tierney (this volume) also observes, efforts to improve readiness for college and careers, and reduce stratification of educational (and thus economic) opportunity, must increasingly occur within a context of scarce public resources. In part because of increases over time in the number of students enrolled, state appropriations for higher education per full-time-equivalent student were about 19 percent lower in 2009–10 than in 1999–2000 after controlling for inflation (College Board 2010). Although there is variation across states, most have also been struggling with the impact of the Great Recession on the availability of state revenues. These challenges were eased somewhat by the availability of federal stimulus funding through the American Recovery and Reinvestment Act of 2009. However, these funds will not be available moving forward. The National Association of State Budget Officers (2010) predicts continued "fiscal stress" for states in the coming years.

When state revenues decline and when the public and political leaders do not support revenue enhancements, reductions in funding for public K–12 and higher education typically follow given the magnitude of the state budget allocated to education and the "discretionary" nature of education funding in most states. Illustrating the widespread pattern, in March 2011 Pennsylvania Governor Tom Corbett's proposed budget for fiscal year (FY) 2012 reflected a 3 percent decrease over FY 2011 in state spending overall, but a 10 percent reduction of in spending for instruction in K–12 public schools ($550 million), including the elimination of prekindergarten and full-day kindergarten programming, and a 52 percent reduction ($625 million) for higher education (Gallagher 2011; Hagerty 2011).

Restrictions on state funding for education reduce the availability of resources for elementary and secondary schools to adequately prepare students academically for college and careers. Reductions in appropriations to public higher education may further reduce educational opportunity, if higher education institutions compensate for reductions in state appropriations by raising tuition or reducing enrollment.

These data and trends raise critical questions about the most appropriate allocation of limited public and private resources for ensuring that today's students are prepared for the jobs and careers of tomorrow. Yet before determining how to allocate public and private resources to best achieve this goal, other more basic questions must first be answered. Among the most important foundational questions are: How do we measure and define the "learning" that is required by employers? What are the roles and contributions to workplace readiness of the many different providers of education and training, including workplaces, high schools, for-profit postsecondary educational institutions, community colleges, and traditional four-year colleges and universities? How can institutional practices and public policies promote the educational preparation of students for tomorrow's jobs?

Purpose of This Volume

Framed in terms of the need to raise educational attainment, initiatives by several organizations have recently focused on various dimensions of workforce readiness. For example, the Lumina Foundation (2011) is supporting efforts to define "the knowledge and skills that students need to acquire to earn associate's, bachelor's, and master's degrees." The Partnership for 21st Century Skills (2009) has developed a framework to guide school districts in integrating "21st century themes" (such as global awareness; financial and business literacy; civic, health, and environmental literacy), "learning and innovation skills" (creativity and innovation, critical thinking and problem solving, communication and collaboration), and "information, media, and technology skills" into core academic subjects (p. 8).

Even with these efforts, however, many questions remain. In particular, prior to this volume, little systematic consideration has been given to how to define and measure workforce readiness, the role of different educational sectors in providing the necessary education and training, or the most effective institutional programs and public policies for stimulating educational preparation for work.

Through a review of existing data and research and some new analyses, the chapters in this volume shed light on these important issues. Although pointing to the need for additional, and more rigorous, research to improve our knowledge of workforce readiness, together these chapters also offer useful insights into what we do know about these issues.

The chapters that follow are organized into three sections. The first section considers how we define and understand "success" in preparing students for the world of work.

In the initial chapter, Alan Ruby reminds the reader that questions about the link between education and work are not new. He also offers a comprehensive discussion of competency-based education, which involves efforts of educators to identify and develop skills that have value in the workplace. Ruby notes the advantages of focusing on "generic" competencies, given the delay between students' choice of curricula and their employment, and the time required for educational institutions to adapt curricula and instruction. He offers "study abroad" as an example of an effort that is intended to provide specific competencies that are perceived to respond to employers' demands for workers in a global economy, but that has not been demonstrated to lead to improved labor market outcomes. This example also points to the challenges of connecting specific educational experiences and curricula with the skills and experiences that employers need and value. In addition, Ruby raises critical questions about the role of the workplace in promoting problem-solving, teamwork, and other capabilities, as well as questions about the measurement of individual competencies.

In their chapter, Katie Barghaus, Eric Bradlow, Jen McMaken, and Sam Rikoon identify challenges that limit current efforts to assess and measure workforce readiness. One issue is the lack of agreement in the literature on how to define workforce readiness, the skills required for readiness (including the distinctions between generic and specific skills), the instructional practices and curricula that best promote workforce readiness, and the outcomes that should be used to define and measure workforce readiness. A second issue is the absence of rigorous empirical research on these topics. Building on a review of four recent examinations of workforce readiness, the chapter offers multiple suggestions to guide future research in this area, as well as recommendations for enhancing state longitudinal data systems so as to make available high-quality data that can be used to substantially improve knowledge of workforce readiness.

Bridget O'Connor then considers the utility of such work-based learning initiatives as career and technical education, often called CTE for high school students. The chapter considers what is known from prior research about the success of work-based learning initiatives in terms of several "domains": student satisfaction, actual learning, application of learning, graduation rates, and earning power. The chapter concludes that, when well-designed

and properly implemented, work-based learning initiatives promise to promote college and career readiness for all students.

The second section of the book considers the roles of different educational providers in preparing students for work. In her chapter, Nancy Hoffman offers critical insights into and recommendations for the system of
career and technical education in the United States. She underscores the
need for improvement by describing the poor performance of the United
States relative to other nations on a number of indicators including youth
unemployment and employment rates, high school completion rates, and
the OECD's PISA assessment (a measurement of college and career readiness among fifteen-year-olds). She also argues that countries that outper-
form the United States on these indicators tend to have policies that support
youth and to have a considerable share of their youth population participating in a vocational education and training program that integrates work
and learning. Hoffman concludes by pointing to "promising practices" for
career and technical education in high schools and community colleges in
the United States that may improve connections between education and
work, particularly for youth in metropolitan areas.

Anthony Carnevale, Nicole Smith, and Jeff Strohl then demonstrate
that, at least in part because of changes in technology, postsecondary education and training is now required for access to middle-class status in the
United States. The authors also predict that the demand for workers with
postsecondary education will continue to exceed supply, building on a pattern that began in the mid-1980s. Carnevale and his coauthors illustrate the
considerable variation in earnings among individuals who earn a particular
degree (associate's degree or bachelor's degree). Their analyses point to the
importance of understanding the relationship between educational attainment and occupation, as well as variations in earnings by major field, when
considering the forces that determine demand for postsecondary education.
While recognizing the dangers of focusing exclusively on earnings as the
measurement of "success" of postsecondary education (arguing that this
focus ignores other outcomes that are valued by individuals and society),
the authors conclude by noting the need for greater alignment of particular
postsecondary educational programs with labor market demand.

In their chapter, Thomas Bailey and Clive Belfield consider the role of
community colleges, with particular attention to the benefits to workers (as
measured by earnings) of certificates and degrees by field of study. Drawing
on both a review of prior research and their own analyses of data from the

Survey of Income and Program Participation (SIPP), the chapter provides useful insights into the labor market returns of community college outcomes. Building on a discussion of how the distinctions between occupational and academic credentials have been exaggerated, the authors conclude by offering recommendations for creating a more appropriate balance between occupational and academic education.

Next, William Tierney discusses the role of for-profit colleges and universities in meeting the nation's education and training needs. While acknowledging the skepticism that many have about how an organization that operates "for profit" can produce educational benefits for individuals and society, Tierney argues that the nation cannot achieve international competitiveness goals without these institutions, especially given recent constraints on state funding for public colleges and universities. Noting that more research is required to fully understand outcomes for students who attend for-profit institutions, Tierney also concludes that, as evidenced by enrollment patterns, for-profit institutions are effectively reaching populations of students that have been historically underserved by traditional colleges and universities, including low-income students and Black and Hispanic students.

In the third and final section, four chapters offer insights and recommendations for institutional practice and public policy.

Based on their review of available rigorous research, Lashawn Richburg-Hayes, Michael Armijo, and Lisa Merrill identify several promising strategies used by K–12 and postsecondary institutions to prepare students for careers. Richburg-Hayes and her coauthors note that only a small share of studies from the larger body of available research use experimental or quasi-experimental research designs to establish whether a program is the cause of improvements in student outcomes. To enhance the contribution to knowledge, the authors recommend that future research studies not only identify whether a particular intervention causes specific outcomes, but also include attention to understanding why an intervention worked, how the program was implemented, and through what mechanisms the program achieved the outcomes. The chapter offers a useful template for conceptualizing research that will improve knowledge of how and why career-pathways interventions work for specific groups under particular conditions.

Acknowledging the importance of postsecondary education and training to labor market outcomes as well as the challenges that limit "college for all," Ronald Ferguson argues that students and their families should be able to choose from among multiple pathways. The chapter proposes a system that offers high-quality pathways to college and careers, pathways that integrate work- and career-related experiences into learning beginning in elementary school, continuing through postsecondary education and training and into adult employment. Ferguson stresses the need for such a system that would recognize and promote opportunity for all youth, but especially youth who are least well-served by the current system (such as students from lower income families, racial/ethnic minorities, low academic achievers). The proposed system envisions involvement from multiple stakeholders, including families, schools, religious institutions, and employers and organizations in the public and private sectors. The chapter offers ten practical and tangible recommendations, along with supporting examples, that states and metropolitan areas could use to develop and sustain such a system.

In their chapter, Laura Wolf-Powers and Stuart Andreason focus on the connections between urban economic development policies and school-to-work policies in the United States. With an emphasis on adult workers without postsecondary education, the chapter describes and critiques the existing system for providing employment training and placement in the United States, concluding that this system appears to have had limited impact on workers' earnings. The chapter then reviews contemporary city and regional economic policy, with particular attention to the promising effectiveness of sector-based initiatives and industry partnerships in promoting workforce development. The authors conclude by suggesting changes to improve the nation's employment and training system for adult workers and better align urban and metropolitan economic development policy with workforce development goals.

In the final chapter, Harry Holzer summarizes the role of programs and policies in preparing youth for employment, particularly in our nation's metropolitan areas. The chapter describes central characteristics of workers and jobs in U.S. metropolitan areas and offers recommendations for promoting stronger connections between education and the workforce. Holzer highlights the many challenges that limit these connections, including the inadequacy of information for students about college and careers, and then points to educational practices that research suggests show promise for improving labor market outcomes. Following a discussion of the unevenness of opportunity within metropolitan areas, the chapter offers recommendations for institutional practices, as well as state and federal public policies, that may improve educational and employment opportunity and outcomes, especially for racial/ethnic minorities and individuals from low-income families.

Following these chapters, I offer a brief conclusion summarizing key themes that cut across the chapters. This chapter highlights implications for institutional leaders, policymakers, and researchers that flow from these chapters.

Preparing Today's Students for Tomorrow's Jobs

Ensuring that today's students have the education and training required for the jobs and careers of tomorrow is critical for reasons of international competitiveness, national employment productivity, and the economic and social status of individuals. Improving the match between educational preparation of workers and the knowledge demands of employers is especially important to the continued economic and social health and vitality of our nation's metropolitan areas. Understanding how to improve readiness is also important given the changing demographic characteristics of the population (for example, the rapidly growing Hispanic population) and increasing constraints on the availability of public resources.

Although much recent attention has focused on the need to increase the educational attainment of the U.S. population, less attention has focused on what types of education and skills today's students, especially those in metropolitan America, require to be ready for the jobs of tomorrow. In particular, little systematic consideration has been given to how to define and measure workforce readiness, to the role of different educational sectors in providing the necessary education and training, or to determining the most effective institutional programs and public policies for stimulating educational preparation for work.

The chapters that follow advance the discourse and state of knowledge on these issues. While identifying some critical areas for additional and higher quality research, the volume also provides a number of useful insights for practitioners and public policymakers. In addition to establishing that more research is required, the chapters in this volume offer valuable insights that educators, educational leaders, public policymakers, and researchers may use to improve the readiness of today's students for tomorrow's jobs in metropolitan America.

I.

Defining Success in Preparing
Individuals for Work

CHAPTER 1

Tinker, Tailor, Soldier, Sailor . . . A Public Policy Agenda on Today's Students and Tomorrow's Jobs

Alan Ruby

This chapter outlines the issues a policymaker looks for when trying to understand the Babel of competing ideas and points of view around the conjunction of two institutions—schooling and work. It begins with the personal because that is where policymakers usually begin, with their own history. The second section aligns personal experience with the structure of schooling and work as it existed fifty years ago, when that history began to form. That examination leads to a brief survey of the way thinking about the relationship between school and work has evolved since just before the rise of compulsory schooling. The survey concentrates on the evolving nature of the idea of "competence" as a way of discussing the bridge between the two social institutions, school and work. It is followed by an examination of some of the factors that shape the value of competencies, and how that value is expressed in the occupational structure of the U.S. workforce. This is followed by a brief examination of the value employers place on graduates with study abroad experience, as a specific example of the dissonance between rhetoric and evidence about the economic utility of specific skills and experiences. The essay concludes with a brief synthesis and argues that the main thing we know about school-to-work transitions is that uncertainty, change, and choice are more important than predetermination, continuity, and tracking.

The Personal

"What do you want to be when you grow up?" As a child living and working on a grape and orange farm in rural Australia I hated that question. Obviously I was going to be a farmer, like my father. I had no desire to run away to sea or to move to "the city" to work in the textile industry. Neither intergenerational nor geographic mobility were on my primary school curriculum, nor on the curriculum of any other Australian child in the 1950s.

Yet, the question seemed to fascinate everyone. I recall being asked by friends, family, the local butcher, and occasionally by teachers. It endured across years, even through six years of agricultural high school and into university. Great Aunt Ollicent never tired of it over twenty years, asking it on every one of her annual visits. The same aunt, mystified by my inability to render her portrait in any medium despite a year of study for an Arts degree, was sure I would come to a bad end. And of course I lacked the skill to explain what I was studying, let alone why.

The question gives a wonderful insight into the era and its economy. There was no notion of trying something out; you were to "be" a farmer for life. There was no notion of changing occupations or sectors, from agriculture to, say, mining. Nor was there any expectation that you would leave the countryside to look for work in the coastal cities. Indeed Uncle Colin was regarded as frivolous and feckless, and definitely unreliable, for changing jobs twice in his lifetime. While "getting ahead" in your field was fine, changing fields seemed alien and unwise.

"Tinker, Tailor, Soldier, Sailor"—the nursery chant we learned as two- and three-year-olds—taught us not just the importance of counting and rhymes, but that occupations were fixed, invariable, and determined by chance. It and its variants (see Opie and Opie 1952: 404–5; and Baring-Gould and Baring-Gould 1962: 216) also taught us the class system and the gender rules of society.

> Tinker, tailor, soldier, sailor,
> Rich man, poor man,
> Beggar man, thief
> Doctor, lawyer, merchant, chief.
> (Opie and Opie 1952: 405)

This personal history lined up with and was shaped by the public policies regulating the school systems of the nation. Those policies were based on assumptions about the transition from school to work.

Aligning Assumptions about Society, Work, and Schooling

Not surprisingly, secondary school organization in Australia in the 1950s and early 1960s reflected the assumption that when young people left school their career destinations were certain. General and vocational, or technical, schools were separate. In the cities, commercial and domestic science schools supplemented agricultural schools. Wherever possible, boys and girls were educated separately and offered slightly different programs of study. Streaming, or sorting children into groups or "tracks," based on ability test results was common both between schools and within schools (Freeman Butts 1955).

The curricula were relatively narrow, with vocationally relevant subjects like bookkeeping, woodworking, wool classing, shorthand, and typing. The few languages that were offered were all European and categorized into Ancient and Modern. Choice was limited and instruction emphasized memory and recall. The encyclopedic acquisition of knowledge and the mastery of long division were esteemed. Students were assessed and ranked in order of proficiency.

For most young people formal schooling ended the year they turned fifteen. Whatever additional job-specific information and skills they needed would be learned in the workplace or in the arduous and long apprenticeships that combined work, learning, and low pay. Entrance to the trades was controlled by guilds, unions, and the available jobs.

Entrance to the professions was not always through university. In some cases it could be gained by a form of apprenticeship—an aspiring lawyer could begin as an "articled clerk" and present himself (seldom herself) for examination after a period of service and tutelage by a practicing lawyer.

Only the elite would finish secondary school and go to university, and the assumption in economic policy was that the national workforce would not need high levels of skill. Other public policy assumptions were embedded in this view of the world, including the ideas that ability was fixed, innate, and measurable, and that jobs were invariant and permanent. The only exception to this rule was for women, who were expected to resign paid employment upon marriage, and in some cases (usually in the public sector) were required to so by law.

This brief survey of public policy and education it is not peculiar to Australia; it applies to all urban industrialized democracies as they grapple with the role of education in the national economy. There is a vigorous debate about the rights and wrongs of organizing and aligning schooling with labor markets or national objectives. Some people take an instrumentalist view that education should serve the needs of the state by equipping individuals for work and economic productivity. Others take a transformative perspective and see education as helping individuals realize their potential and aspirations, celebrating education as an end in itself or as a pathway to a well-developed intellect or mind. The permutations and nuances of these arguments are many. I leave them to others. (For one example, see Partington 1987.)

I accept that education is a public policy domain—it is largely financed or subsidized by public funds and it serves ends that are in the common good. One of those ends is to offer young people the capabilities and knowledge they will need to enjoy fruitful and meaningful lives. Another is to equip school graduates to contribute to the economic productivity of a community. That productivity is enhanced when community members are well-educated and willing to work and learn.

One lens on this debate is the "employability" of graduates. If we accept that access to economic activity is rewarding for the individual and society, we can start to examine how schooling should be organized and learning assessed and certified. One approach is to delineate vocationally specific skills like "animal husbandry" or "shorthand and typing" and prepare students to master them. Another is to offer a broad general education to equip individuals with the foundational skills for learning on the job or in postschool institutions. Yet another is to set out generic skills like "communicating with others" that can be acquired through a variety of disciplines and programs.

In a sense, all three emerge from a way of thinking about the connection between school and work in terms of "competence," where competence is the capacity to satisfactorily perform a role or complete an activity. Competence is a term that suffers from "conceptual inflation" (Weinert 2001), or a surfeit of meanings, because of its frequent use in education and political debates and its relatively long history: it is used as a synonym for "skill," "attribute," and "capability." As we will see, this ambiguity or plurality of meaning has developed from its use as a policy tool in many different settings.

Competencies as a Public Policy Tool

Competency-based education, defined as the construction of educational programs and assessments around units of observable individual performance of a task or process, has its antecedents in "task analysis" approaches to curriculum design. The general idea was that the process of organizing work rationally or scientifically in factories and workshops could be transferred to the development of school-based programs of learning. A role or function in society or the workplace could be broken down into acts or events or tasks that could be used to create a program of learning and an assessment regime based on observed performance. Examples of this go as far back as the 1860s—before the rise of universal basic education. Subsequently, an element of the social efficiency movement fostered scientific curriculum making that would devise programs of study that prepared individuals specifically and directly for social roles. Order, stability, and utility guided the selection of the content and breadth of the curriculum. All three supported the need for efficiency that was embodied in Winslow Taylor's doctrine of scientific management and its concerns for standards and established routines to maximize production and minimize costs. The one best way of producing something could be determined by researchers observing workers, photographing and timing them as they carried out set tasks. Speed would be used to set the best order of tasks, which would increase productivity by saving time and reducing fatigue. Employees would establish a "set of efficient habits" which "changed mental attitudes" (Gilbreth and Gilbreth 1919: 140). The requirements of the workplace could then be codified and communicated through training.

Bobbit, the founder of "curriculum" as a field of practice, used these principles to create a five-step curriculum-making process including job analysis and specifying objectives to ensure that education meet social ends (Kliebard 2004). His process led to a standardized approach for assigning students to the "right" vocational pathways or academic programs that would end in the "right" jobs or colleges. This "scientific" approach, common throughout the 1920s and 1930s, continues to be influential. It is inherent in the behavioral objectives and the scope and sequence curricula of the 1960s, 1970s, and 1980s, and is evident in the English standards of 2005 issued by National Council of Teachers of English in the United States (Tremmel 2006). Its influence is pervasive and can be seen, for example, in the English language curriculum adopted in the 1990s in Singapore (Cheah 1996).

The persistence of this approach over a century owes much to its perceived value in linking education with social or economic utility. It was a way of reducing the "gap" between learning and earning, and a tool to help people move from one type of institution to another. When those transitions are troubled or lagged because of unemployment or structural adjustments in the labor market, competency-based approaches gain popularity.

Of course this is not a new phenomenon. Nor is it peculiar to the United States. The rise of the metropolitan merchant class in Britain and the growth of urban industries in the nineteenth century led to demands for the introduction of commercial law and bookkeeping courses and for commercial languages to be taught in universities rather than classical Latin and Greek (Ray and Mickelson 1990).

"Competencies" became a common part of policy debates in general education in the 1970s and 1980s as industrialized countries concerned about urban youth unemployment and productivity started to reexamine the role of education in economic competitiveness. The National Commission on Excellence in Education's report *A Nation at Risk* (1983) linked school reform with national economic competiveness and fostered renewed interest from the business community in the work of public schools. It was also one impetus for the Department of Labor's advocacy of essential skills and knowledge for all high school graduates expressed in its report, *Learning a Living* (1992). Australia, Canada, New Zealand, and the United Kingdom, which also grappled with significant shifts in economic structures and policies, explored similar changes in their approaches to education. Business groups campaigned for school reform around slogans like "The 4th R: Readiness to Work." The National Alliance of Business used a film of the same name to persuade local business groups in cities across the United States to campaign for more employment-related skills in the curriculum (Ray and Mickelson 1990).

In these Anglophone countries and in most other OECD nations at the time, mass secondary schooling was common and high school completion rates were increasing rapidly or had peaked. Employers, seeking to reduce their own training expenditures, and taxpayers bearing the cost of mass schooling began to express concerns that school graduates were not "job ready," meaning that they were not immediately "employable" and allegedly lacked good work habits and the social skills needed in modern workplaces.

Another reason for the popularity of the competency approach is its apparent simplicity. There is a direct relationship between the content and structure of learning and the skills or knowledge needed by a beginner to be effective in the workplace or occupation. The assessment regime can be simplified to a set of criteria that are observable and binary—what the candidate can do or cannot do. Policymakers, then, can concern themselves solely with outcomes, leaving aside debates about "process," how learning should be organized, and the level of "inputs" necessary for learning to occur.

But some educators, even some who are advocates of competency-based approaches, do not like this simplicity because it is "highly reductionist," dividing and specifying tasks to the point of fragmentation. For each small part, the learner is to be observed performing the activity according to the standard. The task and associated performance criteria often become the "competence" even though the observed behavior is really only part of the process or vocational capability that a person is expected to have (Gonczi 2003).

This and related criticisms have shaped more recent approaches to competence. A major cross-national study lead by the Swiss Statistical agency on behalf of the OECD's Education Division has developed a more comprehensive and holistic approach to defining competence. After an extensive cross-disciplinary process they settled on a definition of a competence as "the ability to meet complex demands successfully or to carry out an activity or task" but supplemented it with the caveat that a competence was embodied in an individual's "internal mental structures of abilities, capacities and dispositions" (Rychen 2004: 21).

The researchers went on to identify three categories of key competencies that are related to broad demands of modern life rather than behaviors tied to general vocational ends: acting autonomously, using tools interactively, and joining and functioning in socially heterogeneous groups. They elaborated all three by including items or elements that refer to interpersonal or emotional qualities. Acting autonomously would include expressing individual identity and asserting one's rights. Using tools would encompass applying languages, symbols, and text to problems in the workplace and in society; participating in diverse groups would include relating to others and the ability and willingness to cooperate (Rychen 2004).

This more comprehensive approach to delineating capabilities that have value in the workplace is attractive to many educators because it moves past knowledge recall as a method of assessing learning and fosters application of knowledge and active-learning strategies. This approach is attractive to employers because it more closely aligns with the activities that individuals are expected to perform in the workplace, either by themselves or in teams. Competencies are attractive to the leaders of social institutions because they describe behaviors and abilities that are essential for effective membership in these organizations or groups.

For policymakers, curriculum designers, and assessors of performance, competencies are constructs that aggregate more highly specified skills into sets that approximate the actions, activities, and tasks that individuals and teams undertake in workplaces and in other social settings. They also reflect sets of capabilities that can be learned or developed rather than being measurements of innate ability. The latter measures all against the same standard and rationalizes occupational stratification in terms of intelligence. The competency-based approach expands individual opportunities by allowing for the acquisition of skill, mobility across occupations, development over time, and the combination of an individual's skills with those of others to complete an activity or solve a problem (Carson 2001).

Just as the developers and advocates of IQ testing were responding to demands from employers and policymakers for tools to guide selection and rationing decisions, the development of more robust definitions of competencies has been driven by a desire for concepts and constructs that align education with other social institutions like "work." Information about the capabilities that might be developed through a course of study or be applied in a social setting could also help individuals make choices about careers, courses of study, and depth of specialization. Similarly, this approach could help employers choose between individuals who have developed different sets of competencies.

In short, competencies are a tool that can help in the transition between school and work. They help educators design programs. They help students select courses and experiences to develop and consolidate their skills and capabilities and they guide hiring and training new employees.

Ideally these competencies and associated measurements would be relevant across different occupational settings, be applicable across various forms of education and training and persist over time. They should be "generic" in the sense that they can be applied to good effect regardless of task or time or trade.

This generic quality is important because the production cycle of formal schooling is lengthy. Individuals are able to, and sometimes are forced to, choose courses and specializations as precursors to post-school destinations as early as six years before graduation. Similarly, curriculum and assessment agencies benefit from the persistent quality of generic competencies as this characteristic provides some certainty that, despite the time required to set up specific curricula or subjects or to make changes in content or in methods of instruction and assessment, the material will still be relevant. And these changes are costly—requiring documentation, materials, and teacher training. The lead time and scale of investments can be justified more easily if the future demand for the skills formed by the programs of study is constant or enduring, or at least predictable.

Does Demand for Job Skills Change?

While essentially a conservative institution dedicated to transmitting values and knowledge across generations, school education does change. One source of change is external events. Things happen in the political, cultural, and economic contexts surrounding education that shift priorities and values.

The most obvious is the general state of the economy, particularly the availability of jobs for school leavers. The general proposition is that education is a "counter cyclical investment"—demand for education goes up when job vacancies go down. Higher education becomes a "warehouse" for human capital especially in areas where unemployment is high. Conversely, in areas where there are plenty of jobs that do not require post-school education, young people are more likely to enter the workforce rather than go to college when compared to their same-age peers in areas of high unemployment (Bozick 2009). The distribution of jobs is not even across or within nations or within cities within nations. Nor, as noted by Laura Perna, Laura Wolf-Powers and Stuart Andreason, and Harry Holzer and other authors in this volume, is access to available jobs evenly distributed among young people, with significant structural unemployment impacting racial groups within the United States (Ryan 2001).

Other broader social and political changes can shape the demand for particular skills or for people with particular capabilities or qualifications. These can be as fundamental as the creation of a new nation, which may shift the importance of particular languages—Portuguese versus Bahasa in East Timor for example, or Russian versus Lithuanian or Ukrainian in the former Soviet Republics.

Discontinuity and change can also come from the creation of new economic entities like the European Economic Community, NAFTA, or the Euro Zone, which change the range of opportunities for the flow of goods and capital, shaping demand for skill, or the European Higher Education Zone, which allows for easier movement of qualifications and skills across national boundaries, changing the labor market composition. (See for example Floud 2006 and Cardosa et al. 2006.) Or it can stem from policy changes as simple as changes in tariffs and taxes, which shift the economic value of skills applied in formerly protected industries and occupations.

Some of these changes have had major impacts on cities through the co-location of established industries and urban areas. This is evident in the history of the textile cities of England where the pathway from home to mill, a "given" for two hundred years, was dislocated by economic integration with Europe beginning in the late 1960s. Youth unemployment rose, school enrollments increased, and public schools with curricula and a culture from a different era were faced with students with low aspirations and few opportunities (Willis 1977). All parties struggled with the change and, in response, governments created youth training and wage subsidies and pressed for new vocational programs. Cities still face these transitional problems. Danson (2005), in a study of "Old Industrial Areas" in Scotland, illustrates how the demand for occupationally specific skills has been replaced by demand for "soft skills" or "future skills" like customer handling, oral communication, team working, and problem solving.

These changes have been most closely observed in occupations that historically required high school diplomas or an equivalent for entrance. Most analytical work in this area tends to focus on the questions: Why does additional schooling increase an individual's income? Why do employers pay more for someone with a diploma?

To address these questions, there are two competing schools of thought: human capital theory and signaling. Both assume that individuals will continue to bear the cost of education up to the point where the marginal return equals the marginal cost, but they differ on their explanations for a wage premium. The human capital group argues that education increases lifetime productivity and this warrants better pay. The signaling group argues that an employer pays a premium because education symbolizes innate ability and the capacity to make better use of training and hence greater productivity.

No matter which theory dominates, the net effect is that successful entrance to the labor market is influenced by years of education or educational credentials. The clearest evidence of this relationship is the fact that in the U.S. economy the premium for having eight years of schooling began to decline in the 1960s as high school completion and college participation increased rapidly (Kroch and Sjobolom 1994). The annual wages, in constant dollars, for employees with only high school diplomas fell from 1980 to 2008 while pay for college graduates increased slightly (U.S. Department of Education 2010). Opportunities for those lacking a high school diploma are also limited; some forecast that less than 10 percent of new and replacement jobs in the 2008 to 2018 period will be open to people with less than a high school diploma (Carnevale, Smith, and Strohl 2010).

Conversely, people with postsecondary education qualifications will have access to a faster-growing pool of jobs than people without awards. The scale is notable: in 2008, three out of ten jobs were in occupations that involved some postsecondary education credentials and these occupations will account for over 50 percent of all new jobs in the 2008 to 2018 period. Increased opportunities through job growth are skewed toward those with formal learning. Conversely, jobs that depend on long-term on-the-job training—more than a year of training—have the slowest growth rates, disadvantaging those who leave school early.

These trends contrast with the BLS projections for 1986 to 2000 which forecast the biggest numerical growth in occupations requiring only high school completion, and that "only 2 of the 10 fastest-growing occupations in terms of absolute job growth" would require postsecondary education (Levin 1994). More recently, Lacey and Wright (2010) project that four of the biggest numerical increases in jobs will be in occupations that need at least some postsecondary education and indeed the greatest numerical growth will be in registered nurses positions. None of the thirty occupations that are expected to be the biggest numerical losers of jobs require postsecondary education. Most of these "losers" are concentrated in production and office and administrative positions with the latter sector losing jobs through technological change and automation. These patterns suggest that the shifts in the skill profiles for jobs in the U.S. economy that Levin was unable to confirm have begun to materialize. Indeed, Carnevale, Smith, and Strohl (2010) argue that the shift toward more skill has materialized already and that BLS forecasts underestimated growth in jobs requiring postsecondary education in the economy in the 1998 to 2008 period by nearly 50 percent.

It is not just access to work that is mediated by education; it is also job stability. The better educated you are, the faster you enter a long-term job, one that lasts for three years or more (Yates 2005).

One consequence of volatility in occupational structures and changes in demand is job turnover. People change jobs, both voluntarily and involuntarily. But little reliable data on "career changes" exists because there is no commonly accepted definition of a "career change." Is the movement from classroom teaching to college advisor a career shift? The clientele, location, and employer are the same but the skill set is different.

With this shortcoming in mind we can look at the number of jobs held in a lifetime. The U.S. Bureau of Labor Statistics (2010) estimates that the youngest "baby boomers," those born in the late 1950s early 1960s, held eleven jobs between the ages of eighteen and forty-four. There are no marked differences between men and women, between different racial groups, or between different levels of education.

On the surface the data in Figure 1.1 suggest a great deal of turbulence in the working lives of younger Americans. When we look more closely, we find that 60 percent of the jobs were held between eighteen and twenty-seven years of age; moreover, the definition of job is employer-based not position-based and is "a period of uninterrupted work." This definition means that a summer job held every year by a college student would count as four jobs. The definition also does not take into account that jobs change around occupants because of process redesign, technology changes, or simple shifts in client needs. This omission and the fact that individuals over age thirty were still "changing jobs" twice every five years suggest that there is a lot to be learned about the ways that education prepares people for productive and personally satisfying working lives that involve occupational mobility.

Thus, from all three perspectives—future opportunities and job growth, time to first stable job, and job turnover—people with more education are better off than those who leave school early. Job entry requirements have increased, and the nature of work has changed to require higher levels of education. The occupational structure of the U.S. economy has changed with growth skewing toward occupations requiring higher levels of education and with lower-skilled occupations losing significant numbers of jobs.

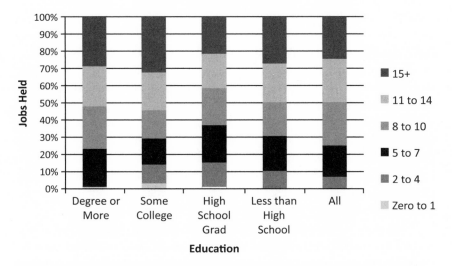

Figure 1.1. Baby boomers and job turnover. *Source*: U.S. Bureau of Labor Statistics 2010.

We are not sure what drives these changes, but innovation, news ways of organizing work, and technology are common explanations. Popular wisdom seems to favor technology as the main force shaping the skills required to perform a particular role.

Technology and the Demand for Skill

The actual impact of technology has been debated. Levin (1994) looked at two claims in this area: 1) that twenty-first century jobs will require individuals to have more education to perform them effectively; and 2) that low-skill jobs in the U.S. economy are becoming higher-skill jobs because of technological change and workplace redesign. He concluded that little evidence linked demand for particular skills with changes in workplaces. The absence of data was due in part to the inadequate knowledge base linking schools and workplace requirements.

Nearly twenty years later the knowledge base has been strengthened. For example, Schone (2009) looks at age bias in new work practices and new technology and Goldin and Katz (2008) have completed a major survey of the relationship between technology and education that illustrates the importance of studying both the supply and demand for skills. But there is still much to be done to identify empirically the knowledge and skill bases required for modern workplaces and to examine the longer-term impact of technology on skill. For example, will technology always be substituting for skill or will it become skill neutral?

Regardless, we should not overestimate the long-term effect on jobs of these changes in technology. Previous waves of economic integration and globalization coupled with rapid and fundamental technological changes like electricity, the steam engine, and the telephone have changed the nature of production and demand for skill. And all of these waves have been followed by periods of stability and certainty (Coatsworth 2004).

The policymaker faced with the immediacy of shifts in employment, the press for competiveness, and short-term political cycles needs information to guide resource allocation and set priorities. Deepening understanding of the interaction between technology, the demand for skill, and the formation and accreditation of skills will be of great help in those policy processes.

Independent of these occupational shifts, some advocates make a case for having educational institutions provide or facilitate specific experiences or skills that make job applicants more employable or worth a premium in a global economy. These arguments are often unsupported by hard evidence, as illustrated in the case of study abroad.

The Economic Value of Study Abroad

Periodically, scholars of globalization argue that young people should leave school or college prepared for an interconnected world where economies are intertwined, where ideas, people, and money move quickly and freely, and work is often done in cross-national and multicultural teams. (See Gardner 2004 for an example.) Various strategies are suggested to educate young people for this "flat world": foreign language learning, courses on global perspectives, and area studies are three examples. A fourth strategy is study abroad, defined as a period of systematic study and immersion in another culture by college students, usually in their junior or sophomore year.

In 2008, roughly 1 percent of all college students took a study abroad course. One factor driving this participation is the perceived economic utility of study abroad. Vande Berg (2007) documents an interest by legislatures and industry groups in the vocational usefulness of study abroad over the past twenty years. A recent survey of over two hundred senior-level U.S. business and industry leaders from enterprises of all sizes found that 60 percent of respondents' companies had personnel policies that valued study-abroad activities. It was not simply that international experience was perceived as a "good thing"; executives believed that recruits' time in other cultures and settings influenced hiring and promotion decisions, initial assignments, and starting salaries (Institute of International Education 2009).

Some claim that study abroad adds to students' second language proficiency, strengthens an individual's sense of global engagement, and influences decisions about further education and careers (Paige et al. 2009; Norris and Gillespie 2009). These qualities are perceived advantages in career development, helping men and women get to the interview stage in private sector job recruitment. Study abroad experience has been perceived to be a factor even when the job vacancy in question did not "specifically require international expertise" (Opper 1991).

While these data are valuable, they would be more useful if triangulated with observed data on the impact of study abroad on initial earnings on graduation and "time to first job." In this way, we could see if the perceived utility and influence are borne out by actual decisions and benefits. However even this data would be limited because it would rely on a model that assumes that results originate "dominantly and directly" from experiences in the specific time spent in another setting (Flack 1976).

One way of limiting the impact of these shortcomings is to examine vocational benefits like time to first job and wage premiums for particular experiences. Of course, these economic outcomes are not the sum of the benefits of study abroad. There are significant personal benefits from these activities although debate continues about how to assess them systematically. (See for example Deardorff 2006 for some insight into the debate about what to measure with regard to intercultural competence and how to measure it, and what outcomes, if any, can be linked to the study abroad experience.)

This example shows the difficulty of fine-grained alignment between an educational experience and access to work and the returns to the individual for particular skills or experiences. It also illustrates that the rhetoric about the value of a particular skill set may shape expressed policies of employers even without empirical data showing that these skills translate into greater financial returns.

This disjunction between advocacy and practice is not confined to the study abroad field but can also be found across the breadth of high school students' employability skills. Using high school students' self-reported data from a representative sample based on Alberta schools, Krahn, Lowe, and Lehman (2002) found that students believed that employers preferred job seekers with good work attitudes and behaviors (40 percent of all responses) rather than basic skills (1 percent of all responses). Students' perceptions contrasted with the reported preferences of employers, who favored basic skills, specific job-related skills, and social skills. Similar mismatches are reported for the higher education sector where employers favor graduates with good communication skills and the capacity to work cooperatively, while university faculty place a premium on professional knowledge and its application (B-HERT 1992).

Study abroad and the other illustrations of the disjunction between the perceptions of employers and students or job seekers highlight the central issue in school-to-work transition: information. How do students and educators know what is needed and valued in the workplace? What opportunities are there, what do they pay, and what is the educational qualification for entrance to these and competing occupations? Employers want to know what students can do, what they can learn on the job, and how quickly they can learn it. Yet there is no easy way or ways for this information to be created, validated, and exchanged.

Synthesis

This information deficit is not a new problem. Looking at the history of formal schooling and curriculum design and the swirl of debates about education reform we can see that the flow of information has been poor: partial, episodic, disjointed, or just not there. The curriculum designers took a "scientific" approach, analyzing existing tasks and existing jobs based on existing technologies, in current forms of work organization. They were not concerned with future demand or the breadth of opportunities open to an individual but with improving the efficiency of current practice and fitting people with jobs. Advocates of vocationally specific preparation programs in schools were concerned with aligning a part of the economy with part of the labor market, and with part of an individual's repertoire of skills. They were not interested in a breadth of preparation or in a changing occupational structure.

The good news is that there have been some encouraging developments. A stronger conceptual basis has developed, allowing more thoughtful conversations about the transition from school to work and what the parties involved can expect from each other. The developmental work that integrates the interpersonal and intellectual capabilities of individuals into sets of competencies that have meaning and value in different occupational and social settings offers a way of exchanging information about bundles of skills with immediate and enduring value, some of which are better learned on the job and others through some form of structured learning. This work also uncouples particular skills from specific occupational destinations and broadens the array of possible first job destinations for individuals.

While the "scientific" curriculum designers focused on today's jobs and efficiency gains and the vocational education advocates aligned parts of the economy and the labor market with part of students' skills, the competencies theorists integrate interpersonal and intellectual capabilities, uncouple skills and occupations, and broaden first-job destinations for individuals. In short, they are linking tomorrow's jobs with today's students.

The policymakers and their advisors confronted with the Babel of data, encouraging developments, competing theories, and partial information probably long for the simplicity of that childhood rhyme, "Tinker, tailor, soldier, sailor," as a decision-making aid. So it is helpful to distill what we do know with a high degree of certainty about the interface of two institutions, school and work. We know that

1. jobs change as economies change and as we create new ways of working together and new tools;
2. people change jobs, voluntarily and involuntarily, and do so often throughout at least the first twenty years of work;
3. people with more education have more job choices and get better jobs faster than those with less education;
4. employers pay a premium for education and use education as one of the criteria in selecting employees;
5. entry standards for jobs in the fastest-growing sectors of the economy are going up; and
6. employers value people with intellectual skills and interpersonal skills, which we can describe as competencies.

There is plenty we do not know about school-to-work transition, but three areas where investigation would be particularly valuable are these:

1. Can skills like the social and emotional capabilities associated with problem solving and teamwork be developed in diverse settings? Specifically, can they be formed in workplaces or other social institutions that are structured, financed, and accredited differently from schools?
2. Can these competencies be fairly and accurately assessed, and individuals' capabilities reported, in accessible and comparable forms that would widen work opportunities or increase mobility?
3. Can education providers incorporate group- and teamwork into courses and programs, assess individual performance in these domains, and report it in a manner that allows fair comparisons to be made between individuals?

All three of these lines of inquiry have the potential to increase access to learning and to widen opportunities for all. This potential is particularly apparent for young people coming of age in U.S. cities where job change is clustered due to the history of industrial concentrations, the density of the flow of ideas and people, and the concentration of knowledge-based enterprises. The ethnographic work in the 1970s and 1980s on urban youth and school-to-work transitions, notably Willis's *Learning to Labor* (1977), was very influential, drawing attention to the challenges for schools and youth as successful participation in schooling became even more important to economic well-being and social cohesion. All of this work takes time.

In the interim we can conclude that a lot has been learned about students and jobs. The heart of what we have learned is that most young people are unlikely to travel fixed career paths. They will change as they learn and add to their skills and knowledge as working adults. They will change jobs and have their jobs change around them. These changes will bring uncertainty and anxiety, opportunity and choice. It is probably time we recast that childhood rhyme and replaced it with

Broker, hedgie, blogger, techie,
Lend or borrow.
Whatever I choose
It's only for tomorrow.

CHAPTER 2

Assessing and Measuring Workforce Readiness: A Discussion toward the Development of a Universal and Valid Measure

Katherine M. Barghaus, Eric T. Bradlow, Jennifer McMaken,
and Samuel H. Rikoon

Over the last fifty years workforce readiness has been studied extensively by academics and educational policy researchers alike. Whether it is immediately after the end of a student's high school educational experience, or in preparation for college and/or graduate-level studies, our educational system is responsible for "preparing and making ready" students for a variety of different occupations and careers. To deliver on this duality (both workforce and higher education preparation), we also need to recognize the differential difficulty in achieving this mission across urban/rural areas in which the size of the school, types of jobs, funding sources, and myriad other factors play a significant role.

To this end, while this term "prepare and make ready" seems obvious and tautological, our survey of extant literature suggests that there is no general agreement on (a) what it means for a student to be ready; (b) what skills are required for readiness, recognizing that the literature tends to separate skills into generic and specific (Bennett, Dunne, and Carré 1999); (c) the best practices to get students ready; and (d) the outcomes that would indicate a successful workforce readiness program. To make matters even more ambiguous, even less is known empirically about this topic.

With that said, critiquing existing literature and stating what has not been done are the easy parts. We recognize that this is a very difficult topic on which to collect reliable data, do anything more than small-scale empirical evaluations, or run experiments where students are "assigned" to different educational treatment conditions. Instead we review four recent works on workforce readiness, using them as a springboard to call for definitive empirical research. We review each of these works to generate research questions, and to help address definitional issues regarding skills, best practices, and needed outcome measures. For clarity we number the topics and questions we perceive as central to understanding workforce readiness. To set the stage for our larger discussion, we first proceed with a review of the open issues as described in the literature. This summarizes four major issues in workforce readiness, beginning with basic definitional concepts and concluding with desired outcomes.

Key Issues from Defining Readiness to Measuring Outcomes

Meaning of Readiness

Much of the ambiguity in the workforce readiness literature arises from the dichotomous ways in which readiness is defined. On the one hand, while many high schools aspire to send a large majority of students to higher educational programs, they must also recognize that many students can't afford higher education, or may choose to pursue what are considered technical/vocational jobs. This dual-purpose mission, of course, puts significant strain on the educational system, which has to jointly train people, academically as well as vocationally. Since our primary purpose in this chapter is to identify questions rather than provide definite answers, we note that the dual nature of "readiness" raises the questions: (Q1) are these necessary skills orthogonal to each other, (Q2) can they both be achieved through one curriculum, and (Q3) what does this imply for curriculum design?

Skills Necessary for Readiness

The literature we reviewed divides skills for readiness into two types: generic and specific. While this categorization is hardly controversial, there is little to no agreement on exactly which skills go into which category. For instance, are theoretical physics skills general or specific? What about architectural drawing skills? The answers depend on the particular field one plans to enter. Much of the literature spends time developing lists of skills for different job areas and subareas. Though somewhat illuminating, these lists do little to formalize definitions of these skills. Instead of pursuing a comprehensive categorization, we use this ambiguity to question whether (Q4) these are meaningful or stable groupings, as the specific skills for various job types are constantly in flux.

Best Practices for Acquiring Readiness

Another dichotomy exists between what are seen as academically oriented "ivory-tower" classes and those that are purely vocational. To us, this dichotomy seems unnecessarily artificial and in fact current practice seems to agree: many of the papers we reviewed discuss emerging programs called "Pathways Programs" (Hoachlander 2008; Orozco 2010). In these programs, schools *integrate* academic courses and vocational training by showing students "academics in action." Academics in action could be students in an advanced engineering class visiting an engineering firm and observing the development and design process, or students in a journalism class visiting a newspaper and discussing story construction. Preliminary evidence suggests that learning by applying theory is extremely promising. If this early data holds, multiple pathways programs may be the vocational tech of the twenty-first century. But (Q5) what evidence will be required to provide robust support for such programs to be adopted more broadly?

Impact of Readiness on Outcomes

The well-known saying "If you cannot measure it, you cannot improve it" (generally attributed to Sir William Thomson, aka Lord Kelvin) is particularly appropriate for understanding workforce readiness. Not only do we as researchers, policymakers, and educators have to be able to measure desired outcomes, but more importantly, we must decide on (Q6) what these outcomes should be. In other words, the field must decide what outcomes and associated measures most directly indicate workforce readiness or a lack thereof. No Child Left Behind (NCLB 2002) has sparked a movement toward using absolute achievement on exams or gain scores as barometers of educational programs' success, similar to gain scores on the National Assessment of Educational Progress (NAEP, http://nces.ed.gov/nationsreportcard), which have historically been used for the same purpose. Regardless of what indicators are selected, it is important not only to compute average gain scores, but also to consider the entire distribution, because average achievement and average workforce readiness could lead to a socially problematic set of outcomes where a larger and larger fraction of students are better equipped yet an equally large fraction are worse off. We now discuss a number of recent papers on the topic and the additional questions they raise.

Review of Four Recent Articles

While a multitude of papers discus workforce readiness, we selected four of the more conceptually and empirically oriented works suggested by authors of other chapters in this volume. We review each of the selected papers below, organizing our review by the four major issues in workforce readiness discussed above. Although the articles pose many interesting open questions, we focus on the key questions outlined above as they are discussed within or informed by these four pieces.

Meaning of Readiness and Skills Necessary for Readiness

An article by Bennett, Dunne, and Carré (1999) explores the extent to which higher education has ceded to business and government the task of fostering students' acquisition of "personal transferable skills" (such as problem solving, teamwork, and communication skills) as well as technical skills (those useful only in specific academic disciplines or within narrow occupational fields). To examine this question, the authors propose a classificatory framework of pedagogical approaches for skill acquisition in use in higher education. They argue that workforce readiness must first be clearly conceptualized. To this end, they draw a distinction between core skills and generic skills, with core skills defined as those specific to higher education disciplines and part of traditional academic preparation, while generic skills are those, such as time management or collaboration, that can be used across disciplines and are more characteristic of vocational training.

The authors do not, however, provide a concrete definition of these skill sets. They conceptualize generic skills as falling into four broad categories: management of self, others, information, and tasks. For each category they provide a list of examples, but note that the framework is flexible and can be adapted according to the needs and preferences of different faculty or disciplines. The authors provide a flexible framework because they are sensitive to prior resistance in institutions of higher education to incorporating generic skill instruction into the curriculum. Furthermore, they hold the view that efforts to fold generic skill acquisition into instruction are more likely to be successful when undertaken (at least partially) from the bottom up.

This article is helpful in framing many of the large questions facing the field of workforce readiness. First, it highlights the lack of consensus that exists in defining what constitutes readiness. Putting aside the related, but distinct, issue of delineating generic from core skills, Bennett, Dunne, and Carré highlight that "readiness" has distinct meanings among various stakeholders: business leaders, university administrations, university faculty, and students. This article suggests that, before we can measure whether readiness is being achieved in academic settings, we need a definition that can be shared across parties as to what readiness actually entails (Q1–Q3).

Second, the authors' framework for delineating core and generic skills draws attention to the need for further discussion around the definition of these skills. While some of the variation in defining these skills may be resolved by the development of a shared definition of "readiness," part of the uncertainty in defining these skills is inherent to the skill division itself. For example, can a set of universally generic skills be resolved, or will the attempt to do so produce such a limited set of skills that are universally necessary for workforce readiness that it bankrupts the conceptual value of generic skills (Q4)? This issue is tied very closely to the question of whether generic skills vary greatly across occupations and fields. Is a generic skill in one area actually a core skill in another? If so, what impact does this have on our ability to measure these areas as distinct constructs?

Third, this article raises the question of how to measure the provision of these skills. Largely a pedagogical issue, provision of skills also relates directly to efficacy, in that understanding how these skills are presented to students can later be used to assess the effectiveness of different pedagogical approaches. There may be reason to think that not all approaches are equal in fostering student mastery of these skills. The authors present a model of pedagogical approaches for the delivery of generic skills that includes five elements: disciplinary content knowledge, disciplinary skills, workplace awareness, workplace experience, and generic skills. Through fieldwork (interviews and classroom observations) the authors have identified six patterns to the provision of generic skills, ranging from no explicit focus to the attainment of generic skills being the desired outcome of instruction. This model may be a useful starting point, as one approach to measuring skill provision, but it also raises a number of important questions about developing such measures, specifically: to what extent is such a model reliable across university settings, as the sample presented in this article was somewhat limited; how exhaustive are these pedagogical classifications more generally; and what do we know about how these approaches vary systematically across disciplines or student ability groups? Before we can begin to use pedagogical approach as a mediating variable in studies of workforce readiness, we must first understand what is being measured.

Finally, this work raises the question of how we should conceptualize, and ultimately measure, generic skill attainment. Will we have one standard of generic skill proficiency for all students, or will we allow for variation in certain areas across disciplines (much as we currently place more weight on quantitative, rather than verbal, GRE scores for prospective engineering students)? While answering such a question is fraught with numerous difficulties in design (for example, generic skill attainment is confounded with major selection and pedagogical approach), we must discuss and address it if we are to develop a valid outcome measure of skill acquisition. While providing more questions than answers, this article does offer a fairly concise overview of the issue and areas of disagreement. Furthermore, it advances a framework that may be useful in fostering dialog on this topic. Thus, perhaps by undertaking such a discussion with all stakeholders, first steps toward advancing the field can be put in motion. At the least, such an exchange will help to elucidate the degree to which consensus exists and also to provide preliminary areas important to measuring generic skill attainment.

A position paper by the Business Higher Education Round Table (B-HERT 2002) defines and discusses generic skills and provides explanations for the increasing attention to this topic. The paper first defines generic skills as a range of abilities, "attitudes, values, and dispositions . . . that are increasingly viewed as important in higher education" (B-HERT 2002: 3). The paper then considers the reasons generic skills are important, including (a) increasing demand for graduates with generic skills, (b) economic and technological shifts that require workers to have generic skills to be successful, and (c) recent calls from educators for more emphasis on generic skills.

All of the reasons offered for the importance of generic skills point to the issue of workforce readiness or "employability," defined as the ability not only to obtain and sustain employment, but to continually improve one's productivity, and thus earning potential, by "competing effectively in the job market" and being able to acquire new skills (B-HERT 2002). Naturally, the next question posed is, "how do we determine what generic skills are needed for workforce readiness/employability?" The authors note that a common approach for addressing this question is to survey employers about valuable employee attributes. However, the use of employers' perceptions of what skills are needed to increase employability has limitations. For example, it is unclear how employers determine which generic skills are important. Thus, the paper concludes that further research should investigate how employers determine which generic skills are desirable.

The paper further argues that generic skills lead not only to greater employability, but also to improved learning, because "the strategies needed to develop generic skills are also the ones that lead to good learning outcomes" (B-HERT 2002: 6). Thus, if the development of generic skills is incorporated in education, learning in general will improve, and the "employability gap" could be closed without undermining "substantive" education (B-HERT 2002). This proposition leads to the question of how to include the development of generic skills in education. The paper provides some examples of how this is being done in Australia (for example, by developing "statements of graduate attributes"), but notes that more work is needed (Q2 and Q3).

In addition to defining generic skills and arguing for their importance, the paper focuses on the measurement of generic skills. Specifically, the paper highlights how the holism and contextuality of generic skills complicates any attempt at measurement. The authors argue that, while it is helpful to think about generic skills individually when trying to understand them, their intertwined nature cannot be ignored; in other words, generic skills also need to be considered holistically (B-HERT 2002). Furthermore, generic skills are influenced by the context in which they are used. Different occupations require different generic skills and the same occupation in different environments requires different generic skills (B-HERT 2002) (Q4). These characteristics suggest that measuring isolated skills says nothing about an individual's "capacity to integrate generic skills" and "to frame an appropriate response to a given contextual situation" (B-HERT 2002: 7). Thus, the paper poses the following important questions:

- How do we effectively measure generic skills given their intertwined nature and the importance of context?
- What is the "appropriate level of generality" (by discipline, occupation, or specialty) when defining and measuring generic skills?

A final measurement question raised by this paper pertains to the type of measurement (for example, multiple-choice test, observation, or survey) most appropriate for measuring generic skills. The use of multiple-choice tests to assess generic skills is questionable (B-HERT 2002). Such tests assume that understanding the concept of a generic skill indicates the ability to utilize it appropriately and effectively (B-HERT 2002). However, the paper argues that conceptual understanding is a necessary but insufficient condition for the ability to appropriately use generic skills (B-HERT 2002).

These measurement concerns beg the question of how to measure generic skills better. One possible approach is to employ a randomized design and multiple methods of data collection. For example, to study teamwork skills, individuals could be randomly assigned to groups in which they are asked to perform a collaborative task. Upon completion of the task, each group member would be asked to rate the others' ability to work in a team. In addition, raters could be trained to observe the groups and rate each member's ability to work collaboratively. Using both surveys and observations would allow for triangulation of the measurement of teamwork. To further strengthen this study, one member from each group could be randomly selected to move to a different group where they would perform another task and teamwork skills would be rated again. Such a design would make it possible to assess the selected individual's ability to work in a team independent of the specific context (task and team members).

Finally, the paper poses the question of which generic skills are necessary for three key levels of educational attainment: "(1) commencement of undergraduate study, (2) completion of undergraduate study, and (3) completion of postgraduate study" (B-HERT 2002: 11). The paper posits that the generic skills needed to begin undergraduate study include communication, numeracy, "information literacy", critical thinking, and interpersonal skills (B-HERT 2002). At the completion of undergraduate study, students should have generic skills "such as critical thinking, problem solving, analytic capacity", the ability to make value judgments, ethical behavior, and technological fluency (B-HERT 2002: 12). Generic skills needed at the completion of postgraduate study include "independent and critical thinking" (B-HERT 2002: 14). Although several "foundational generic skills" are offered for each level, the authors note that this question still requires further research (Q4).

The work of Bennett, Dunne, and Carré (1999) and B-HERT (2002) raises many questions related to the meaning of workforce readiness and the skills necessary for readiness. However, the key questions raised by these articles are (Q1) whether academic and generic/vocational preparation are orthogonal to one another, (Q2) whether they can both be achieved through one curriculum, (Q3) what this implies for curriculum design, and (Q4) what skills are necessary for readiness? The next set of articles takes this line of research several steps further by focusing on how to implement best practices for acquiring readiness and how to study the impact of readiness on outcomes.

Best Practices for Acquiring Readiness and the Impact of Readiness on Outcomes

In Edith Aimee Orozco's (2010) dissertation, "A Comparison of Career Technical Education: 16 Career Pathway High School Participants with Non-Participants on Academic Achievement, School Engagement, and Development of Technical Skills," she compares the outcomes of students who received a traditional education with those of students who were exposed to Pathway Educational (PE) methods. PE methods provide traditional academic coursework along with electives focused on the acquisition of career or technical skills. Orozco found that on objective tests of academic achievement, a self-report of engagement, and a self-report of technical skill development, the scores of students in the PE methods were higher, even after controlling for ethnicity, socioeconomic status, gender, and location (Q6).

There is much to like about this dissertation: First and foremost, it appears to be one of the first major empirical studies that looks at the benefit of an integrated educational format that blends academic and practical knowledge. Second, it does not rely on one single measure (such as academic achievement) but rather looks at multiple measures collected in a multi-method approach (test scores and surveys in this case). Finally, rather than act as a definitive source to answer these questions, this work appropriately notes its limitations and is really a "call for more research" to understand the benefits of a PE method.

With that said, this dissertation draws other conclusions that support the basic tenets of our chapter:

- Empirical research on PE methods is scarce, as suggested by the modest number of empirical papers cited.
- Studies that do exist suggest an *association* between PE methods and achievement, but no more than that.
- Broad-based experimental or quasi-experimental methods applied to this issue are needed.
- At the moment, the public policy implications of these findings are merely suggestive of the need for increased state-level investment.

This dissertation also provides guidance on designing an optimal experiment. First, control variables are critical, as PE methods are likely to have differential effects across age, race, socioeconomic background, etc. Thus, these dimensions should be considered in the collection of information at the individual-student level to allow for their use as controls and to allow for studies employing matched-pair research designs. Second, the outcomes of interest (student achievement, engagement, technical skills acquired) are related to study dropout, with students assessed as being lower on these measures less likely to participate or graduate. Hence, more sophisticated methods than a pure ANCOVA approach (taken in this dissertation) will be needed to make sure that self-selected populations are not analyzed. Third, while test scores and perceived benefits are important to both students and society at large, long-term longitudinal studies are needed to assess the economic benefits of a PE program in terms of increased attendance of higher education programs, increased salary upon employment, and other societally beneficial outcomes. This suggests that PE programs cannot be evaluated in isolation, but rather need to be linked to individual-level datasets that track students over time (such as the National Assessment of Educational Progress studies).

Lastly, while it is not mentioned in this dissertation or much of the extant research, one should not take the construction of a PE program as a given. The choice of topic areas, the amount of vocational/technical material within an everyday curriculum, the set of pathways, and their linkage to more traditional academic subjects (such as math and science) are all open to debate. Although many researchers, evaluators, and policymakers may want to focus on outcomes, more work needs to be done to design the optimal programs themselves. Unresolved issues include what educational governing bodies would need to be involved, and what level of proof they would need to be convinced of the value of PE methods (Q5).

An article by Hoachlander (2008) summarizes the theoretical and empirical motivations for high schools and their students to focus on adopting "multiple pathways" in their curricula. Multiple pathways refers to a strategy where students simultaneously enroll in traditional academic coursework along with one or more electives concentrated on the acquisition of career or technical skills. Based on national statistics regarding the high prevalence of career and technical education (CTE) courses taken by American high school students, the article characterizes an ideal implementation of the multiple pathways approach to secondary education and discusses the potential benefits for student outcomes (Q5 and Q6).

The underlying logic of recommending multiple pathways in high school is that advanced academic knowledge is of limited utility if students are unable to connect the material learned in traditional courses to the practical working world. Explicit instruction in both core skills derived from academic study and also generic skills helps students integrate their knowledge in the manner they will be required to in the workforce. Hoachlander sees the implementation of multiple pathways in American high schools as a method of ensuring that academic coursework retains its rigor without losing its relevance to the real world contexts students find themselves in upon graduation. Schools operating in the multiple pathways framework are responsible for the provision of both work and college readiness equally, in effect providing an answer to the age-old student question, "Why do I need to know this?" (Hoachlander 2008). The implementation of multiple pathways is purported in this article to lead to a wider range of possible postsecondary opportunities for students than either traditional academics or CTE alone, and also to have a positive impact on academic achievement. All components of the program are designed to be highly demanding, with supplemental services provided should students require support beyond in-class instruction.

Hoachlander (2008) describes several examples of schools and states implementing a multiple pathways approach, and cites evidence from the empirical literature that multiple pathways should be aimed at college-bound and vocationally oriented students alike, given the strategy's purported benefits in terms of both future earnings and academic achievement. While space limitations preclude a detailed review of the evidence provided in support of multiple pathways, a review of this article raises several important questions for future research in the area.

Perhaps of greatest importance to any proposed future study of multiple pathways is the measurement approach taken in assessing the quality and implementation of the programs themselves. With variation occurring naturally based on the delivery strategies of high schools, districts, and states the field appears to lack a standardized assessment device to facilitate their accurate comparison. This is a crucial issue because we will be unable to understand the (overall or domain-specific) breadth, quality, or implementation fidelity of a multiple pathways approach without a systematic appraisal of its characteristics. Such an assessment might take the form of a specifically targeted survey or observational rating protocol, but could also potentially make use of existing administrative data.

Once the above assessment is developed, it could be utilized to answer the question of whether the multiple pathways approach leads to positive student outcomes (either in terms of academic or career performance). Based on the literature cited by Hoachlander (2008), no studies of these effects had been conducted to date. Thus, a pressing need exists to design and carry out rigorous research evaluating the effectiveness of multiple pathways curricula. Hoachlander (2008) reports that national survey data have shown an association between CTE coursework and positive outcomes such as academic achievement and future earnings. Likewise, anecdotal reports have been a valuable mechanism for learning of specific challenges within particular contextual environments. This data is limited to simple associations, however, and should not be considered substantive evidence for the independent contribution of the multiple pathways approach.

One plausible design for studying such effects is the cluster randomized trial (with schools as the unit of randomization) comparing business as usual to an integrated multiple pathways curriculum. With appropriate statistical power, such studies would be valuable for their utility in appropriately disentangling the effect of a multiple pathways approach to secondary education from the myriad other influences on student achievement. Quasi-experimental approaches to evaluation research might also be considered. For example, a multiple time series design would offer the benefit of permitting a relatively clean comparison of outcome trends before and after the implementation of multiple pathways, along with comparisons to samples lacking such a program.

Hoachlander's article makes the assumption that students taking more CTE are doing so because they are interested in career preparation, but there are several other plausible factors that might lead to this phenomenon, as well as to their higher performance on standardized achievement tests. Among these is the possibility that students with higher levels of ability or motivation take more courses in general. This phenomenon may explain the data Hoachlander (2008) cites from the National Education Longitudinal Study finding an association between enrollment in CTE courses and reduced high school dropout rates. Students enrolled in more courses might simply be more motivated to educate themselves and stay in school. High enrollment in CTE may also result from student interest in "career" skills for the purposes of developing a hobby, or the fact that their friends are enrolled in such courses. Many students may also enroll in CTE courses simply to fulfill general elective requirements for high school graduation. We should not make the mistake of attributing lower dropout or other positive outcomes to CTE without first conducting rigorous research on the topic.

The work of Hoachlander (2008) and Orozco (2010) raises many questions related to how to implement best practices for acquiring readiness and how to study the impact of readiness on outcomes. The key questions raised by these articles are, (Q5) what evidence will be required to provide robust support for multiple pathways (and other readiness programs) to be adopted more broadly, and (Q6) what are the desired outcomes of workforce readiness initiatives?

All four of the reviewed papers highlight important questions that need to be addressed in the workforce readiness literature. To that end, we use what we have learned from this selective literature review to suggest a framework for designing a dataset optimally suited to addressing the knowledge gaps identified.

A Data Wish List

In recommending best practices for gathering data on workforce readiness and testing interventions to improve readiness, it is helpful to bear in mind two broad frameworks for empirical evaluation. First, in true field experiments the randomization (and thus, probabilistic equivalence) of study groups to treatment and control conditions permits an unbiased estimate of an intervention's effect on the treated subsample (Shadish, Cook, and Campbell 2002). Conducting such trials outside a laboratory is notoriously challenging for myriad reasons, including (in no particular order) ethical issues, practical or financial feasibility, implementation fidelity, and attrition, to name a few. These are particularly pronounced when the target settings and samples of such field trials involve public schools and their students (Boruch 1997). In direct response to the above challenges, a relatively robust set of methods facilitating the rigorous analysis of data resulting from observational studies has coalesced in recent years (Rosenbaum 2010). These methods attempt to mitigate the threats to causal inference inherent in the statistical comparison of non-equivalent study groups defined to a nontrivial degree by selection bias. Our point here is not to review experimental or quasi-experimental methodology in detail. We simply note that while true experimentation would be preferred for its parsimony and support of causal inference, observational studies (particularly longitudinal ones) of interventions to improve workforce readiness are also informative so long as they employ rigorous analytic strategies.

A natural requirement of rigorous field studies is that their measurement and data management strategies rise to or exceed the quality standards set for their design and implementation. This implies the development of and adherence to detailed procedures for common tasks such as scale development and scoring, the collection and coding of data, and the protection of identifying information. Ensuring the reliability and validity of any data collected is essential to supporting confidence in any inferences drawn from them. Gathering higher-quality data, however, typically increases the cost of research. Thus, a balance must be struck between conducting idealized field studies and implementing efficiencies to the extent that we retain the ability to draw justifiable conclusions from our data. We see no reason that the historical link between increased quality and cost need persist ad infinitum, and perceive a midpoint between the above two extremes at which much of the important scholarship on workforce readiness will occur. The need to keep costs in line while maintaining sufficient data quality should motivate the centralization of data collection and dissemination efforts. These should avoid potential redundancies, in addition encouraging the widespread availability and usage of the resulting data. In fact, much of the data infrastructure required to reliably assess readiness status (and its susceptibility to manipulation by policy or other interventions) may already be in place at the state level.

As of fiscal year (FY) 2009, the U.S. Department of Education's Institute of Education Sciences (IES) had awarded grant funding to forty-two states (including the District of Columbia) for the development of Statewide Longitudinal Data Systems (SLDS). Such data warehouses are at varying stages of development but will eventually collect a wide range of information pertinent to issues of workforce readiness (such as standardized test scores, electronic transcripts with course enrollment and completion data, and graduation status; IES 2009). Already used to indicate warning signs for high school dropout (Neild 2009), SLDSs may soon become the state-of-the-art in designing mechanisms to track the progress of students through formal schooling and their eventual engagement in the workforce. Along these lines, a majority of states have planned the integration of postsecondary educational and workforce-related data within their developing SLDS (IES 2009). While clear definitions of what this data entails are available only from individual states, the very inclusion of educational and workforce indicators clearly indicates the priority placed by IES on facilitating the capability of both policymakers and researchers to track longitudinal workforce readiness information across and within states using existing administrative records. The use of extant resources speaks directly to the above-mentioned potential for rigor and efficiency to serve as complementary rather than competing goals. Some individual cities and collective groups of local communities have also embarked on initiatives to develop similarly integrated data systems (KIDS: Fantuzzo et al. 2006; Youth Data Archive: London and Gurantz 2010).

While there is ample reason to be cautious in assuming the quality and accuracy of administrative data on educational outcomes and workforce readiness, we are encouraged by IES's specification of six key SLDS features targeted directly toward ensuring maximal validity. Examples include the development of a formal data audit system, storage of comprehensive metadata on the history of any changes made to the SLDS, and a comprehensive data dictionary (IES 2009). Apart from technical issues of data quality, another raised consistently by those considering any kind of field research is the pressing need to secure buy-in from local stakeholders and those participating in the research (Boruch 1997; Rossi 2004). Several factors point to this being a less salient issue with regard to statewide data systems, not the least of which are their centralized administration and existing or future legislative mandates for the annual reporting of school performance data (such as the No Child Left Behind Act of 2001). Further, requests to make use of SLDS data or other resources are handled by a centralized administration, avoiding the need of individual researchers to secure buy-in at the student, teacher, school, or district level.

We now consider how our guiding questions might be optimally answered using ideal student-level data collected on a longitudinal basis. Considering the broad set of skills deemed necessary to enter the workforce across different fields, we ask (and answer):

Q1: Are these skills orthogonal to each other?

A1: Psychometrically rigorous assessments of both academic abilities and the prevalence of psychosocial characteristics should go a long way toward informing this question. Coupled with appropriate data on workforce or postsecondary educational engagement, researchers can employ multivariate analyses to develop typologies or profiles of the specific skills defining successful performance across the range of careers. In this light, the orthogonality vs. dependence between individual skills (within and across fields) becomes a relatively straightforward measurement question, answerable given adequate data.

Q2: Can these skills be achieved by students all exposed to the same curriculum?

Q3: What does the answer to Q2 imply for future curriculum design?

A2–3: The simple answer to Q2 is likely to be "No." It seems every new issue of educational trade publications and practice-oriented academic journals alike offers the promise of a new, highly effective curriculum effective for the vast majority of students. Putting aside for the moment that remarkably few of these have ever been subjected to or met evidence standards for rigorous evaluation (IES 2008), it has long been recognized that students exhibit differential learning strategies and thus may be expected to be differentially susceptible to curricular interventions. This is putting aside the issue of curricula developed for students with special needs (whether intellectually challenged or gifted) and physical disabilities. The future of curricula designed to enhance workforce readiness should make use of the results of studies seeking to answer Q1. They should be informed by and seek to enhance the optimal skill set for a given career area, specializing their content to the degree necessary to prioritize the development of such competencies.

Q4: In light of the above questions and our ever-modernizing work environments and economy, how stable is the set of ideal skills for successful performance in a given domain/career?

A5: This question is answerable only with appropriate longitudinal data. Given reliable data on the skill profiles exhibited by those succeeding in different career pathways over time, quasi-experimental methods may be used to compare their prevalence across career and geographic areas. Of course, previously unrecognized skill profiles are likely to emerge over time in response to market or technological demands. The regular utilization of infrastructure such as a SLDS offers the opportunity to observe such patterns (and apply any salient interventions) in near real time as opposed to only retrospectively.

Q5: What evidence will be required to provide robust support for a multiple pathways approach (or any other proposed curriculum) to be adopted more broadly?

A5: Here we see yet another advantage of SLDSs. Given that the ability to generalize research findings is in large part a function of the sampling method from which the data are generated (Shadish, Cook, and Campbell 2002), SLDSs offer the invaluable benefit of census-level samples. The fact that an SLDS contains observations for all students attending school and/or working in a given state by definition permits the generalization of findings based on the system's data to that same population. Short of multiple confirmatory randomized field trials, one could not hope for better evidence in support of the adoption of an effective curriculum than longitudinally stable, positive impacts observed vs. matched control groups in a SLDS. Further, the large sample sizes inherent in SLDSs should imbue analyses using their data with statistical power sufficient to gauge the effectiveness of policy or curricular interventions within most demographic minority subgroups.

Q6: Given the necessary measurement techniques, the fundamental question arises, "What *are* the specific student outcomes it is desirable to assess?" Rephrased, what outcomes most directly indicate workforce readiness (however it is ultimately defined) or a lack thereof?

A6: We do not yet possess the proper evidence to answer this question definitively, but, as mentioned above, potential candidates for desirable outcomes may include the following:

1) performance on standardized academic assessments;
2) GPA in a particular subject relative to the student's school or local peers;
3) school attendance rate;
4) disciplinary record (or lack thereof);
5) participation/performance pattern in extracurricular activities or elective coursework.

These are only a basic set of potential indicators. We await the results of future research to define the most salient indicators of readiness across different fields in a more concrete fashion.

In summary, from the perspective of an idealized set of research methods and available data, the following recommendations may be made. First, readiness must be investigated and assessed using more sophisticated empirical methods than have been employed to date. These need not necessarily be purely experimental, but also cannot consist solely of ANOVAs on non-equivalent, non-matched groups. Modern methods for conducting observational studies offer an excellent pathway to robust research, aided in no small part by the very large sample sizes inherent to statewide or other administrative data systems. Second, longitudinal data will be essential for answering many of the most pertinent questions regarding the stability of skills or skill profiles supporting workforce readiness. Third, rather than reinventing the proverbial wheel, SLDSs currently in existence or development should be augmented to include reliable and valid data informing the issue of workforce readiness. After ensuring the protection of identifying information, these data should be made unconditionally accessible to the research community at large.

Conclusions and Final Thoughts

This chapter has focused on what is known about measuring workforce readiness. While there are many unanswered questions in this field of study, including perhaps the most fundamental of definitional consensus, we argue that much can be gained and some of these unanswered questions can be advanced by bringing extant, higher quality, data to bear. We do not advance any new frameworks for understanding readiness but instead summarize the main questions the field needs to address in order to advance measurement and eventually evaluation of readiness. We propose drawing upon SLDSs as a first step to help provide more context as the field considers these questions.

We envision the advancement of measurement around readiness as an iterative process, whereby evaluation of existing data on student paths and course-taking may help further the dialog and consensus for what is necessary for readiness, much as has recently occurred in the area of curriculum standards with the release and adoption of the Common Core State Standards. Greater consensus and clarity around what readiness entails would, in turn, lead to opportunities to create better measures that are both more sensitive and specific to the desired outcomes. Development of these measures could occur on the smaller scale, and they could eventually be transferred to the state and national scale after ample evidence has been amassed and careful review by the field has occurred. Once the field has a set of valid measures around readiness, any number of trials to examine potential programs to boost workforce preparation could ensue and readily be compared to one another on a host of shared outcomes. While this approach may or may not lead to the use of a uniform approach to readiness, it would at least allow the field to evaluate differential program effectiveness on common metrics and to make decisions about program utility with greater transparency and accuracy.

Finally, we think that improved measurement around readiness can better advance the discussion and measurement of lifelong outcomes, which include not just those skills or attributes that the field determines are necessary to be well-prepared for the workforce, but also what the impact of having this skill set is once one enters and progresses in the workforce proper. Obviously, causality will be a difficult issue to address in this sort of work, as ethically individuals cannot be limited or forced to obtain a certain level of readiness. However, as discussed above, much improvement in quasi-experimental methods has occurred in recent years that may help to advance our understanding of what leads to positive life-cycle outcomes. Moreover, the implications of improved measurement work may be less about determining cause and effect than about creating clarity around the extent and impact of readiness, that is, to what outcomes does readiness actually relate; and around those discussions of what society may desire as outcomes, that is, the moral and practical implications of what goods and goals should be achieved by readiness (the *what is* versus the *what should be*). This may be less an area for academics and researchers than for policy-makers, but better evidence on readiness and how it relates to outcomes can only help to improve the quality of discussion and, in theory, the resulting policy.

Workforce readiness is certainly a fertile topic of debate. At its heart, readiness relates to the age-old discourse on the purpose and goals of education. While that debate is likely to continue for centuries more, there can be little argument that modern economies do indeed need a prepared workforce. Whether such preparedness is the responsibility of schools or other entities may be the subject of discussion, but we should at least be working toward a commonly held approach to measuring such readiness. While our review of the literature shows that much work remains to be done toward this end, we have suggested a number of ways in which this endeavor may be started, and are optimistic about the mutual benefit that will be derived by its undertaking.

CHAPTER 3

Work-Based Learning: Initiatives and Impact

Bridget N. O'Connor

Perhaps the foremost challenge in reforming urban education is ensuring that all students have the resources they need to succeed. Public high school students in urban areas, where their more wealthy counterparts often attend private schools, are at a disadvantage. Socioeconomic status, which includes the support of responsible adults and family income, is a strong predictor of a student's success in school (McNeal 2011). Yet we continue to focus urban school reform efforts on creating smaller classes and improving teaching. The smallest class with the best teacher will have little effect on a student's success if that teacher is the student's sole support system (Nocera 2011). What can be done within the curriculum to ensure that we give students academic credentials and at the same time engage the entire community in ensuring that high school graduates are not only academically prepared but also ready to enter the work world?

An approach used in the past was traditional vocational education, which in the United States emphasized preparation for specific jobs. Unfortunately, vocational education programs were frequently dumping grounds for underachieving students from low socioeconomic backgrounds, who were also often minorities. Such programs had a long history of doing the right things badly or just doing the wrong things. Recall when students in auto shop worked on cars with outdated technologies, or when a career preparation program existed for which there was no sustainable career, such as traditional secretarial science.

Such tracking of students into vocational programs for low wage, increasingly scarce jobs understandably created a backlash against vocational education that resulted in policies intended to eliminate vocational tracks and prepare all students for college. Combined with efforts to increase high school graduation requirements, these educational policies steadily squeezed out opportunities for all non-academic coursework. A one-size-fits-all curriculum based on traditional academic disciplines increasingly directed students toward one result: to get into college. This approach did not take into account diverse individual motivation; or unequal skills in language, math, and science; or uneven aptitudes. It did not take into account the impossibility of preparing *all* students for one type of postsecondary path or the importance of ensuring that learning has context, meaning, and is applicable outside of the classroom.

In this chapter, I first describe some of today's much-improved work-based learning (WBL) initiatives at the secondary level, often called career and technical education (CTE), and then discuss what we know about their impact. The discussion will include issues related to identifying appropriate learning measures and outcomes. The overall thesis is that well-designed and effectively implemented WBL initiatives focus on helping students see the relevance in what they learn and provide students with access to the support of responsible adults. Relevance and access can help guarantee that students will be prepared to enter postsecondary education and/or the workforce. (For further discussion of work-based learning, a type of workplace learning, see Nancy Hoffman's chapter in this volume.)

Work-Based Learning Initiatives

The world in which students live is not a compilation of discrete classes. While discussing the limitations of Watson, the IBM computer that challenged *Jeopardy* contestants, *New York Times* columnist Stanley Fish articulated a view that is relevant here: "The worlds we live in are already built; we don't walk around putting discrete items together until they add up to a context; we walk around with a contextual sense—a sense of where we are, what is at stake and what our resources are—already in place; we inhabit worldly spaces already organized by purposes, projects and expectations" (Fish 2011: first paragraph). WBL initiatives can bring the world to the student or take the student to the world.

Table 3.1 offers a listing of initiatives that fall under the work-based learning rubric. Note that some, such as career education and mentoring programs, are designed to heighten career awareness. Others, such as career academies and career majors, result in skill development through integrating academic learning with workplace skills and problems. Still other initiatives involve actual work—sometimes for pay and other times not-for-pay. Non-paid work includes service learning and working in school enterprises (for example, the school bookstore). For-pay experiences can include cooperative education, after school jobs, and ideally, internships.

Perhaps the most well-known of these initiatives is the internship. Long the staple of professions such as engineering and publishing, internships are opportunities for students to experience the world of work *in* the world of work. Effective internships are a match between the needs and time commitments of the sponsoring organization and the student. In the typical internship process, an organization develops a job description that includes tasks, location, and time commitment for the position and students apply for the job. Arguing that WBL was an educational reform movement, Bailey, Hughes, and Moore (2004) noted the challenges of recruiting employers and ensuring that resultant work experiences were viable learning experiences. They recommended that someone should take responsibility to generate positions and develop a repository for internships and part-time jobs. Such "coordinators" can also help students work through the application process. They, along with other stakeholders, can also take responsibility for sustaining, supporting, and evaluating student performance in these jobs (Bailey, Hughes, and Moore 2004).

The importance of *paid* internships is a mantra of many successful programs. A paid internship is evidence that the organization expects value from the student intern and the intern sees his or her contribution as adding value to the organization. Given that money issues are incredibly important to many students, and perhaps essential to low-income youths' efforts to remain in school, paid internships can be a win-win for both employer and student.

Paid internships are the culminating activity of many career academies. Career academies are career-specific programs that operate as schools within schools, offering specialized curricula designed to supplement the academic curricula. They are often described as having strong partnerships with both the schools that support them and the business or industry that their programs represent. Because they bring cohorts of students together and provide

Table 3.1. Categorization and Definitions of Work-Based Learning Initiatives

Learning Initiative	Definition
1. CAREER AWARENESS	Programs designed to make students aware of the wide range of occupations open to them
a. Career education	Classes or seminars overviewing a wide range of career choices
b. Career fair	School-wide exhibition showcasing career options
c. Mentoring programs	Matching students with adult mentors in the community
d. College and career planning	A sequence of activities that enable students to prepare for the futures beyond high school
2. SKILL DEVELOPMENT	Opportunities to develop specific skills as part of classwork
a. Problem solving in academic classrooms integrated with career education	Teachers use work-based problems to motivate learning
b. Career academies	Schools within a school or separate small school organized around a broad career theme
c. Career majors	All students within a specific school explore a wide variety of careers, but organize their coursework around a broad career area
d. Tech-prep	Four-year programs that combine the last two years of high school with the first two years of community college
3. WORK-LIKE EXPERIENCES (NON-PAID)	Non-paid work outside of the traditional school curriculum
a. School-based enterprises	Students "work" within the school
b. Service learning	Students provide services to the community
c. Internships (can be for pay)	Students experience a variety of jobs outside the school
4. EMPLOYMENT (PAID)	Work experiences where students receive money for work performed
a. After-school job placement	School helps student obtain jobs
b. Cooperative education	Part-time jobs offered as part of vocational training
c. Apprenticeships	Students learn specific skills while working with an adult who coaches

Source: Adapted from O'Connor 2002.

intensive adult scaffolding, career academies can be ideal places to introduce students to the workplace (O'Connor and Ponti 2008).

How a high school district goes about implementing internships, or any of the initiatives described in Table 3.1, is largely dependent on its size, access to resources, and the participation of the community in which it exists. Location may expand or limit choices. Theobald (1996) explained that a large urban school district may have a range of paid cooperative work programs and job placement services for students who want part-time employment. Rural school districts, on the other hand, tend to have fewer options. Suburban schools, he said, may be in the best position to ensure rich, useful work-based learning experiences, as they tend to have relatively high degrees of parental involvement and, at the same time, access to city resources, including potential employers.

The section that follows describes what we know about the impact of some of these initiatives in reaching the goal of preparing an individual for the workplace.

The Impact of Work-Based Learning Initiatives

Determining appropriate outcome measures for WBL requires first having realistic learning goals that educators, parents, and the public in general support. What are hallmarks of successful programs? Is a program successful if learners consider the program useful and motivational? If participants score higher on a test of knowledge than non-enrolled students? If trained evaluators ensure the validity of curricular offerings? If graduation rates are higher for participants than for students not in the program? If participants are more likely to be employed or earn higher wages than those not in the program?

In this section, I summarize what we know about the impact of WBL initiatives, organized around the four domains of WBL program evaluation identified by Donald Kirkpatrick (1994) and adding a fifth domain. These evaluation domains are: student satisfaction with programs (reaction); the actual learning that takes place (learning); the application of what was learned outside of the classroom (behavior); graduation rates (organizational impact); and, an additional category, earning power upon completion (labor market outcomes).

Reaction

Student reactions to their school-based experiences at the secondary level are not heavily documented. Reaction—student attitudes toward or satisfaction with their instructor, curriculum, class, or program—is important to students' engagement in their schooling. While scholarly debate about whether such data are reliable and valid is long and complex, schools, particularly at the college level, often use reaction data to assess student satisfaction with all facets of their learning experiences. Although limited to descriptive analyses, the one study discussed here suggests that today's students are, overall, not satisfied with their school lives.

This study, the Million Voice Project, is supported by the Pearson Foundation in partnership with the Quaglia Institute. Through the Million Voice Project's website (http://www.millionvoice.org), teachers and/or researchers can order surveys and post data that measure high school students' perceptions of their educational experiences. A report on the Quaglia Institute's website (accessed April 14, 2011) provides preliminary findings from over 500,000 American students and lists several gaps that must be closed to improve student engagement and academic success:

- relationships: students desire to do well in school, but they do not believe their teachers think they will;
- participation: students think school can be fun and beneficial to their future, yet they do not feel engaged in school;
- expectations: students believe they have leadership abilities, but they do not believe their school fosters development of this skill.

Although data from this survey are currently being analyzed, these preliminary findings suggest that schools are not living up to their students' expectations and that they can do much better. Because WBL experiences can create or enhance student engagement with their teachers and other involved adults, such initiatives may help reduce gaps such as those listed above.

Learning

Any discussion of learning outcomes must recognize that it is the whole person—body and mind—who experiences and learns. Peter Jarvis articulated this spirit when he defined learning as

> the combination of processes whereby the whole person—body (genetic, physical, and biological) and mind (knowledge, skills, attitudes, emotions, beliefs and senses)—experiences a social situation, the perceived content of which is then transformed cognitively, emotively or practically (or through any combination) and integrated into the person's individual biography resulting in a changed (or more experienced) person. (Jarvis 2006: 13)

This definition is consistent with Beach's definition of learning transfer, which describes learning as not simply a transfer of knowledge, but a movement of "the entire human being, including his or her identity and social participation" (Beach in Konkola 2007: 214). Such a perspective is useful as the goal of WPL initiatives is to integrate and transfer what is learned from the school environment to the workplace.

Even as early as 1916, John Dewey posited that we learn through our experiences and that we build knowledge based on what we already know. Meaningfulness in what is learned is essential to learner engagement and motivation to complete tasks. This approach implies that measuring the value of work-based learning initiatives goes beyond competency development and standardized testing for content to include attention to how knowledge is applied in ways that integrate a variety of skills and disciplines, or have systemic value.

The impact of learning in CTE programs has been measured by studies comparing academic outcomes of those participating to outcomes of those in control groups who did not participate. Academic outcomes are typically measured by standardized test scores or nontraditional evaluation strategies, such as portfolios, discussed further below.

These studies typically consider such questions as: Are year-to-year improvements in SAT standardized test scores indicative of learning? When learners meet or exceed established standards (which are actually minimum expectations), what does that tell us? Matters related to standardized test administration, content variations, and interpretation of results have been debated in relationship to the overall fairness of tests (Olson and Sabers 2008). For standardized testing, the issues continue to be related to developing valid, reliable measures that can be easily scored and interpreted so that findings are useful to administrators, teachers, parents, students, and other stakeholders.

Standardized tests are often deemed unfair to minorities or students with lower socioeconomic backgrounds. In addition, how the tests are implemented can often make comparisons between and among groups difficult. The debate continues as to whether there should be a set of national academic standards, implying that textbooks would need to be standardized and teachers would have to likewise be evaluated on their own content knowledge and on the success of their students in learning what is being taught (Ornstein and Hunkins 2009). Teacher-developed tests, long used to determine course grades, are often inappropriate in comparing learner groups.

That said, academic content specialists for reading and mathematics have developed standards that stress knowledge comprehension and, in some cases, performance or application of concepts. Standardized testing for WBL skills and knowledge, on the other hand, may be more difficult since the workplace is a moving target. While professions and industries do not know exactly what students need to know or do to be considered workplace ready, they are in a good position to partner with schools to create assessments that could indicate the degree to which a student has mastered content in job-related areas.

One of the most widely lauded benefits of WBL is its impact on academic achievement and/or specific occupational skills. WBL may be embedded into academic courses through classroom speakers, discussions with adults, and real-world projects as part of academic curricula (Larson and Vandegrift 1998) or, alternately, academic skills may be embedded into occupational curricula. In both cases, academic and CTE instructors will ideally work together to determine goals and evaluation criteria.

In one randomized trial, researchers through the National Research Center for Career and Vocational Education (NRCCVE) investigated the impact on student learning when volunteer CTE teachers partnered with math teachers to develop math-enhanced CTE curricula (Pearson et al. 2010). After one year, students in the math-enhanced CTE sections outperformed control groups on two of three standardized measures of math achievement while advancing their occupational knowledge. This math study was followed by an intervention with reading strategy instruction whereby two different models of content-related reading instruction were compared with a control group. Reading comprehension and vocabulary were statistically improved in the two intervention groups. A science-in-career and technical education study is currently underway (Pearson et al. 2010). These initial efforts showed that academic achievement was improved when CTE classes were purposefully integrated with academic subjects.

Work experience during high school can translate to success in postsecondary education and life as well. A longitudinal case study of thirty-four British students who entered college with vocational qualifications reported that their work experiences influenced their learning—not only while they were in school, but in their later ability to lead fulfilling lives and careers (Shaw 2011). Konkola et al. (2007) described a case in occupational therapy education in which students interviewed therapists to identify a useful project. Then, teachers and therapists worked to create the project, which students worked on with assistance from the therapists and teachers. Such collaboration blurs the boundaries between school and work.

A student-centered approach to evaluating learning outcomes is portfolio development, where students document what they did, how they did it, and what doing it meant to them. Thus, portfolio development adds context to content and gives students an opportunity to demonstrate and reflect on what they are learning. By giving all students, whether they consider themselves college bound or not, the responsibility not only to demonstrate what they have learned but also to reflect on what their learning means, portfolios can provide motivation and buy-in to goals. Students themselves are involved in the assessment process as they "collect, reflect, and select pieces for inclusion," thus enabling "teachers to 'sit beside students' rather than 'standing over them'" (Stefanakis 2002: xxii). Portfolios also provide useful feedback to teachers, parents, and any other adults who may be helping the student achieve. Adult scaffolding is important because, while the aim is to ensure that students are independent and self-reliant, adults need to help students in choosing appropriate goals; provide a wide range of learning experiences to support those goals; and provide continuous feedback. Thus, the portfolio development process itself is a learning and communication opportunity.

While research on K–12 portfolio effectiveness is limited, one study shows that teachers were more likely to use the technique when they had training in its use and adequate support in its implementation (Viggiano

2009). Equally important, teachers who have used portfolios in elementary and secondary school classrooms have found them to be a valuable method of serving a wide range of students from both a cultural and cognitive perspective (Stefanakis 2002). Additionally, portfolio evaluation, while time-consuming, can be a very useful way to assess learning even when what is being learned does not fall in the conventional academic realm. As such an approach presents the world of work and the world of school as intertwined, not as distinct entities, portfolios could form the basis for systemic change that puts learning into context.

Behavior

The third evaluation domain, behavior, assumes that the outcome of a learning initiative is best measured outside of the learning environment. Here, behavior is defined first as attitudes toward work and then as workplace and college readiness. Changes in behavior are often demonstrated through case studies or studies comparing behaviors of those completing programs to those in control groups who did not participate.

Attitudes toward work, including professionalism, work ethics, and other attitudes, are difficult to define, let alone measure. While most of us take for granted the ability to show up on time, dress appropriately, and follow business etiquette, these skill sets are not always in new graduates' toolkits. However, we have known for some time that learning such skills in schools and within the context of work can improve attitudes toward work and contribute to personal growth (Bailey and Merritt 1997; Flynn 1995; Porter and Bradwick 1996; Rhoder and French 1999; Walker 1995).

Measuring individuals' attitude changes as a result of an intervention is different from measuring their reaction or satisfaction. The Work Self-Efficacy Inventory (WS-Ei) measures both cognitive and behavioral outcomes of work experiences including co-ops, internships, and new work experiences (Raelin 2011). The inventory (available at http://www.mindgarden .com/products/wsei.htm) is further described as measuring

> a range of job behaviors and practices referring to beliefs in one's command of the social requirements necessary for success in the workplace. Its theoretical underpinning is that individuals with

higher work self-efficacy are more likely to undertake, and to be successful in, workplace performance. Furthermore, work accomplishments, in turn, increase self-efficacy through a feedback loop tying subsequent performance to augmented self-efficacy beliefs. Work self-efficacy can be developed through work-based learning provided through formal experiential activities within higher education and industry. (Raelin 2011)

The constructs measured by the instrument include confidence in being able to learn on the job, problem solving, coping with stress, fulfilling one's work roles, being a team member, being sensitive to others, managing politics, and being able to manage oneself in the workplace overall. Individuals may take the test either online or on paper. Sample survey items can be found on the website. Such data can be useful feedback to internship developers and evaluators.

One approach to trying to develop work-related attitudes and behaviors in low-income urban youth is offered by Year Up, a nonprofit organization founded by social entrepreneur Gerald Chertavian. Active in eight U.S. cities, Year Up links community colleges and employer mentors to serve 4,000 disadvantaged minority youths with a high school or equivalency degree. This six-month training program is followed by a six-month internship in a large corporation. Year Up pays students $200/week to help ensure that they complete the program and helps them find mentors. Employers pay Year Up about $22,750 per student for a six-month internship (Bornstein 2011). Year Up focuses on not only hard skills, but also soft skills, which its founder calls "harder skills": writing appropriate email notes, working as a team member, making eye contact, and being proactive at work. Year Up Founder Chertavian has been cited as saying:

> It's how you make eye contact, it's how you dress, it's how you shake hands, it's how you make small talk at a Christmas Party. It's when we speak, are you nodding your head? Are you leaning in and asking questions? It's knowing how to introduce yourself. It's knowing what's appropriate for conversation. All of those things are learned. If you don't have that context, boy, it feels real foreign to go through the security gate at Fidelity and exist in that environment. (Chertavian, in Bornstein 2011: paragraph 14)

Evidence of the program's success is that since its inception, Year Up has a completion rate of about 70 percent and within four months, approximately 84 percent of graduates have either enrolled full time in college or secured a job with a starting wage of $15 per hour, or roughly $30,000 per year (Bornstein 2011).

Employers are important stakeholders in any attempt to ensure that students are prepared for the workplace. In a survey of 217 employers in four industry groups (manufacturing, financial services, nonfinancial services; and nonprofits), respondents were asked to comment on three types of training for new workforce entrants: workforce readiness, job-specific training, and career development. Although it is unclear exactly how much money is spent on each of these training categories, 46 percent of respondents reported spending 19.1 percent of their overall training budget on workforce readiness training. The majority of training dollars went to job-specific training (61.3 percent) and career development (19.7 percent) (Casner-Lotto, Rosenblum, and Wright 2009). These data show that employers have much at stake in the workplace readiness of their employment pool—and undoubtedly would prefer that individuals were ready for the workplace before they are hired.

In a comprehensive survey of the perceived workplace readiness of both high school and college graduates, 283 employers at mid-market organizations (organizations with revenues of $100 million to $1 billion) cited high school graduates as "falling short in overall preparation for entry-level jobs" (The Conference Board 2008: 6) and specifically deficient in written communications, professionalism/work ethic, critical thinking, problem solving, and oral communications. Six respondents were interviewed; one, the human resources director at Cyra/Com, said that the high school students recently hired "lack[ed] an overall understanding of professional etiquette" (The Conference Board 2008: 24). To address this situation, the Tucson-based organization partnered with a local high school to develop and implement a workforce readiness curriculum. Although evaluation of the program is ongoing, its promise is suggested by the program's efforts to invite other area high schools to participate (The Conference Board 2008).

As would be expected, the workplace opportunities that students can get through schools tend to be better than those they find on their own. In a large longitudinal research project conducted in the San Francisco Bay area, researchers followed 256 students (half male/half female, 53 percent African American, 21.6 percent Latino, 16.5 percent Asian, and 8.2 percent White) who participated in a three-year biotechnology education and training program. Of the twelfth graders who participated in the program, which combined high school and community college courses and included paid internships, all graduated from high school and 90 percent continued on to postsecondary education (Ryken 2004: 39).

The U.S. Department of Education's National Center for Education Statistics (NCES) published data from a longitudinal study of graduates from the class of 2004; it described the educational and work status of those who participated in CTE occupational programs and those who did not, two years later (2006). The data described student participation in coursework that was taken in twelve broad areas, including business, communications and design, engineering technologies, health sciences, and engineering technologies. Participation was defined as having taken either a two- or three-credit class. While 81 percent of the students who took no occupational classes continued their education, almost 70 percent of those who took at least a three-credit class and 74.4 percent of those who took at least a two-credit class enrolled in postsecondary education (U.S. Department of Education 2011). These data indicate that those students who took two or three occupational credits continued their education beyond high school at rates somewhat comparable to those who did not take any occupational coursework.

Organizational Results

Organizational results are those that indicate that an intervention has systemic value, improving outcomes at the school level. A commonly used measure of organizational results is graduation rates. As discussed in the introduction to this volume, the United States has experienced dismal high school completion rates. Some data show that, in fact, "one in four American students does not graduate from high school on time, if at all" (Bottoms 2008: 16). Students drop out of high school for many reasons, but reasons often include boredom or a lack of self-confidence in learning what is being taught (which itself is often disguised as boredom).

Research on the impact of CTE programs on high school graduation rates is posted on the Association for Career and Technical Education's website. As of December 17, 2010, the listed studies indicate that occupational programs, because they provide learning experiences seen as relevant to the learner's life, can keep students motivated and thus keep them in school. For example, a study funded by the Gates Foundation showed that 81 percent of students who dropped out said that "more real world learning" could have influenced them to stay in school. The website also describes a 2000 Oregon State Legislature study that found that small learning communities within large high schools, such as career academies, reduced school dropout rates.

One of the country's largest career academies is The National Academy Foundation (NAF), which supports four career academies across the nation. On their website (accessed December 20, 2010), NAF reported that it "has academies in 21 of the 25 largest school districts in the United States," and that "90 percent of their enrollees graduate from high school and that 80 percent go on to college." The Manpower Demonstration Research Corporation (MDRC), created by the Ford Foundation and federal agencies, has been studying NAF career academies since 1993. Their website (accessed May 31, 2011) reports the results of research involving randomized, controlled field trials that followed 1,400 students from nine different high schools from the ninth grade through several years after graduation. Survey data, observation data, student transcripts, and standardized test scores showed that career academies improved the labor market prospects particularly of young men, and the entire group had graduation rates and postsecondary credentials that were equal to those of the control groups (Kemple and Willner 2008).

Labor Market Outcomes

In terms of labor market outcomes associated with participating in WBL programs, most studies focus on wages. For example, the National Academy Foundation reported on its website (accessed December 20, 2010) that its graduates made $16,704 (or 11 percent) more a year than a control group who did not attend the Academy. Moreover, they found that young men's earnings over the period studied were $30,000 (or 17 percent) more than the control group. Likewise, in a comparison of students who participated in the Year Up program with those who had applied but had not been accepted, The Economic Mobility Corporation (EMC) reported that as a result of obtaining jobs in more lucrative information technology or investment operations with partner firms, those who participated had wages above the national median, averaging $19.69/hour (Bornstein 2011).

Summary and Concluding Comments

In this chapter, I describe and discuss a variety of WBL initiatives that either bring the world of work to the secondary school classroom or take students to that world. Ranging from ways to learn about careers, to programs designed for occupational knowledge and skill development, to paid and non-paid work experiences, there are numerous WBL options for a school system to consider.

The studies described in this chapter indicate the promise of WBL in high schools. WBL initiatives may have benefits to participants' satisfaction, their academic learning, their ability to enter the workplace, a school's graduation rates, and students' earning power. For example, one study cited in this chapter (Pearson et al. 2010) showed that when CTE and academic teachers teamed up to revise CTE curriculum, students' academic as well as occupational learning achievement rose. Cases of nonprofit and private for-profit organizations offering programs that promote workplace readiness indicated that these sectors can make an impact when they partner with schools and community organizations (The Conference Board 2008). The chapter also describes the success a career academy can have at improving graduation rates and labor market outcomes of its graduates (Kemper and Willner 2008).

Given the evidence that WBL improves student learning and engagement, why aren't these programs more widespread? Part of the answer is that traditional vocational education did this task badly, and it is hard to change these long-standing perceptions. Work-based learning programs, however, are not this traditional vocational education; they are approaches intended to keep all students engaged in their education as well as to provide entry into internships and/or paid employment. Well-designed and properly implemented approaches may initiate a possible career trajectory and may provide preparation for life as well as work.

Successful, well-designed initiatives initially require champions as well as resources that are often beyond a school's reach, such as internship coordinators and job placement offices. Moreover, WBL initiatives must be integrated into the overall curriculum and provide value to *all* students, whether or not they plan to go to college. The goal is not to segregate or "track" less-able students into specific careers. Instead, the goal is to replace the perception that school is a place where facts are served with the understanding that school is an environment in which students learn how to learn, unlearn, and relearn skills they will need to hone throughout their lifetimes.

The successful WBL programs discussed here have similarities: motivated students, scaffolding from responsible adults (including parents and potential employers), and measurable results. Successful WBL programs often involve employers and other members of the community; the responsibility for learning does not lie solely with the teacher. Engagement from a multitude of responsible adults is likely especially important for inner city schools that need additional resources, and for the low socioeconomic status urban youths they serve who need additional encouragement. Today's WBL can help break down the barriers between school and work, providing new opportunities for learning for all students. It isn't school *to* work; it's school *and* work.

II.

The Role of Different Educational Providers in Preparing Students for Work

CHAPTER 4

Improving Career and Technical Education in the United States

Nancy Hoffman

To do productive work is a fundamental human need. Work attaches citizens to the public world and increases the health and well-being of families and communities. A significant task for any society is to support and guide young people as they explore occupations, test themselves in the work world, and determine how they will contribute to the economy. Under the best vocational education systems, such as those in the Germanic and Nordic countries, Australia, and New Zealand, young people complete the portion of their education that is "all school" at around age fifteen or sixteen. As they mature from later teenage to about age twenty, they enter a period of "learning to work," which integrates school and experience in a career area and ends with a nationally recognized qualification. By their early twenties, young people enter their careers, often transitioning seamlessly from integrated work and learning into full-time roles in their apprenticeship or internship companies.

Across developed countries, educators, policymakers, and economists recognize that the new "knowledge economy" demands higher levels of training and different skills than the twentieth-century high school or upper secondary school provided. (Upper secondary schools generally start at age sixteen and end around nineteen; students exit with a qualification more like a two-year community college technical degree than a high school diploma.) Young people with aspirations to white collar, "middle skill" jobs in high-growth areas such as health care, high tech, engineering, and finance, as well as those choosing the old trades, need more sophisticated skills and knowledge than ever before. Some countries are doing well by young people, preparing most for good jobs requiring twenty-first century skills, protecting them from unemployment in the current economic crisis, and transitioning them into the labor force smoothly and relatively quickly. This is not the case in the United States.

This chapter first presents data that shows that strong vocational education and training systems (here called VET) correlate with low youth unemployment, low rates of labor market inactivity, smooth transitions into the workforce, and high upper secondary school completion rates. In addition, strong vocational education systems tie young people to the economic needs of their regions, since local employers are the ones who make apprenticeships and other forms of workplace learning available to them. In metropolitan areas with large concentrations of youth and many employment options, strong VET systems provide structure, guidance, and incentives for young people to connect to appropriate employers.

The chapter goes on to offer observations about vocational education or what is now called *career and technical education* (CTE) in the United States. (The U.S. Department of Education changed the terminology from vocational education and training—the term used in other parts of the world—to CTE in 2006.) It points to CTE's challenges as states and districts attempt to implement a system that will serve urban youth who are eager to work, but have few ties to a confusing and difficult-to-penetrate job market. They also lack the advantages of a post-high school, multi-year period of transition that is afforded their more affluent peers, for whom a bachelor's degree is simply the next agreed-on step to adulthood. The chapter then suggests that some models of CTE are promising, but that the United States has a long way to go to create a mainstream, well-regarded system that transitions young people choosing CTE smoothly into productive employment.

Indicators of Youth Status in the Labor Market

The economic crisis in the United States is having an enormous impact on the well-being of many people, and is impacting youth disproportionately, especially in metropolitan areas where young people compete with adults for low-skill jobs. As in other downturns, young people are more vulnerable to unemployment, and more likely to move in and out of the labor market in temporary jobs rather than securing stable employment (Scarpetta, Sonnet,

and Manfredi 2010: 9). In 2008, the United States had a youth unemployment rate of about 11 percent, while the average calculated by the Organization for Economic Cooperation and Development (OECD), the international
organization that provides comparative data on trends in its thirty-two
member countries, was 14.4 percent. By July 2010, the U.S. rate of youth
unemployment had risen above the OECD average to about 19.1 percent,
and it is continuing to rise while unemployment as a whole hovers between
9 and 10 percent. During that same year, youth unemployment rates were
substantially lower in Australia, Austria, Canada, Denmark, Germany, Japan, Korea, the Netherlands, Norway, and Switzerland (lowest at 4.5 percent
in March 2010). Those countries had lower rates before the recent recession
and smaller than average increases after (Scarpetta, Sonnet, and Manfredi
2010: 13). Given the shaky economies of some members of the comparison
group such as Greece, Ireland, Italy, Portugal, and Spain, the United States
should and could be higher up the rankings.

An additional indicator of youth distress in the labor market is the percentage of young people who are inactive; they are not job seekers and are
neither in education nor in training. The latest figure (2006) for such young
people (who are often called "NEET") showed that this group comprised 11
percent in the United States, a figure just above the OECD average (Scarpetta, Sonnet, and Manfredi 2010: 13).

As for transitioning youth from schooling to stable first employment
(within five years of leaving education), data from OECD's *Jobs for Youth
Review* puts the United States a little above average among sixteen OECD
countries studied (OECD 2006–11). The United States does better than some
European countries with what the study calls *high performers*—young people
employed 70 percent or more of the time in the five years after leaving school.
More U.S. students return to school after time in the labor market, but nearly
one third of U.S. youth fall into the categories *youth left behind* and *poorly
integrated new entrants*. *Left-behind* youth spend most of the five years in
unemployment or inactivity; and *poorly integrated new entrants* move in and
out of employment, unemployment, and inactivity, signaling difficulties in
settling on a promising career path (Scarpetta, Sonnet, and Manfredi 2010:
14). This is a large group numerically in the United States because of the size
of the youth population, and a cause for concern in a country with a very
limited social safety net and few job protections for those who do land work.[1]

With low skills and no high school diploma, entry into the job market is
nearly impossible today. But the drop-out rate from high school has reached

epidemic proportions in many urban areas of the United States. In 2009, the most recent date for which data is available, 2.1 million young people went to school in what have come to be called "drop out factories," high schools that lose more than 40 percent of their students between ninth and twelfth grades (Balfanz 2011). Twelve OECD countries now have higher percentages of upper secondary school completers than the United States, so not only are their secondary completion rates higher, their young people are completing additional years of schooling and getting skills with viability in the labor market. Among the high performers, countries with strong VET pathways such as Austria, Germany, and Switzerland have the majority of students in VET systems and graduation rates above 90 percent. (Quintini 2009)

Along with the lack of a diploma, young people in the United States may be experiencing trouble finding jobs in an increasingly competitive market because they are not achieving academically at acceptable levels, nor are they trained in the technical skills required for many metropolitan job markets. On the OECD's PISA assessment, which tests a sample of fifteen-year-olds across a wide range of countries every three years in math, science, and literacy, the U.S. performance has been consistently mediocre. In the most recent round of testing (2009) the United States scored only a small increment above average. With its attention to applying knowledge, PISA provides a better indicator of college and career readiness than many traditional discipline-based tests of content.

Countries that are doing much better than the United States by their young people—supporting them to achieve academically at higher levels, keeping them in school, and, most importantly, structuring the transition from school to work so that almost everyone has training for an initial career and enters the workforce smoothly—share two characteristics. First, they have special youth policies that view younger generations as important to support, protect, and engage with as an investment in future prosperity. Second, in partnership with employers and unions, they educate from 40 percent to 75 percent of their young people in vocational education systems that link education and regional labor market needs and include substantial learning in the workplace.

Youth policies send strong signals to young people, their families, and employers that society has a collective responsibility to prepare its members for productive adulthood. Some youth policies include guarantees of schooling coupled with work experience while others include sanctions for non-participation. Almost all allow employers to pay a training wage to young people who are learning in the workplace while completing upper secondary school, and increasingly, countries are requiring students to stay in school or in a combination of school and work until they complete a qualification or reach age eighteen.

In regard to learning in the workplace, in the best VET systems, curriculum and assessments replicate authentically the messy, problem-based, people-intense, and time-limited world of work. VET teachers "identify *occupational situations* which are significant for the work activity and also have a potential for learning" and structure competences to be assessed around them (Fischer and Bauer 2002: 142). The informing orientation of VET pedagogy is authentic, problem-based rather than discipline-based learning. In short, the smartest and quickest route to a wide variety of occupations for the majority of young people in the successful countries is a vocational program that integrates work and learning.

To sum up, while most teens in the United States and elsewhere stay in school because they want to prepare for a job, other countries are doing much better than the United States in helping young people who are not headed for a four-year degree prepare for and enter stable employment. In the more successful countries, the explicit goal of upper secondary VET is to provide the education and training young people need to prepare for a specific career or calling. In the United States, the goal of high school CTE is to help young people explore careers so they don't drop out of high school. This distinction may seem subtle, but it is not. An education system that, in partnership with employers, holds itself accountable for preparing youth for careers and moving them into productive roles in the labor force has a different orientation than one that is largely school-based, disconnected from employers, and focused on skills and knowledge needed for college-level study. For young people who go on to a community college where career preparation *is* a goal, with a few exceptions, employers are not engaged, little learning takes place in workplaces, and linkages between curriculum and labor market requirements are frequently haphazard.

CTE in High Schools

The data above are useful in putting the United States' results in international context, and indicating that much better outcomes are possible, but an enormous challenge is how to reorient and build from the current CTE options so that they provide meaningful work-based learning, and better link urban, low-income youth who are headed into the labor market with high school and community college degrees with the jobs in their metropolitan labor markets. (See Bridget N. O'Connor's chapter in this volume for further discussion of work-based learning.)

A significant proportion of American high school and college students intend to pursue employment that does not require a baccalaureate. Many begin by enrolling in career and technical programs at the secondary level. About one in five high school students in the United States concentrates in occupational education programs (NCES 2008). Among 2005 high school graduates, more occupational education credits were earned than credits in fine arts or languages. Among CTE high school graduates who go on to postsecondary study, most choose an industry certificate or a community college associate's degree in an applied field (Skinner and Apling 2006). Some CTE graduates go immediately to work, and a small number pursue a four-year degree. Other post-high school options are short-term training programs, delivered either in for-profit or community-based organizations, or a registered apprenticeship that combines some training with work.

As Thomas Bailey and Clive R. Belfield also discuss in their chapter in this volume, at all postsecondary levels (certificate, associate's, and bachelor's), more students concentrate in career fields than academic subjects. Over 40 percent of college freshmen start in community colleges and most of these enroll in occupational programs. The trend has been away from CTE *program* concentrators toward more academic education at both the high school and postsecondary levels. But occupational *course taking* and credits have increased at the postsecondary level and held steady at the secondary level, signaling that, while students may not sign up for a CTE program, most take at least one career-focused course showing that they are interested in exploring career options (NCES 2008).

The wide range of careers targeted by CTE programs is reflected in the diversity of delivery mechanisms used to instruct CTE students. Programs and courses offering career preparation at the high school level are delivered in many different forms. The comprehensive high school, the legacy of the expansion of high school education to a wide range of young people in the 1950s, still predominates, especially where population density can support only a single high school. Such a school would have academic and CTE tracks, although some proportion of CTE students would likely be placed in academic courses with their college-prep peers.

In many urban areas, large schools have been broken down into smaller learning communities, academies, or even separate schools with their own principals housed in a single large building. Such smaller entities often have career themes—media, health careers, leadership, social justice, business, information technology, and the like. While these often sound like career preparation programs, most are not intended to lead directly to work after graduation. There may be internships, a partnership with an employer, or a community service opportunity, but work-based learning is rarely available to all students for extended periods.

CTE is also delivered through vocational technical schools devoted to career preparation, including high schools in large urban areas devoted to a single career area (such as automotive technology or aviation science). Sometimes such vocational technical centers serve students who are transported there for parts of the school day. In urban areas particularly, vocational schools have high proportions of low-income students of color, newly arrived immigrants, and students with special needs.

Despite the existence of a varied CTE high school delivery system, the system as a whole faces persistent challenges:

- High school programs cannot meet the academic and technical standards that students need to master in order to enter into post-secondary programs without remediation.
- Community college programs have high rates of entering students who do not meet prerequisites or who fail to complete after enrolling because of their life circumstances and because the college's academic and social supports are stretched thin.
- Inadequate communication and poor alignment of secondary and postsecondary programs and curricula in a region make it difficult for high school students to understand the options available to them and what it will take to gain entry into programs with labor market payoffs.
- Employers are not engaged in designing technical programs to meet their needs or in sending clear signals to students about skills, attitudes, behaviors, and opportunities for exposure and experience that can maximize employment options.

The impact can be seen in the results for students. At the high school level, employment and earnings gains from participation in high school CTE programs are weak: no relationship has been found between the earnings of men working full-time six years after completing high school CTE programs and the occupational courses they took in high school; for women, the impact was negative (NCES 2008). (An exception to these employment outcomes is the record of the career academies, small career-themed programs that have been found to result in significant employment and earnings increases for low-income males. (See Kemple 2008; Kemple and Snipes 2000.)

CTE in Community Colleges

Recognizing the limits of high school CTE and accepting the notion that high school CTE should be exploratory, U.S. educators and policymakers have increasingly advocated for placing in-depth technical training in community college rather than in high school. The argument is that students need stronger foundational or basic skills than ever before: math, computer skills, writing, and critical thinking are required for many occupations. Educators believe that these skills cannot be taught in high school to the necessary levels simultaneously with high-level technical skills; vocational high schools are best at introducing career choices and giving students a taste of work in various fields. Today, most advanced career and technical education is delivered to postsecondary students via four-year colleges, community colleges, or technical colleges, as well as proprietary institutions or for-profit institutions. Instruction includes both traditional classroom delivery and, increasingly, online courses. States are providing advanced college-level CTE courses to high school students via tech-prep and dual enrollment classes in both traditional high schools and such new models as early college high schools.

The community college CTE sector is difficult to characterize. Community colleges offer an enormous range of programs and fill multiple missions—preparing students to transfer to four-year institutions, mounting adult basic education programs, tailoring programs for incumbent workers for employers. As for occupational programs, with many specialties and subspecialties and wide variation in requirements across colleges in the same system, good data about CTE programs is hard to come by (Shulock, Offenstein, and Moore 2011). The most extensive recent research concerns developmental education and credential completion rates and sets out clearly why the sector needs substantial improvement if it is going to serve the needs of urban youth looking for credentials that will be viable in their regional labor markets. Nearly 60 percent of all entrants are placed into non-credit remediation, many of them recent high school graduates. Indeed, fewer than 25 percent of developmental education students complete a certificate or degree within eight years of enrolling. Many never get beyond a remedial math course. Indeed, about two-thirds of entering students have skills so weak that their ability to ever complete a college level course is in peril (Bailey 2009). And even if students succeed in placing into credit-bearing courses, most enter without a clear career focus, leaving them vulnerable to costly errors in course taking and academic drift. Community colleges, in general, do a poor job of providing information to help young people chose a program of study (information such as course requirements, length of time to complete, or employment prospects) (Rosenbaum, Deil-Amen, and Person 2006).

There are additional hurdles for urban youth. Most of the programs in such high-demand fields as health, information technology (IT), engineering, media, and finance have prerequisites such as college-level mathematics, biology, introduction to IT, and the like for entry. Although community colleges are open admission, these programs are not. That is, students can only apply to enter these programs after successfully completing key general education courses. High-demand programs of study like nursing are competitive, with limited slots available. With competition for entry, priority tends to go to students who already have B.A.s, work experience, or are transferring in substantial college level work. This is despite the fact that there is a substantial economic payoff to earning a long-term (thirty credits or more) certificate, and for their economic futures, young people should be entering and completing such programs (Carnevale, Smith, and Strohl 2010). Consistent with data in the chapter in this volume by Anthony P. Carnevale, Nicole Smith, and Jeff Strohl, recent data from Florida confirms that graduates with a well-chosen two-year associate in science degree earned $10,357 more on average than baccalaureate graduates of the State University System (Miami Dade College Forum 2011).[2]

Across the sector, certificate and degree completion rates are dismal. Recent evidence from a California study shows that while community colleges mount career programs in high wage fields—the researchers studied information technology, engineering technology, engineering, and nursing—those who complete the programs, and few do, are older and do not need developmental courses (Shulock, Offenstein, and Moore 2011). While more research is needed, this study and other anecdotal evidence suggests that high schoolers with low to middling grades who make it into credit-bearing courses may not get through anatomy, math, basic IT courses, and similar prerequisites, and so are excluded from advanced technical training. Nonetheless, career education is strong in many community colleges so there is much on which to build.

National Education Policy Related to CTE

Given the picture above, how is the nation addressing the disconnect between the evident desire of young people to enter the labor market and an education system that is failing to help them achieve that end? After years of work on improving high school graduation rates and college matriculation, the nation is focused on the *completion* of a postsecondary credential, including the bachelor's degree but with particular emphasis on the associate's degree or certificate conferred in a community college. The logic is as follows:

- The United States has fallen behind because, though we produce a high number of bachelor's degrees, we lag in the production of associate's degrees.
- To increase degree production, the country will have to better educate the most challenging segments of the population—students who are first-generation college goers, students of color, low-income students, and English language learners.
- Many of these students now do not complete high school, graduate poorly prepared for college, never exit from community college remedial courses, and/or do not complete a credential.
- While the American dream asserts that these students should have the choices of their more affluent and better-prepared peers—specifically, to earn a bachelor's degree in four years on a residential campus—many will end up in community colleges.
- These students will choose, be counseled, or be tracked into programs leading either to a transfer degree or, more likely, to a career-oriented program.

So despite the worrisome record of community colleges as a source of career education for young people, the policy community is depending on them as the engines of job training and upward mobility. Except for for-profit institutions, as William G. Tierney discusses in his chapter in this volume, there really is no other choice. As is often the case when the U.S. economy falters, students are flocking to community colleges, exposing just how stretched those institutions are in meeting their goal of producing graduates ready to enter the labor market with the appropriate skills and training. As Tierney also notes, many of the community colleges serving heavily populated areas have turned away applicants for lack of seat space. In California, for example, community colleges turned away 140,000 students in 2010–11 and anticipate turning away an additional 140,000 in the 2011–12 academic year (California Community Colleges Chancellor's Office 2011).

While the emphasis on completion is long overdue, it is only as the fiscal crisis drags on into 2011 that policymakers, educators, and families are asking not only what a completed college degree is worth, but whether some credentials are a better bet than others. That is, in a recent Heldrich Center study of 571 B.A. recipients graduating between 2006 and 2010, only 56 percent of those who got their diplomas in spring 2010 had a first job. And 40 percent of the jobs landed by those who graduated in the entire four years studied did not require a bachelor's degree. This kind of data is shifting the spotlight from "college for all" to "college for what" (Godofsky, Zukin, and Van Horn 2011). It is then a good moment for policymakers and educators in the United States to strengthen career pathways—and to consider work-based models more like those in countries that have strong vocational education systems.

But policy proposals that focus more attention on helping low-income urban youth prepare for high-skill jobs in their local communities through more effective high school and community college vocational programs have reawakened debates about tracking. Should all young people be on a pathway to a postsecondary credential? Is that an appropriate aspiration? If a postsecondary credential—the majority view—then does the call for "college for all" mean that everyone needs a bachelor's degree, or is a community college degree with an occupational or technical focus an acceptable postsecondary option? At both the secondary and postsecondary levels, CTE comes with considerable stigma based on history. Secondary school systems have used CTE as the route for non-academically inclined students with weak high school preparation, and since many such students are poor, of color, and have not had access to the opportunities and choices of their more advantaged peers, CTE has raised issues of social justice. Civil rights activists among others fault school systems for pushing low-income young people and young people of color into low-quality high school and community college CTE programs while more affluent young people get a liberal arts education. A review of the literature on occupationally focused community college outcomes concludes that "choosing an occupational major may have negative effects on earning an associate's or bachelor's degree" (Offenstein, Moore, and Shulock 2009: 5).

As I write, the country is in the midst of a heated debate about CTE, sparked in part by a new report from the Harvard Graduate School of Education, *Pathways to Prosperity*, which argues that the country needs a more robust set of options (in addition to traditional four-year college) for the wide variety of young people—not only low-income students—who respond to applied learning, do not want to sit in classrooms for four years after high school, and want to try themselves out in adult workplaces sooner rather than later (Symonds, Schwartz, and Ferguson 2011). In addition, as *Pathways to Prosperity* points out, only 40 percent of twenty-seven-year-olds currently hold a postsecondary credential today; thus even if the country were to succeed in credentialing 55 or 60 percent of the adult population by 2025—the goals set out by the White House and several major philanthropies— simple math leaves 40 percent still without a credential beyond high school.

In a recent article in *The Nation*, Dana Goldstein asks whether "sounding the call for a more intellectual version of 'career and technical education,' or CTE, one that infuses traditional vocational training with the academic rigor and ethic of college prep," is the way forward (Goldstein 2011: 1). Such debate is healthy, but it puts major pressure on educators responsible for CTE to come up with improvement strategies that would comprise this more intellectual version if CTE is going to overcome the legacy of tracking. Shorthand for that version of CTE might begin with the ideas of John Dewey and a long line of progressive educators who have argued that learning is most powerful when it involves reflection on action in the real world.

Commenting on the CTE debate, Mike Rose, who has written widely on the cognitive demands of physical labor, put the challenge this way: the distinction between manual and abstract-minded ways of thinking "emerged out of a cluster of troubling beliefs about knowledge, education, and the social order, and these beliefs continue to constrain our educational imagination."

He also argued that "it would be foolhardy to dismiss labor-market realities, for many low-income students are in immediate financial need. These students can commit to postsecondary education only if it leads to a decent wage and benefits" (Rose 2011). The best CTE programs are intellectually challenging, whether focused on the old trades like automotive technology or new professions in IT or finance; they also provide work-based learning experience that gives students a leg up in the job market. Before coming to these model programs, I briefly describe the state of work-based learning.

Work-Based Learning

Most educators, particularly CTE educators, would agree that some form of applied or work-based learning linked to labor market needs should be included in students' pathways; and many understand that workplace learning, a type of work-based learning, can be both specific and broadly contextualized. But, as Bridget O'Connor in this volume discusses, in the United States, work-based learning opportunities in companies that might later employ program graduates are the exception, not the rule. Opportunities for internships and service learning—both workplace kinds of experience—are more available to well-connected and outstanding students than to the average to lower-achieving high schoolers who would likely benefit most. Selective colleges are known to give an edge in admission to students who have had demanding internships in high school, but many of these internships are competitive and unpaid, and therefore not available to low-income students who are seeking paid work. In postsecondary education where work experience in a student's chosen career area (a summer job in a scientific research laboratory or in a financial services firm) might be the distinction between one student's job application and that of another graduate, again low-income young people are often shut out because they do not have the social capital to land these kinds of paid opportunities (Perlin 2011).

Although students may not have school-related internships, many high school students work or want to. Research confirms that employment in the teen and young-adult years can have a very positive impact on future prospects for employment and earnings, and teens who work in high school are less likely to drop out. Conversely, low-income teenaged men who do not find work are more likely to get into trouble with the law, while their female counterparts are more likely to become single mothers. The percentages of teens and young adults who are working are now at the lowest levels recorded since the end of the 1930s Depression (Symonds, Schwartz, and Ferguson 2011). The current youth employment crisis affects the youngest and least advantaged cohort first because they are the least well-prepared for jobs.

Promising Practices in CTE

Given this picture—a low-income youth population concentrated in metropolitan areas with dismal job prospects and an inadequate education system—the United States needs to make a greater investment in the CTE models that are already proving their potential in the labor market or are at least designed to do so. In this concluding section, I briefly describe initiatives in high schools, some with pathways to community colleges that are carefully preparing young people for careers—taking into account the career-specific knowledge needed, providing strong foundations in reading, writing, and math, and getting students at least some of the experiential learning and real time problem-solving that makes a difference in the labor market.

At the high school level, cutting-edge career and technical education (CTE) bears little relationship to traditional vocational education programs that are sometimes little more than schools of last resort for students who were not going to succeed in college prep. National initiatives such as career academies, Project Lead the Way, High Schools that Work, and Linked Learning—a more recent California initiative—combine the broad academic foundation needed for further education with some depth of study in a career area.

According to MDRC research, the career academy movement, the largest "modern" CTE program now some 7,000 schools strong, helps graduates achieve higher earnings as adults. The academies introduce students to career themes, and typically include workplace learning (Kemple 2008). Project Lead the Way introduces high school students to engineering using a rigorous, uniform curriculum, national assessments, professional development for teachers, and extensive project-based learning, and can be installed within a traditional high school. It has now spread to over 3,000 high schools. High Schools That Work (HSTW), developed by the Southern Regional Education Board, has grown into the nation's largest effort to integrate challenging academics and CTE. The newest of the modernized CTE models is Linked Learning, an ambitious California initiative that goes beyond career exploration in high school to provide engaging career concentration in areas of high demand in specific labor markets in the state—engineering, biomedical and health sciences, energy, information technology, manufacturing, natural resources, and the like.

With aspirations to engage employers and to place students in serious internships, Linked Learning has established a special teacher preparation program, since teachers who enter CTE from the work world may not have the skills to work in such programs, and traditionally trained teachers often do not. Sounding very much like the best European VET models, Linked Learning requires its teachers to "design meaningful instructional tasks based on real-world problems, stay abreast of changes in their field, identify cross-sections between academic and career-technical focuses, coordinate school and workplace learning, simulate workplace environments, identify career paths, and understand labor trends and projections" (Hoachlander 2008).

Two high-performing networks for high school age young people—Cristo Rey and Year Up—have commonalities with European apprenticeships: substantial work experience is a requirement for everyone, and students are socialized to understand and perform well in a business culture. Both serve primarily low-income urban young people. Through its Corporate Work Study Program, Cristo Rey has its students work one day a week in hospitals, universities, law firms, research labs, and private businesses. Serving high school graduates ages eighteen to twenty-four entering the workforce with weak skills, Year Up provides technical and professional skills, college credits, an educational stipend, and a six-month corporate internship.

Some high school CTE programs have certification and licensure requirements that include clinical or workplace experience that is evaluated as part of completion requirements designed to meet state, national, or even international standards. City University of New York (CUNY) is starting a new community college designed according to an entirely new work and learning model; students will prepare for a limited number of careers in high-need and high-value areas in New York City.

States are also linking high school and postsecondary education to support college-level credit in high school through dual enrollment and accelerated whole school models such as early college high schools. The recent rapid

growth in dual enrollment programs and the promising development of a
national network of some 250 Early College High Schools (ECHS) suggest
that some of the barriers that have prevented better cooperation across the
secondary/postsecondary boundary are beginning to break down. There are
now over 53,000 young people in the ECHS network, the majority low-income
students and students of color. Over 40 percent are graduating from high
school with at least one year of college credit, and nearly a quarter with an
A.A. degree. About one-third of the programs have a STEM focus, with young
people equipped to enter the job market after the A.A. if they want to. North
Carolina's Learn and Earn schools offer ECHS STEM- and career-focused
models, with strong political support and employer participation, that other
states and districts could adapt to suit their education and employment needs.[3]

Several national philanthropies are turning their attention not just to
completion, but to improved access to career preparation for young adults.
New programs draw on a body of rigorous research about the I-BEST approach (Integrated Basic Education and Skills Training) developed by the
Washington State Board for Community and Technical Colleges (SBCTC)
that demonstrates that retention improves if students are enrolled in a program of study with basic skills embedded in their first occupation-related
courses. Other research-based design features include fewer choices among
postsecondary courses, more structure, and accelerated time to completion
(Rosenbaum and Person 2006; Offenstein, Moore, and Shulock 2009;
Wachen, Jenkins, and Van Noy 2010; Jenkins 2011). In addition, community
colleges that have strong links to employers and provide service learning
and internships are taking up the challenge of ensuring that urban young
people are given the information, academic preparation, and guidance they
need to take advantage of such opportunities.

Possibilities for Progress

So where do these examples leave us? No one has to convince young people
that completing high school and attaining a community college degree or
certificate with some work experience in the chosen career field is a must today, and a good investment even if you want to go on to a four-year institution or graduate school. The problem is that excellent but scattershot
opportunities for young people do not constitute a system. A promising

strategy to engage U.S. employers in building a stronger CTE system is to begin with community colleges rather than with high schools. The primary labor market is not set up to absorb sixteen- to eighteen-year-olds in any substantial numbers, even as trainees, and most employers would be skeptical that young people at that age could make a productive contribution to the company's bottom line, whatever the evidence from Switzerland or Germany. Our employers are more likely to provide work and learning opportunities for young people already enrolled in community college—a signal of perseverance and initiative.

A second lever for building a system of career education in the United States is to acknowledge that a high proportion of students are already both working and learning. As described in Laura Perna's (2010) edited volume, the problem is that in all but a handful of cases, these two activities are competing with, rather than complementing, one another. Except for those institutions that offer "cooperative" programs in which the institution organizes job placements aligned with a student's academic program, paid student employment (as distinct from unpaid internships) is disconnected from the academic program, and students are forced to fit their work schedule around their academic course schedule rather than being able to plan these two sets of activities in an integrated fashion. Most students are not in "student-friendly" workplaces.

The ultimate goal should be to build career pathways that pick students up in high school and carry them through to a postsecondary occupational certificate or associate's degree. Programs that span grades eleven to fourteen would not only align our CTE system with the age span covered in most strong VET systems, but would enable a more efficient use of scarce federal and state funds that are now divided between secondary and postsecondary levels. In summary, for either high school or community college programs, the following are important building blocks and characterize best practices today:

- employer and business leader engagement in the design and support of effective pathways to careers;
- structured pathways with clear requirements, timelines, and outcomes leading from high school though postsecondary credential completion;
- opportunities to engage young people in workplace learning;

- effective career counseling and guidance, including scaffolded exposure to employers and career pathways beginning in the middle grades;
- new institutional structures at the regional labor market level to provide coordination, quality assurance, and sustainability.

Because the career and technical education system serves so many of the country's most vulnerable and least privileged young people, particularly in urban areas, its weaknesses are especially troubling. High school CTE and community colleges have become the United States' de facto job training system, but a much more outcome-focused, efficient, and effective system is needed. CTE is one road that can put young people on the path to careers with middle-class wages, but it has a long way to go, and political and practical barriers to address, to realize its potential.

CHAPTER 5

Postsecondary Education and Economic Opportunity

Anthony P. Carnevale, Nicole Smith, and Jeff Strohl

The New Consensus: Postsecondary Education Is the Legitimate Arbiter of Economic Opportunity

Education has always played both a social and an economic role in the United States. Since the industrial revolution, Americans have looked to education to help reconcile the equality implicit in democratic citizenship with the inequality natural to market economies. After the closing of the frontier in the late nineteenth century, education became an important route to economic success. In the post-World War II era, education gradually evolved into the preferred and the most well-traveled route to good jobs. While not new, the correlation between education or training after high school and career success has strengthened dramatically since the 1980s.[1] Education and economic opportunity are more closely linked than ever. Today, the overwhelming consensus is that access to postsecondary education or training is necessary for access to the middle class—and the data support this consensus. The recession of 2007 accelerated this trend, both through the elimination of many good jobs that required high school or less and through the strengthening of the importance of postsecondary education. Social policy analysts and commentators are now rightfully worried that workers without any postsecondary education will fall behind in the twenty-first-century economy (Cohen and Balz 2011).

This new reality finds wide support in American society because, in theory, using access to postsecondary education to drive economic opportunity and career choice allows us to expand merit-based opportunity without surrendering individual responsibility. The consensus view that educational achievement is the legitimate arbiter of economic opportunity is even stronger because it complements an American preference for a relatively open economy and limited government. In other words, the education consensus has allowed us to anchor economic opportunity in a merit-based system driven by individual responsibility without the government's being too heavy-handed with either the economy or the labor market.

The growing role of postsecondary education and training as the arbiter of economic opportunity seems fair. Individual performance appears more salient than social markers in determining the college access and success that lead to good jobs. But our emphasis on individual performance in education masks the underlying social structures that sort and rank students long before the college admissions offices get involved. The education consensus is not entirely fair because access to education is not fair.[2]

The American success formula rests on the notion that merit-based opportunity represents a just means for allocating social benefits. Yet both merit and opportunity are powerfully influenced by coincidences of birth that give some children advantages over others. In a society where people start out unequal, educational achievement measured by test scores and grades can become a dodge—a way of laundering the money that comes with being born into the right bank account or the right race or ethnicity (Rothstein 2004). We know that more advantaged students go to college and graduate at much higher rates than equally qualified students from working families and low-income families. The American postsecondary system is becoming a dual system with the less advantaged half of the nation's students concentrated in the least selective four-year colleges and in community colleges. White students and the relatively more advantaged postsecondary students are more and more concentrated in the most selective colleges (Carnevale and Strohl 2010).

This unavoidable reality is readily apparent long before the selective college admissions process. According to Alden Thresher, a former admissions director at MIT and chair of The College Board:

Though the prim college regulations . . . have been evolving for three centuries . . . most of the real screening has all along been done by the accidents of socioeconomic origins, early environment, and the various levels of aspiration habitually characterizing particular groups and subcultures . . .

. . . [T]he sorting process involves the interaction of sociological forces of many kinds. Some are so familiar and so subtle in their operation as easily to escape notice; they come to be taken quite for granted, on the principle that the last thing a fish would ever notice is water. (Thresher 1989: 4–5)

The seminal work of Eric Turkheimer and his team at the University of Virginia shows that for most low-income children, there is little relationship between innate abilities measured in childhood and aptitudes developed by the time they are of college age (Turkheimer et al. 2003). In other words, if you come from a poor or working-poor family, chances are you will not be able to "be all you can be." Conversely, Turkheimer and his team find that measured differences in innate abilities as children account for most of the difference in the developed aptitudes among college-age middle- and upper-income adolescents. For the most part, kids who come from families that make more than $60,000 a year do get a shot at being all they can be.

But fair or not, the link between education and success is based on more than mere cultural biases or political convenience. Economic and technological changes have spurred increasing demand for postsecondary education and training.[3] Technology and increased productivity from education continue to drive growth in the economy as a whole, with the results that

- the fastest-growing occupations—such as STEM (science, technology, engineering, and mathematics), health care, and managerial professionals—require workers with disproportionately higher education levels; and
- over time, all occupations are increasingly requiring more education.

About 28 percent of the increase in demand for postsecondary education is because of new occupations requiring postsecondary education or the growth of occupations that already required high levels of education (author's calculation from 1980 and 2010 March Current Population Surveys).[4] The vast majority (72 percent) of the shift toward postsecondary requirements, however, comes from the demand for higher skill levels in occupations that previously did not require postsecondary education or training. A "foreman" or "manufacturing supervisor" in the 1960s, for example, has since morphed into a variety of new occupations that now require postsecondary education, including today's "manufacturing engineer." The high school-educated insurance agent of the fifties becomes the college-educated insurance broker or financial services advisor of the twenty-first century.

As a result of these shifts, our grandparents' high school economy has given way to the modern postsecondary economy. More and more, postsecondary education and training have become the threshold requirement for access to middle-class status and earnings, in good times and bad. Postsecondary education is no longer merely the preferred pathway to middle-class jobs—it is, increasingly, the *only* pathway.

College Is the Key to Middle-Class Earnings

But what does it mean that postsecondary education and training is the only pathway to the middle class at a time when economists fret that the American middle class is actually shrinking? In the thirty-seven-year period shown in Table 5.1, the share of middle-class people with some college or an associate's degree declined from 53 percent to 45 percent. The key to understanding this phenomenon is discerning where those people are going when they leave the middle class. Note that the share of people with some college and associate's degrees in the top three income deciles *increased* from 28 percent to 35 percent, while the share in the lowest deciles remained constant at around 20 percent.

Therefore, while it is true that the middle class is declining, a more accurate portrayal of the American class dynamic would be to say that the middle class is dispersing into two equal and opposing streams of upwardly mobile college-haves and downwardly mobile college-have-nots. High school dropouts, high school graduates, and people with some college but no degree are on the down escalator of social mobility, falling out of the middle class and into the lower three deciles of family income. In 1970, almost half (46 percent) of high school dropouts were in the middle class. By 2007, the share of dropouts in the middle class had fallen to 33 percent. In 1970, 60 percent of high school graduates were in the middle class. By 2007,

Table 5.1. Education Distribution across Household Income Deciles (1970–2007)

1970	Lower-Income Class (Lower 3 Deciles)	Middle-Income Class (Middle 4 Deciles)	Upper-Income Class (Upper 3 Deciles)
High school dropouts	39%	46%	15%
High school graduates	22%	60%	18%
Some college/associate's degree	19%	53%	28%
Bachelor's degree	16%	47%	37%
Graduate degree	13%	46%	41%
2007			
High school dropouts	59%	33%	7%
High school graduates	35%	45%	19%
Some college	29%	45%	26%
Associate's degree	20%	45%	35%
Bachelor's degree	14%	38%	48%
Graduate degree	9%	30%	61%

Source: Carnevale, Smith, and Strohl 2010: 3.

Note: Postsecondary education has become the threshold requirement for a middle-class family income. In the older data (1970), the education code in the questionnaire did not distinguish between associate's degrees and some college (which includes those with a few college credits and those who have completed postsecondary vocational certificates). In later years, the questionnaire specifically separates these two divisions.

the share had fallen to 45 percent. The share of people with some college but no degree in the middle class has fallen from 53 percent to 45 percent between 1970 and 2007.

Over that same period, people with college degrees (associate's, bachelor's, and graduate degrees) have either stayed in the middle class or boarded the escalator upward to the highest three family income deciles. The share of people with bachelor's degrees in the middle class declined from 47 percent to 38 percent, decreasing by nine percentage points. But the share of people with bachelor's degrees in the top three income deciles jumped from 37 percent to 48 percent. Meanwhile, the share of people with graduate degrees in the middle class declined from 46 percent to 30 percent—a decrease of 16 percentage points. But, clearly, the people leaving the middle class with graduate degrees were leaving for higher wages, as the share of people with graduate degrees in the top three income deciles increased from 41 to 61 percent.

Lifetime Earnings from College Are High in the Long Term

While the economic return on college may drop off in the short term, as it has in the current recession, lifetime earnings from college are high in the long term. College-educated workers earn more—but what is a degree really worth over a lifetime? A 2002 Census Bureau study estimated that in 1999, the average lifetime earnings of a bachelor's degree holder were $2.7 million (2009 dollars), 75 percent more than the amount earned by high school graduates in 1999 (Cheeseman Day and Newburger 2002). Today, we find similar numbers—but since 1999 the premium on college education has grown, to 84 percent. Figure 5.1 below illustrates the differences in median lifetime earnings by degree level, showing a steady progression in lifetime earnings from $973,000 for high school dropouts to $3,648,000 for professional degrees.[5]

But what if people took the money they spend on college, and instead of spending it on their education, they invested it in blue chip long-term government bonds? The investments would grow over a lifetime. Would the investment be more valuable than the college degree? The financial payoff from college over forty working years is often measured differently, because money in hand is more valuable than money in the future. To adjust for that, we calculate what economists and financiers call the *present value* of degrees (PV) and can therefore do a hypothetical cost-benefit analysis of attending college as opposed to investing the college costs. If we start today and look forward to earning $1 million in additional pay over forty years that result from our college investment, then the present value tells us how much money is required today at an assumed interest rate to yield that amount in the future. Assuming an interest rate of 2.5 percent (the real interest rate of long-term government bonds), then a conservative estimate of the present value of the lifetime average marginal return from a bachelor's degree over a high school diploma is about $300,000. To determine if a college degree is worth it, we must simply ensure that the discounted cost of the degree[6] is less than $300,000 expressed in today's dollars.[7]

However, the economic costs of attending college should also include the indirect cost of income forgone while students are in school, plus the direct costs of tuition, books, and other necessities.[8] Two-thirds of students pay less than $15,000 per year for college, and more than 75 percent of students attend four-year colleges that cost less than $24,000 in tuition and fees per year. Less than 5 percent of college students go to schools that cost more

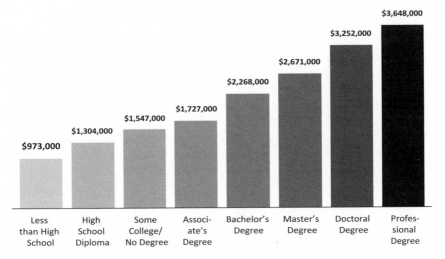

Figure 5.1. Estimated median lifetime earnings by education level. *Source*: Carnevale, Rose, and Cheah 2011: 3.

than $39,000 per year, according to the College Board (and two-thirds of students who attend these schools don't pay the full sticker price) (Baum and Ma 2010).

For argument's sake, we have taken the larger of those estimates that the majority of students pay into consideration for our calculations. Our conclusion: over the length of a four-year degree, the estimated cost is around $80,000.[9] Therefore, costs for college are well below the median expected net returns of $300,000.

Not only is college worth the cost in sheer economic terms, but it also provides other economic benefits as well, such as career choice and employment stability. Workers with college degrees had the lowest unemployment rates over the past three years (as they have historically), receiving the best possible shelter from the recession of 2007. They also have the best prospects for being hired in the recovery. They are the most trainable and adaptable workers in both good and bad economic times. This means that high school graduates and dropouts (without postsecondary education or training) are much more at risk of being left behind as the economy plods forward in the long march back to normalcy.[10]

A college education does not make one immune to economic recession, of course. When it rains long enough and hard enough, everyone gets a little wet.

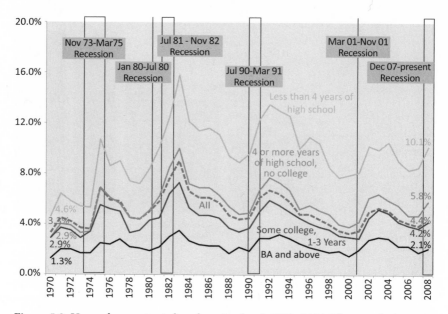

Figure 5.2. Unemployment rate by education level, 1970–2008. Those with the most postsecondary education have the lowest unemployment rates. *Source*: Bureau of Labor Statistics, Employment Situation, various years.

In our current economy, where 59 percent of the population has at least some college education, even the most highly educated have lost jobs, and many college graduates are scrambling for the reduced pool of jobs available to them. Unemployment rates at all education levels have climbed during the recession, and the unemployment rate of those holding bachelor's degrees and above reached a peak of 5.1 percent in November 2010 before declining again.

Still, as Figure 5.2 shows, workers with a postsecondary education have been significantly better off than those with less education in every phase of the economic cycle. The figure, which uses annual unemployment data between 1970 and 2010, shows that those holding bachelor's degrees were three times less likely to be unemployed than workers with no high school diploma. In economic downturns, then, college degrees still make the best umbrellas, and college campuses still provide the best shelters, as well as the launching pads for jobs and careers that will survive the recession.

The tangible benefits to postsecondary education, then, are clear. What's more, demand for postsecondary education has been increasing for decades and the future promises more of the same.

The Demand for Postsecondary Education
Will Continue to Increase

The notion that everyone needs at least some postsecondary education is not without expert critics, but the debate may already be purely academic, as our mass postsecondary education system has already arrived. Nowadays, more than 60 percent of Americans go on to some kind of education or formal training after high school. Access to postsecondary education and training has become the essential goal for education reform in the K–12

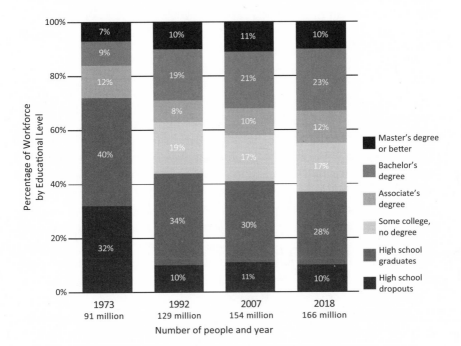

Figure 5.3. Distribution of jobs by education level, 1973–2018. By 2018, about two-thirds of all employment will require some college education or higher. *Source*: Carnevale, Smith, and Strohl 2010: 14.

system, and middle-class employability is now emerging as a key standard of educational adequacy in the postsecondary system.

The statistics bear this out. Since the early 1970s, the American economy has transformed from one that featured more jobs for high school dropouts than for college graduates, to one where the share of jobs for dropouts has plunged from roughly one-third to 11 percent. The future promises more of the same, as shown in Figure 5.3: by 2018 almost two-thirds of all jobs will require at least some form of postsecondary education. In 1973, there were 25 million jobs that required[11] applicants to have at least some college education (28 percent of all jobs) (Figure 5.3). By 2007, that number had nearly quadrupled to 91 million jobs, or 59 percent of all jobs in the U.S. economy.

The share of workers with an associate's degree, certificate, or some college has more than doubled, from 12 percent to 27 percent of the workforce. The percentage of workers with bachelor's degrees has also more than doubled, from 9 percent in 1973 to 21 percent in 2007. Graduate degree holders have increased at a slightly slower pace, going from 7 percent to 11 percent over the same period.

The proportion of jobs available to workers with no postsecondary education and training has fallen commensurately with the increasing demand for workers with postsecondary education and training. This declining share of opportunities for workers with some high school education, or their high school diploma, is now highly segregated by occupational cluster. For example, by 2018, an estimated 61 million jobs will be available for prime age workers[12] with a high school diploma or less (37 percent of all jobs), compared to 101 million jobs for workers who will need at least some postsecondary education (63 percent of all jobs). Of those 61 million jobs, 87 percent will be found in only three of the sixteen career clusters: food and personal services, sales and office support, and blue collar career clusters. These particular clusters are characterized by either declining job opportunities or low wages. In addition, the rate of wage increase for people with high school or less education has also been stagnant.

The proportion of workers who will need an associate's degree, postsecondary certificate, or some college will increase from 27 percent in 2007 to 29 percent in 2018. The share of workers who must have bachelor's degrees will climb from 21 percent to 23 percent, while the number of jobs requiring graduate degrees may decline slightly, from 11 percent to 10 percent over the same period (Carnevale, Smith, and Strohl 2010: 13–14).

The Role of Colleges and Universities Is Vital, Especially as the On-Ramp to a Larger System of Work-Based Learning

Among other things, higher education acts as an important gateway for accessing other parts of the postsecondary learning system. Postsecondary education provides entry to jobs that offer the most employer-provided training, plus access to the most powerful, flexible workplace technology (Krueger 1993; Eck 1993). Education, training, and technology tend to be *sequential and complementary* in producing productivity and earnings. Higher levels of formal education not only increase access to jobs that provide further training, they also increase access to technology that complements, rather than replaces, skills. Use of such technology—desktop computers, for instance—tends to increase both worker autonomy and pay. Less-educated workers tend to use technology that substitutes for skill.

But formal college is only a piece of the postsecondary education and training puzzle. In fact, colleges and universities represent only 35 percent of the entire postsecondary education and training system. The rest consists of formal and informal employer-provided training programs, military training, and a variety of other venues for postsecondary learning (Figure 5.4).

Non-degreed learning systems are also important to access and success in the workforce. Postsecondary training programs that result in certificates, test-based licenses, and certifications are commonly missed by both education and labor data sources. Typically, education data only count people who have passed through educational institutions in pursuit of formal degrees, while labor market data exclude certificates or industry-based certifications. Moreover, both sets of data ignore the role played by formal and informal learning outside the traditional education system, including industry and occupational licensure, apprenticeships, and employer-based training.

Technology Is Driving the Demand for Postsecondary Attainment

As noted above, demand for postsecondary education in the workforce is rising—and it is technology that is driving the shift toward increasing postsecondary requirements. The economic history of the United States is one of lock-step progression between technology and educational attainment. In the nineteenth and twentieth centuries, electricity and the internal combustion

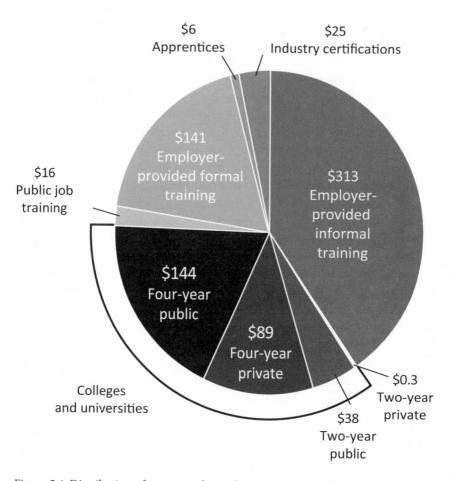

Figure 5.4. Distribution of postsecondary education programs by program type (dollars in billions). Formal postsecondary programs make up 35 percent of the $772 billion postsecondary education and training system. *Source*: Carnevale, Smith, and Strohl 2010: 2.

engine drove the rise of manufacturing and America's shift away from an agrarian economy. Today, computers and related inventions are driving the information revolution and transforming the U.S. economic landscape once again. Just as the industrial revolution was critical to building a mass K–12 education system to feed workers into the manufacturing industries, the information revolution is spurring the development of a mass postsecondary system to fill the needs of sophisticated new industries, such as computer systems design.

Integral to this trend is a concept in labor economics known as *skill-biased technological change*. This simply means that technological development and the organizational changes that come with it favor workers with more education because they have the expertise needed to handle more complex tasks and activities. Demand for these workers, in turn, grows across the board as the technology spreads throughout the economy.

Computer-based technology adds new kinds of value that were simply impossible in previous economic eras. In the old industrial economy, the dominant competitive standard was mass production of standardized goods. The dominant outcome metric was material-based productivity: cost-efficiency through reducing inputs required to produce a given level of output. In the postindustrial economy, productivity is still supreme, but it has been joined by a growing set of competitive standards including quality, variety, customization, convenience, customer service, speed, novelty, and social responsibility (Carnevale 1991).

The penetration of information technology has fueled a fundamental change in how employees are organized. The new format emphasizes flexible networks accountable to common performance standards. As a result, production processes are now just as likely to use goods and services produced by other organizations as those produced in-house. These flexible networks, which now dominate the knowledge economy, require communication and information technologies that allow organizations to connect easily with one another and with their customers.

Increases in organizational complexity lead to an ever-increasing bias toward skilled and educated workers because workers need more knowledge and training to handle that complexity. Increases in educational attainment, in turn, result in efficiency and productivity gains when better-trained workers are paired with the technologies that make the networks possible. The result is predictable—demand for employees with better preparation goes up.

On the flip side, information technology can depress demand for workers with only high school diplomas or less. Available evidence shows that information technology tends to substitute for the narrow and repetitive work tasks that require low-skilled workers in many industries—which is why many lower-level jobs tend to disappear forever in recessions. Prior to the 1991 recession, roughly one-third of laid-off workers with high school educations or less reclaimed their old (or comparable) positions during recovery periods. In the past two recessions, the numbers have been even smaller. Jobs created in recent recoveries looked nothing like the jobs lost, and the people hired for those new positions looked nothing like the people laid off from the old ones. In the past two recessions, the typical job loser was a high school-educated male in a traditionally male job, such as manufacturing or construction, working in the middle of the country. In the past two recoveries, the typical job gainer was a female with a postsecondary education who lived on either coast and worked in a service occupation—particularly health care, education, or professional and business services.

We Are Still Underproducing Postsecondary Talent

Technology has shifted the economy, bringing about structural change, and we now need more postsecondary talent than ever. The forces of supply and demand have contributed to the resulting underproduction. On the supply side, we have failed to produce postsecondary degrees at a steady rate (Goldin and Katz 2008; Carnevale and Rose 2011). From 1915 to the early 1980s, the supply of college-educated workers in the workforce rose steadily by 3.1 percent a year because more people were going to school and because less-educated workers were gradually being replaced with more-educated workers. Starting in 1985, however, the increase in college-going youth slowed down to a crawl, when compared with their immediate predecessors. But the net replacement of less-educated retirees with more highly educated young people still meant that the relative supply of workers with postsecondary education still grew by 2.5 percent a year from 1980 to 1990.

As the workforce gradually became more educated, however, increasing overall attainment levels beyond what was there became more difficult after 1990. This is because the overall education level of retirees was progressively higher and the difference between the education levels of new entrants and that of retirees shrank. Consequently, the supply of college-educated workers rose by 2 percent per year from 1990 to 2000, and fell to 1 percent per year from 2000 to 2010.

While the rate of increase in the supply of college-educated workers has fallen, the demand for college-educated workers has continued to rise. The movements of demand, however, have been following a different logic. De-

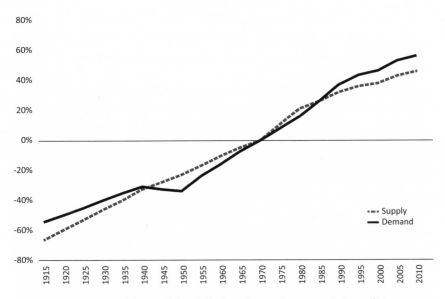

Figure 5.5. Supply and demand for skilled workers relative to 1970 conditions, 1915–2010. *Source*: Carnevale and Rose 2011: 19.

pression and war in the early twentieth century resulted in slow-growing demand for skilled workers in those years, even as more young people stayed in school longer, and increased their human capital. Relative demand for skilled labor grew by 1.7 percent per year from 1915 through 1950 (Figure 5.5). Starting in 1950, the long boom of the 1950s and 1960s was followed by the computer and Internet revolutions starting in the 1980s. The yearly growth of demand for skilled workers between 1950 and 2005 was an impressive 3.6 percent.

While the supply and demand story for postsecondary education is complex in its details, the long-term trend is clear. Demand has increased steadily, but supply fell off after 1984. As a result, the wage premium for postsecondary education and training has risen precipitously since the 1980s, bringing growing earnings inequality along with it. The future promises more of the same. Our own research at the Georgetown Center on Education and the Workforce suggests that at the current trend rate, the wage premium for bachelor's degree holders will grow from the current

84 percent to a whopping 93 percent by 2025, even with a trend increase of almost eight million new college degrees (Carnevale and Rose 2011).

Relative Wages Are a Conclusive Indicator of Demand for Postsecondary Workers

Economic theory demonstrates that wages are a marker of productivity and tells us that employers will pay more for workers who strengthen the bottom line. This reasoning has been countered by the argument that the increasing demand for postsecondary education is not related to what employers *need* but what they can get, and those employers are just hiring empty degrees, devoid of additional value. This perspective, however, ignores the basic economic principles of supply and demand at work in the labor market. Even more importantly, this argument flies in the face of good market reasoning. Employers might err and hire empty degrees once or twice, but they will not continue to do so over a long period. In general, employers have no incentive to pay a higher wage unless they are obtaining higher productivity, or they want to either guarantee a worker's tenure or provide a premium for special skills or training in tight labor markets.

Wages by education level traditionally behave as human capital theory predicts: higher education levels correlate with higher wages (a proxy for higher productivity). This trend has remained unchanged, with few exceptions, for the last several decades. What's more, the best available data on the hiring and pay practices of American employers has indicated that, for the past thirty years, employers have been paying increasingly more for more highly educated workers relative to their high school-educated counterparts. Economists call the pay of bachelor's degree holders relative to their high school educated counterparts the "wage premium." This wage premium paid to holders of bachelor's degrees and above acts as an indicator of the relative demand for workers with bachelor's degrees and above versus non-degree holders.[13] In a free market, wages, or annual earnings, are a measure of worker productivity. It is hard to imagine that rational employers would continue to hire degrees if they were not obtaining commensurate productivity gains.

In the 1970s, the wage premium for college-educated workers declined as the supply of these workers grew dramatically with a surge in college attainment. A declining wage premium indicated that relative supply exceeded relative demand for college-educated workers. This quickly changed

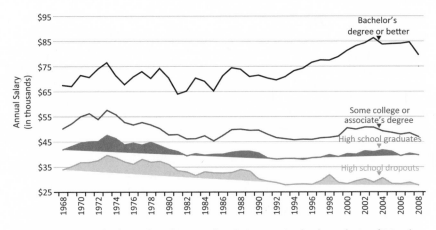

Figure 5.6. Annual salaries by education level. *Source*: Author's analysis of March Current Population Survey data, various years.

in the wake of the recession in the early 1980s as information technology began to transform the economy from an industrial base to one focused primarily on services. This trend peaked in the 1990s as the wage premium for college-educated workers spiked dramatically. Rising wages over time indicate excess demand or a short-term inability of supply to meet demand for a particular skill. In other words, the supply of educated workers is not keeping up with demand, and as a result, employers must invest more of their profits in order to acquire the skills and talent their work requires.

Figure 5.6 clearly illustrates the point that postsecondary education has led to a consistent earnings advantage for over a generation. For the great majority of Americans, it is necessary to obtain at least some college—a postsecondary certificate or an associate's degree—to earn wages above the national median. By obtaining a bachelor's degree, a worker contributes the greatest percentage jump to his or her earning power—84 percent over a high school graduate.

From an Economic Perspective, All Jobs and All Degrees Are Not Equal

Most data, including our own, understate the importance of postsecondary education and training because they treat all jobs as if they had similar characteristics.[14] However, not all jobs are created equal. Low-wage service jobs account for about 20 percent of the workforce but only 14 percent of the hours worked in the economy (Autor and Dorn 2009). Moreover, these jobs are commonly in industries with large shares of part-time work, or characterized by very high turnover.

Some jobs available to workers who lack postsecondary experience provide opportunities for these workers to settle into a career and earn a sustainable wage,[15] particularly jobs in manufacturing, professional and business services, and some technology positions. The best opportunities, though, for those out of high school are in male-dominated fields. Over 80 percent of workers in manufacturing, architecture and construction, and transportation, distribution, and logistics are male.

Many of the low-wage service jobs, however, are highly transitional; young people commonly take jobs in food services or other low-skill occupations as they work themselves through school or toward better, more skilled jobs they can turn into a career. Roughly half the workers in low-skill, low-wage occupations move into higher wage categories within five years.

As an illustration, there are many more doctors who used to be cashiers than there are cashiers who used to be doctors, but the statistics treat the two jobs equally. For every new job for cashiers that will open up between 2008 and 2018, there will another thirteen job openings to replace cashiers who leave the occupation. By way of contrast, for every new job for physicians, there will only be 0.8 job openings to fill the jobs of physicians who leave the occupation (Carnevale, Smith, and Strohl 2010).

Yet jobs data treat openings for low-skilled positions the same as openings for long-term career jobs. This data issue exaggerates the significance of low-skilled jobs and, in turn, underestimates the demand for postsecondary education and training. Ultimately, about 11 percent of Americans are stuck in low-wage low-skill jobs in the bottom quartile of wage distribution (Carnevale and Rose 2001). In other words, as robust as the demand for higher education and training may seem in our forecasts, in reality it may actually be greater.

All jobs are not created equal and neither are all college courses, certificates, and degrees. The traditional degree hierarchy from high school to Ph.D. doesn't hold up when measured from an earnings perspective. On average, higher degree levels bring higher earnings, but there is a lot of overlap in earnings by degree level. Figure 5.7 demonstrates that, depending on

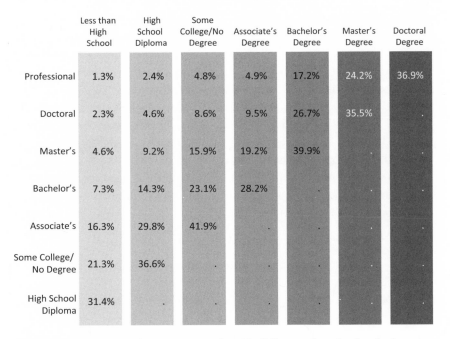

	Less than High School	High School Diploma	Some College/No Degree	Associate's Degree	Bachelor's Degree	Master's Degree	Doctoral Degree
Professional	1.3%	2.4%	4.8%	4.9%	17.2%	24.2%	36.9%
Doctoral	2.3%	4.6%	8.6%	9.5%	26.7%	35.5%	.
Master's	4.6%	9.2%	15.9%	19.2%	39.9%	.	.
Bachelor's	7.3%	14.3%	23.1%	28.2%	.	.	.
Associate's	16.3%	29.8%	41.9%	.	.	.	.
Some College/ No Degree	21.3%	36.6%	.	.	.	.	.
High School Diploma	31.4%	.	.	.	.	.	.

Figure 5.7. Earnings overlap among people with different education levels. Some people earn more than their more highly educated counterparts. *Source*: Carnevale, Rose, and Cheah 2011: 6.

industry and occupational choice, the link between better education and higher wages can sometimes be unclear. For instance, 28 percent of workers with an associate's degree make the same amount or more than their colleagues with a bachelor's degree. About 23 percent of workers with some college but no degree earn the same amount or more than employees with a bachelor's degree, and 40 percent of those with bachelor's degrees earn the same amount or more than their counterparts with a master's degree (Carnevale, Rose, and Cheah 2011).

There is also much greater variation in earnings within degree level than between degree levels. For example, while bachelor's degrees bring an 84 percent earnings advantage over high school degrees, the difference between the earnings of the top and bottom bachelor's degree majors (for example, high school counselor and petroleum engineer) is four times the difference between high school degrees and bachelor's degrees (Carnevale, Strohl, and Melton 2011). For the most part, college degrees are worth the cost and the debt burdens. After all, college costs only accumulate over two to four years and earnings returns accumulate over several decades. Nonetheless, some awards and degrees are not worth the cost and debt burden, as the ongoing tensions between the federal government and for-profit schools have demonstrated (and as William G. Tierney discusses in his chapter in this volume).

In addition, there is always mismatch between people's skills and available jobs. Many people end up with the wrong degree in the wrong place at the wrong time. Others choose occupations that do not maximize earnings returns from their certificate or degree.

The complex and dynamic relationships between postsecondary programs and the labor market suggests the need for information to better align postsecondary programs and jobs.

Occupation Matters

The knowledge-based economy has not only shifted demand for postsecondary education, it has fundamentally reshaped the way that we think about careers. As we have moved from the industrial-based manufacturing economy, where a job was defined by the workplace, plant, and industry, work has become defined more by the tasks a worker performs. Today, the predominant unit of analysis for understanding the economy is occupation.

Although education matters enormously in determining earnings, an individual's earnings are not dependent solely on educational attainment. Occupation—the job someone works in—matters, too. Of course, occupation and educational attainment are closely linked, with some occupations requiring more education than others. Demand for workers with postsecondary qualifications is tied tightly to occupations and the skills they require, and more loosely to the industries in which the occupations reside.

Understanding the relationship between education and occupation is critical to understanding the forces driving demand for postsecondary education. Occupation is a simple, shorthand way of expressing all the tasks performed in a particular job and therefore the skills and level of formal education needed. While there is variation, occupations generally have similar requirements regardless of industry. Accountants, for example, perform comparable tasks whether they are working for a mining company or a hospital—and the training required to do the work is virtually the same. As a result, the education requirements for occupations are relatively homogenous.

To speak about the educational requirement of an industry is not really meaningful, because industries are conglomerates of many different occupations and levels of educational demand. The day when people left high school, went to work in the local industry, and then worked their way up through a wide variety of occupations is disappearing. Starting out straight from high school on the loading dock or in the mail room and climbing to the CEO's corner office is no longer an option. Individuals who work in multiple occupations within a single industry over their lifetime are becoming rarer and rarer.

This is partially because of the increasing complexity of work today, which requires more specific education and training focused on a particular occupation (labor market specialization). More often now, education, training, and work are focused on the occupation, and careers reflect workers' ascension of an occupational hierarchy. Some occupations are tied tightly to particular industries (such as nurses in health care), but more and more occupations are dispersed broadly *across* industries.

In Figure 5.8, we show average wages for broad education levels in each of our ten occupational groupings. The best-paying jobs at the top of the education distribution overall are still doctors and nurses in the health-care professional and technical occupations, while managers and CEOs in managerial and professional office jobs rank second for the size of their wage premiums. STEM jobs also pay well at every level of the educational distribution, a trend that remains consistent across time. Someone with an associate's degree in a STEM occupation makes more than a master's degree holder working in education.

While better education correlates to better pay across the board, this dynamic is especially significant in low-earning jobs. Workers with some college, for instance, receive a 13 percent bump in salary over high school graduates in food and personal services occupations and a 10 percent increase in health-care support occupations. Occupations that require the least amount of education for its workers still pay low wages, however—even at the top of that education distribution. For example, college graduates earn only about $33,000 in health-care support and $35,000 in food and personal services occupations. Although there are benefits to more training in these occupational groupings, there are still wage ceilings that make it impossible to climb comfortably into the middle class. The average wages of workers in food and personal services with various levels of educational attainment has actually declined in real terms since the 1980s (Carnevale, Smith, and Strohl 2010: 105).

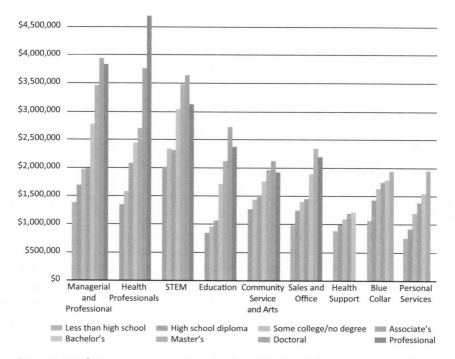

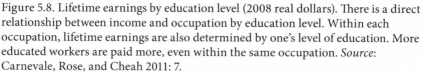

Figure 5.8. Lifetime earnings by education level (2008 real dollars). There is a direct relationship between income and occupation by education level. Within each occupation, lifetime earnings are also determined by one's level of education. More educated workers are paid more, even within the same occupation. *Source*: Carnevale, Rose, and Cheah 2011: 7.

Occupational choice also matters at the highest education levels. A graduate degree in health-care professional, managerial, and STEM occupations gives workers a wage premium vastly superior to that of a comparable degree for workers in food and personal services occupations. Ultimately, occupation-specific human capital ties people to their occupations and can result in substantial wage premiums for specialized tasks. Occupational choice is highly correlated to earnings, regardless of educational attainment levels. High school dropouts in managerial and professional office and STEM jobs, for instance, still earned twice as much as high school dropouts in health-care support or food and personal services jobs.

Further, workers with bachelor's degrees in managerial and professional office or STEM occupations earned more than employees with graduate degrees in blue collar, community services and arts, education, health-care support, and food and personal services occupations, on average. In general this pattern holds true for all levels of education.

Majors Matter

Finally, examining the earnings of individuals by undergraduate major also demonstrates that educational attainment is not the only factor driving earnings. Different majors have different economic value. While going to college is undoubtedly a wise decision, what you take while you're there also matters a lot. Economic returns on different majors run a wide gamut—primarily because different majors lead to different occupations. At the extreme, the highest-earning major (petroleum engineering) earns 314 percent more at the median than the lowest-earning major (counseling psychology). As shown in Figure 5.9, the highest median earnings at the aggregate level are in engineering majors ($75,000) and computers and mathematics majors ($70,000), while the lowest-earning majors are psychology and social work ($42,000) and education ($42,000) (Carnevale, Strohl, and Melton 2011).

Commodification or Intrinsic Value? Higher Education Does Not Need to Choose

It is no secret that the U.S. economy has changed since the late 1970s. Manufacturing's decline is just a symptom of the larger change recently wrought by technology. As a result, postsecondary education is now required in the majority of jobs—an estimated 63 percent of all jobs by 2018 (Carnevale, Smith, and Strohl 2010). Moreover, postsecondary education and training is the key to accessing the middle class, higher-paying jobs, and advanced training.

But what does the increasing demand for postsecondary-educated workers mean for our educational institutions, which are struggling to integrate their potentially contradictory missions of educating students for work and educating them for citizenship?

The increasing economic value of knowledge is both a boon and a burden for educators. As the economic value of higher education grows, the scale and scope needs to increase commensurately. The good news is that the knowledge economy also forces a mass democratization of higher education,

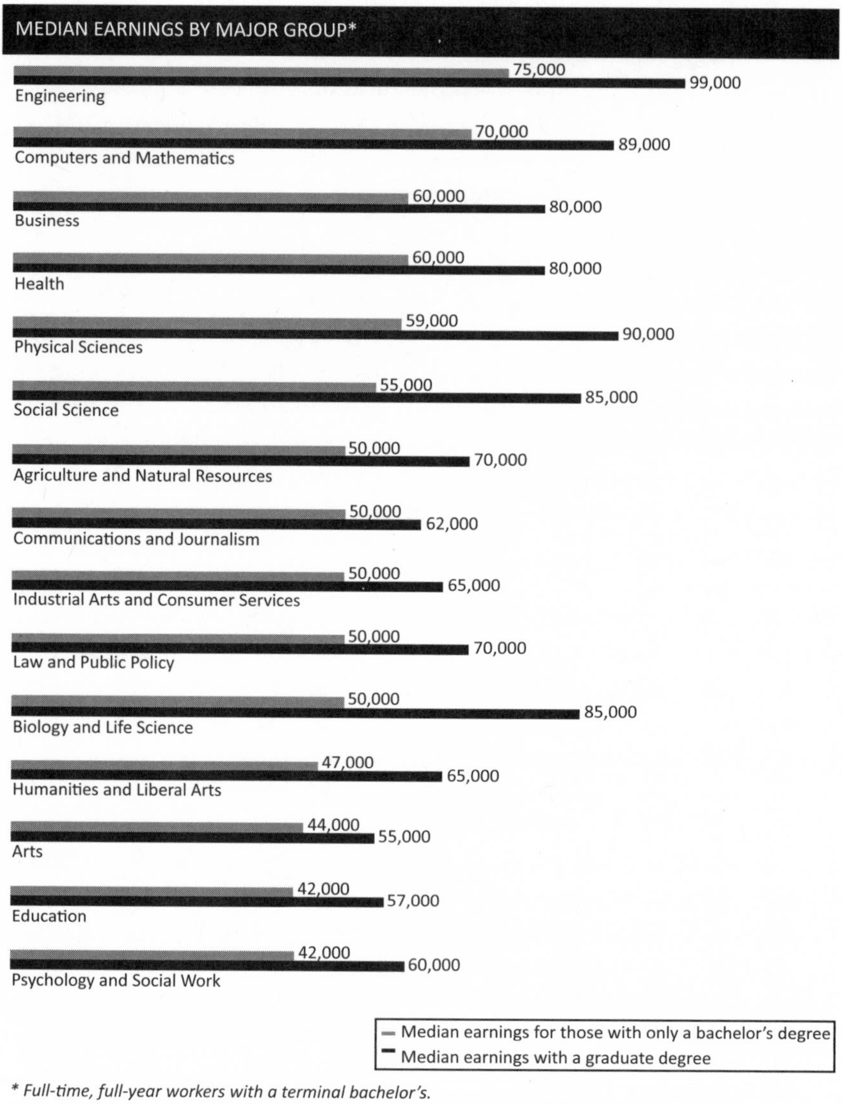

MEDIAN EARNINGS BY MAJOR GROUP*

Engineering
75,000
99,000

Computers and Mathematics
70,000
89,000

Business
60,000
80,000

Health
60,000
80,000

Physical Sciences
59,000
90,000

Social Science
55,000
85,000

Agriculture and Natural Resources
50,000
70,000

Communications and Journalism
50,000
62,000

Industrial Arts and Consumer Services
50,000
65,000

Law and Public Policy
50,000
70,000

Biology and Life Science
50,000
85,000

Humanities and Liberal Arts
47,000
65,000

Arts
44,000
55,000

Education
42,000
57,000

Psychology and Social Work
42,000
60,000

— Median earnings for those with only a bachelor's degree
— Median earnings with a graduate degree

* Full-time, full-year workers with a terminal bachelor's.

Figure 5.9. Median earnings by college major. There is extreme variation in the median earnings of workers with bachelor's degrees by their college major. (Analysis of data from the 2009 American Community survey.) *Source*: Carnevale, Strohl, and Melton 2011: 5.

because access to college has become the threshold requirement for middle-class earnings and status in postindustrial America. In very short order, college has become a mass system and is asked to meet the standards of both democratic accountability and economic utility. Demand has grown faster than traditional institutions have been able to keep up, and as a result, enrollment in for-profit higher education has grown exponentially. But the standards of accountability in a mass democratic institution and the vision of a selective college apparatus are fundamentally at odds.

The political landscape highly favors postsecondary education and, by extension, as other authors in this volume argue (O'Connor; Hoffman; Wolf-Powers and Andreason), has largely ignored career and technical education (CTE) at the high school level and above. What then do we do about the 37 percent of our workforce who drop out of high school, or who will only attain a high school diploma and have little chance of entering a postsecondary program? As Ronald Ferguson also argues in this volume, career pathways out of high school that explain to Americans entering college how to maneuver the postsecondary education system, or how to climb the ladders and lattices required to get to the "next steps" in the workforce, are not well-developed.

The major political obstacle to this connection of career and technical training is fear of "tracking"—a toxic policy that hinders the nation's quest to make the American Dream accessible to all its citizens, in particular for minorities, inner-city youth, or those from low-income communities. CTE programs do serve a great purpose for our nation's youth, as they help to make connections between young adults and postsecondary opportunities. Without discussing these options in a directed way, as with CTE, many minority and low-income youth will lack the resources needed to make good decisions about postsecondary education and workforce choices.

As Tierney argues in this volume, for-profit institutions are here to stay. They have been extremely successful in reaching the non-traditional student;[16] and in providing access to low-income communities, minority populations, adults over twenty-six, and adults with children. The foresight of for-profit institutions in making key market connections between the classroom and the workforce surpasses that of CTE programs, which face similar curriculum challenges. Many for-profit institutions collaborate closely with business to design curricula to meet workforce needs.[17]

Some believe that the increasing value of education may force a reckoning of narrow economic needs and broader educational goals, resulting in a "commodification" of education, where the social value is stripped away and education is reduced to a mere product that can be bought, sold, or hired. Hence the outcry of critics who lament that college students these days do not study enough Plato. They are not entirely off the mark. Education has intrinsic as well as extrinsic value. The temptation to provide narrow vocational training rather than more general learning is strong in a market economy, especially in our current budgetary environment. In theory, the increasing power of economic markets in higher education can promote underinvestment in the value of knowledge for its own sake, underinvestment in the value of self-knowledge, and reduced concern for the broader cultural and political value of knowledge in a democratic political system.

As the economic value of education increases, we will need to remember that education, especially higher education, concerns more than dollars and cents. It should do more than provide new technology and new foot soldiers for the American economy. Higher education is a crucial anchor for the professions in their struggle to maintain their professional values and standards in a world increasingly driven by the narrow valuation of cost efficiency and direct earnings returns—the medical professions are an obvious case in point.

Many jobs now require preparation that sounds a lot more like liberal education and professional education than narrow job training. Postindustrial careers are defined by unique sets of applied knowledge, values, skills, and interests that far exceed what one can find in postsecondary course catalogues, let alone in the narrow training programs characteristic of the industrial era.

Even beyond these considerations, however, educators in both secondary and postsecondary institutions have a cultural and political mission to ensure that there is an educated citizenry that can continue to defend and promote our democratic ideals and freedom of thought. Streams of inquiry that trace back to various sources from Theodor W. Adorno to Seymour Martin Lipset demonstrate convincingly that, once nations achieve a basic level of wealth, tolerant political attitudes and political participation depend more on education and less on traditional metrics for economic class. Moreover, the same streams of research suggest that more general forms of education, as opposed to narrow vocational or technical schooling, tend to promote tolerance and undermine the development of authoritarian personalities.

We need to aspire to a dual bottom line in American higher education. There is a pragmatic balance to strike between postsecondary education's

growing economic role and its traditional cultural and political independence from economic forces. Ultimately, however, the inescapable reality is
that ours is a society based on work. Those who are not equipped with the
knowledge and skills necessary to get, and keep, good jobs are denied full
social inclusion and tend to drop out of the mainstream culture, polity, and
economy. In the worst cases, they are drawn into alternative cultures, political movements, and economic activities that are a threat to mainstream
American life. Hence, if secondary and postsecondary educators cannot
fulfill their economic mission to help grow the economy and help youths
and adults become successful workers, they also will fail in their cultural
and political missions to create good neighbors and good citizens. And increasing the economic relevance of education should, if done properly, extend the ability of educators to empower Americans to work in the world,
rather than retreat from it.

Conclusions

The economic role of education, especially postsecondary education, has
become central to the American social contract; education provides upward
mobility that helps us reconcile the equality implicit in democratic citizenship with the inequality that market economies create. Over the past three
decades, computer technology has automated repetitive mental and physical
tasks. Well-paid jobs that only required a high school education are declining, replaced by jobs requiring some form of postsecondary education and
training. As a result, by 2018, at least 63 percent of all jobs will require education and training beyond high school.

Over the past three decades, postsecondary education and training have
become the new arbiters of access to middle-class earnings. The increase in
lifetime earnings of those with postsecondary education relative to the
earnings of high school graduates, which has been rising ever since the
1980s, now stands at roughly $1,547,000 for people with some college but no
degree; $1,727,000 for people with associate's degrees; $2,268,000 for people
with bachelor's degrees; $3,252,000 for people with doctoral degrees; and
$3,648,000 for people with professional degrees. This growing lifetime earn-
ings premium is the best evidence of increasing demand for education.

The growth in demand for postsecondary education and training shows
no signs of slowing. At the same time, the difference in earnings by degree

level has been superseded by a much broader variation in earnings based on the relationship between particular curricula and occupations. For example, 28.2 percent of workers with associate's degrees earn more than the average bachelor's degree holder. And while the difference between high school and bachelor's degree earnings is 84 percent, the difference between the median earnings for the lowest and highest paid bachelor's degree majors is 314 percent.

As demand for skilled and educated workers continues to increase in the years ahead, the need to better align postsecondary programs with labor market demands for particular skills will also increase. The relationship between postsecondary education and training and earnings has become both more important and more complex. Aligning student transcript data with employer wage data is now prudent policy. These pressures are changing the postsecondary system from one focused on access and completion in general, to one focused on employability and earnings differentials tied to particular curricula.

CHAPTER 6

Community College Occupational Degrees: Are They Worth It?

Thomas Bailey and Clive R. Belfield

This chapter provides a broad overview of the economic consequences of occupational higher education in the United States, with a particular focus on community colleges. The apparent contrast between employment-focused occupational or career education on the one hand and academic or liberal arts education on the other has been the basis of a long-standing controversy about the role of higher education and what it should be and do to serve society most effectively. This tension has taken on more urgency as U.S. higher education has increasingly come under criticism from policy-makers, researchers, and the public. U.S. colleges and universities, which until only ten or fifteen years ago were acclaimed as the best in the world, are now widely criticized and seen as falling behind postsecondary systems in many other countries.

In their 2008 book, Goldin and Katz describe an almost century-long "race" between education and technology: wages and economic growth depend on how well workers can keep up with changes in the complexity of job tasks. In earlier eras, the workforce kept up by increases in high school graduation rates and subsequently by increases in college enrollment and degree completion. These increases not only promoted economic growth but spread the benefits of that growth widely throughout society. But these trends have stalled in recent decades, potentially leading to faltering growth and innovation and a reversal of the post-World War II trend toward educational equality. And while the international comparisons have focused on the percentage of the population with a college credential, recent research by Arum and Roksa (2011) suggests that even those American college students who persist do not learn very much. The growing criticism of American higher education is accompanied by a consensus that new technology and work organization actually require a deeper and more flexible education system. This system will need to keep up not only with technological change but also with the changing nature of work organization and labor contracts.

Higher education also has responsibility for retraining adults who either failed to acquire skills in high school or in earlier rounds of higher education, or whose skills have become obsolete. Many working adults need new skills but are unable to take time out from employment. Job loss during the Great Recession (from December 2007 to June 2009) has further highlighted the need for adaptability and retraining, as older workers who lost their jobs in the Great Recession need new skills. The college student population, or potential population, also includes those persons who acquired little human capital during high school and need vocational training, remediation, or even a high school diploma. This last group is particularly clustered in urban areas, where demographic changes—in population ages and immigrant status—are interacting with low-quality schooling and high dropout rates to create cohorts of persons who are under-prepared for the world of work (Tienda and Alon 2007).

In seeking to design an education system that can prepare students for the changing demands of the labor market and can strengthen the skills and human capital of low-income and first-generation college students, education reform is often conceptualized as a tension between a higher education system focused on specific preparation for particular careers and one that provides a broader, more academic education under the assumption that more specific skills can be learned on the job. Although we cannot fully reconcile this tension, we argue that a sharp distinction between academic and occupational skills is misleading and distorts reality.

Our chapter is structured as follows. We begin with a general discussion of career-focused and academic education, arguing that the distinction between the two forms of education has been exaggerated. We then describe occupational credentials across the higher education system, with a focus on community colleges both as providers of associate's degrees and as providers of a large proportion of vocational certificates. The next section reviews the evidence on the labor market returns to these credentials and considers its implications for metropolitan workers. We then present our own analysis of the returns to community college certificates and occupational and academic associate's degrees. In this analysis, we use the Survey of Income and Program Participation (SIPP) data from 2008, which has not been used previously to analyze community college outcomes. We analyze pathways and labor market returns for vocational certificates and associate's degrees across workers in metropolitan and non-metropolitan areas. We conclude by considering how policy might help create an appropriate balance between academic and occupational education and enhance labor market opportunities for students in occupational programs. We also discuss the implications of the Great Recession.

Occupational and Academic Education

Describing the Dichotomy

American educators have argued about the balance between occupational and academic education for at least a century. Advocates of academic education argue that occupational education is too narrow for the dynamic nature of modern technology and workplace demands, that it fails to prepare students to adapt to changing skill demands, and that it abandons the general goal of education to prepare an educated citizenry. According to this perspective, students learn these broader skills through a general education or liberal arts curriculum comprised primarily of science, social sciences, and the humanities. Advocates of occupational education argue that a general academic education does not teach students valuable labor market skills. Although the academic perspective seems to enjoy intellectual support, especially among academics and other commentators, in practice occupational education seems to have carried the day, at least in terms of numbers. As we shall see, the large majority of degrees and certificates conferred by institutions of higher education are in what the U.S. Department of Education refers to as "career" programs or majors. Plus, as we argue below, even this lopsided ratio between occupational and academic degrees understates the dominance of occupational preparation nationally.

In the past, controversy was often focused on vocational education in secondary school. High school vocational education was initially designed for students who were not going to college, to prepare them for jobs. But as a consensus grew in the late twentieth century that everyone needed at least some college to have a chance to obtain a decent job, high school programs that failed to prepare students for college lost favor. Vocational (now called technical) education in high school had to either lead directly to postsecondary occupational programs (this was one goal of the tech prep program) or to teach academic skills through contextualized instruction. (These were strong underlying goals of the 1994 School to Work Opportunity Act. See Bailey and Merritt 1997.)

A related trend emerged in occupational education in community colleges in the late 1990s. Many occupational programs in community colleges had been designed to prepare students for work immediately and, because they were not transferrable to a four-year institution, these programs were referred to as "terminal." But in some areas, educators perceived that employers began to favor bachelor's graduates where they had previously hired associate's degree holders. Colleges and state legislators responded by merging state technical college systems that granted certificates or non-transferable associate's degrees and comprehensive community college systems that included many transferable programs. These mergers took place in Minnesota, Louisiana, Indiana, and other states. So-called "career pathway" programs were designed to allow students to intersperse periods of education with periods of work to allow continued opportunities for occupational mobility. The goal was to allow students to earn a two-year degree, for example, and spend some time working, but with the ability to return to college to earn a bachelor's degree without losing the credits that they had already earned. This created a design problem in that the optimal content of the first two years of a four-year degree in, say, accounting, was not necessarily the same as the optimal content of a two-year accounting degree designed to prepare someone for immediate work. The conflict generally involved the value of academic or general education courses in these vocational programs.

Perhaps a similar dilemma can be seen at the four-year level, in which some educators are suspicious of four-year occupational degrees. In this case, the argument is often that college should be about more than work preparation—it should also be about citizenship and cultural growth. Even when attention is focused on work preparation, the relative roles of general skills and specific competencies taught in undergraduate career programs such as business are debated.[1] One of the sharpest examples in this area concerns teacher education. The Teach for America approach suggests that a student with a strong liberal arts education and a short summer training program can be as effective a teacher as a graduate of a college teacher education program (Xu, Hannaway, and Taylor 2007).

Moreover, the academic versus occupational argument is complicated by the dual role that any level of education has in preparing students for work immediately after that level of education and preparing them for subsequent levels of education. Focused occupational education comes under attack most often when the associated jobs tend to need additional education. High school vocational education fell out of favor when labor market information suggested that students needed at least some college to get a good job. At the other end of the educational hierarchy, professional and graduate degrees provide explicit occupational preparation. No one argues that surgeons or lawyers would be most effective if graduate or professional school consisted of a general liberal arts curriculum in which they learned to "problem solve" and "work in teams." Graduate education usually combines very specific occupational preparation with some form of guided or mentored experience. Thus most academics or journalists, who look askance at undergraduate occupational programs, had their occupational education in graduate school. In general, liberal arts education is the education that students get in the levels of education that precede their highest level, at which point in most cases they get focused occupational preparation.

The discussion is further confused when academic education is in fact specific occupational preparation for some jobs. As Dewey wrote in 1916, "Many a teacher and author writes and argues in behalf of a cultural and humane education against the encroachments of a specialized practical education, without recognizing that his own education, which he calls liberal, has been mainly training for his own particular calling" (Dewey 1916).

Many teachers and almost all professors, for example, studied academic disciplines at the undergraduate level that are of direct relevance to their employment. These academic disciplines might seem "liberal," but they actually represent early occupational training.

Over the last two decades, the argument that employers and the labor market demand general skills, not specific skills, has enjoyed a great deal of support. CEOs on the lecture circuit often argue that they want people who know how to learn; they can teach the specific skills. Generally, the concept of "skills for tomorrow's jobs" elicits a call for better general education so that students will be able to adapt to the ever-changing demands of the contemporary workplace. But enrollment trends do not support this perspective, or at least not the version of it that suggests that these skills can best be

learned through a traditional college education with a significant component of liberal arts or academic subjects. There is growing enthusiasm for
very specific occupational certificates that often have minimal general education content. Indeed one of the advantages of these programs is that they
often do not have academic prerequisites and therefore do not require students with weak academic skills to undergo remediation. Remediation has
been shown to be a huge barrier to college persistence and completion (Bailey, Jeong, and Cho 2010). In certificate programs, remediation is sometimes
incorporated into substantive courses, but in general, certificate programs
get students in and out quickly with a specific job goal. Whatever these students may lose in general skills is compensated by a greater probability of
completion and better access to jobs. At least for students with weak academic skills and adults returning to school to upgrade skills, certificate
advocates argue that trading off the amorphous benefits of general skills
for a concrete job is well worth it.

Occupational Credentials

The Classification of Instructional Programs (CIP) categorizes degrees as
either "liberal arts (academic)" or "career (career and technical for sub-
baccalaureate)" programs (National Center for Education Statistics [NCES],
n.d., Postsecondary taxonomy). Academic programs include fine/perform-
ing arts, humanities, interdisciplinary studies, letters/English, mathematics, science, and social and behavioral sciences. Everything else is classified
as a career program—most of these have occupational-sounding titles such
as agriculture, business management, consumer services, and so forth. By
this classification, postsecondary education is already overwhelmingly occupational: 98 percent of certificates, 62 percent of associate's degrees, and
60 percent of bachelor's degrees are in career education (NCES n.d.: Table
P84).[2] Table 6.1 shows that, in 2006, across all postsecondary institutions
there were 2.02 million awards in career education, compared with 0.89
million awards in academic education (70 percent versus 30 percent). Approximately half of all awards in career education are bachelor's degrees,
one-quarter are associate's degrees, and the remaining one-quarter are certificates. Table 6.1 also shows that award growth has been more or less uniform across each category: over the last decade, all award types have grown
by approximately 30 percent. In fact, there has even been a slight trend in

Table 6.1. Number of Undergraduate Credentials Awarded by All Title IV
Postsecondary Institutions

Group	Numbers in 2006	Percentage Growth Since 1997
Total, all undergraduate credential levels	2,913,819	29%
Career education	2,022,885	30%
Academic education	890,934	28%
Bachelor's degrees	1,485,242	29%
Career education	895,248	32%
Academic education	589,994	24%
Sub-baccalaureate credentials	1,428,577	30%
Associate degrees		
Career education	460,197	23%
Academic education	283,997	36%
Certificates		
Career education	667,440	34%
Academic education	16,943	14%

Source: NCES n.d., Table P79.

which bachelor's degrees have become more vocational (with career education growing at 32 percent, compared with 24 percent for academic education) as associate's degrees have become less so (growing at 23 percent and
36 percent, respectively). The trend in associate's degree growth probably
results from an increase in transfer students, who often shift to career degrees once they enroll in a four-year college.

Among bachelor's degrees, associate's degrees, and certificates, certificates are the fastest growing award. Between 2000 and 2009, they grew by
44 percent while total degrees and certificates grew by 39 percent. But within
certificates, short-term certificates (less than one year) were by far the fastest growing segment, growing by 56 percent during the decade (Bailey 2011:
Table 1). At two-year public institutions, almost half of all awards conferred
are certificates (see Table 6.2). However, since certificates take less time
than associate's degrees, they account for about one-quarter of total college
activity (student hours) at two-year public institutions.

Table 6.3 shows higher education awards by field of study (career education only). Perhaps the most striking conclusion from Table 6.3 is the broad
overlap in provision across institutional types. With the notable exceptions

Table 6.2. Awards Conferred by Public Two-Year Colleges (2009)

	Associate's Degrees	Certificates		
		Total	< 1 year	1+ year
Awards conferred				
Total	509,615	365,637	218,476	147,161
Percentage	58%	—	25%	17%
Percentage of all such awards by Title IV eligible institutions	65%	45%	51%	39%

Source: Bailey 2011.

that we mention below, four-year institutions offer a substantial amount of instruction in fields that certificate-providing institutions also offer. It is therefore possible to imagine an integrated system where enrollees might progress from a certificate to an associate's degree up to a bachelor's degree in the same field.

That said, Table 6.3 makes clear that certificates in health care dominate the certificate market. Across all institutions, they constitute 45 percent of all certificates awarded, with almost twice as many awarded in 2006 as in 1997. Health programs also account for one-third of associate's degree awards.

Table 6.3 also shows the shifting balance within a given field across certificates, associate's degrees, and bachelor's degrees. For certificates, the next largest field is manufacturing and construction-related fields (at one-fifth); although the number of these certificates has grown since 1997, the number of associate's degrees in the same field has fallen. A more consistent trend is toward consumer services career education: 15 percent of certificates and 7 percent of associate's degrees (and 5 percent of bachelor's degrees) are awarded in this field; but the numbers have grown substantially since 1997 across all award types.[3] Finally, the nature of business credentialing has shifted upward over the period 1997 to 2006. Table 6.3 shows that business certificates fell by 38 percent yet associate's degrees and bachelor's degrees in business rose significantly.

Although community colleges are a large part of the certificate market, they are not fully dominant. Table 6.4 shows that community colleges confer 46 percent of all certificates. Their market share is greatest in agriculture and natural resources (88 percent); protective services (85 percent); business (67–69 percent); and engineering technologies (64 percent). For the largest

Table 6.3. Awards by Field of Study

Field of Study	Certificates			Associate's Degrees			Bachelor's Degrees		
	N	%	% Change 1997–2006	N	%	% Change 1997–2006	N	%	% Change 1997–2006
Health sciences	298,480	45%	97%	145,126	32%	34%	91,973	10%	7%
Manuf., constr., repair, transport	112,812	17%	15%	31,285	7%	-16%	8,279	1%	57%
Consumer services	99,641	15%	43%	33,456	7%	130%	44,428	5%	46%
Business	51,062	8%	-38%	90,775	20%	7%	278,432	31%	39%
Protective services	27,541	4%	37%	26,539	6%	31%	35,319	4%	40%
Computer/information sciences	20,946	3%	-24%	32,081	7%	185%	47,480	5%	92%
Engineering, arch., science tech.	18,001	3%	9%	35,803	8%	-10%	91,041	10%	10%
Marketing	10,795	2%	521%	7,053	2%	305%	38,733	4%	85%
Public, legal, and social services	7,779	1%	53%	16,497	4%	15%	33,912	4%	20%
Education	6,925	1%	304%	14,528	3%	37%	107,238	12%	2%
Agriculture and natural resources	5,200	1%	4%	6,550	1%	10%	23,053	3%	57%
Communications and design	8,258	1%	22%	20,504	4%	47%	95,134	11%	70%
Total	667,440	100%	34%	460,197	100%	23%	895,248	100%	32%

Source: NCES n.d., Table P80.

Table 6.4. Sub-Baccalaureate Awards Conferred by Field Among Career-Technical Students at Two-Year Public Colleges (2007)

Field of Study	Number of Awards	% of All Awards in That Field
Agriculture and natural resources	4,849	88%
Protective services	24,996	85%
Business management	21,080	69%
Business support	13,136	67%
Engineering, architecture and science technologies	12,516	64%
Manufacturing, construction, repair, and transportation	77,442	58%
Education	3,720	58%
Computer and information sciences	10,321	56%
Public, legal, and social services	3,979	50%
Communication and design	4,393	47%
Marketing	4,195	43%
Health sciences	117,603	37%
Consumer services	26,561	26%
Total	324,791	46%
Number of awards conferred by all U.S. institutions	835,070	22%

Source: NCES n.d., Table P89.

field—health sciences—community colleges provide only 37 percent of all awards. Whereas private, non-profit colleges provide very few certificate programs, the for-profit sector is a significant competitor with the public institutions. For-profit institutions provide almost 38 percent of short certificates and almost half of all long (more than one-year) certificates (Bailey 2011: Table 1).

Returns to Community College Courses

Evidence on the Returns

The return to an associate's degree—as measured using the human capital earnings framework—is strongly positive. In our review of eighteen separate studies (Belfield and Bailey 2011), the unweighted average earnings premium

Table 6.5. Annual Earnings Gains over High School

Credential	Males	Females
Associate's degree[a]	13%	22%
Vocational certificate Grubb 1997	7%	24%
Marcotte et al. 2005[b]	8%	20%
Jepsen et al. 2009	9%	3%
Jepsen et al. 2009[c]	22%	41%

Source: Belfield and Bailey 2011: Table 1.

[a]Returns to an associate's degree is the unweighted average across 18 studies.
[b]Marcotte (2010) found no statistically significant returns using NELS.
[c]Returns to a vocational diploma.

(the additional income earned by an associate's degree graduate compared to a high school graduate) is 13 percent for males and 22 percent for females (see Table 6.5, row 1). This is the average across all associate's degrees and workers of all ages. However, studies have found that returns differ by subject area. On average, research indicates that occupational associate's degrees have higher earnings, suggesting that academic community college degrees may be most useful if students transfer and go on to earn a bachelor's degree. But this varies within both academic and occupational areas, with health and quantitative fields yielding the strongest returns.[4]

Also, wage gains to community college education have grown over recent decades. For example, Marcotte, Bailey, Borkoski, and Kienzl (2005) find higher gains using a more recent dataset (NELS over NLSY, SIPP, or NLS). Thus, our unweighted averages—based on older surveys such as the NLSY79—might actually be understatements.

While returns to occupational associate's degrees may be as high as or higher than those to academic degrees, the *ex ante* expected benefits of the degrees also depend on the probability of completion. Alfonso (2006) found that associate's and bachelor's degree students with occupational majors had lower graduation rates (in part because of lower transfer rates). However, Bailey, Kienzl, and Marcotte (2004) suggested that the relationships vary by student characteristics, with disadvantaged students having higher graduation rates when they major in an occupational field.

Despite the proliferation of occupational certificates and the growing interest in them, only four studies have estimated the returns to these awards.[5] Table 6.5 shows that these studies find strongly positive returns compared to high school degrees: for males, the return is 7–22 percent, and for females it is 3–41 percent. In related work, Jacobson (2011) found that certificates yield a higher boost in earnings than an equivalent number of college credits without a credential. As with degrees, areas of concentration make a difference, even for students who do not complete their certificate. Using UI data from Washington state in the 1990s, Jacobson, LaLonde, and Sullivan (2005) estimated returns of 10 percent per year for students in quantitative or technically oriented vocational courses and 3–5 percent for less quantitative courses.

Certificates appear to provide good economic benefits, at least in some fields, and the unadjusted probability of completion is much higher for certificates than for associate's degrees. Although the National Center for Education Statistics does not publish graduation rates by degree type, it is possible to infer these rates by comparing graduation rates for colleges that predominantly confer certificates to those that focus more on associate's degrees. Institutions with the highest graduation rates tend to be technical colleges that confer mostly certificates and few associate's degrees. Indeed, of the fifty two-year institutions with the highest graduation rates for the 2005 cohort as reported by the Integrated Postsecondary Data System (IPEDS), only thirteen granted any associate's degrees. In a similar vein, public institutions classified as "less-than-two-year institutions" (the highest degrees conferred by these institutions are certificates taking less than two years) had an average graduation rate of 71 percent for 150 percent of normal program completion time (Bailey 2011).

Methodological and Conceptual Issues in Estimating the Real Benefits of Career Education

Clearly, many questions remain unanswered with respect to career education in the form of either an associate's degree or vocational certificate.

First, to identify the causal impact of education it is important to control for personal characteristics. This is particularly important for certificate holders, who may not resemble the "typical" student. For example, they are disproportionately female and may have considerable work experience before they obtain a certificate. Students entering a specific short-term occupational program probably have more clearly defined goals than students who enter a general program in college. Students may also be motivated to obtain a certificate because of deteriorating current work opportunities or licensing requirements. These factors might explain differences between completion rates for certificates and associate's degrees.

Second, certificates and occupational associate's degrees serve two very different roles. It is conceivable that certificates could function as a first step into higher education that would subsequently lead to higher degrees. As noted above, the fields of study overlap, which suggests the possibility of constructing sequential educational ladders that start with certificates and lead to higher-level degrees, perhaps with an intervening period of work (this model is referred to as "career ladders"). Although this model sounds reasonable, it has been difficult to implement, and no labor market evidence exists on the returns to "stackable" certificates. One difficulty has to do with how to combine occupational and academic material in a career ladder or stackable credentials model. In practice, at least, very few students move on to higher-level degrees from certificates.

Certificates may also serve a labor market role inconsistent with a conception of education as a sequence of ever-higher degrees. Students with associate's or bachelor's (or even graduate) degrees may return to college for certificates seeking very specific skills. Thus, in many states, certificate programs serve a role similar to that of continuing education, which is often not connected to any formal degree. In these cases, the value of the certificate may interact with degree attainment, and that interaction effect may vary across education levels: high school dropouts, for example, may gain more than college graduates from having a vocational certificate. Few studies have examined these interactive effects in detail.

Third, but related to the above, is the so-called diversion effect: certificates or occupational associate's degrees may provide short-term benefits but may limit options for future study.[6] These programs might represent a barrier to transferring to a four-year program or—conditional on transfer—might represent a barrier to completing a four-year program.[7] While a great deal of research suggests that starting in a community college reduces a student's chances of completing a bachelor's degree, little research analyzes the effect of enrolling in a particular program in community college.

Fourth, certificate programs are shorter and have higher completion rates than associate's degree programs.[8] Shorter courses yield higher net returns for a given earnings gain because they require less time out of the labor market. If certificate students are also more likely to complete, then their *ex ante* expected returns would be even higher, assuming that there is an additional value to completing a degree (the so-called sheepskin effect).

Courses at community colleges are also considerably cheaper than those at four-year institutions and typically have links with local employers such that their students may secure a job offer more quickly. Certainly, the returns may be biased even more toward vocational courses if these are shorter, cheaper, offered at more convenient times outside the working day, or linked with job placements.

Finally, the benefits of human capital are not restricted to the labor market (see Belfield and Levin 2007). Educated persons reap a host of other benefits (such as enhanced health and consumption choice efficiency), and society gains positive externalities (less crime or welfare reliance). These externalities are one justification for government subsidy of education such that fields with low positive externalities should receive lower subsidies. For individuals, even if the earnings gains are small, other benefits may be sufficient compensation. However, these other benefits may vary with the type of education; it seems more likely that a broad education that enhances general cognitive functioning would yield more of these benefits than vocational certification or even occupational degrees. The latter types of award may convey few positive externalities—they are more akin to indicators of competency in a particular task than to indicators of cognitive function. As such, occupational degrees and certificates may have a lower social rate of return.

General Labor Market Issues

Demand-side issues. Occupational degrees prepare students for particular types of jobs. Certainly the value of those degrees and how they compare to academic degrees, or how much academic content they should have, depends on the demand for these jobs.

Critically, vocational subjects often lead to licensure or certification in a trade or profession. In some cases, students must complete a specified occupational associate's degree or certificate to be eligible to sit for a certification assessment, and certification requirements set the optimal mix of academic and occupational instruction. Kleiner and Krueger (2010) estimate that almost one-third of the workforce holds a license and that possession of a license may increase wages by 15 percent. It may be that licensure drives up wages by artificially restricting the labor supply. But if the licensing or certification system is effective in protecting consumers or guaranteeing the quality of service, then these earnings gains reflect productivity rather than labor supply restriction. However, since licensing requirements do vary substantially by state (in cosmetology, for example), it is unlikely that these requirements always ensure optimal competencies.

Research on the specific skills for occupations that are expected to be in high demand is somewhat ambiguous. On the one hand, predictions of the demand for labor are made in terms of occupations and the skills embodied in these occupations (for example, nursing). See Carnevale, Smith, and Strohl 2010. It would seem that these skills can only be acquired through occupational training (such as learning how to draw blood) or through the content of each specific field of study. On the other hand, policy documents emphasize general skills and behaviors: as summarized in a 2009 report by the Council of Economic Advisers (CEA), "a range of behaviors that reflect 'greater student self-awareness, self-monitoring, and self-control' are key indicators that students are able to . . . succeed" (p. 10).[9] Although as the CEA report suggests, contemporary changes in required skills are often thought to require more general skills, an argument can be made that these changes in fact will lead to a greater emphasis on occupational credentials. First, jobs are becoming more complex and specialized, such that they cannot be performed without proper training. Second, for consumers many services are "experience goods," whose quality cannot be guaranteed *ex ante*: a credential (such as a medical diploma) is a signal of quality. Third, as highly skilled workers change jobs more frequently, prospective employers will rely on occupational credentials in making employment decisions. Finally, as government regulations increase, formal and verifiable credentials will be used more extensively. According to this reasoning, the need for occupational credentials is likely to grow.[10]

Supply-side issues. On the supply side, Table 6.3 suggests that—at least in terms of fields—students can choose from a range of program durations and institutional types. Thus, the career education market—broadly defined— appears to be reasonably competitive. Moreover, there may be more competition in terms of entry and exit of providers: given their shorter duration and indeed their lack of articulation, institutions may find it easier to introduce new certificate programs (as opposed to new degree programs), or to close down ineffective ones. Such flexibility may be advantageous if there are rapid changes in the labor market.

However, the flexibility of occupational certificates may mean that it is hard to evaluate the quality of a particular certificate *ex ante*. There may be few prior graduates who can attest to the value of the certificate, and fewer or weaker quality controls on providers. Certificates might therefore be of low quality, and quality may vary across providers. We have already emphasized that occupational programs do not easily fit together. The problem is compounded by the fact that students do not always receive clear information that would enable them to make straightforward choices about what to study and at which type of institution (Scott-Clayton 2011).

Different institutional types—for-profit institutions, comprehensive community colleges, technical colleges—combine academic and occupational instruction in different ways. In the two-year sector, and especially for certificates, for-profit colleges are very important in some states. The for-profits have the reputation of focusing on specific job preparation without a strong emphasis on general or academic education. Rosenbaum, Deil-Amen, and Person (2006) argue that graduation rates for occupational students are higher at private (for-profit and not-for-profit) career colleges than at community colleges. At the institutional level, for-profit two-year colleges have higher graduation rates than community colleges, but most of the for-profits confer certificates. Public two-year technical colleges that confer only certificates also have very high graduation rates. But these higher graduation rates for both the two-year for-profits and the technical colleges may be the result of their focus on certificates, which we have seen have much higher completion rates, rather than their institutional type per se.[11]

Metropolitan area issues. In most of the above discussion, we have not distinguished metropolitan or urban residency from other residency types. Many of the features and trends apply across all population densities, and state policies—rather than urban economies—drive certification requirements.

However, some aspects of this analysis are especially salient for metropolitan areas. First, the returns to higher education are greater in urban areas, and this correlation is interpreted as "human capital is more valuable in cities." This greater value may reflect greater productivity spillovers across educated workers, although the extent of such spillovers is sensitive to empirical formulation.[12] Second, for-profit institutions are located primarily in areas with higher population densities, so students in these areas should have more providers to choose from. In combination, these two factors suggest that education policy should be more straightforward in metropolitan areas: skills are more valuable, job opportunities are greater, and college options are more plentiful. Investments in occupational programs should be more likely to pay off.

However, the countervailing factor—demography—is salient. The demography of attainment is different in cities: most of the so-called "high school dropout factories" are in urban areas, much higher proportions of students have limited English proficiency, and in general school quality is relatively low (Tienda and Alon 2007). Moreover, although degree holders earn more in cities, many of these persons acquired their education outside the city and migrated in to get work. These educated workers have then displaced urban workers with weaker credentials. The metropolitan challenge therefore includes many of the issues raised above, but also includes a broader social challenge to raise the educational capabilities of cohorts of high school students. These students will need considerable resources to succeed in the labor market: as well as a high school diploma and GED— and then with high probability, remedial education—many will need counseling and support to complete an associate's degree.

Current Returns to Occupational Programs

Analysis Using SIPP

We update the research literature on the economic benefits of academic and occupational education by using the most recent wave of the Survey of Income and Program Participation (SIPP) data from 2008 (waves 1 and 2). The SIPP is a continuous series of national panels, with 36,000 interviewed households in the 2008 panel; the sample is a multistage-stratified sample of the U.S. civilian non-institutionalized population. The SIPP covers labor force, program participation, and income in each wave. This Survey has information on terminal education levels, including whether the individual has a vocational certificate. The second wave includes a topical module that asks persons with higher education qualifications what their field of study was. In this wave, individuals are assigned to mutually exclusive categories of certificate, associate's degree, or bachelor's degree status. We use the standard human capital approach to estimate earnings premiums.[13] The SIPP data are up-to-date with a large sample and the best national data to estimate the returns to field of study.[14] Information also exists on whether the individual lives in a metropolitan area. Our results can then be compared to an earlier exercise using SIPP by Grubb (1997).

First, we estimate the general returns to education using the standard human capital framework. We note again here that evidence of significant returns to associate's and bachelor's degrees is in itself evidence of returns to occupational programs because these constitute the majority of such degrees. In conjunction, we look at the labor market effects of vocational certificates. Our second estimation looks within each level of education to see whether academic or career education yields higher labor market returns and which fields yield the highest returns. For each estimation we report results for the full sample, for samples split by metropolitan versus non-metropolitan residence, and by gender. We also include a set of covariates and use the SIPP sampling weights (see Table Notes for details).

The Returns to Education

Vocational certificates. In this section we examine the returns to education using the standard Mincerian framework. In our first estimation, we interpret a certificate as a qualification above high school but mutually exclusive of any other higher education qualification (we assume certificate holders do not have an associate's degree, for example).

For separate equations for metro versus non-metro and by gender, the coefficients on each attainment level are presented in Figure 6.1 (see Table 6.9 for the full set of specifications). A clear earnings advantage exists for higher levels of attainment over being a high school dropout. Certificates and "some college" have very similar premiums, but both are higher than the premium for high school graduation. The "some college" category is highly heterogeneous and includes students who may have taken a course or two at a community college and those who have accumulated two or three years of credits at a four-year institution. Certificates make particular sense for men, while going from a high school degree to a certificate has only a small effect on earnings for women. In contrast, the associate's degree represents a larger increment over a high school degree for women than it does for men. Figure 6.1 also shows the two general findings: returns to education are lower for nonmetro than metro residents and the gap increases with education level (as shown by Wheeler 2004), and returns are higher for females than for males.

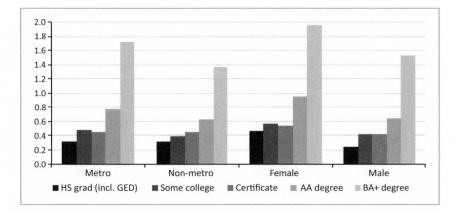

Figure 6.1. Earnings premium over high school dropout (percentage factor). *Source:* SIPP 2008 data; see Table 6.9 for coefficients and model estimation. The figures use percentage factors (not coefficient values) on the vertical axis. That is, a value of 1 denotes earnings that are 100 percent higher than those of the default category (high school dropouts).

However, vocational certificates are not always part of a fixed sequence of educational credentials: GED holders can obtain them, as can bachelor's degree holders. Previous analyses of certificates have focused on the returns to certificates when they are the highest degree attained and have not distinguished between a student with a bachelor's degree and a certificate and one with only a bachelor's degree. Fifteen percent of all individuals in the SIPP sample (including high school dropouts) have an occupational certificate. Two-thirds of those have no other degree. Thus, for these students, a certificate is in effect a terminal degree. Since certificate instruction has very little general education, these students learned their general skills in high school. However, one-third of all certificate holders have a higher degree. For these individuals, any returns to a certificate may in fact be partially the returns to the other qualification.

We model the relationship between earnings and educational attainment, with vocational certificates interacting with degree attainment (see Table 6.10 for the full specifications). Completing a certificate does increase earnings above those earned by high school graduates, thus the earnings for the groups "high school graduate plus certificate" and "some college plus certificate" are both above the high school graduate earnings (and these results are statistically significant). On the other hand, individuals who combine certificates with associate's degrees or with bachelor's degrees earn less than those who have those degrees without a certificate, and this relationship holds in both metro and non-metro areas and for both women and men.

Unfortunately, these data do not indicate whether students earned their certificates before or after their "higher" degrees. If students with higher degrees do return to get a certificate, then this might offer an explanation for the lower earnings of students who combine higher degrees and certificates. Perhaps older students with degrees decide to seek a certificate either if economic changes have made their jobs obsolete, or if they find that their initial degrees have little value in the labor market. Thus the lower labor market premiums for students who combine certificates and degrees may result more from the circumstances that motivate older students to seek certificates than from the labor market value of those certificates.

Associate's and bachelor's degrees in academic or career fields. We now turn to specific fields of study to examine whether the labor market returns to certificates and associate's degrees are concentrated in particular disciplines or occupations. Here we use the subsample from the second wave of SIPP 2008. As an initial investigation, we classify individuals as having either an academic or career qualification (using NCES categories). In Table 6.6 we report the coefficients for career education over academic education at both the associate's and bachelor's degree level. As shown in column 1, individuals with degrees in career education earn approximately 5 percent more than individuals with degrees in academic disciplines. This differential remains when the sample is split by metropolitan residence status, although because the sample sizes are smaller the effect is less precisely estimated. Notably, career education pays off significantly for females: women with career associate's degrees earn approximately 14 percent more than those with academic associate's degrees.

Field of study. Now we divide the academic and career education groups by discipline. Here we are able to include estimates for individuals with vocational certificates as well as associate's degrees.[15]

Table 6.7 shows the returns across vocational credentials relative to a credential in a service industry (such as hotel management). Across the full sample, vocational awards in computing, business, police/protective services, and construction are associated with higher earnings; notably, returns for vocational certificates in health are statistically insignificant. When we disaggregate by metropolitan area residence, few fields emerge as espe-

Table 6.6. Log Monthly Earnings: Associate's Degree Holders and Bachelor's Degree Holders Only

	Full Sample	Metro Residents	Non-Metro Residents	Female	Male
Career associate's degree field relative to academic field	0.053	0.051	0.092	0.142	−0.044
	[0.029]*	[0.033]	[0.065]	[0.039]***	[0.043]
Observations	3,877	2,972	9,05	2,206	1,671
R-squared	0.12	0.12	0.1	0.06	0.14
Career bachelor's degree field relative to academic field	0.046	0.046	0.046	0.085	0.015
	[0.020]**	[0.022]**	[0.050]	[0.030]***	[0.027]
Observations	8,315	6,938	1,377	4,242	4,073
R-squared	0.09	0.1	0.09	0.03	0.09

Source: SIPP 2008, wave 2.

Note: Career associate's degree field is agriculture, computing, business, education, health, communications, engineering, policy, vocational, and visual arts. Career bachelor's degree field is agriculture, business, computing, education, health, communications, and art/architecture. Persons with non-zero earnings aged eighteen to sixty-five only. Specifications also include experience; experience squared; marital status (married/single); ethnicity/race (White/Hispanic); and immigrant status. Models (1)–(3) include gender. SIPP sample weights applied. Robust standard errors in brackets.
*$p<0.1$. **$p<0.05$. ***$p<0.01$.

cially beneficial. Females who get business certificates earn more than those with service sector certificates; health certificates are also associated with higher earnings but the variance is wide. Males, on the other hand, get similar advantages regardless of the field of certificate.

Table 6.8 shows the returns across fields for individuals who have an associate's degree. The reference field is social sciences (academic). Only a few fields of study—either occupational or academic—have returns that are statistically different than those in the social sciences. Across the full sample, health and computing degrees yield the highest earnings; education and agriculture have the lowest, with associate's degrees in arts also having low returns. This last result affirms the general evidence reported above. Again, the differences are attenuated when the sample is split by metropolitan residence status. Notably, females obtain earnings premiums in health and computing

Table 6.7. Log Monthly Earnings: Vocational Credential Holders Only

	Full Sample	Metro Residents	Non-Metro Residents	Female	Male
Vocational field relative to service industry					
Computing	0.204	0.165	0.398	0.206	0.165
	[0.103]**	[0.124]	[0.161]**	[0.170]	[0.120]
Business	0.238	0.252	0.203	0.343	0.044
	[0.098]**	[0.118]**	[0.145]	[0.147]**	[0.137]
Police	0.214	0.23	0.118	0.13	0.161
	[0.121]*	[0.143]	[0.216]	[0.268]	[0.134]
Construction	0.201	0.208	0.208	0.244	0.102
	[0.093]**	[0.113]*	[0.132]	[0.208]	[0.104]
Other	0.156	0.141	0.226	0.213	0.076
	[0.090]*	[0.110]	[0.115]**	[0.145]	[0.104]
Health	0.128	0.142	0.092	0.222	−0.159
	[0.097]	[0.115]	[0.153]	[0.143]	[0.207]
Mechanical	0.12	0.121	0.14	0.131	0.021
	[0.095]	[0.115]	[0.139]	[0.261]	[0.106]
Cosmetology	−0.073	−0.025	−0.249	−0.009	0.034
	[0.104]	[0.123]	[0.178]	[0.152]	[0.210]
Observations	4,461	3,368	1,093	2,203	2,258
R-squared	0.12	0.11	0.18	0.04	0.09

Source: SIPP 2008, wave 2.

Note: Persons with non-zero earnings aged eighteen to sixty-five only. Sample does not include persons with associate's degrees or above . Specifications also include experience; experience squared; marital status (married/single); ethnicity/race (White/Hispanic); and immigrant status. Models (1)–(3) include gender. SIPP sample weights applied. Robust standard errors in brackets.
*$p < 0.1$. **$p < 0.05$. ***$p < 0.01$.

but have lower earnings with degrees in arts, education, and agriculture. For males, the only fields where earnings are statistically different are education and agriculture.

Metropolitan issues. Overall, our analysis with the SIPP affirms that human capital is more valuable in metropolitan areas. Insofar as education yields a positive return on average, we should therefore expect community college programs to be a particularly good investment for urban residents. We also find that in metropolitan areas wage gaps increase as education levels increase. Given the importance of demography, however, this finding may not be unambiguously beneficial: the big payoff is from at least an associate's degree but many urban high school students may not be able to complete such a degree.

Table 6.8. Log Monthly Earnings: Associate's Degree Holders Only

	Full Sample	Metro Residents	Non-Metro Residents	Female	Male
Associate's degree field relative to social sciences					
Health	0.203	0.165	0.382	0.277	0.018
	[0.043]***	[0.048]***	[0.096]***	[0.052]***	[0.086]
Computing	0.114	0.12	0.067	0.246	0.029
	[0.056]**	[0.062]*	[0.120]	[0.085]***	[0.071]
Engineering	0.063	0.058	0.063	0.214	−0.012
	[0.063]	[0.066]	[0.183]	[0.170]	[0.068]
Sciences	0.056	−0.005	0.327	0.058	0.018
	[0.077]	[0.086]	[0.176]*	[0.093]	[0.128]
Communications	−0.039	−0.129	0.621	0.314	−0.313
	[0.192]	[0.213]	[0.156]***	[0.218]	[0.278]
Business	−0.005	0.004	−0.003	−0.008	0.026
	[0.042]	[0.046]	[0.099]	[0.058]	[0.060]
Police	−0.077	−0.111	0.063	−0.049	−0.12
	[0.162]	[0.207]	[0.151]	[0.154]	[0.209]
Vocational	−0.029	−0.045	0.024	0.004	−0.058
	[0.056]	[0.064]	[0.110]	[0.096]	[0.069]
Visual arts	−0.052	−0.106	0.202	−0.008	−0.117
	[0.095]	[0.101]	[0.282]	[0.122]	[0.134]
Arts	−0.068	−0.095	0.02	−0.146	0.041
	[0.060]	[0.067]	[0.141]	[0.078]*	[0.096]
Education	−0.191	−0.203	−0.138	−0.139	−0.341
	[0.071]***	[0.080]**	[0.148]	[0.078]*	[0.172]**
Agriculture	−0.283	−0.203	−0.27	−0.145	−0.31
	[0.136]**	[0.185]	[0.198]	[0.471]	[0.144]**
Observations	3,877	2,972	905	2,206	1,671
R-squared	0.13	0.14	0.13	0.08	0.15

Source: SIPP 2008, wave 1.

Notes: Persons with non-zero earnings aged eighteen to sixty-five only. Specifications also include experience; experience squared; marital status (married/single); ethnicity/race (White/Hispanic); and immigrant status. Models (1)–(3) include gender. SIPP sample weights applied. Robust standard errors in brackets.
*$p < 0.1$. **$p < 0.05$. ***$p < 0.01$.

In looking across fields of study, our analysis shows similar returns for metropolitan and non-metropolitan residents. The lower returns to an associate's degree in education and health for metropolitan residents relative to non-metropolitan residents are perhaps unsurprising. Presumably, these reflect institutional factors such as collective bargaining and unionization and these factors may be outside the control of urban policymakers.

Conclusions

Lessons for Policy from the Evidence

Are community college occupational degrees worth it? Our preliminary answer is that on average both certificates and associate's degrees are associated with an increase in earnings above the earnings of a high school graduate. The large majority of certificates are in occupational fields and, within associate's degrees, occupational awards are at least equivalent to academic awards; and our analysis of SIPP (along with other research) suggests that on average the returns to occupational degrees are higher than those for academic degrees. On the other hand, these two categories are heterogeneous: occupational degrees combine nursing and cosmetology; and academic degrees combine studies in the humanities or arts, which have low returns, and technical fields that have much higher returns. This diversity may explain the generally mixed conclusions of comparisons between academic and occupational associate's degrees.

Making a sharp distinction between academic and occupational (or career) areas is also misleading: it treats a longitudinal process as a cross section. In most cases, academic and career instruction are not substitutes but complements—the former prepares students for subsequent levels of education while the latter occurs immediately prior to entering the workforce. This pattern is consistent with a finding that, for those who stop at an associate's degree, an occupational award probably makes more sense than an academic credential. Calls for more academic education in preparation for a particular occupation are more or less synonymous with calls for more education—adding more general education to necessary occupational instruction.

The lower the level of the degree, the more difficult it is to combine academic and occupational instruction: programs simply have less time in which to educate students. This tension is particularly common in programs that attract adult students. These students usually have very specific goals and less time for general educational exploration. In these cases, determining the necessary academic and vocational skills is particularly important. To the extent that high school provides a stronger academic foundation, it will be easier to arrive at an optimal balance for short-term occupational programs.

Educators are working toward designing so-called career pathway programs and ladders that allow students to alternate between work and school. This model recognizes the circumstances of students who cannot attend school full time well into adulthood. The problem, though, is that an education that shifts gradually from academic to occupational instruction is inconsistent with an education that consists of several discrete pieces, each leading to a particular job or occupation. This may be why career pathway models or programs for stackable credentials have been difficult to implement, and why so few students who earn certificates move on to higher degrees. The associate's (A.D.N.) and bachelor's (B.S.N.) nursing degrees are an apparent example of a sequence of degrees that allow individuals to move back and forth between work and education. But this is deceptive. The A.D.N. programs solve the problem of general education by requiring substantial general education prerequisites for admissions—college level courses that a B.S.N. student would often take in the first two years.

Coordinating program levels to facilitate this type of educational process would require a differentiation between academic prerequisites for specific occupational courses and academic courses or experiences that provide more general skills and competencies. It would also require the different institutions or departments to work together to jointly redesign their programs with this type of mobility in mind.

For the most part, the measurement of the returns to degrees is based on measuring the earnings premium for individuals who have completed those degrees. But we have seen that for those who start degree programs the probability of completing the degree differs by program and degree level. The expected earnings benefit for a student who starts a program should take into account the probability of completing that program relative to the probability of completing an alternative program. This may be particularly important for community college students with very weak academic skills, who often get lost in remedial classes and never emerge into college-level instruction. If the overall completion rate for certificates does reflect the probability of completion for an individual in a particular program, then certificate programs look more attractive. This is especially true for men who, according to our estimations using the SIPP, do not experience a large increase in earnings going from a certificate to an associate's degree. One problem with a strategy of guiding these students into certificate programs is that few students move on from these programs. A redesign of certificate and associate's degree programs to facilitate transfer, as we suggested above, might address this criticism.

Final Thoughts on the Great Recession

A program that perfectly balances occupational and academic instruction to produce the most effective professional will not lead to an earnings premium if no demand exists for those skills in the labor market. In prior decades, demand has been strong. But the Great Recession from December 2007 to June 2009 has caused the most serious labor market disruption in more than half a century, and some changes appear to be structural rather than cyclical.

Overall, the Great Recession washed through the labor market in the same way most recessions do: raising unemployment levels among the lowest skilled and least experienced workers. Of course, it has washed through very powerfully and in concentrated ways on these groups. In terms of impacts, it has affected the same groups as have past downturns. That said, the Great Recession is distinctive in some ways.

First, the housing crisis has substantially impaired labor market flexibility as workers cannot move to find new jobs. Whereas in the past workers might have moved to find a job that matches their skills, because they cannot sell their homes they may now have a greater need to change their skills to match jobs in their local labor market. This restriction clearly reduces labor market flexibility, putting a premium on general skills that might facilitate retraining. At the same time, it reduces the value of specific occupational credentials if employment in those occupations is unavailable locally.

Second, the Great Recession has accelerated the change in the nature of the employment contract. Long-term attachment to a firm has become less common as the employment relationship has become more precarious, uncertain, intermittent, and variable (Kalleberg 2009). This change also puts a premium on flexibility: workers must be prepared to change careers. However, in this case specific occupational credentials may be advantageous, assuming that relevant jobs are available, because these credentials will signal to employers what skills workers have.

Third, the rise in unemployment has been concentrated among permanent job losers and the long-term unemployed. The Great Recession has also closed off labor market participation to many marginally attached workers, those people who are already only intermittently working or looking for work. In principle, job retraining might help these workers find employment, but the structural changes appear to be profound, and these workers may find themselves at the end of a job queue for a declining number of jobs. It is asking a great deal of a retraining program to strengthen these workers' skills adequately. It is unlikely that education programs—unless they are extensive—can address much of the damage to this population caused by the Great Recession.

Structural changes in the economy, labor market, work organization, and technology over the last decades have created a need for both more specialization and more adaptability. Under these circumstances, it has become more difficult to plan and implement an optimal combination of academic and occupational instruction. The Great Recession has compounded the problem while severely reducing the resources available to solve these problems. Simply adding more of both kinds of education for everyone is not an option. A successful strategy will combine a better understanding of the appropriate balance between academic and occupational skills, new methods of relating and combining instruction in the two areas, and inter-institutional cooperation that can lead to a more effective instructional division of labor.

Appendix: Additional Tables

Table 6.9. Individual Earnings

	Log Earnings (Previous Month)			
	Metro	Non-Metro	Female	Male
Relative to dropout				
High school graduate (incl. GED)	0.28	0.271	0.38	0.224
	[0.009]	[0.017]	[0.013]	[0.011]
Some college	0.39	0.33	0.455	0.348
	[0.010]	[0.019]	[0.014]	[0.012]
Vocational certificate	0.371	0.375	0.435	0.348
	[0.011]	[0.020]	[0.015]	[0.013]
Associate's degree	0.576	0.486	0.667	0.498
	[0.011]	[0.020]	[0.015]	[0.013]
Bachelor's degree or higher	1.003	0.858	1.086	0.93
	[0.010]	[0.018]	[0.013]	[0.011]
Observations	141,987	39,555	86,768	94,774
R-squared	0.27	0.21	0.21	0.27

Source: SIPP, 2008, wave 1.

Note: Persons aged eighteen to sixty-five only. Specifications also include experience; experience squared; marital status (married/single); ethnicity/race (White/Hispanic); and immigrant status. Models (1)–(2) include gender. SIPP sample weights applied. Robust standard errors in brackets. All coefficients statistically significant. $p < 0.01$.

Table 6.10. Individual Earnings Interacted with Certificate

	Log Monthly Earnings			
	Metro	*Non-Metro*	*Female*	*Male*
Relative to dropout HS graduate	0.266	0.244	0.36	0.21
	[0.009]	[0.016]	[0.013]	[0.010]
HS graduate + certificate	0.347	0.283	0.405	0.301
	[0.013]	[0.021]	[0.016]	[0.015]
Some college	0.377	0.304	0.436	0.334
	[0.010]	[0.019]	[0.014]	[0.012]
Some college + certificate	0.408	0.446	0.448	0.426
	[0.013]	[0.027]	[0.017]	[0.017]
Associate's degree	0.586	0.464	0.674	0.493
	[0.012]	[0.021]	[0.016]	[0.014]
Associate's degree + certificate	0.515	0.448	0.586	0.465
	[0.015]	[0.030]	[0.020]	[0.017]
Bachelor's degree	1.003	0.851	1.082	0.927
	[0.009]	[0.018]	[0.013]	[0.011]
Bachelor's degree + certificate	0.857	0.623	0.902	0.793
	[0.017]	[0.039]	[0.022]	[0.022]
Observations	141,987	39,555	86,768	94,774
R-squared	0.27	0.21	0.21	0.27

Source: SIPP 2008, wave 1.

Note: Persons aged eighteen to sixty-five only. Specifications also include experience; experience squared; marital status (married/single); ethnicity/race (White/Hispanic); and immigrant status. Models (1)–(2) include gender. SIPP sample weights applied. Robust standard errors in brackets. All coefficients statistically significant.
$p < 0.01$.

CHAPTER 7

The Conundrum of Profit-Making Institutions in Higher Education

William G. Tierney

Recently, Greg Davis, a columnist for the American Federation of Teachers (AFT), critiqued the $35 million community college "Completion by Design" initiative, a project created by the Bill and Melinda Gates Foundation and endorsed by President Obama's administration. Davis asserted that the initiative ultimately would harm the poor. He argued that an undertaking aimed at completion in organizations where almost a quarter of the students were dropouts would cripple community college budgets and exclude those very students that community colleges were designed to serve. The logic was that those students who are most at risk of not completing a degree are the students community colleges should serve, and by emphasizing a "completion" agenda, community colleges would be less desirous of having such students on their campuses. Such a point is particularly germane with regard to urban community college students, insofar as the majority of these students are first-generation, low-income people of color. The implication of the article was that any initiative aimed at college completion, without an inherent understanding of the risks associated with such students, was at best flawed, and at worst anti-democratic (Davis 2011).

The article, published in spring 2011, came at the same time that critics of for-profit colleges and universities (FPCUs) pointed out abysmal graduation rates, above-average defaults on student loans, and below-average placement in jobs to which the students aspired (Burd 2009, 2010). Although the socioeconomic profile of FPCU students is largely equivalent to that of community college students, the interpretation by FPCU critics was quite different from that in the AFT article. The vast majority of students at both types of institutions are urban students and people of color. But to the critics of FPCUs, high dropout rates at FPCUs were evidence of deceitful practices on the part of those organizations.

In these examples, two different organizational types face similar problems and serve a similar clientele, but the explanation of the problems is entirely different. One organizational type—the community college—should acknowledge that dropouts go with the territory of their constituencies; the takeaway is that community colleges are doing the best they can. The other organizational type—for-profit colleges and universities—should stop their deceitful practices and, in doing so, decrease their dropout problem.

Community colleges have their share of critics, just as for-profits have their defenders (although the latter are largely consultants paid by the for-profit industry). What has struck me, however, are the parallel universes I travel in when discussing and analyzing for-profit higher education. The problems are often the same at community colleges and for-profit institutions—cost, completion rates, employability, and financial aid—but the tenor of the discussion is distinctly different and the conclusions reached are equally distinct. These discussions come at a particularly vexing time for those working in the postsecondary sector. On the one hand, people argue that the United States needs to increase access to higher education and increase funding for public colleges and universities; on the other hand, many lament the rise of for-profit colleges and universities and seek to curtail their growth, if not entirely eliminate the sector. Meanwhile, public fiscal support is declining both in overall numbers and on a per full-time equivalent (FTE) basis and, as a result, participation in the public postsecondary sector is not increasing nationwide; and in some states it is actually decreasing. By contrast, the for-profit industry is the fastest growing sector in higher education in the United States.

The divergence in how these conversations have evolved stems from two distinct, but related, issues. First, there are those who are philosophically opposed to education as a profit-making enterprise. For almost a generation a large body of work has criticized the increasingly corporate mentality in higher education and bemoaned the use of words such as "consumers" when speaking of students (Slaughter and Rhoades 2004). From this perspective, education is a public good and profit is an anathema. In contrast, some writers maintain that actually the difference between non- and for-profit institutions is not as significant as many assume (Horn 2011). Others suggest that what makes an educational organization more productive has little to do with public/private or nonprofit/for-profit status and more to do with good management (Cota, Jayaram, and Laboissière 2011). Although there is a good deal to say about the idea of higher education as a public good, and its differences from private for-profit higher education, I have said it elsewhere (Tierney, Hentschke, and Ragusa 2011) and will focus my comments on the second issue: what we know about FPCUs with regard to their academic and economic performance.

Conceivably, if for-profits were able to increase access to higher education for low-income, first-generation individuals and enable them to graduate and attain good jobs at a rate higher than their public and private nonprofit counterparts, then the criticism of them might be muted, but not eliminated (as skepticism of their for-profit status would likely persist). However, largely because of their growth over the last decade, cursory analyses of their performance have raised several concerns, which shall be my focus here. Because so little is known about FPCUs, I first consider how they function, which is at odds with traditional colleges and universities in terms of basic issues such as governance, curriculum, and admissions. I then consider what we think we know but, I suggest, we do not. For example, there has been a great deal of discussion about FPCU admissions practices, but the research about these practices is relatively thin; my point here is to suggest that before offering general conclusions about a sector we first need to have a more convincing understanding of how the sector functions. I then conclude with a discussion of what we need to know about academe's fastest growing sector—both in the nation and in urban areas. I preface all of these points by arguing that an analysis of the for-profit sector is important not only in order to understand that particular sector, but also because the access, participation, and attainment goals that have been set for the country cannot be reached without the constructive participation of the for-profit industry.

Setting the Postsecondary Stage for 2020–25

Higher education in the United States has long sought to nourish the intellect and advance an individual's civic engagement. Its purpose, however, has largely given way to a concern for the economic well-being of the individual and society. Although one might debate the philosophical merits of reducing a postsecondary degree or credential to monetary advantage rather than civic advancement, the fact is that education has always been a way to improve one's social and economic well-being. Such has been particularly the case in large urban areas, where institutions have tried to help lift individuals out of poverty. For over a century, for every Harvard University that has sought to train the mind, there has been a training school for barbers, beauticians, and any number of other trades. The manner in which we analyze the economic return (for example, a salary) to an investment (such as federal and state funding and individual loans) largely excludes any consideration of education as a non-monetary undertaking.

The rationale for a postsecondary degree as an economic boost to individuals and society, although debatable as the sole purpose of higher education, is compelling, and is largely the sine qua non for for-profit higher education. FPCUs market themselves in a manner that emphasizes the economic gains a consumer will realize when he or she earns a degree. General education, distribution requirements, and degrees in the humanities and social sciences are largely absent in for-profit education. Courses are focused, degrees are within reach, and success suggests not simply the attainment of a degree, but a job. The criticism of FPCUs centers not on their inability to stimulate learning for learning's sake, but on the claim that they do not provide individuals with the necessary educational tools to improve their economic well-being and instead saddle them with debt.

Most critics of for-profit higher education and students of higher education and the economy assume that getting a degree or certificate pays off for both the student and the taxpaying citizen. We know, for example, that the salaries of college graduates, defined as those holding a bachelor's degree, are almost 50 percent more than those of individuals who have some college, but no degree; a college degree holder earns almost two-thirds more than an individual who only has a high school degree (Klor de Alva and Schneider 2011). As described in the introduction to this volume, during the recent economic downturn, all educational groups suffered rises in unemployment, but those with bachelor's degrees encountered less unemployment than those who only had a high school degree.

Although graduates from selective institutions earn more annually and over a lifetime than those who attend less selective institutions, individuals who attend the least selective sorts of institutions—two-year community colleges, trade schools, and for-profit institutions—also benefit from significant returns. And despite a tightening in the economy, the time and money invested in obtaining a college degree still provides positive returns to the consumer regardless of where he or she goes—an elite national private university, a local community college, or a for-profit college or university (Hentschke and Tierney forthcoming).

Additionally, attendance at postsecondary institutions is good for the taxpayer, the state government, and the federal government. Postsecondary graduates earn higher salaries and pay more in taxes. The estimated return to the taxpayer from someone earning a bachelor's degree ranges between $15,000 and $20,000 (Klor de Alva and Schneider 2011). Attendance at every kind of postsecondary institution appears to generate benefits in terms of additional tax dollars. We also know that those who are college-educated contribute to growing industries and create additional jobs. The Lumina Foundation (n.d.) believes that the United States has to increase attainment of two- and four-year college degrees and credentials from 39 percent to 60 percent—educating nearly 800,000 more college graduates per year over current rates—by 2025 to remain globally competitive. In California, for example, by 2020 the state will likely have a shortage of approximately 1 million college-educated workers (Johnson 2009). If the state does not fill those jobs, the jobs will presumably be moved out of state or to another country (Tierney and Hentschke 2011).

Curiously, not everyone agrees that a postsecondary degree is profitable: critics come from both ends of the ideological spectrum. Marxists offer an intellectual critique of work and the economy. A Marxian analysis suggests that further education is largely a part of credentialing; the requirement for more credentials represents little more than capitalism's ability to frame societal needs in a manner that enables the powerful to remain powerful. In this light, the poor in the early twentieth century were encouraged to get a high school degree and, as a result, going to college became more important. Now that going to college is encouraged, the rich and powerful will attain a better degree and so on. For-profit organizations bolster this argument because they promise individuals greater wealth while the class structure remains in place (Brown, Lauder, and Ashton 2010).

At the other end of the ideological spectrum, conservative economists, such as Richard Vedder, and conservative higher education analysts, such as Jane Shaw and George Leef, argue that higher education does not need to be expanded. They point out, for example, that one-third of all Domino's pizza delivery drivers in Washington, D.C. have a college degree (Shaw 2010), implying that those drivers do not need a degree; they suggest that the deluge of articles and studies claiming that America needs more people participating in higher education is largely a ploy by postsecondary cheerleaders to garner more public monies (Leef 2006). For-profit education is often the hero in this analysis insofar as the analysis assumes that market-based organizations are more effective than organizations on the public dole.

Both analyses, however, stand in contradistinction to several research studies that project job shortages if the country does not better educate its people. Insofar as employment occurs on a state level, I use California as a case in point. California is a useful example because of its size (its economic recovery is essential to the country's economic recovery) and because it has long been thought of as an example to other states and countries with regard to how higher education should function. Figure 7.1 shows that, in California as in other states, with higher education levels there is greater participation in the workforce (see Figure 7.1).

The Public Policy Institute of California confirms what I pointed out above: college graduates in the state of California earn almost twice as much per hour as high school graduates (Johnson 2011). Further, not only do college graduates earn more, but the need for a better-educated workforce will

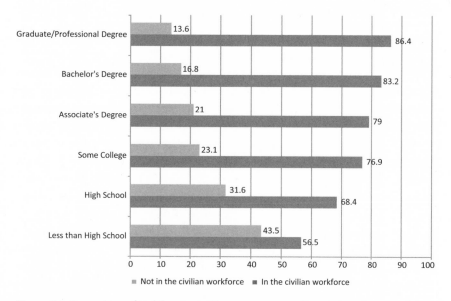

Figure 7.1. Percentage of California civilians ages twenty-five to sixty-four participating in the workforce by level of education, 2000. *Source*: Jones and Kelly 2007.

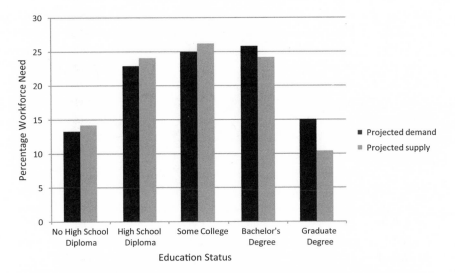

Figure 7.2. California workforce projections for various education levels in 2025.
Source: Johnson 2009.

continue to grow. If states such as California do not address this need immediately there will not be enough working adults with some form of postsecondary education to meet the projected demand for workers with more than a high school degree (see Figure 7.2). Such news is not new. Indeed, multiple analyses project shortfalls for California and other states (see Table 7.1), as well as metropolitan areas like Philadelphia (as described in the Introduction to this volume).

Similarly, The Georgetown University Center on Education and the Workforce projects that by 2018 in the country in general, and in California in particular, over 60 percent of workers will need to have a postsecondary education in order to meet workforce demands (Carnevale, Smith, and Strohl 2010). Projections in Iowa, Colorado, and the District of Columbia show comparable percentages (62, 67, and 71 percent respectively) of jobs that will require a postsecondary education in 2018. The use of the word "postsecondary" is purposeful. I am not suggesting, based on these various reports, that all students need a two- or four-year degree. Rather, approximately one-half of the postsecondary attendees may earn a certificate in a profession—programs in which for-profits excel.

Table 7.1. Studies Projecting Shortfalls in Educated Workers in California

Source	Out-year	Basis for the Goal	Degree Mix	Age Group	Target Goal	Gap in California above Current Production Levels
Public Policy Institute of California	2025	Labor force and CA rank relative to other US states	BA and above only	25–64	41%	1.00 million
Georgetown Center for Workforce and Economy	2018	Labor force	Some postsecondary, all credentials and degrees	25–64	61%	1.33 million
Lumina Foundation "Big Goal"	2025	International leadership	Some postsecondary, all credentials and degrees	25–34	60%	3.40 million
Obama Administration	2020	International leadership	Some postsecondary, all credentials and degrees	25–34	CA's share of a national goal to get to 60%, adjusted to reflect state variations in attainment	1.13 million
California Workforce Advisory Board	2016	CA workforce/ skill needs	All skill areas including on-the-job, certificates, and degrees	24–64	Not expressed as a target, good source for occupation-specific areas	CA's needs for replacement workers will be as great as new job growth

Source: Adapted from Carnevale, Smith, and Strohl 2010; Johnson and Sengupta 2009; Tierney and Hentschke 2011.

In California, because of the expected retirement of well-educated workers, the assumption is that the state will have 3.3 million jobs requiring postsecondary credentials (Tierney and Hentschke 2011). Current projections show that the state will have only 2.2 million workers qualified for these jobs. Other states with large populations—Texas, New York, and Florida—will have 2.2, 1.8, and 1.6 million jobs respectively that will require a post-secondary credential (Carnevale, Smith, and Strohl 2010). Deficits in participation in higher education and attainment of a college degree are most stark among the state's racial and ethnic minorities. Mirroring national trends, African American and Latino students also remain the most at risk of dropping out of high school, not transitioning to college, and not completing a postsecondary degree. Although such points pertain to the entire state, the most significant concerns lie in the large metropolitan areas, as these areas typically have considerable populations of low-income people of color.

To exacerbate the problem, as President Obama has pointed out, the United States now lags behind other industrialized countries with regard to college participation and attainment (see Table 7.2). For 2006, the most recent year for which there are complete data, the United States was number three in the percentage of the population aged twenty-five to sixty-four that had earned a degree, but number fourteen in the percentage of graduates among traditionally aged students (Organisation for Economic Co-operation and Development [OECD] 2009, 2010b). We are falling behind in the global race for human capital development, placing the country at risk for economic decline. The President, as well as the leaders of the Lumina and the Gates Foundations, has called for the United States to regain its competitiveness over the next decade and once again to be the number one nation in the world in terms of college access and attainment (see Table 7.2). For the United States to reach such an ambitious goal, the states must strengthen their efforts in multiple ways—not only by increasing the number of students who attend a postsecondary institution, but also by increasing the numbers of students who are college-ready at the end of secondary school, who remain in college once they enroll, and who transfer from two-year to four-year institutions. Obviously, to reach such goals, the country's larger states need to redouble their efforts, particularly in urban areas within states where college participation is particularly low among the urban poor.

Accordingly, I am suggesting that in order for the nation and individual states to reach international competitiveness goals and meet projected labor

Table 7.2. U.S. Tertiary Education Participation Indicators and Ranking Among
OECD Nations, 2006

Indicator	Percentage	Ranking
Attainment rate, ages 25–64	39.5%	3rd
First-time entrants as a percentage of the population in the corresponding age group	64.0%	10th
Graduation rate as a percentage of graduates to population at typical age of graduation	35.5%	14th

Source: Adapted from OECD 2009, 2010a, 2010b.

market demands, three related, but distinct, education goals—all of which
are ambitious and all of which necessarily involve for-profit higher education providers—must be achieved. The country's leaders have argued for an
increase in the *participation rates* in higher education; this measure refers to
the overall percentage of a population that enrolls in higher education. A
second goal has been to increase college *completion rates*. Completion refers
to students who actually begin a program of study and complete a degree.
The third goal pertains to increasing America's *attainment rate*. Attainment
is the percentage of the working population who earn a degree.

I also wish to suggest that increasing participation, completion, and attainment rates, *in combination*, is vital to the nation's economic well-being.
However, a significant increase in *any*, let alone all, of these rates is ambitious, especially at a time when the nation is in considerable fiscal difficulty
and trying to trim federal and state budgets. Indeed, if state governments
were flush with revenue and there were no need to increase participation,
completion, and attainment rates in institutions of higher education (IHEs),
then a discussion about the role of for-profit higher education might seem
peripheral. But this is not the case.

Between 2008 and 2018, demand for college-educated workers in almost
half of the states will grow two to three times faster than demand for high
school graduates or dropouts. In six states (Indiana, Massachusetts, Maine,
Michigan, Minnesota, and Ohio), jobs that require a college education will
grow five to seven times faster (Kelly and Strawn 2011). California, for example, is estimated to need an additional 100,000 students each year for the next
decade in order to meet the estimated worker shortfall (Johnson 2011). In the
past, such a problem might have been solved by building additional public
campuses and increasing the number of students attending public-sector

institutions. Instead, however, the University of California and California State University systems intend to admit fewer students overall in the next year, and fewer in-state students. The community college sector is considering admitting 400,000 fewer students (Tierney and Hentschke 2011). In Minnesota, the state reduced the higher education budget by $47 million; as a result, 9,400 students lost their financial aid grants and the remaining students saw a 19 percent drop in the size of their grants (Minnesota Budget Project 2010). The reality is that at a time when states need to increase college participation, the public sectors are cutting back. Without the active involvement of the private non- and for-profit sectors there is simply no way to reach the education levels that will enable the United States to be a leader in college access, completion, and attainment.

What We Know: The Rise of For-Profit Higher Education

For-profit colleges and universities are growing more rapidly in numbers of both institutions and students than traditional colleges and universities (Hentschke, Lechuga, and Tierney 2010). In 1967, approximately 6.9 million students attended U.S. degree-granting institutions. Less than 22,000 of these students, or less than one-third of 1 percent, were enrolled in for-profit degree granting institutions at the time (Tierney and Hentschke 2007). Forty years later, by 2007, the number of students enrolled across all institutions had nearly tripled to over 18.2 million. At the same time, the number of students attending for-profit degree granting institutions had increased to nearly 1.2 million or approximately 6.5 percent of the total (Tierney and Hentschke 2007). Moreover, these data reflect degree programs only, and do not include institutions that offer only certificates. If non-degree, certificate-granting for-profit institutions and their students are included in these statistics, the market share of for-profit institutions has been estimated to be approximately 9 percent at the turn of the century (Ruch 2001) and higher still today (Weisbrod, Ballou, and Asch 2008). FPCUs also have higher proportions of first-generation, low-income, women, and students of color than public or private four-year institutions, and in some instances parallel or exceed the racial and ethnic minority percentages in community colleges (Jez 2011).

The student body is increasingly composed of "the new majority"—what used to be labeled non-traditional students. FPCUs largely tailor their services to the working adult who desires to attend school on a part-time basis. These institutions also cater to low-income individuals, which is a matter of concern to many and a matter of pride to others, a discrepancy that I discuss below. In short, a significant percentage of FPCU students come from populations considered to be "at-risk," and if the country is to increase college going, more students from these very populations will need to attend college.

The share of degrees produced in the United States by FPCUs has grown from less than 1 percent forty years ago to nearly 10 percent today (Tierney and Hentschke 2007). Another way to view relative sector growth is to compare compound annual growth rates (CAGR): for-profit enrollment has increased from 214,000 in 1990 to approximately 880,000 in 2004 (CAGR of 11 percent), a rate considerably higher than that of all public and private nonprofit colleges and universities (with CAGR in the low single digits). Estimates suggest that growth in the for-profit higher education sector will continue, even though estimates of the educational value of the sector compared to traditional IHEs are unclear. In California, for example, for-profits have more FTEs (20 percent of the FTE population) than the University of California (9 percent), California State University (17 percent), and private nonprofit sector (7 percent) (Jez 2011). Only the California community college system has more FTEs than the for-profit sector.

Unlike traditional colleges and universities, FPCUs offer certificates as well as associate's and bachelor's degrees. In California, for example, FPCUs award about half of all short- and long-term certificates (Jez 2011). Master's and doctoral degrees are largely confined to business, law, and education; degrees that require an expensive infrastructure, such as medicine or dentistry, are rarely offered. Undergraduate degrees tend to focus on courses in the professions rather than the humanities. Some institutions capture niche markets such as graphic design, culinary arts, and fashion design. The areas of study with the largest enrollments are consumer services, apparel and textiles, manufacturing and construction, and health sciences. The courses are more compressed and more likely to take place year-round, as compared to the leisurely academic pace with summer interlude found at traditional institutions. Evening, summer, and online courses are common; even very early (6:00 A.M.) or very late (11:00 P.M.) classes are offered in order to meet the needs of a specific niche of students.

Students find out about FPCUs differently from how they would find out about traditional colleges and universities (TCUs). FPCU students generally do not visit campuses as they might if they were applying to public or private nonprofit institutions. Instead, students often learn about FPCUs by way of the institutions' advertising: a "cold call" from an admissions center; print, radio, and television advertisement in a market that the traditional institutions largely avoid; or through social media. The message is almost always on job attainment or greater wealth for the prospective "consumer." Whereas a TCU may tout a beautiful campus or the camaraderie of the student body, FPCUs market themselves as efficient purveyors of a product that will improve the economic well-being of the prospective applicant.

At FPCUs, tenure is largely absent and shared governance is missing. Indeed, the faculty at FPCUs are more likely to be part-time professionals who teach as an add-on to their regular employment. Because the professional staff is part-time and untenured, course offerings reflect the needs of the market. The administration of a for-profit institution hires and fires individuals based on their professional competence and the need for their services. In terms of faculty responsibilities, research and service are nonexistent (Hentschke, Lechuga, and Tierney 2010).

Teaching is much more constrained at a FPCU than at a TCU. At FPCUs, faculty do not deviate from the syllabus or established educational outcomes. Generally, curriculum designers—not the individuals teaching the classes—at FPCUs develop, update, and amend standard curricula that all faculty teach. As a result, the institution—not the professorate—owns the curricula (Hentschke, Lechuga, and Tierney 2010).

Although many, but certainly not all, classes are online, the learning outcomes are more homogenous across sections of a particular course than the heterogeneous teaching and learning at a TCU (Hentschke, Lechuga, and Tierney 2010). Further, students at FPCUs have very little leeway in the courses that they take. The curriculum is prescribed and those who work in FPCUs see general education and distribution courses as "extraneous." The focus of FPCUs is less to foster the ubiquitous "love of learning" one hears about in a TCU, and instead to develop the skills required to perform a particular job.

The Holy Grail for FPCUs is accreditation, for without some form of accreditation, an institution is unable to tap into federal monies and, increasingly, state funds. Whereas a decade ago less than ten states provided in-state funding for students attending FPCUs, in 2011 the number was over twenty. In California, for example, 50 percent of for-profit students receive Pell grants (Jez 2011). The Higher Education Act requires institutions to be accredited and to meet certain requirements if their students are to receive federal student financial aid. As a result, FPCUs seek accreditation in a number of ways—some by the old-fashioned way of applying for accreditation, and others by other means, for example, by acquiring a troubled, accredited nonprofit institution and then dramatically changing and expanding the institution via online offerings and organizational remodeling.

The governance structures of FPCUs differ from those of the public and private nonprofit sectors (Bennett, Luchessi, and Vedder 2010). FPCUs are either privately held or publicly traded companies. Their boards comprise investors who intend to make a profit, and who are well compensated for their time. While public institutions may be required to include particular constituencies or political appointees on their boards, for-profits have no such requirements. Unlike their private nonprofit counterparts, FPCU board members are not philanthropists expected to contribute to the institution. Board discussions at FPCUs revolve more around the business and fiscal processes of the institution than the academic and student side of the organization.

The regulatory framework also differs. Regulation for public and private nonprofit institutions has been relatively light on the federal level and more focused at the state level. For-profits, however, have received considerable attention from the U.S. Department of Education and the U.S. Congress. State boards largely have not included for-profits in their postsecondary oversight. Instead, FPCUs are regulated by individual state agencies, such as the department of education in Minnesota or the department of consumer affairs in California. Until recently, FPCUs were represented by federal and state organizations whose roles were primarily lobbying. Although TCUs also have lobbyists, most postsecondary associations (such as the American Association of University Professors and the Association of American Colleges and Universities) have historically focused on faculty, curriculum, and governance rather than lobbying.

Finally, FPCUs have come in for a good deal of criticism. Congress has begun to investigate their practices, as have the U.S. Department of Education and several state agencies. Newspapers, blogs, television shows, and websites have offered a cascade of information about shoddy business practices, which seem to haunt the sector. Some critics, such as Senator Harkin of Iowa, believe in the adage "where there is smoke there is fire," and suggest that examples of unethical practices are emblematic of the entire industry. Others, however, suggest that it is impossible to indict an entire industry based on singular examples. What remains unknown is whether FPCUs retain and graduate students in a manner akin to, or better than, TCUs.

FPCUs are growing rapidly and serving predominantly non-traditional student markets in urban and metropolitan areas. FPCUs increasingly offer degree programs identical in title to those offered in TCUs (Tierney and Hentschke 2007), but, by their very nature as for-profit businesses, employ different business models. Research has not yet indicated whether these "new" entrants into higher education provide educational services that are more effective or productive than TCUs, but the evidence is clear that they are capable of growing their capacity to accommodate significant growth in enrollments, unlike TCUs. Thus, the infusion of FPCUs into the higher education market has the potential to increase participation in higher education.

What We Think We Know about FPCUs

Although the problems are linked, the majority of the criticisms of for-profit higher education—other than the underlying philosophical concerns—fall into three categories. *Admissions criteria* refer to how students are recruited and admitted. *Debt burden* pertains to the amount of debt a student accrues when he or she attends a for-profit and what happens to that debt. *Gainful employment* speaks to the ability of the for-profit graduate to get a job for which he or she has been trained. In what follows, I outline the concerns that have been raised based on available data.

Admissions Criteria

One concern is that for-profits act more like companies than educational organizations in how they attract students/customers to their institutions. During the 1992 reauthorization of the Higher Education Act, Congress prohibited colleges from providing any commission, bonus, or other incentive payment based directly or indirectly on success in securing enrollments to admissions officers. At the time, several reports pointed out that for-profit trade schools were simply enrolling unqualified low-income working adults in order to garner profit for the institution. Recruiters were paid based on "head count"—how many potential applications they could turn into applicants and then convert into students. The legislation that banished incentive bonuses was intended to deter flim-flam artists from attracting students in order to tap into the financial aid a student could get, rather than focusing on a student's educational interests. The second Bush administration created "safe harbors" (in other words, loopholes) that essentially gutted the regulations. Incentives and commissions were back on the table as viable options for for-profits and they made full use of them. Further, by the time the safe harbors were created the technology had improved to the point that, as with non-education businesses, stand-alone companies and venture capitalists could create call centers that produced data banks of names for "lead generation."

Undoubtedly some institutions have engaged in false advertising and shoddy business practices. Two for-profits in California, for example, each had to pay over $5 million to settle a lawsuit about false advertising and unlawful business practices (Tierney and Hentschke 2007): they allegedly presented inaccurate salary and employment information to prospective students. A Colorado institution paid $7 million to the federal government because the institution encouraged students to cheat on entrance exams and, again, gave false information about jobs to prospective applicants (Tierney and Hentschke 2007). The Apollo Group, parent company of the University of Phoenix, paid the federal government $67 million to resolve a lawsuit pertaining to the violation of the rules governing safe harbors, although they did not acknowledge wrongdoing (Tierney and Hentschke 2007). This payment followed a $9.8 million payout to the government in 2004 from a report pointing out other illegal admissions practices: the concern then was that the Apollo Group's high-pressure sales culture did not care about student or program quality but rather about getting "asses in classes."

In large part because the federal government has been unable to put forth new comprehensive guidelines monitoring admissions criteria, close to twenty states are now considering legislation that would regulate admissions practices at FPCUs. The vast majority of information about admissions practices, however, is not based in research or any systematic study of the for-profit sector. Instead, there has been a steady drumbeat of allegations and findings on individual institutions. Some institutions, such as the University of Phoenix, have not acknowledged wrongdoing but instead have paid fines to make lawsuits go away.

For-profits' admissions practices are portrayed as dramatically different from those in the nonprofit sectors. Hawkins and Modar (2011), for example, write: "Prospective students at non-profit institutions may interact with a wide range of institutional representatives—current or former students, faculty, admission officers, financial aid officers, alumni—all of whom (or none of whom) may have played a part in influencing a student's decision about whether to enroll. If an admission officer performs badly—misrepresenting the institution, not being able to answer questions accurately, ignoring calls, not showing up to work—he or she may be subject to negative evaluations or eventually released. But for those who perform well, evaluations and salary increases are determined within the context of the individual's contribution to the operation of the whole."

The authors claim that recruiters do not receive money solely based on "headcount" (Hawkins and Modar 2011). While constructing a class is critical in any college or university, TCUs do not reward or sanction an admissions office strictly on the number of students recruited. The authors know that admissions officers do more than simply recruit individuals because nonprofit institutions are members of the National Association of College Admission Counseling (NACAC), which issues standards for admissions. Admissions counselors also have training specific to higher education, and recruiting is but one part of the job. A wealth of research on admissions and counseling large bears out the authors' claims.

At the same time, while criticizing the idea of recruiting, the nonprofit industry is complicit in the trend toward hiring recruiters in foreign countries to attract students either for foreign campuses or for online courses. Words such as "consumer," "lead generation," and "admissions conversion" have become common on many public and private nonprofit campuses. On the one hand, we have a great deal of research about the nonprofit sector. On the other hand, we have a flood of legitimate critiques of individual organizations without any systematic research to see how widespread the wrongdoing is among FPCUs. We also see an accretion over time of business practices being employed by nonprofit institutions, which once ridiculed such terms and practices.

Debt Burden

The amount of debt that a student incurs, and sometimes defaults on, can be troubling. Students enroll for a college degree with the assumption that they will be better off than they were before they started the program. When a student drops out or does not complete a degree and has incurred thousands of dollars of debt, then the student is generally worse off, not better. When students default on loans, taxpaying citizens—via the federal and state government—are left repaying the loan to an institution that may have had a part in the student's problems. At a time when the country needs more people enrolled in higher education in order to secure better paying jobs that in turn contribute to the economy, a student saddled with debt, and no degree, places the country in a worse situation than if the student had not even tried to get a college education.

Some obvious points are worth noting insofar as they scaffold the concern about students' monetary burdens from attending for-profit institutions. Students who complete a degree are more likely to pay back their loans than non-completers regardless of institutional type. Students who attend for-profit institutions pay considerably more in tuition than students who attend comparable private nonprofit or public institutions; they also are likely to amass greater debt. Compared with TCUs, FPCUs have substantially more students who are part-time, low-income, working-class adults who are the first in their families to attend college. FPCUs also have a higher percentage of students of color than comparable private nonprofit and public institutions. Students with the characteristics of those who attend for-profit institutions are less likely to complete college, more likely to have trouble paying back their loans, and more likely to default on their loans, regardless of institutional type (Klor de Alva and Schneider 2011). That is, a low-income, first-generation, working-class student, for example, is more likely to default on a student loan than someone who is upper-class and comes from a family with college degrees. These points together create substantial concern about the loans students accumulate when they attend a FPCU. When we also factor in the questionable admissions practices of for-profit institutions the concern only deepens.

Again, the problem arises not only with questionable institutional practices but also with the constituency being served. Several individuals have come forward with lawsuits claiming they were duped into agreeing to loans that had high interest and/or penalty fees that the recruiter did not explain. One of the purported strengths of a for-profit also can be seen as a weakness. When students apply to a TCU they generally file for loans and grants on their own. Although the process may be cumbersome, presumably the individual learns about the costs that he or she will incur while filing for the loan (although this assumption is untested). At a FPCU, however, the recruiter is likely to file for loans on the student's behalf. Obviously, when someone asks, "Is financial aid available?" the simple answer of "yes" requires an explanation. But allegedly, students are often left in the dark with regard to the interest rates they will pay, the added costs of transaction and origination fees, the consequences of defaulting on a loan, and even that the loan must be repaid.

Analyses by the College Board (Baum and Steele 2010) suggest that close to 60 percent of bachelor's degree recipients at for-profit colleges graduate with more than $30,000 in loans. Such an amount is astronomical when compared with the debt accrued by students who attend a community college, but it is even one-and-a-half times more than that of students at higher-cost private colleges, and three times more than that of students at public four-year universities. Even 20 percent of students who only earn an associate's degree from a FPCU graduate with a debt load of at least $30,000.

Critics claim that the for-profit industry is engaged in predatory practices. FPCUs respond that loans and defaults are in large part due to the constituency they serve. The problem with the currently existing research is that it is either microscopic (institution-specific) or macroscopic, such that all institutions are folded into one. The cost of a degree, even when loans are considered, is also made to seem much simpler than it actually is. That is, most analyses focus on the costs to the individual and overlook the cost to the taxpayer/citizen. A student who pays $1,000 in tuition is said to incur a cost of $1,000 regardless of the institution he or she attends. However, public higher education receives state subsidies; for-profit institutions pay taxes. To calculate the true cost of a degree to the taxpayer/citizen we need to consider not only the base cost for tuition and a loan; we must also take into account the subsidies that account for a considerable portion of public higher education. In short, we actually know little about the cost of a degree and the burden incurred by taxpayers when students take out loans to go to a for-profit rather than a public not-for-profit institution.

A recent report brings into question whether most students who attend for-profit institutions actually end up in debt. Using national data sets, the report concludes, "during the first decade after graduation, no matter what the level of selectivity, the net financial returns are, on average, higher for public and for-profit institution bachelor's graduates than for graduates of not-for-profit colleges and universities" (Klor de Alva and Schneider 2011: 8). The authors go so far as to suggest that graduation and employability rates are higher among for-profit than community college graduates. In short, the report brings into question the relatively simple studies that, to date, offer gross characterizations of different sectors. However, because the report was produced by the University of Phoenix's research arm, many question the findings.

Gainful Employment

The burden of debt in some respects is irrelevant if the job attained upon completion of college pays enough for an individual to repay the loans. A U.S. Government Accountability Office (GAO) (2010) report highlighted how recruiters at some for-profit institutions promised potential students well-paying jobs upon the completion of a degree, but the salaries they suggested a person would make were fabricated. In one instance, students recruited to a school to study culinary arts were led to believe that they would earn a degree and land a job as a chef earning a good salary, but instead they ended up working in a fast food restaurant as dishwashers. Although these individuals may indeed have gotten jobs in the culinary industry, the degree proved worthless and the salary did not enable them to prosper, let alone pay off the loans they accumulated while in school.

Gainful employment is a deceptively simple idea. If an institution trains students for specific jobs, then those jobs should be available upon completion of the degree and students should be prepared to assume those jobs. The problem, of course, is how one measures gainful employment. In the Higher Education Act of 1965, Congress allowed colleges that offered vocational programs to define for themselves what the term meant. Hence, someone who studies to be a chef and ends up as a dishwasher is gainfully employed. The *New York Times* reported that one institution, for example, recruited students into a criminal justice program where enrollees thought they would end up working in the FBI making $50,000 per year, but instead they ended up as security guards making an hourly wage (Lewin 2010).

As a result, the U.S. Department of Education has tried to implement rules regarding the definition of gainful employment. The term will be defined using some combination of the ratio of debt that graduates assume relative to their earnings and the rate at which they are able to repay their loans. The implications of this definition can be considerable. If for-profit institutions do not meet the criteria they may lose federal student aid. Up to one-third of all for-profit institutions could be affected. Public and private two- and four-year nonprofit institutions are absolved from any concerns about whether their graduates get good jobs, although vocational institutions would be included.

What We Need to Know about FPCUs

Decisions about whether the for-profit industry will continue to play a growing role in educating postsecondary students to meet the international competitiveness and workforce demands, or whether it will be significantly restricted or regulated, must depend in large part on investigation into the performance of FPCUs. My assumption is that the credibility and perceived quality of these institutions is enhanced when their internal operations and business practices are visible and verifiable. Thus, the focus of research into the for-profit higher education sector needs to identify practices that promote institutional transparency to students, regulatory bodies, employers, policymakers, and other educators, and inform the issues I have discussed.

The overarching research agenda should be to design assessment and accountability systems to enhance institutional effectiveness in the pursuit of societal goals. Based on my knowledge of the industry, my own previous research, and extensive discussions with researchers and policy analysts knowledgeable about the industry, I have identified six issues that need critical exploration. In what follows, for each of these issues I sketch what the problem is, what the program of investigation might be, and how one might go about studying the topic based on the problems I have earlier outlined. These research topics are germane for FPCUs throughout the country, but also might be best focused on urban areas insofar as most students at FPCUs are in urban areas. The research areas derive from the problems that are currently being debated and are critical to understanding whether the for-profit sector should be allowed to grow or be curtailed.

I. FPCUs' Capability for Conducting Innovative and Ethical Admissions Practices

PROBLEM

As noted, all students, but first-generation students in particular, most of whom live and work in urban areas, may not receive accurate information about the costs and benefits of applying to college and the likelihood of degree completion. Misinformation results in students' accumulating unmanageable debt and being unable to meet loan obligations, at an enormous cost to themselves and the citizenry more generally. At the same time, to reach new populations, standard admissions practices may require redirection.

PROGRAM

Undertake a study of admissions practices to determine allowable and ethical practices for recruiting potentially "at-risk" students. Engage in comprehensive analyses of the recruitment and admissions practices in FPCUs to determine which practices are most effective in supporting precollege students' college readiness, including their knowledge and understanding of student financial aid.

II. FPCUs' Ability to Enhance Students' Access, Progression, and Program Completion

PROBLEM

An increasing number of students face challenges in accessing and successfully completing degree and certificate programs. Effective tracking and evaluative mechanisms are needed to compare student access, progression, and completion rates in FPCUs with those in other postsecondary sectors.

PROGRAM

A fruitful analysis would identify pedagogical and/or institutional practices that are most effective in achieving the highest levels of college access and degree completion, particularly for populations of students who are educationally underprepared. Although a wealth of methodologies might be employed, one possible avenue is to engage in comprehensive analyses of the pedagogical and/or institutional practices in FPCUs compared with those in TCUs. The purpose would be to determine which practices are most effective in supporting students' college access, degree progress, and completion.

III. FPCUs' Capacity to Address Student Remediation

PROBLEM

More than two-thirds of all students in higher education in general, and in urban areas in particular, require some form of academic remediation. Students in need of remediation are often the most at risk in terms of dropping out and defaulting on loans, but they are overwhelmingly the new populations who must be tapped to increase postsecondary participation. Effective means and measures are required to track dropout and retention rates and identify students in need of remediation at FPCUs, as well as to understand why completion rates rise and fall in different sectors.

PROGRAM

Remediation is a problem across all sectors, but is particularly important among students that FPCUs attract—urban, first-generation, low-income students of color. An undertaking to describe and empirically analyze pre-college preparation programs run by FPCUs to bring students to grade level, and to investigate those in-class and out-of-class pedagogical practices that facilitate remediation in reading, writing, and mathematics, would be of considerable benefit. For this project, one might analyze the pedagogical and/or instructional practices in high schools, TCUs, and FPCUs to determine which practices are most effective in supporting precollege students' college readiness and enabling access to postsecondary study without remediation.

IV. FPCUs' Success at Lowering Student Default Rates and Ensuring Student Loan Repayment

PROBLEM

A high percentage of students attending for-profit institutions appear either to default on their loans or to assume a debt burden beyond their financial means post graduation.

PROGRAM

The need exists to describe and then analyze loan default and repayment rates for students in the for-profit sector relative to the rates of comparable students in the public sector. One approach may be to engage in comprehensive analyses of the advisement and financial aid delivery practices to determine which practices are most effective in supporting college students financially, including helping them understand the options that exist with regard to loan repayment.

V. FPCUs' Success at (a) Enabling Gainful Employment for Their Students and (b) Meeting Employer Needs

PROBLEM

A key criterion for success in a FPCU is how well graduates are able to gain jobs and, once they have jobs, how well they are prepared for them.

PROGRAM

Research should investigate short- and long-term job placement rates and employer satisfaction. Such a study might begin with career counseling and employment support practices in FPCUs compared to TCUs, to determine which practices most effectively support college students' employment readiness and job success, using student-, graduate-, and employer-focused inquiry with a large-scale, mixed methodological multivariate design.

VI. FPCUs' Ability to Develop Adequate Governance Standards and the State's Ability to Implement Useful Regulatory Procedures and Processes

PROBLEM

Different states have different policies governing FPCUs that ostensibly offer better or worse regulatory control. FPCUs have different ways of functioning in accordance with these policies that either enhance or decrease institutional transparency. Clearly, if FPCUs are to grow and play a role in increasing the economic competitiveness of the country, then a regulatory framework needs to be put in place that better enables states to monitor institutional effectiveness.

PROGRAM

A researcher might undertake cross-agency, cross-state analyses of different states and FPCUs in an effort to recommend best practices nationally. One approach may be to conduct case studies across various states in an effort to identify and understand best practices.

Conclusion

Like other chapters in this volume, this chapter assumes that, for the United States to remain competitive, postsecondary access, completion, and attainment rates must increase over the next decade. Such an assumption is of particular importance in inner cities, where a significant increase in college attendance among low-income, first-generation youth, and working adults will need to occur if the country is to reach the goal of a better-educated citizenry.

If this assumption is correct, then the nation faces a dilemma. The public higher education sector and the private nonprofit sector do not have the capability to increase their capacity much beyond current levels. Or rather, the public sector to a significant degree, and the private nonprofit sector to a lesser extent, *could* increase capacity, but unless these sectors radically reform the way they function, and/or states dramatically increase funding, such increases will not happen. Indeed, in some states (such as California) the absolute number of students educated by the public sector is likely to decrease.

As a result, the country needs a vibrant and viable for-profit postsecondary sector. As I noted at the outset, I appreciate the philosophical concerns about profit-making companies involved in providing what has historically been seen as a public good. I also understand the legitimate concerns of those who have read about, or unearthed, unscrupulous practices by for-profit colleges or universities. Certainly one role of the state is to ensure that the citizen is protected. To the extent that consumers have been defrauded or promised something they did not receive, the state must have a capable regulatory body that protects the consumer and ensures regulatory compliance by FPCUs. However, whether a particular institution ("company") should be fined or put out of business is one issue; whether the entire industry is corrupt is another. At present we lack valid, reliable data about the fastest growing postsecondary sector in the country: FPCUs. Although we certainly have instances of malfeasance by a number of for-profit colleges and universities, we do not have the data to prove corruption at a systemic level.

Researchers are fond of saying at the end of a manuscript, "More research is needed." Such a statement frequently comes across as a justification for an individual to do more research rather than advancing a particularly pressing theoretical or public policy need. In the case of for-profit higher education, however, more research truly is needed. Given the current fiscal and philosophical stance by the citizenry of the United States, it is in the best interests of the nation to ensure that we make decisions about the reform and regulation of the for-profit sector that enable the growth of FPCUs and thus bolster the economic health of the country.

III.

Implications for Institutional
Practice and Public Policy

CHAPTER 8

Strengthening the Education and Workforce Connection: What Types of Research Are Required to Determine How Well Career Pathways Programs Prepare Students for College and Careers?

Lashawn Richburg-Hayes, Michael Armijo, and Lisa Merrill

Globalization, technological change, and the rise of a knowledge-based economy have spurred the need to improve educational attainment and ensure a rising standard of living for American citizens (Council on Competitiveness 2008). As a result of these changes, employees require greater knowledge and skills to compete for new labor market opportunities across the nation and the world (Carnevale, Smith, and Strohl 2010). As described in the introduction to this volume, business and education leaders nationwide have called for the United States to better prepare young people to be career and college ready after finishing high school, and for all working-age adults to attain some postsecondary training (Business Roundtable 2009; The Bill and Melinda Gates Foundation 2009; Lumina Foundation 2009; National Governors Association 2011; Council on Competitiveness 2008). These leaders recognize that national and global demographic trends signal trouble ahead if we maintain the current course.

Unfortunately, our current system for providing education and workforce training is not likely to rise to the challenge of adequately preparing the current and future workforce for jobs that guarantee a living wage for several reasons. First, as Anthony Carnevale and his colleagues describe in this volume, a high school degree alone will not provide the skills needed for today's workforce. In fact, there is a fairly well-established decline since the 1970s in the real average earnings of full-time workers with a high school diploma or less (Mishel, Bernstein, and Allegretto 2007), making a high school diploma a poor choice of terminal degree. Second, while unprecedented numbers of students are attempting college, rates of college completion have not changed for as long as statistics have been kept (Eaton 1997). While there are many explanations for the lack of change in college graduation rates, underpreparation for college-level work and the financial burdens of college represent two large barriers. Finally, our educational system does not provide adequate access for workers to pursue additional education or training. The most affordable institutions are often not flexible enough to be convenient for workers who are students, and financial aid programs often penalize the working poor student by assuming that the bulk of the previous year's income will be available to cover education costs (Long 2007).

The above shortcomings of our educational system may disproportionately affect low-income populations and those living in urban areas. While population growth in cities and low-income suburbs has increased rapidly, growth in employment opportunities has lagged behind (Holzer and Stoll 2007). Since low-income people, minorities, and immigrants in urban areas are less than half as likely to enroll in college as people living in suburban areas (Richardson and Bender 1986), the result is a combination of lower educational attainment and fewer employment prospects. If the urban areas are segregated by income or race as well, education and employment outcomes may be further depressed (Cutler and Glaeser 1997).

Career pathways appear to be a promising strategy to address these issues. Defined as a series of connected education and training programs combined with support services, career pathways are geared to securing employment within a specific industry or occupational sector, with each step along the pathway designed to prepare the participant for the next level of employment and education (Jenkins 2006). The career pathways model differs from traditional occupational skills training in that participants can enter and exit the career pathway at various points, yet the pathway eventually leads to employment in specific occupations in a specific sector. The idea behind career pathways is not new; it emerged over two decades ago out of the separate efforts of career and technical education programs in high schools, workforce development programs, and professional and technical education programs at community colleges as an institutional response to a changing student body (Agrawal et al. 2007). Since that time there have been numerous initiatives advancing career pathways models, such as the College and Career Transitions Initiative (Warford 2006), the National Career Pathways Network (Institute for a Competitive Workforce and National Career Pathways Network 2009), and the Ford Foundation's Bridges to Opportunity Initiative (Bridges to Opportunity 2008). While there are a number of guides, toolkits, and best practice resources for developing and operating career pathways, little rigorous evidence is available about the effectiveness of the components that comprise career pathways or the effectiveness of the career pathways framework itself. However, rigorous research that has been conducted on initiatives that share aspects of the career pathways model may be helpful in thinking about possible effects from a fully functional model. Such career pathways-like initiatives are spread across distinct research areas that may not overlap (for example, K–12 education and workforce development). This chapter gathers the causal evidence on some of these initiatives to answer two questions: What are some effective K–12 and postsecondary institutional practices and strategies for preparing students for career success that mimic aspects of career pathways? What evaluation design components would best contribute to our knowledge of the effectiveness of career pathways programs in preparing students for college and career success?

The chapter consists of two parts: The first segment reviews selected strategies that share aspects of career pathways and that seem promising in preparing students for academic and career success. The second segment discusses evaluation design components that may best contribute to our knowledge of why such programs are effective or not effective.

Summary of Evidence on Academic and Career Pathways

Academic and career pathways are a set of coherent, articulated, academic and career courses that may begin in high school or college and continue on to industry-recognized licenses or certificates, an associate's degree, or a baccalaureate degree and beyond (Hughes and Karp 2006; Hull 2005; Offenstein, Moore, and Shulock 2009). Career pathways are often developed, implemented, and maintained through partnerships between high schools, colleges, or universities, on the one hand, and employers, on the other (Hull 2005). Ideal pathways should prepare all students, including adult learners, for rewarding careers, and allow for multiple points of entry and exit so that workers can gain skills as needed throughout the course of their career (Hull 2005; Agrawal et al. 2007). By streamlining and structuring the transitions within and between high school and postsecondary education, career pathways present a promising strategy to improve education productivity, academic outcomes, and social mobility for students of all skill levels and backgrounds.

Given that there are very few large-scale career pathways models for which rigorous evidence is available, we focus on both true career pathways and programs that share some components of career pathways (yet would not be considered career pathways according to the above definition). To find empirical studies, we contacted experts in the field and asked them to recommend articles. We supplemented these sources by searching multiple meta-search databases such as JSTOR, ERIC, and Google Scholar using evaluation design key words, such as *randomized control trials*, *experimental*, and *quasi-experimental*, as well as content terms. Then we used references from these articles to direct us to new empirical evaluation studies.[1] Table 8.1 provides a summary of the studies discussed.

As mentioned by authors of other chapters in this volume, one promising type of school-to-work strategy to improve educational and work outcomes for students in high school is career academies. Career academies are small learning communities that offer students career-related and academic curricula, as well as work experience with local employers (Kemple and Scott-Clayton 2004). Sharing many aspects of career pathways, career academies typically do not yield industry-recognized certification—a critical element of career pathways.

Developed more than thirty-five years ago, career academies now operate at scale in over 2,500 high schools (Quint 2006). Students in career academies are guided by career themes, such as health care, finance, technology, communications, and public service, that strive to integrate vocational training with the rigorous academic curricula required for graduation (Maxwell and Rubin 2001). Four-year follow-up results from a random assignment evaluation of career academies operating in nine sites across six states suggest that career academies have positive effects on reducing dropout rates, improving attendance, and increasing academic course taking and student engagement, as well as increasing the likelihood of on-time graduation, but have no effect on completion (Kemple and Snipes 2000).[2] Eight-year follow-up results found an 11 percent (or $2,088) increase in

Table 8.1. Summary of Research

Study	Target Group	Intervention	Sample	Summary of Results
Kemple 2008; Kemple and Snipes 2000	9th or 10th graders in high schools operating career academies	Career academies: Small learning communities (30–60 per grade) operating in high schools that combine academic and technical curricula around a career theme in grades 9 or 10 through grade 12.	1,764 youth with 959 (54 percent) in the program group and 805 (46 percent) in the control group. The program operated in 9 career academies at high schools in six states.	Program produced sustained earnings gains that averaged 11 percent (or $2,088) more per year for Academy group members than for individuals in the non-Academy group—a $16,704 (in 2006 dollars) boost in total earnings 11 to 12 years after random assignment. No impacts on educational attainment for the full sample. For students at high risk of school failure, substantial positive impacts including decreased dropout rates, increased attendance rates, and increased number of academic and vocational credits earned.
Maxwell and Rubin 2001	Students who ever participated in a career academy	Career academies	Administrative records on 10,000 students (14 participated in career academies) from inner-city schools in one large urban school district.	Study used a non-random comparison group. Reported that program had significant effects on high school GPA, average number of hours worked, and the percentage of students attending a four-year college.

(continued)

Table 8.1. (continued)

Study	Target Group	Intervention	Sample	Summary of Results
Millenky, Bloom, and Dillon 2010	Young people between the ages of 16 and 18 who have dropped out of (or been expelled from) school, are unemployed, drug-free, and not heavily involved with the justice system	National Guard Youth ChalleNGe: 17-month intervention with 3 phases: a 2-week boot camp; a 20-week residential program on a military base, and a 1-year non-residential mentorship	3,074 with 2,320 (75.5 percent) in the program group and 754 (24.5 percent) in the control group. Program operated in 10 sites.	Program group members were more likely to earn a GED or high school degree (61 percent versus 36 percent) and earn college credit (25 percent versus 9 percent) than control group members.
Cave et al. 1993	17 to 21 years, economically disadvantaged school dropouts with poor reading skills	JOBSTART: Provided education and vocational training, support services, and job placement assistance.	2,312 youth randomly assigned to two groups. Program operated in 13 sites.	Program group members were more likely to earn HS diploma or GED (42 percent versus 28.6 percent) and more likely to participate in some education or vocational training (94 percent vs. 56.1 percent). No impacts on earnings for the full sample
Burghardt et al. 2001; Schochet, McConnell, and Burghardt 2003	16 to 24 years, U.S. citizenship, family income, selective service registration, and residency in the state of the program. Applicants must show ability to benefit and have no serious medical or behavioral problems	Job Corps: provides basic education, vocational skills training, health care and education, counseling, and residential support. Program has open-entry, open-exit philosophy, with most participants staying an average of 8 months	15,400 youth randomly assigned to a program group (9,400 or 61 percent of the total) or a control group (6000 or 39 percent). Program operated in over 100 different centers.	Program increased education and training among program group members (93 percent versus 72 percent) 48 months after random assignment. Program group members were more likely to earn a GED (42 percent versus 27 percent). The program increased earnings (although the amount of the increase varies by data source).

Study	Target Group	Intervention	Sample	Summary of Results
Jenkins, Zeidenberg, and Kienzl 2009; Zeidenberg, Cho, and Jenkins 2010	Adult students requiring basic skills	Integrated Basic Education and Skills Training (I-BEST) program: Integrating instruction in basic skills with instruction in college-level professional-technical skills, I-BEST seeks to enable basic skills students seeking occupational training to enroll directly in college-level coursework.	77,147 students across three cohorts (2005 through 2007), with 1,390 (or 1.8 percent) participating in the I-BEST program.	Quasi-experimental analyses suggests enrollment in I-BEST had positive impacts on earning any college credit and certificate/degree attainment. No effects on persistence or labor market outcomes
Maguire et al. 2009	Adult students with sixth- to tenth-grade reading and/or math levels, depending on individual site requirements	Sectoral Employment Impact study: Sector-focused training, career match processes, integrated skills training, strong link to local employers, and individual support services	1,286 people, with half (or 643) randomly assigned to the program group.	Program group members earned 18.3 percent (or about $4,500) more and were more likely to work than control group members over the 24-month study period. Program group members were more likely to work in jobs that offered benefits (between 50 and 60 percent versus 40 and 50 percent) and higher wages.

(continued)

Table 8.1. (continued)

Study	Target Group	Intervention	Sample	Summary of Results
Jastrzab et al. 1996; Jastrzab et al. 1997; What Works Clearinghouse 2010	Low-income, at-risk young adults, aged 16 to 26	Youth Corps: students engage in full-time community service activities along with academic, classroom experiences and vocational and life skills. The average program length is 4 to 5 months.	626 students, 383 randomly assigned to the treatment group.	Results are from follow-up survey information collected fifteen months after the begining of the program. According to the follow-up, the program group worked more hours (2,000 compared to 1,500), with slightly higher average wages ($6.66 vs. $6.26) and lower arrest rates (17 percent in the program versus 12 percent in the control group). A cost-benefit analysis shows a $597 benefit to society ($9,540 program cost, $7,824 social benefit, and $2,313 individual wage increase).

earnings over the eight-year period among career academy participants, with the earnings gains being concentrated among young men (Kemple 2008).

Maxwell and Rubin (2001) examined the potential of career academies to improve school and work outcomes for students from inner-city schools in one large urban school district. Using information on 10,000 students over three cohorts and employing a comparison group design, they found that career academies had a statistically significant positive effect on high school GPA, average number of hours worked, and the percentage of students attending a four-year college, controlling for all other variables. Students not in career academies had dropout rates two times higher than those who were enrolled in academies. According to this study, career academies had no significant effect on wages, working in a field related to the high school program, average hourly wage, or high school graduation.[3]

One of the best-known career pathways programs at the postsecondary level is the Washington State Board for Community and Technical Colleges' Integrated Basic Education and Skills Training (I-BEST) program. I-BEST is geared to increase the rate at which adult basic skills students advance and complete college-level occupational programs (Zeidenberg, Cho, and Jenkins 2010). I-BEST programs combine a basic skills instructor and an occupational instructor to team teach basic skills using materials that are of interest to the student and aligned with a given workforce program (Jenkins, Zeidenberg, and Kienzl 2009). A series of these integrated courses in a specific professional/technical field provides students with a structured pathway to industry-valued certificates and employment in a specific field, as well as preparation for further college-level education leading to a degree (Wachen, Jenkins, and Van Noy 2010). Quantitative analyses of I-BEST programs (Zeidenberg, Cho, and Jenkins 2010; Jenkins, Zeidenberg, and Kienzl 2009) using propensity score matching and multivariate regression analysis (including difference-in-differences analyses) suggest that I-BEST is an effective model for improving student outcomes.

Another set of programmatic interventions that have similar components to career pathways concentrates on developing a path for those who are not enrolled in educational institutions and may have deviated from the traditional education and training trajectory. These alternative pathways target individuals who have limited career options because they dropped out of high school or they have not developed the knowledge and skills necessary for gainful employment. Nonprofit or government programs such as Youth Corps, Job Corps, the National Guard Youth ChalleNGe Program,

JOBSTART, and Youth Build share some components of career pathways, such as combining academics and career preparation to lay the groundwork for success in the labor market.[4]

Rigorous, randomized experiments demonstrate that the Youth Corps, Job Corps, and ChalleNGe programs provide meaningful employment gains for high school dropouts. Funded by federal youth development programs such as the National and Community Service Act of 1990, the Youth Corps Program includes 120 independently run programs in twenty-one states. All Youth Corps participants receive a stipend while they work toward a GED or high school diploma and conduct community service activities that range from tutoring children to repairing houses (Jastrzab et al. 1996). An evaluation using an experimental design found that program group members were more likely to have worked for pay, worked more hours, and were less likely to be arrested than control group members fifteen months after random assignment. The impacts for certain subgroups, such as African Americans, were particularly large. For example, 91 percent of African American male participants were employed after completing the program compared with 62 percent of African American males in the control group. The corresponding figures for African American females were similarly large, with 90 percent of African American female participants employed compared with 60 percent of African American females in the control group (Jastrzab et al. 1996).

Job Corps has been geared to increase the self-sufficiency of disadvantaged youth since its inception in 1964. Job Corps is targeted to youth between the ages of sixteen and twenty-four, and most participants are high school dropouts. Like other youth job training programs, Job Corps provides intensive education, training, and support services. Unlike other programs, the services are provided in a residential setting and participants can start and stop the program as they desire (there is no prescribed participation treatment period). While the services vary by program and participant, on average participants enroll in Job Corps for eight months and live on site, where they engage in individualized, computer-based academic instruction along with training in a specific work trade. Career counselors assist students in job placement and continue to support students for sixth months after placement. The National Job Corps Study randomly assigned over 15,400 youth to program and control groups and found that the program increased enrollment in education or training programs among Job Corps members (93 percent enrolled versus 72 percent enrolled) forty-eight months after random assignment. Program group members were more likely to earn a GED (42 percent versus 27 percent) and more likely to earn a vocational certificate. By the fourth year, the average weekly earnings for Job Corps participants was 12 percent (or $22 per week) higher than non-participants (Burghardt et al. 2001; Schochet, McConnell, and Burghardt 2003).

Like Youth Corps, the National Guard Youth ChalleNGe Program is a federal government program targeted to youth disconnected from education or the workforce. The program operates in over twenty-seven states and has served over 90,000 participants since its inception over two decades ago. Blending military and educational experiences, participants in ChalleNGe go through three phases over seventeen months. The first is a two-week long assessment and induction period that occurs on a military base. During the second phase, which lasts twenty weeks, the participants continue to live in barracks, like military recruits, while they enroll in academic and career and life skills courses. The last phase is a one-year non-residential mentorship program to transition participants into a more traditional pathway, through entry into either secondary educational institutions or careers. An experimental evaluation of ChalleNGe shows that program group members were more likely than control group members to earn a GED or high school degree (61 percent versus 36 percent) and to earn college credit (25 percent versus 9 percent). Program group members were also more likely to be in school, employed full-time, or in the military than control group members (72 percent versus 66 percent) (Millenky, Bloom, and Dillon 2010).

Unlike Youth Corps and ChalleNGe, JOBSTART was developed and evaluated by a nonprofit research organization. Modeled after the residential Jobs Corps program, JOBSTART provided education, vocational training, support services, and job placement assistance to seventeen- to twenty-one-year-old economically disadvantaged school dropouts with poor reading skills. JOBSTART substantially increased educational attainment, with 94 percent of program group members receiving some type of education or training compared with 56.1 percent of control group members in the four years following random assignment, but did not result in a change in earnings for the full sample (Cave et al. 1993).

While the above studies largely focus on youth, the Sectoral Employment Impact study focused largely on adults. Using a random assignment design, the study evaluated whether well-implemented, sector-focused training programs could affect the earnings of low-income disadvantaged workers and job seekers. The study evaluated outcomes generated by three separate organizations that had operated workforce programs for at least three years.

While each organization's sector focus and approach was different, they all had established career match processes, integrated skills training, and individual support services (such as assistance with childcare, transportation, and housing). The study found that program group members earned 18.3 percent (or about $4,500) more and were more likely to be employed than control group members over the twenty-four month study period (Maguire et al. 2009). In addition, program group members were more likely to work in jobs that offered benefits.

There are several new initiatives currently in the formative stages that more closely reflect the definition of career pathways provided earlier. These programs will greatly expand the availability of career pathways and broaden what is known about the effectiveness of such frameworks. For example, several states are currently examining pathways to connect pre-college coursework to career and technical coursework. Along these lines, the Southern Regional Education Board (2009) proposed that all students should be required to pass reading, writing, and mathematics exams; however, students specializing in career and technical education should be offered an option to pass state-approved, nationally recognized employer certification exams in place of additional academic exams. Similarly, the Ohio Board of Regents and the Ohio Department of Education are working to develop a system of stackable certificates to help low-skilled adults eventually complete at least one year of college with an advanced technical certificate (Community Research Partners 2008).

In terms of broadening our knowledge of program effectiveness, the Office of Planning, Research and Evaluation in the Administration for Children and Families of the U.S. Department of Health and Human Services launched the Innovative Strategies for Increasing Self-Sufficiency (ISIS) project in 2007. The goal of ISIS is to find and evaluate (using experimental designs) intervention strategies that further employment and economic self-sufficiency among low-income families across at least six sites around the nation (Fein 2009). It is envisioned that the project will test multiple types of career pathways (ranging from narrow to comprehensive programs) and pathways approaches for different target populations and occupations/sectors. In 2010, The Center for Economic Opportunity and the Mayor's Fund to Advance NYC launched WorkAdvance, a program geared to boost the earnings of unemployed and low-wage working adults by helping them prepare for and enter quality jobs in selected sectors with opportunities for career growth. Funded by the Corporation for National and Community

Service through a Social Innovation Fund grant, this sector-focused advancement initiative provides pre-employment services, occupational skills training, job development and placement, post-placement services, and financial assistance (Corporation for National and Community Service 2011). The project seeks to evaluate programs operated by several different providers through a random assignment research design.

Evaluation Design Ideas to Further Increase Knowledge

While it is too early to gauge the ability of these various efforts to improve academic and labor market outcomes, the number of initiatives and the quality of the planned research suggests that much more will be known about effectiveness over the next five years. The remainder of this chapter discusses additional evaluation tools geared to improve research on career pathways.

Before discussing the tools, it is important to note that the methodology for assessing whether a program works or not is critically important in evaluation, and the most sound methodology should be employed to permit interpretations that are either causal or as close to causal as possible. Causality is established when an intervention proceeds an event, is shown to be related to the event, and other explanations for the relationship are implausible (Shadish, Cook, and Campbell 2002: 105). Designs using random assignment (also known as randomized controlled trials or RCTs), in which eligibility for the intervention is determined essentially by a flip of a coin, are considered to be the gold standard of evaluation because the methodology ensures causal interpretations of whether something works by controlling "selection" into the intervention. That is, when executed properly, random assignment results in only one explanation for why a student is eligible to participate in an intervention: they were assigned by chance and the likelihood of that assignment is known. As such, RCTs produce reliable estimates of program impacts, or the value added by the intervention over the status quo. While random assignment is the best methodology available to permit causal interpretations, the method also has a few drawbacks: RCTs are often are context-specific, resulting in findings that may not easily generalize to other places (low external validity), they can be very expensive to mount, and they are not appropriate for all questions. For career pathways programs in particular, random assignment may result in a very long enrollment period as it will take several cycles to recruit the required number of students for the study given that programs typically serve thirty to sixty participants and random assignment studies often require 1,000 partici- pants for sufficient power to detect impacts (Bloom 1995).

As a result of the desire for better causal inference and to overcome the shortcomings of RCTs, there has been an increase in quasi-experimental methods such as regression discontinuity designs and matching estimators, particularly propensity score matching techniques. There are now several excellent reviews on which methods are the preferred approaches for certain questions and how to implement them (Reynolds and DesJardins 2009; Caliendo and Kopeinig 2008). However, these approaches also have draw- backs: most methods require a number of strong assumptions that are often not satisfied in practice; execution can be complex and difficult to explain; and, despite the complexity, the question of selection bias often remains.[5] Most discouragingly, several recent papers that use these methods fail to replicate experimental results (for example, see Bloom et al. 2002 in the wel- fare context; Peikes, Moreno, and Orzol 2008 for a study of employment promotion).

While random assignment designs address the question of causality, even these designs often provide little explanation of how and why interventions do (or do not) work. Using an analogy from Shadish, Cook, and Campbell (2002: 9), a RCT can tell you whether the flip of a light switch causes illumination, but it will not reveal that the mechanism underlying the relationship between the switch and illumination is the closing of an insulated circuit. That is, with- out additional components, a simple experimental design does not identify the mechanism(s) that relates the independent variable (or treatment) to the outcome of interest (say, earning a credential). As a result, RCTs can result in "black box" evaluations in which the mechanisms and conditions associated with the intervention remain unknown, which in turn prevents a clear under- standing of what is necessary to replicate findings.

To improve upon the pathways research reviewed earlier, we suggest that program design and evaluations be accompanied by at least three additional research questions:

1. Why would one expect the intervention to work? That is, are the in- tervention components reasonable given the research literature and can they be reasonably expected to achieve the program goals?
2. What mechanisms are believed to generate the outcomes?
3. Was the program implemented as designed?

These suggested research questions assume primary research and employment of the strongest methodology (such as random assignment and regression discontinuity) appropriate for the questions being answered.[6] The purpose of these additional components is to help researchers gain more knowledge of the components and mechanisms that generate findings. Each research question is discussed further below.

Why Would One Expect the Intervention to Work?

This research question highlights the need for program designers and evaluators to be explicit about the role that theory and previous research play in program creation, as well as the need for clarity about the goals that the program is expected to achieve. Three tools can be used to help answer this question: driver diagrams, logic models, and a protocol to measure planned treatment contrast.

DRIVER DIAGRAMS

Adapted from the field of improvement research, a driver diagram is a visual tool that helps document the current theory of how to improve a problem or system (Langley et al. 2009). The driver diagram typically consists of three components: the primary outcomes or goals that an intervention is hoped to affect, the key drivers from the literature that illuminate the barriers that prevent or block goal attainment, and the change concepts or components that are employed to address specific barriers.[7] When a driver diagram is used at the start of the design phase of an intervention, it may be useful to include two additional components: a column of predictions of the effects of the change concepts on the primary outcomes of interest, and a column of estimated costs for reasonable combinations of components.[8] The column of predictions may help in the decision-making around which components to include in the treatment and may further help in discussions of strength of the intervention and treatment contrast (discussed below). The inclusion of an anticipated cost column would encourage designers to think critically about cost effectiveness from the beginning, and such considerations may result in the removal of an expensive component in exchange for another (or others) that is more sustainable.

Figure 8.1 illustrates a driver diagram for a hypothetical career pathways program. Note that the key drivers and change concepts in the diagram are

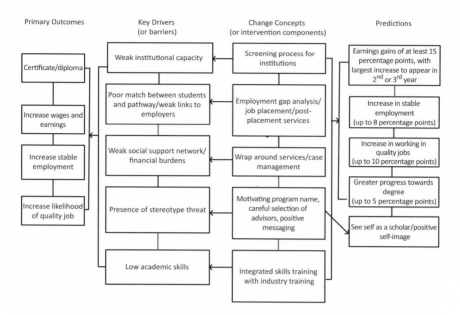

Figure 8.1. Driver diagram for a hypothetical career pathways intervention.

derived from research on programs with components similar to career pathways. While this diagram does not do so, the research studies could be listed in the above boxes as a way to summarize the literature, while the diagram itself visually shows the connections between the proposed components and various research studies that inform those components. Implemented early in the research timeline, the driver diagram will generate a summary review of the literature and spark reflection on the merits of proposed components *before* an intervention is launched, which may prevent the replication of weak ideas.

What Mechanisms Are Believed to Generate the Outcomes?

Logic models provide a visual representation of how resources, activities (the intervention components), and outputs (process measures that verify components were enacted) are expected to lead to outcomes, to describe the theory of change underlying a program. Using a logic model during the intervention development process helps illuminate assumptions and forces researchers to add needed components to the evaluation agenda in order to adequately test the underlying theory of change (Frechtling 2007). Adding the hypothesized mediators to a logic model—or the mechanisms theorized to translate outputs to outcomes—can further help researchers avoid "black box" evaluations. That is, illumination of these ideas can help further research into *how* and *why* interventions work (or don't work). For example, the theory of change underlying career pathways holds that integrating vocational training and basic skills for learners with skill deficits in incremental, sequential steps will result in progress through both career and academic coursework, attainment of industry certifications, and stable employment in a high-quality job (see Figure 8.2).

The logic model shows that four factors are expected to mediate the relationship between the intervention components and the outcomes: the strength of the employer linkage to the career pathways program, credit attempts,

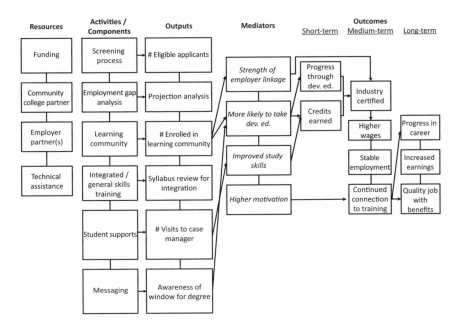

Figure 8.2. Logic model illustrating the theory of change underlying the hypothetical career pathways intervention.

improvement in study skills, and greater academic and/or career-related motivation.[9]

Once the theory of change is developed and the intervention components are finalized, the next step in improving research involves a thorough understanding of the intended strength of the intervention and the planned treatment contrast—two very important evaluation concepts. The strength of a treatment refers to the intensity with which the researcher intends that the treatment be delivered (Sechrest et al. 1979). This inherently involves the planned dosage of the intervention. A strength tool or protocol could be employed in the design phase of a project as an a priori designation of what the intervention's designers view as a high, moderate, or low level of intensity for each activity. For example, a strength tool would pre-specify the minimum number of case management visits, years of experience an institution has operating a pathways program, and other parameters that the designers believe will result in a high, moderate, or low intensity career pathways program *before* any program data are analyzed. This pre-specification encourages designers to think critically about the components and the level of effort that must be expended (or the amount of services that must be received) in order to elicit the predictions specified in the last column of the driver diagram (Figure 8.1). Use of a strength tool also helps to prevent revisionist history during the analysis phase of a project, since the tool is developed and implemented prior to the analysis of program data.

While pre-specification of intensity partially helps to strengthen the design of an intervention, thinking about this concept relative to the status quo, or comparison condition, is also important, so that resources are not wasted evaluating interventions too weak to generate impacts at conception (Cordray and Pion 2006). That is, the newly planned services must provide value above and beyond the services currently available to students. The connection between strength and treatment contrast is illustrated in Figure 8.3.[10] The figure shows that the planned intervention services should be significantly different from the services that already exist. This difference represents the planned contrast in treatment of the intervention and should be determined prior to the assignment to treatment.[11] The strength tool discussed above is a way to document ex ante the dosage levels necessary for the component to be deemed to be implemented at a high, moderate, or low level. For example, students in

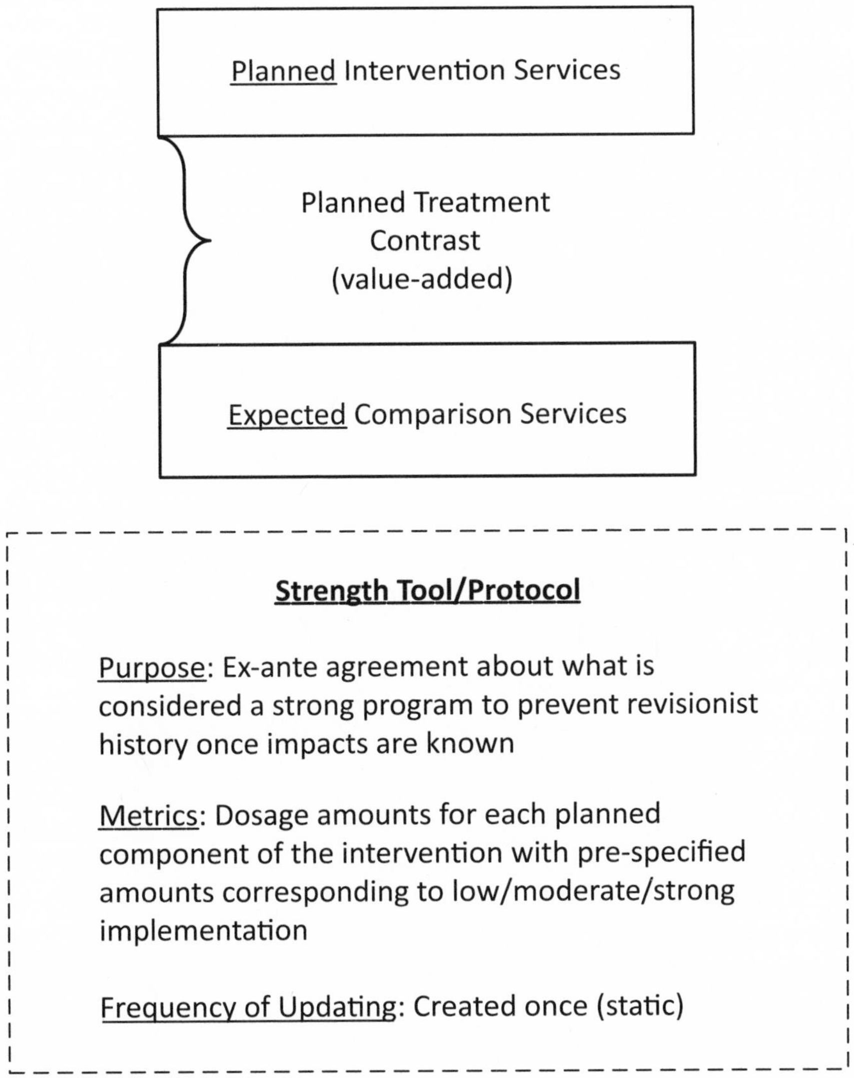

```
┌─────────────────────────────────────┐
│                                       │
│     Planned Intervention Services     │
│                                       │
└─────────────────────────────────────┘
          ⎫
          ⎬    Planned Treatment
          ⎬         Contrast
          ⎬       (value-added)
          ⎭
┌─────────────────────────────────────┐
│                                       │
│     Expected Comparison Services      │
│                                       │
└─────────────────────────────────────┘
```

Strength Tool/Protocol

Purpose: Ex-ante agreement about what is considered a strong program to prevent revisionist history once impacts are known

Metrics: Dosage amounts for each planned component of the intervention with pre-specified amounts corresponding to low/moderate/strong implementation

Frequency of Updating: Created once (static)

Figure 8.3. Planned treatment contrast. *Source:* Adapted from Bloom, Weiss, and Hill 2011 with contributions from the research team of the Performance-Based Scholarship Demonstration (Reshma Patel, Alissa Gardenhire, and Katherine Morriss).

a proposed career pathways program may be expected to meet with a case manager every month. If the intervention is slated to last six months, there should be six such visits. Based on the literature, consultation with experts in the field, and the knowledge that students in the expected comparison condition have two such visits, this amount of contact may be deemed "moderate." Similarly, two visits may be deemed "low" while eight or more visits may be deemed "high." These specifications are predetermined before the program is implemented and provide a way to explicitly account for the knowledge gained from prior research as well as knowledge of the expected comparison context.

Was the Program Implemented as Designed?

When conducting a program evaluation, it is worthwhile to remember that treatments are delivered in real world settings and are rarely standardized in practice; they often comprise multiple components that may not be implemented in their entirety, or at all; they are sometimes delivered by unmotivated staff; and their delivery can be influenced by context that is outside of the researcher's control (Sechrest et al. 1979). In other words, many things can happen in bringing an intervention from conceptualization into practice. Since an evaluation will only measure the effectiveness of what was actually implemented, it becomes quite clear that researchers need to pay as much (if not more) attention to the quality of implementation as is paid to the quality and analysis of quantitative data.

The second suggested research question addresses whether the program actually implemented is strong relative to the originally designed program and whether the program evaluated is a fair representation of the originally designed program (fidelity to design).

IMPLEMENTATION FIDELITY

Implementation fidelity refers to the integrity with which the delivered intervention adheres to the designed intervention, that is, the degree to which the program implemented in practice reflects the original design. Implementation fidelity is important because a poorly implemented program may fail to produce impacts, but the failure may not truly reflect whether the original design would have resulted in improved outcomes. As a result, researchers might prematurely abandon otherwise good ideas. Therefore, evaluators and designers should ensure that programs receive a "fair test," which means that programs are evaluated first in their strongest form (Sechrest et al. 1979). Fidelity can be assessed along at least three dimensions:

- Adherence to the program model: This aspect of fidelity measures whether the program is being delivered to participants as intended. Research questions that relate to this dimension include: *Was the program implemented with a high or low level of fidelity? Were program components provided as intended? Did provisions change over time?*
- Exposure to the intervention (or actual dosage): While the internal validity of a RCT is maintained even in the instance that program group members do not fully receive the treatment, such a situation does not ensure a fair test of the program.[12] This aspect of fidelity measures whether actual dosage approximates the designed level of dosage. Research questions that relate to this dimension include: *Do program group members participate in activities at the planned levels? Do these participation rates change over time? Does participation vary by subgroup?*
- Intervention differentiation: This aspect of fidelity ensures that participants that are intended to receive the treatment do so and those that are intended to be excluded do not actually participate. The principal concern here is to ensure that crossovers are kept to a minimum. Research questions that relate to this dimension include: *Do control group students receive intervention services? If so, at what rates? Does this change over time? Does participation vary by subgroup?*

Two tools may help address these seemingly innocuous, but very complex research questions about the above dimensions of fidelity: the offered strength tool/protocol and the realized strength tool/protocol.

OFFERED STRENGTH TOOL/PROTOCOL TO MEASURE ADHERENCE TO THE PROGRAM MODEL

As noted above, despite the best intentions, intervention components may not be offered as designed and/or the expected status quo services may change.[13] Furthermore, changes may not settle to a steady state in response to the treatment, but may continue to fluctuate over time, increasing or decreasing in response to a number of factors outside of an evaluator's control.

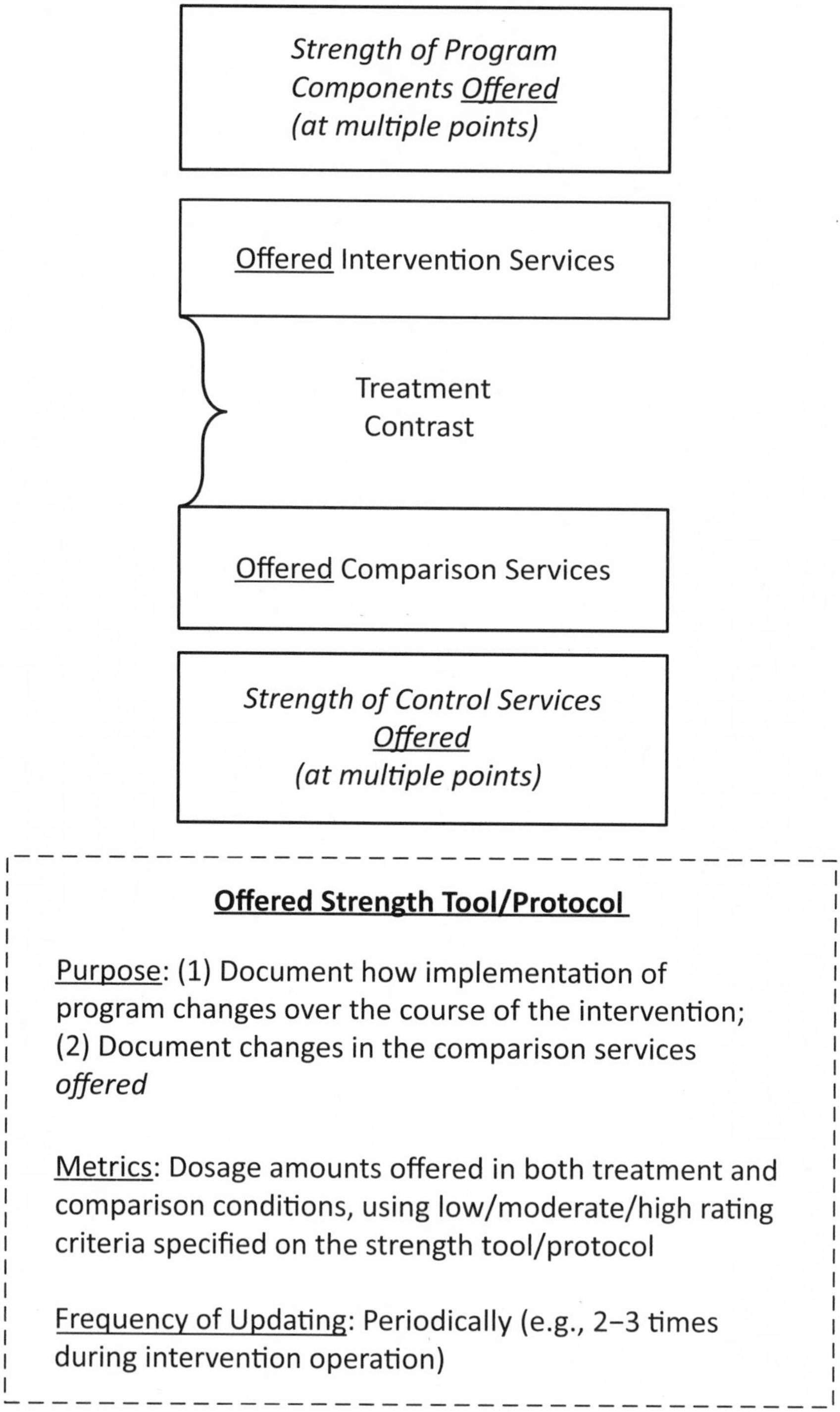

Strength of Program
Components *Offered*
(at multiple points)

Offered Intervention Services

Treatment
Contrast

Offered Comparison Services

Strength of Control Services
Offered
(at multiple points)

Offered Strength Tool/Protocol

Purpose: (1) Document how implementation of
program changes over the course of the intervention;
(2) Document changes in the comparison services
offered

Metrics: Dosage amounts offered in both treatment and
comparison conditions, using low/moderate/high rating
criteria specified on the strength tool/protocol

Frequency of Updating: Periodically (e.g., 2–3 times
during intervention operation)

Figure 8.4. Treatment contrast—comparison of services offered. Adapted from
Bloom, Weiss, and Hill 2011 with contributions from the research team of the
Performance-Based Scholarship Demonstration (Reshma Patel, Alissa Gardenhire,
and Katherine Morriss).

In this case, the treatment contrast (or the difference in the offered treatment services and the offered status quo services) may be either larger or smaller than the planned treatment contrast discussed above and the differences may vary over time. Figure 8.4 illustrates the difference in offered services.

In order to capture the change in treatment contrast over time, a variation of the strength tool—the offered strength tool/protocol—may be employed to document the components of the intervention that were offered over time and to simultaneously document the comparison services that were offered over the same period. For example, if comparison case management services are provided through an annual federal grant, non-renewal of the grant may result in the average number of visits declining from two within a six month period to one visit. If it is also the case that the intervention service hires more case managers during this period (perhaps the same managers let go from the comparison service), then the number of case manager visits among students participating in the intervention may increase. If these dynamic changes occurred, the treatment contrast would be larger than the planned treatment contrast.

REALIZED STRENGTH TOOL/PROTOCOL TO MEASURE EXPOSURE TO THE INTERVENTION (OR ACTUAL DOSAGE) AND INTERVENTION DIFFERENTIATION

Despite being eligible to participate in an intervention, students may not show up or may show up initially and later drop out. Similarly, ineligible students (those assigned to the comparison condition) may receive intervention services. That is, actual treatment group and comparison group participation may differ from what was initially planned. Figure 8.5 illustrates this idea. The figure shows that the difference in actual receipt between the intervention condition and the comparison condition (the realized treatment contrast) may be larger or smaller than either the planned treatment contrast shown in Figure 8.3 or the treatment contrast shown in Figure 8.4.[14]

Conclusion

As described in other chapters in this volume, a sense of urgency for increasing the numbers of skilled workers has fueled research on the educational pipeline from K–12 to postsecondary and resultant labor market outcomes. This chapter presented evidence from several rigorous evaluations

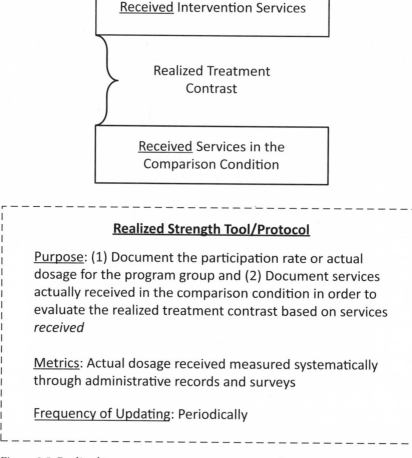

Figure 8.5. Realized treatment contrast—comparison of services actually received. Adapted from Bloom, Weiss, and Hill 2011 with contributions from the research team of the Performance-Based Scholarship Demonstration (Reshma Patel, Alissa Gardenhire, and Katherine Morriss).

of programs that share components of career pathways and revealed that the framework of providing integrated academic and vocational training seems promising in increasing earnings and stable employment. The review also suggests that the use of random assignment designs is indeed feasible in this area.

While the evidence base has been strengthened by these past experimental studies, there are a considerable number of new programs currently being implemented. Research on these programs should answer the standard questions of whether interventions work and, if so, for whom and under what conditions. However, to make the most of these new studies and planned evaluations, more information is needed about the design and implementation of the programs, since failed implementation of an intervention provides no information about the effectiveness of the original design (Cordray and Pion 2006). In addition, insight is also needed into why certain strategies work (through what possible mechanisms). For example, the research questions discussed in the second half of the chapter could help solve the puzzle with regard to the large impacts found for African American males in the Youth Corps study, and the concentrated earnings gains among men in the career academies study.

In sum, developing protocols that assess intervention components and taking snapshots of differences between the treatment and comparison conditions periodically over the course of an intervention can greatly improve the ability of researchers to answer questions of *why* or *how* a program did or did not work. This chapter described five tools that can be added to a researcher's toolkit:

1. driver diagrams: to document the origin of components and impact predictions;
2. logic models: to document the theory of change and finalize intervention components;
3. strength tool/protocol: to measure planned strength and planned treatment contrast;
4. offered strength tool/protocol: to measure the treatment contrast, or differences in offered services in the intervention and comparison conditions; and
5. realized strength tool/protocol: to measure actual participation differences.

This chapter also described why it is useful to set various benchmarks at program inception (high, moderate, or low) for participation levels or take-up of each intervention component, to help maintain researcher objectivity. These a priori benchmarks can then be compared with the observed levels measured periodically throughout the program implementation using the above tools.[15] This comparison will provide an indication of whether the program's implementation mirrored the planned implementation and whether change occurred over time. It is worth noting that the a priori benchmarks of high, moderate, and low should be set such that they reflect the likelihood of generating high, moderate, or low impacts.

In conclusion, while researchers have paid much attention to quantitative methodology (and rightfully continue to do so), it is time that equal attention be paid to the questions about program design and implementation highlighted in this chapter. That is, the time is ripe for the education and workforce training fields to realize that poor design and failed implementation are also subject to the well-known adage applied to data analysis: garbage in yields garbage out.

CHAPTER 9

Conceiving Regional Pathways
to Prosperity Systems

Ronald F. Ferguson

Since its inception, our nation has undergone several major phases in the collective responsibility we assume for our young. Initially, education was a private affair. Indeed, it took a century to achieve broad agreement that government should be responsible for schooling (Tyack 1974). Thomas Jefferson proposed the idea soon after the American Revolution. He understood that citizens would under-invest in education because they would fail to consider the full societal benefits. Gradually over the nineteenth and early twentieth centuries, Americans came to agree with Jefferson.

By the middle of the twentieth century, state and local governments across the nation had accepted responsibility for educating children. Every healthy child in America was required to attend school at least through eighth grade. High school graduation was the primary goal, since a stable middle-class lifestyle was achievable in the 1950s and 1960s for high school graduates.

Now, half a century later, high school graduation is no longer sufficient. Anthony Carnevale and his coauthors demonstrate in this volume that most jobs that pay a living wage require more than a high school degree. A consensus is developing that young people from every segment of the society and every region of the nation should complete high school and then undergo additional certification for the world of work.

Unfortunately, our system is underdeveloped. School-to-career arrangements are often like street systems with potholes, detours, dead ends, and missing road signs. Too frequently, young people get lost in the maze. Then they arrive in early adulthood lacking the skills and orientations to exercise the rights and responsibilities of citizenship and to succeed in jobs that pay living, middle-class wages.

If we can agree on the basic proposition that all youth should complete high school and that most should earn some form of postsecondary certification in order to become career ready, then the challenge before us is to conceive and implement the institutional arrangements—the Pathways to Prosperity systems—that are required. The time has come for the next great leap forward in the collective responsibility we assume for our young.

Despite the quite laudable "college for all" movement that has become ubiquitous in schools and the media over the past few years, our current pathways system is working poorly for youth who lack the skills or desire to achieve four-year college degrees. Huge numbers of American youth reach late adolescence unfamiliar with the mainstream world of work, not headed to college, and with no understanding of the pathways by which they might transition from adolescence into productive adulthood. By the time they reach their late twenties, less than a third of young adults have four-year college degrees, and only about 40 percent have any type of postsecondary degree. Even if we doubled the percentage with college degrees, which is unlikely in the near-term future, there would still be millions needing alternatives that are poorly developed in the current system.

As other chapters in this volume argue, pretending that all youth are headed for college success is unfair to young people for whom other options would be better. Of course, one could argue that high schools are not designed to prepare all students for college, that traditional tracking, grading, and curriculum structures were designed for the very purpose of preparing only a select few students for higher education (Tyack 1974). Farrington and Small (2008: 5) assert that prospects for realizing the college for all goal are limited by "[h]undred-year-old structural mechanisms designed to draw academic distinctions among students" for the purpose of sorting some students into college and others into the blue-collar labor market. Certainly, we should oppose any forces that are pushing students away from preparing for college when college would be their best option. However, we should also oppose the practice of pushing students toward college when other postsecondary options might fit them better and offer superior prospects for success. Admittedly, there are risks. But students and their families should have multiple pathways from which to choose.

This chapter is fundamentally about system design. It builds upon the *Pathways to Prosperity* report (Symonds, Schwartz, and Ferguson 2011) that my colleagues and I at the Harvard Graduate School of Education released in February 2011. That report proposed that the United States needs a more complete, high-quality pathways system with multiple pathways, expanded roles for employers, and a compact with youth. It gave examples from European nations that are ahead of the United States in how well they prepare their youth for careers.

Central to the design of a pathways system should be a scaffolded sequence of work- and career-related learning experiences. That sequence should begin in late elementary school, around the fifth grade, and should continue through young adulthood. Employers and other adult organizations, including religious and civic groups, should play a much greater role than they currently do in cooperation with schools and other institutions. The chapter outlines ten strategic threads of a Pathways to Prosperity strategy to mobilize our collective will and build our capacity to prepare more young people for success in the twenty-first century.

A Twenty-First-Century Social Contract

To achieve these reforms, we need a new social contract that defines public and private sector roles and responsibilities in a Pathways to Prosperity system for youth. The urgency of developing such a system is increasing as our population shifts toward a mix in which people of color, many of whom are poorly served by current arrangements, become the majority of the nation's electorate and workforce. Multiple high-quality navigable pathways to prosperity are needed to prepare youth from all racial, ethnic, and social class backgrounds for success as parents, citizens, and workers. With this kind of comprehensive, "positive youth development" aspiration in mind, the Committee on Community-Level Programs for Youth (2002) proposed a new social compact to provide the following types of youth development experiences:

- physical and psychological safety;
- structure;
- supportive relationships with adults;
- social opportunities to belong;
- positive social norms;
- skill building opportunities;

- community networking opportunities; and
- opportunities to practice new skills.

These are the features of positive youth development systems. All young people deserve these experiences in all of the formal and informal settings where they learn and grow, but especially in their homes, schools, religious institutions, and workplaces.

The greatest and most challenging reforms will entail new commitments to legions of underprepared and disconnected young people who either fail to complete high school or complete high school without the wherewithal to connect with the world of work or postsecondary learning. These youth are disproportionately children of color, but Whites are amply represented as well. Young people in this category often have few marketable skills, few social network resources to expose and connect them to opportunities, and few supports to help them succeed on the job if and when they are fortunate enough to become employed. Accordingly, their unmet needs include marketable skills, information about their options, financial assistance, and ongoing supports to help them navigate the transition from adolescence into adulthood. For some youth, families can supply these resources. But for many millions—perhaps half the youth of the nation—family supports and resources are not enough.

I regard the pathways challenge and social contract to be aspects of a larger social movement. I call it the movement for excellence with equity (Ferguson 2008). Although they may be messy conglomerations, all successful movements contain distinct goals, strategies, policies, programs, projects, principles, and practices. Inside the broader movement, the pathways goal is that young people should begin identifying "possible selves" and career options as early as late elementary school and commence moving along experiential pathways that interest them. As they learn more about options and move through middle and high school and into postsecondary education or training, they should narrow their focus and successfully transition into the adult world of work. Supported by the business community and various other organizations, such a sequence of experiences might play out along the following timeline:

- Grades five and six: Businesses and other institutions authorize and enable their employees to visit fifth- and sixth-grade classrooms where they tell their life stories, beginning when they were the children's ages.[1] Registries of schools and visitors are organized to maintain this system at scale.

- Grades seven and eight: A few times during the school year, students take field trips to employment sites and go behind the scenes in organizations that they might otherwise never see or imagine. Information about careers and the world of work are integrated into these experiences and also into the core curriculum at school.

- Grades nine and ten: Employers authorize, encourage, and enable employees to visit schools to help counsel youth concerning career preparation. Young people are invited individually or in small groups to visit employment sites that interest them. Information about careers and the world of work becomes more deeply integrated into the core curriculum at school. Career and technical elements are routinely available in the high school curriculum, with participation depending on skill and interest.

- Grades eleven and twelve: Options for combining paid work and learning expand greatly. Schools work with employers to integrate work and learning, especially for youth not skilled or interested enough to make four-year college the best near-term choice. Employers loan employees to supplement the career counseling that schools provide.

- Grades thirteen and fourteen: High-quality workforce preparation programs in community colleges and other institutions work closely with employers to help youth develop marketable skills, logistical knowledge, and networks of contacts. Registries track youth for several years after training in order to document their experiences, diagnose the need for additional supports, and identify ways to refine the system.

- Grades fifteen and sixteen: Youth who chose to do so have accumulated enough basic education courses to enable them to move along to four-year colleges. Others move into the adult world of work.

Organizing and maintaining a system with these features is no simple task. Figure 9.1 provides a template of system components, featuring senior power brokers who use their influence to put the system in place. Public sector systems will be important—for example, we need publicly funded entitlements for post-high school education and training. However, what the public

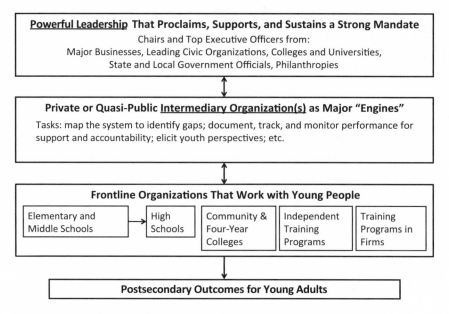

Figure 9.1. Key elements of a regional pathways system.

sector can achieve will be insufficient without expanded roles for private sector organizations.

Together, public and private sector leaders need to ensure that the tasks outlined above are performed more routinely and more effectively. The system needs to support a variety of roles in the types of intermediary organizations that Figure 9.1 envisions:

- system developers—public and private sector organizations that help build capacity and maintain quality. These organizations assist education and training institutions with funding, curriculum, professional development, staff recruitment, and so on.
- system regulators and monitors—public and private sector organizations that set rules for the delivery of particular types of services, monitor performance, and hold institutions accountable.
- businesses and associated intermediaries that help build and support the system—private sector organizations that help identify labor market trends, develop curricula for schools and training

organizations, provide internships, assist with instruction at particular education or training sites, and provide problem solving supports to help young workers succeed on the job.

The current system has within it a range of education and youth development organizations that support young people through key age-and-stage transitions beginning in early adolescence. They could be better integrated in a well-functioning system. They include

For Early- to Middle-Adolescence Transitions

- extended families
- middle schools
- out-of-school time programs
- religious institutions

For Middle- to Late-Adolescence Transitions

- comprehensive high schools
- career and technical high schools
- alternative high schools
- second chance programs (Job Corps, YouthBuild, Year Up, others)
- employers that hire high-school-aged youth into internships

For Late-Adolescence to Early-Adulthood Transitions

- community colleges
- technical colleges
- postsecondary apprenticeship programs
- four-year colleges and graduate schools
- the military
- employers who hire young adults

All of these entities play important roles in every region of the nation. They need to be integrated into a well-functioning pathways system.

Need for a More Elaborate System

The following pages present ten strategic threads that are important for developing robust and sustainable systems of pathways in states and metropolitan regions. Each thread represents a feature of effective systems that leaders need to understand and take into account as they re-conceive local systems. Exactly how leaders incorporate these threads into their strategies will need to be tailored to the specific resources and relationship patterns that have grown out of each region's distinctive history.

Thread #1: Powerful Leadership

Initiating and sustaining the institutional structures we need requires high level, powerful leadership drawn from the top ranks of major corporations, universities, and governmental organizations. The most effective people combine passion with competence, and also have the wherewithal to attract other powerful people to join forces with them. Such people have the authority to set priorities and allocate institutional resources without asking permission. Others understand that there are benefits to cooperating with such people, and penalties for resisting. These are people with the name recognition, skills, and personalities to effectively cultivate both a sense of urgency and a sense of possibility. They have major influence on resource flows and strong records of past accomplishment.

For example, Orrin Ingram, CEO of Ingram Industries Inc., and Tom Cigarran, CEO of Healthways, Inc., are prominent Nashville businessmen. In 2004, they spent $700,000 of their own funds to found a nonprofit organization named "Alignment Nashville." Their purpose was to align the priorities of the Metropolitan Nashville Public Schools (MNPS), local businesses, and the region's nonprofits (Hess and Downs 2011). The business, education, and nonprofit leaders that Alignment Nashville convened agreed that MNPS was not preparing students well enough for the twenty-first-century economy. They identified a lack of educational relevance for high school students as a key problem, concluding that "school needed to look more like real life" (Hess and Downs 2011: 24). Mobilizing quickly, staff from Alignment Nashville, the Nashville Chamber of Commerce, and the Mayor's office helped MNPS draft a grant application for a U.S. Department of Education Smaller Learning Communities (SLC) program. Their successful application brought in over $6 million for SLCs based on the career academy model.

Nashville now has 12 academy high schools that operate two to five career academies each. The district boasts a total of 46 academies and 117 business-academy partnerships (Sparks 2011). Indeed, a theme in the successful grant application was that local business and civic leaders would remain engaged (Hess and Downs 2011). The Alignment Nashville high school committee has six industry-linked partnership councils with business representation. The councils "advise MNPS of significant trends in the industries, assist in the development of new academies, and connect MNPS with potential partners and resources" (Hess and Downs 2011: 29). A key feature of these arrangements is that Alignment Nashville invited only people with executive power in their home organizations to serve on the partnership councils.

Another example built on powerful leadership is Strive, based in Cincinnati and northern Kentucky. Its declared purpose is to "develop the best educational system in the world from preschool through college" and "ensure that every student in the region succeeds" (University of Cincinnati 2006). Its senior leadership includes local school superintendents, college presidents, elected officials, civic leaders, and other executives from education, business, and nonprofit sectors.

The person most responsible for pulling leaders together for Strive was Nancy L. Zimpher, then president of the University of Cincinnati. One person told us, "People would show up just because she asked and expected them to do so." A press release from the University of Cincinnati on August 18, 2006, has the heading "President Launches 'Strive' Educational Partnership" (University of Cincinnati 2006). It shows President Zimpher with her arms outstretched in front of a group of other education, business, and political leaders that she had helped convene for the launch.

Thread #2: Instigators

Instigators are people who work, often behind the scenes and with limited formal authority, to plant seeds of change and to propose and refine the ideas that effective leaders then promote. Indeed, many of the people who may read this chapter will be instigators. Learning details about the roles that instigators play can be difficult because their effectiveness often depends on their remaining in the shadows, supporting others who make the announcements and take the credit. Nonetheless, the instigators are the idea people. Their ideas become critically important catalysts for the work that others carry forward.

Potential instigators may not realize that this is a role that they can play. They may underestimate the value of communicating their ideas in forms that others can understand, appreciate, and pass along. Researchers constitute a prime category of potential instigators. Through their work in think tanks and universities they have access to a broad range of ideas and intellectual resources. They often have the skills to organize ideas in useful ways. Further, they may have the scheduling flexibility to participate in working groups of instigators that distill and refine the concepts around which others will later organize. Instigators contribute ideas that people with power help bring to fruition.

One especially prolific instigating force related to the Pathways to Prosperity agenda is the Berkeley-based organization ConnectEd: The California Center for College and Career. Established in 2006 through a grant from the James Irvine Foundation, ConnectEd supports the development and dissemination of Linked Learning, a high school improvement approach that creates "programs of study that connect learning in the classroom with real-world applications outside of school" (http://www.irvine.org). Each high school student in a Linked Learning program pursues a "pathway" that "connects strong academics with real-world experience"—a comprehensive study that integrates "rigorous academic instruction with a demanding technical curriculum and field-based learning—all set in the context of one of California's 15 major industry sectors" (http://www.irvine.org).

ConnectEd builds awareness of the Linked Learning approach through the publications, videos, and other resources on its website, http://www.connectedcalifornia.org. In addition, it publishes research on the social and economic benefits of Linked Learning. ConnectEd instigated the Linked Learning Alliance, a statewide coalition of education, industry, and community organizations committed to transforming the way California's high schools operate.[2]

Thread #3: Highly Skilled and Dedicated Staff in Powerful "Engines"

Pathways systems need powerful organizations—I like to call them "engines"—that drive the change process and help sustain the scope and quality of the system's ongoing work. Strive and Alignment Nashville aspire to become engines. A key feature of engines is that they are *not* frontline organizations working directly with youth and families. Instead, their role is to support and hold accountable the organizations that work directly with youth and families. In addition, they should monitor the mix of organizations doing frontline work to ascertain that they are well matched to the region's needs and have the capacity to perform effectively. Threads 4 through 10 below describe some of the functions that engines should perform.

Perhaps the most essential quality of successful engines is that their staffs are skilled and dedicated enough to play their roles effectively. They need to be at least as skilled and talented as the vast majority of people in the organizations with which they interact. They also need courage. Their main functions entail, on the one hand, helping people and organizations to achieve things that they could not have achieved on their own, and on the other hand, holding them accountable for keeping their promises and playing their roles well. Of course, engines may divide these functions across multiple actors or departments; and there may be multiple engines, each of which specializes in particular functions. The point is that the engines perform vital system-building and maintenance functions.

My view is that engines need to be private sector organizations in order to protect them from control by elected officials. If the pathways system becomes too identified with one political party or too embroiled in partisan politics, the broad support that it needs from the employer community and from all political parties might be undermined. The best way to address this challenge is unclear. Perhaps the main engines should be quasi-public organizations with boards appointed jointly by public and private sector leaders, and staffs held strictly accountable to those boards. In the end, what matters most is that they are professionally operated organizations with clearly defined duties and that they perform extremely well in service to the pathways mission.

Thread #4: Clear Central Themes That Provide Focus

Enlisting and sustaining participation by employers and other stakeholders requires having a few central themes that people can wrap their minds around and not be overwhelmed. By "themes," I mean compelling facts and ideas concerning the urgency of the work, and pertaining to the structures and routines needed to establish and maintain an effectively operating system of pathways to prosperity. These compelling facts and ideas continually remind people why they are making the required sacrifices.

There are many ways to frame the central themes. In Cincinnati and Northern Kentucky, Strive's framers crafted "the Strive Promise." It focuses on what leaders called "five key goals and initial strategies." The five are

1. *Every child will be **prepared** for school from birth through early childhood education.* United Way of Greater Cincinnati's Success By 6 initiative will lead efforts to ensure every child is prepared for and has access to high-quality early childhood programs.

2. *Every child will be **supported inside and outside the school walls.*** Resources, programs, and services that support students and families will be coordinated at the district and school levels through the creation of schools as Community Learning Centers and Family Resource Centers. These will provide expanded academic enrichment opportunities for children along with such services as youth development activities, art, music, and recreation programs and counseling.

3. *Every child will **succeed academically.*** Existing teacher training and professional development programs will be aligned and improved to attract and retain the most talented and committed educators to Cincinnati and Northern Kentucky.

4. *Every student will **enroll** in some form of postsecondary education.* Financial barriers to college will be eliminated and trained adults will provide guidance to students to raise their aspirations and enable them to apply to and be accepted in an institution that meets their career objectives.

5. *Every student will **graduate and enter a career.*** Colleges will provide comprehensive student support services, especially to first-generation students, and expand co-op opportunities (Cincinnati Public Schools 2011).

Note that the fourth of these is central to the pathways agenda.

Generating effective central themes to drive the development of a Pathways to Prosperity system requires avoiding what Keith Westrich, Director of College and Career Readiness at the Massachusetts Department of Elementary and Secondary Education, calls "third-rail" words.[3] He warns us that the phrase "vocational education" incites opposition from stakeholders who worry about racial and social class biases in past educational tracking practices. Westrich reminds us of the need to be clear that college and career readiness is a *both/and*—not an *either/or*—proposition, a crucial emphasis echoed in the first guiding principle of Linked Learning: "Pathways prepare students for postsecondary education *and* career—both objectives, not just one or the other" (ConnectEd; italics in original). The success of any movement to build a regional Pathways to Prosperity system will depend upon the careful use of language.

In Massachusetts, the crafting of messages has taken a promising form in a recently released report from the Massachusetts Workforce Investment Board (MWIB), entitled *Preparing Youth for Work and Learning in the 21st Century Economy* (MWIB 2010). The report marks the culmination of an effort of the MWIB Youth Committee that began in 2007 in response to a gubernatorial directive. Their charge was to assess the existing youth employment system and recommend improvements. The report asserts the following vision: "All youth develop the 21st century academic and professional skills critical to career success in our evolving economy. Secondary and postsecondary credentials are an important part of this vision which applies to both in-school and out-of-school youth" (MWIB 2010: 5).

The report then breaks down the vision into three explicit recommendations, each accompanied by action steps to guide policy and implementation. The three recommendations are

1. Increase the number and quality of work experiences and career exploration activities for both in-school and out-of-school youth.
2. Organize collaboration among education, workforce, and human service agencies at both the state and regional levels.
3. Pilot a "multiple pathways" approach in selected regions that combines the education, workforce development, and human service support necessary to address the state's dropout crisis by creating new avenues to educational attainment, economic security, and upward mobility for all youth (MWIB 2010: 5).

These are very general statements. Nonetheless, they are clear statements around which stakeholders can organize to make progress toward achieving the pathways vision.

Thread #5: Streamlined and Coherent "Curriculum"
for the Change Process

Building a Pathways to Prosperity system will require giving stakeholders clear images of the roles that the system needs them to play. People in many cases will need to play roles for which they have not been prepared—they will need to do things that they have never seen done. Therefore we need materials to help stakeholders understand their roles and learn to play them.

ConnectEd has organized resources on its website into a comprehensive ToolKit—a portfolio of resources to help guide stakeholders in designing and implementing high quality Linked Learning pathways (http://www.connect edcalifornia.org/landing). The ConnectEd ToolKit offers a navigable collection of publications, videos, links to external resources, and upcoming professional development sessions structured around four essential elements: pathway design, engaged learning, system support, and evaluation and accountability. Importantly, the four elements that comprise the ToolKit match the four organizing principles of the Certification Criteria for Linked Learning Pathways, discussed below. This consistency of language and structure enhance coherence and render the ToolKit more accessible and actionable.

The first component of the ConnectEd ToolKit, Pathway Design, contains a wealth of resources to guide the process of designing quality pathways "with a structure, governance, and program of study that provides all students with opportunities for both postsecondary and career success" (http://www.connectedcalifornia.org/base/toolkits/index/area:1). Also included in the Pathway Design module is an Advisory Board Manual, which describes how to operate a business and community advisory board as a key aspect of pathway design.

Second in the ConnectEd ToolKit is the Engaged Learning section, which addresses the difficult work of creating pathways curricula with the requisite levels of rigor in both academic and technical learning standards. Integrating such complex instructional strategies presents a significant challenge, so it is not surprising that the Engaged Learning module is the most resource-rich section of the ConnectEd ToolKit. The section includes guidance for developing work-based learning experiences along with preparation for postsecondary options, representative of the approach's balanced emphasis on both college and career.

The third piece of the ToolKit, System Support, discusses district-level policies and practices that cultivate an authorizing environment in which quality pathways can thrive. The System Support model emphasizes leadership and human capital considerations for successful implementation of quality pathways and for long-term sustainability.

The final section addresses Evaluation and Accountability, outlining practices to ensure that a pathway is in fact improving student outcomes. The module also addresses how to use data to drive continuous improvement of a pathway by tracking students through formalized postsecondary follow-up practices.

Impressive as it is, the ConnectEd example represents only a narrow slice of what we mean by a curriculum for the change process. It pertains to one program, not the whole system. Stakeholders in other parts of the system will benefit from similar supports, many of which remain to be designed.

Thread #6: Organizational Structures with the Capacity to Teach and Motivate Adults

The pathways system needs routines and structures inside various public, private, and nonprofit institutions that help people to learn their roles—including but not limited to roles as teachers, trainers, and supervisors—and to feel motivated to play them effectively. The system needs mechanisms for coaching, observing, and sharing that make it difficult for individuals in key positions to avoid participating in the change process.

For example, when Strive in Cincinnati focused on improving outcomes for youth in the K–12 system, it created a structure for learning. Each participating organization was assigned to one of fifteen different Student Success Networks (SSNs), with each network defined by a particular type of activity, such as tutoring or early childhood education. According to Kania and Kramer (2011: 36), "Each SSN has been meeting with coaches and facilitators for two hours every two weeks for the past three years, developing shared performance indicators, discussing their progress, and most important, learning from each other and aligning their efforts to support each other." Because almost all of the local funders in the region require their grantees to participate in Strive, it is difficult for participating organizations to stand aside and avoid the learning.

Similarly, recall the career academies program that stakeholders collaborated to create in Nashville. Teachers needed new skills to play the roles that the academies required. According to Hess and Downs (2011), the Nashville

Chamber of Commerce helped match teachers with local businesses for "externships" and arranged stipends. The Chamber, a business organization called PENCIL, and Alignment Nashville each assigned staff to help organize meetings and coordinate participation of the business community in helping adults to learn the roles they would need to play to make the career academies successful.

Thread #7: Patient but Tough Accountability

The system needs tools and routines for monitoring practices and outcomes, targeting assistance where needed, sometimes replacing people or organizations that fail to improve.

Accountability will operate differently depending on whether the actors are in for-profit firms, governmental organizations, or nonprofit organizations. For nonprofit organizations, funders have a key role to play. In the case of Strive, for example, most Cincinnati area funders have aligned their criteria for evaluating grantees. As a result, no matter who their funders might be, organizations know that their performances can be easily compared against other organizations that play similar roles and provide similar services. Funders as a group can track progress on particular metrics for the region as a whole, and they can identify which of their grantees are contributing (or not contributing) to the observed trends.

Accountability in for-profit firms and governmental organizations will need to operate through normal channels. Boards of directors and executive officers will need to be clear with employees concerning the expectations and rewards that go along with participating in the pathways system. Forms in which employees might serve and support the pathways system are many, ranging from volunteer activities on the one hand, to assignments carried out as formal duties on the other.

No matter which sector they represent, people who control resources in a regional pathways system need to make it clear that results matter. They need to make sure that performances are monitored, that people and organizations needing remedial support to improve actually receive the support that they need, and that continuing support depends upon demonstrated improvement.

Thread #8: Institutionalized Data Gathering, Including
Data from Young People

There should be mechanisms for gathering and organizing data, including a regional registry for young people who choose to have their progress tracked and to benefit from associated information or counseling services. Information could be collected on schooling status, job status, and academic or career credentials achieved or desired. Youth could report on the places they applied for work and the responses they received. They might also register their career aspirations, extracurricular interests, and job preferences. Personal and group identifiers might include age, years of formal schooling, disability status, English as a second language status, race/ethnicity, gender, and others.

Kania and Kramer (2011) describe how what they call *collective impact* initiatives should use data to achieve alignment. They write, "Collecting data and measuring results consistently on a short list of indicators at the community level and across all participating organizations not only ensures that all efforts remain aligned, it also enables the participants to hold each other accountable and learn from each other's successes and failures." As an example, they describe how all of the preschool programs in Strive use the same measures to track results. Analysis of those results led to a new project that effectively reduced summer learning loss in the months leading up to kindergarten. Benefits of collecting common data extend beyond just preschool programs. Kania and Kramer report, "Each type of activity requires a different set of measures, but all organizations engaged in the same type of activity report on the same measures. Looking at results across multiple organizations enables the participants to spot patterns, find solutions, and implement them rapidly" (Kania and Kramer 2011: 40).

Thread #9: Data-Driven Decision Making and Transparency

In order for data to be useful, mechanisms must be in place to use it. A well-functioning regional pathways system should include analysts to track trends in strategically important indicators and to produce reports tailored for busy decision makers. The data for tracking trends should come from many sources, not just the regional registry outlined above. Decision-making groups in the pathways system should be encouraged to specify the types of analyses they need for making their decisions. Their requests should influence both the types of data collected and the types of analyses produced.

There should be a "dashboard" maintained on a public website where anyone who wants to know can track the progress on featured goals. Goals could be defined by age group. Dashboard entries might show, for example, the percentages of youth in the region being reached with career-exposure experiences appropriate for their ages.

In addition, career-exposure programs and projects might be developed in response to the interests expressed in registry entries. Or imagine that the youth registry tracked the types of reasons employers gave when turning young people down for jobs. A pathways system could create mechanisms for working with employers and young people to design ways of overcoming the problems thus identified, in order to make good job matches. Similarly, if identifiable problems seemed repeatedly to result in quits or fires, those might become the focus of professional development for frontline supervisors, to prepare them to work with young employees more effectively across a particular sector of the economy.

A major emphasis of our Pathways to Prosperity report was that regions need ways of integrating work and learning from high school through postsecondary levels. This integration will require rethinking curricula and designing supports to help young people choose pathways to pursue. There will surely be imbalances, with excess demand for some opportunities and excess supply for others. A major challenge is to design and implement the pathways system in ways that fairly and transparently allocate opportunity, especially across segments of the community representing different racial, ethnic, and socioeconomic status groups.

Transparency is important because many people do not trust the traditional mechanisms. Each segment of the community will have their antennae up to detect favoritism or disrespect. Less advantaged groups or communities of color will worry that the system is tracking their children toward the most menial opportunities and hoarding the best opportunities for Whites or for the children of the well-to-do. Even between different nonwhite groups, say, Hispanics and Blacks, there may be sensitivities concerning whether one group or the other is being favored by particular decision-making processes. Transparency can help allay such concerns.

Thread #10: Community Involvement and Resources

Leaders in a Pathways to Prosperity system should engage a broad range of stakeholders. It is important initially for a small group to take the lead in order to assemble resources and set things in motion. Some core defining features must be nonnegotiable. But success requires much broader participation. Leaders need to strike a balance so that all key stakeholder groups feel included and respected.

For example, the top-down nature of Strive's introduction ignited some criticism. In a recent interview conducted for this chapter, Strive Executive Committee Chair Kathy Merchant opined,

> When it comes to stakeholders, it is important to make it a grass-roots, not a grass-tops movement. We call ourselves an overseeing body, the executive committee. I prefer to call it a committee of executives to keep it more of a social movement than a rigid hierarchy. These are the leaders in the community who hold the levers of change. They can make things happen without going through others. . . . [But] we have a weakness in engaging others like parents at the grassroots level. We are back-filling now because there is a point of tension with some in the community feeling, "They have done this 'to us' instead of 'with us.'" The inclusion question is important.

Merchant's perspective here is understandable, given her position as the leader of Strive's core intermediary organization. After all, one aspect of her job to is to engage people from all levels of the community and convince them that their views are respected and influential. At the same time, it would be a mistake to believe that so much change would be brewing in the region without powerful leaders having decided to just do it—just make it happen!

Power matters. But there is a division of roles that needs to be understood. As the system-building process matures, influence should become more widely shared. Stakeholders should have opportunities to present their views and debate competing perspectives. Tensions will be inevitable as pressures are exerted from the top down, middle out, and bottom up. If a critical mass of stakeholders at any level of the system becomes too dissatisfied, prospects for success will be greatly diminished. Conversely, if a broad cross section of the community sees progress and the region develops a strong sense of efficacy surrounding its Pathways to Prosperity system, success becomes sustainable.

Conclusion and Call to Action

Social and economic vitality in twenty-first-century America may depend more than we want to acknowledge on how good a system we build for school-to-career transitions. In too many instances, our school-to-career system resembles a road system with dead-end streets, potholes, and roads to nowhere. For some youth, we have an interstate highway system leading to four-year college graduation, but many youth lack the interest or where-withal to travel that road. In contrast, many other parts of the system are in disrepair and difficult to navigate. There, young people who search for roads to success often get lost for years. This is unfair. We need a well-maintained and navigable system for all youth, not only some youth.

This chapter concerns how states and metropolitan regions can provide better pathways to prosperity for adolescents and young adults. Around the time of fifth grade, we should introduce children to the amazing variety of careers and "possible selves" to be considered as they think about their fu-tures. Then, without constraining their choices, we should provide a se-quence of career-related learning opportunities until they join the workforce as young adults in the careers that they have chosen.

To create and sustain the pathways system that this chapter envisions, highly influential stakeholders who lead major institutions in business and government will need to spearhead support for key intermediary institutions, which we have called "engines." These essential leaders are people with name recognition who have the power to direct resources, and the skills and person-alities to cultivate not only a sense of urgency, but also a sense of possibility. They may rely for some of their best ideas on people that we call "instigators," some of whom have no formal authority and will never get the credit. In-formed by instigators and driven by their conviction that the work is impor-tant, dominant leaders of major institutions need to set up organizations that serve as engines. The engines are not direct service providers. Instead, they play system-building and support roles for other organizations. They need to employ highly talented staffers to help organize, support, and assure the qual-ity of the critically important work upon which this chapter has focused.

We also need a change of mindset. There was a time in American history when multiple pathways into the workforce served clearly discriminatory purposes. They were designed to transport some youth into the most pleasant and lucrative employment opportunities, while channeling others into the dirtiest and lowest-paying alternatives. Privileged segments of our population were favored because of their racial, ethnic, and social class backgrounds, and others were restricted to the lowest rungs of the economic system. Measured skills were different between groups because of historical differences in opportunities to learn. In too many cases, those differences were used as excuses for favoring one group over another in hiring decisions, even when the skills were irrelevant for performing the jobs.

Today, academic skills still correlate highly with family background characteristics. However, more than in the past, academic skills really do translate into economic productivity.[4] So, in the interest of equity, closing academic achievement gaps between students from different family backgrounds remains my greatest preoccupation.[5] Academic achievement gaps perpetuate economic opportunity gaps.

But achievement gaps are only part of the problem. We should be honest with ourselves about the reasons that job market outcomes are so much worse for some youths than for others. Our unwillingness or inability to cope effectively with disparity has caused us to under-develop school-to-career supports for a large segment of our youth population. We have been in denial about the need to identify youths for whom the traditional four-year college is probably not a good fit and to help them identify alternative roads to career success. And let us be clear that these youth do not come only from less-advantaged households. The fact is that parents from all walks of life, including many of us who have highly successful business careers or teach at elite universities, have children for whom four-year colleges are not the best options.

When I hear the "college for all" slogan, I think four-year college. Some of my valued colleagues want the phrase to connote all types of post-high school career preparation. Whatever the semantics we ultimately settle upon for the meaning of the word "college," let us agree that all youth deserve multiple career pathways from which to choose and high quality supports for making their choices. To make this happen, every one of us can be an instigator, and some can do much more.

CHAPTER 10

Aligning Secondary and Postsecondary Credentialization with Economic Development Strategy, or "If Low Educational Attainment = Poor Metropolitan Competitiveness, What Can Be Done about It?"

Laura Wolf-Powers and Stuart Andreason

Several chapters in this volume consider the role of public policy in improving connections between education and the labor market. Of particular concern in these chapters are the education and employment of students in poor school districts in America's central cities and inner suburbs—school districts in which a majority of students come from low-income, low-wealth households. As Goldin and Katz succinctly put it in the final chapter of their book *The Race between Education and Technology*, "it is important to recognize that schools are essentially failing particular students. Those left behind by the system are mainly minority children in inner-city schools who become the youths who are not college ready (2008: 348).

These are the students who grow up in poor households, in neighborhoods where the vast majority of their peers are also poor. They enter primary school at a disadvantage, and they leave the K–12 system (as dropouts and graduates alike) with low levels of literacy and analytical skill. Even when well-positioned to benefit from postsecondary education, they face enormous barriers to financing this investment.

Table 10.1 shows key educational attainment and poverty statistics, as well as public high school graduation rates, from the largest twenty-five central cities in the United States by population. Within this group, nine cities—Baltimore, Dallas, Detroit, El Paso, Houston, Los Angeles, Memphis, Philadelphia, and San Antonio—fall both below the group average for educational attainment (as measured by the proportion of the population over twenty-five years of age with a bachelor's degree) and above the average for household poverty rates. Cities with high poverty rates and low rates of educational attainment are in a particular bind, because the needs of their populations far outstrip the resources available from the tax base. Political leaders, policy-makers, and agency executives in these places must "solve simultaneously" for the challenge of raising revenue to support city services and the challenge of creating economic opportunity for those left behind in the knowledge economy. To take one example: the city of Philadelphia has a population of about 1.5 million and a working-age population of about 990,000. Of the working-age population, 22 percent have not obtained a high school degree, and by one estimate 550,000, or over half, are functionally low-literate. Accordingly, Philadelphia has both one of the lowest labor force participation rates (45 percent) of any U.S. city and one of the highest poverty rates (24 percent). Significantly, it is not low labor force participation alone that drives poverty in Philadelphia, but low earnings as well. According to the Philadelphia Workforce Investment Board, 40 percent of working adults in the city earn poverty-level wages as measured against the Pennsylvania Self-Sufficiency Standard for a family of four (Philadelphia Workforce Investment Board 2007, 2009).[1] An important part of the explanation for these low wages is that for the relatively small number of jobs in Philadelphia that can be filled by functionally low-literate workers, the supply of workers substantially exceeds the demand.

This status quo carries grim implications for Philadelphia and its peer cities, as well as for the metropolitan regions that contain them.[2] Not only do individuals remain poor, but local and regional economies stagnate. Scholars have convincingly shown that since service industries began to assume prominence in the urban economic base, economic growth and fiscal stability have been most durable in places where a combination of innate advantage and shrewd public policy has produced an educated and adaptable workforce (see Glaeser 2005; Glaeser and Saiz 2003; Glaeser and Shapiro 2001; Gottlieb and Fogarty 2003). Figure 10.1 demonstrates the strong relationship between education and economic health as a "place" phenomenon

Table 10.1. Educational Attainment and Poverty Measures in the Twenty-Five Largest U.S. Cities by Population

City	Local HS District Graduation Rate (%)	% with Less than HS Degree	% with a BA or Higher	% of Households in Poverty	% of Children in Poverty
New York	63	21	33.1	17.7	27.3
Los Angeles	44.5	26.8	29.4	16.8	27.9
Chicago	51	21.2	31.7	18.5	30.6
Houston	52.9	26	28.3	17.4	31.5
Phoenix	68.2	21.7	24	14.5	26.3
Philadelphia	64.4	20.8	22.1	22.3	34.2
San Antonio	47.3	21	23.4	17.4	26.6
San Diego	63.7	13.7	40.6	11.3	17.3
Dallas	50.8	28.1	28.2	18	33.6
San Jose	76.4	18	35.7	9	13.1
Detroit	37.9	23.9	12.1	29.6	46.5
San Francisco	57.1	14.4	51.1	11	12.2
Jacksonville	50.8	13	24.3	13	19
Indianapolis	27.6	16.3	27.7	15.3	25.3
Austin	58.9	15.7	43.5	14.5	25.1
Columbus	44.7	13	32.5	17.2	27.7
Fort Worth	56.5	22.3	25.2	15.2	24.1
Charlotte	60.5	11.9	39.8	11.3	17.4
Memphis	51.2	18.6	22.8	20.7	36.9
Boston	60.7	15.8	42.9	18.7	27.8
Baltimore	41.5	23.1	24.9	19.1	28.4
El Paso	60.6	27.6	20.9	23.9	35.6
Seattle	77.3	7.9	54.3	11.9	12.4
Denver	61.1	16.7	39.3	15.7	26.4
Nashville	45.2	15.2	32.9	14.1	25.6
National Average	**71.3**	**15.5**	**27.5**	**12.8**	**18.6**

[1]Data from US Census American Community Survey, 2005–2009 Averages.

[2]Graduation rates are percent on-time, four-year graduations, with no GED, in 2005, derived from NCES data using the Urban Institute Cumulative Promotion Index, by the Learning to Finish Calculator by Pew Partnership for Civic Change (2008).

[3]NYC graduation rate from NYC DOE, "Mayor Bloomberg and Chancellor Klein Announce That High School Graduation Rate Rises to All-Time High of 63 Percent, Marking the Eighth Consecutive Year of Gains."

[4]Universe for educational attainment is population ages twenty-five years and older.

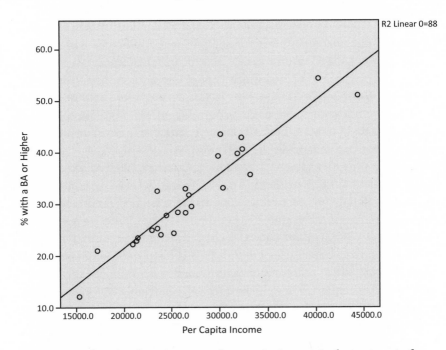

Figure 10.1. Educational attainment and per capita income in the top twenty-five U.S. cities by population. *Source:* Data from U.S. Census Bureau American Community Survey 2005–2009 estimates.

in addition to an individual one. While human capital is less of a factor when other elements of competitive advantage (warm climate, low taxes, newer infrastructure) are present, the presence of a college-educated populace is especially crucial to the successful adaptation of older industrial cities. In a fascinating study for the Federal Reserve Bank of Philadelphia, Jeffrey Lin (2009) demonstrates that "new work"—occupations born of innovation and technological change—has concentrated in metropolitan regions with high endowments of skill. Conversely, the disamenities associated with a high proportion of unskilled residents (such as high taxes, high crime, and a profound disconnect between the sources of local taxes and their uses) drive the decline of low human capital cities by making them less attractive to middle-class and affluent households. Metropolitan regions containing declining cities appear to suffer slower population and income growth than their counterparts in which the inner cities are more competitive for regional population and jobs (Voith 1998; Hill and Brennan 2005).

How can public policy contribute to the alleviation of this crippling problem? Other chapters in this volume review the game-changing potential of policy changes around career and technical education at the high school level and around administrative and economic access to postsecondary schooling for adults. The purpose of this chapter is to examine options in the economic development policy sphere, where, as noted above, increasing recognition of human capital as a major source of innovation and competitive advantage has made the attraction and development of a skilled workforce a priority (Kresl and Fry 2005; Markusen 2008; Markusen and Schrock 2008; Wolf-Powers 2004). To set the stage for a discussion of existing and potential links between economic development and labor force development policy, we examine the current "second chance" employment training and placement system, the chief resource for adults who have emerged from secondary school without the skills they need to obtain and maintain work and to achieve economic mobility over time. We then examine the state of contemporary city and regional economic development policy, which is linked with workforce policy through sector-based initiatives and industry partnerships, but currently quite tenuously. We conclude by recommending changes in both the second chance workforce system and urban and metropolitan economic development practice that would render the connections between them less fragile.

The Public Workforce System in Crisis

Currently in the United States, an out-of-school individual who seeks assistance from the public sector in obtaining work or training for work encounters a largely federally funded, largely locally managed system—mediated by state government—that operates under the rubric of the Workforce Investment Act of 1998 (WIA).[3] WIA has four titles. Title I, administered by the Employment and Training Administration in the U.S. Department of Labor, is the largest, and contains job development and training programs for adult, youth, and dislocated workers.[4] Title II, administered by the Office of Vocational and Adult Education in the U.S. Department of Education, supports adult basic education and literacy programs. Title III funds the state-based labor exchange services originally authorized by the Wagner-Peyser Act of 1933, while Title IV transfers money to states for vocational rehabilitation of people with disabilities, again through their education departments.

Although consolidated under the banner of workforce investment, these programs continue to operate under distinct bureaucratic regimes; only occasionally, for example, do Title I employment-oriented programs succeed in achieving complementarity at the program level with literacy and basic education initiatives administered by federal and state departments of education.[5]

The public face of the workforce system is a "One-Stop Center," a physical location intended to consolidate at a community level the array of labor market services authorized by the raft of titles and programs described above. A visitor to a One-Stop Center accesses a hierarchy of services in a specific sequence. First come "core services," including job search and placement assistance, labor market information, and an initial assessment of skills. If the core services do not result in job placement, a user is offered "intensive services": more comprehensive assessments, development of an individual employment plan, and group and individual counseling. Depending on the integration of the education and labor departments in a given state, academic remediation and literacy instruction may be available at the One-Stop Center as well.

Occupational training becomes an option under WIA Title I only after core services and intensive services are exhausted with no placement resulting. Training services typically come in the form of an individual training account (ITA), which an individual can use to access a certified training program of his or her choosing at a community college, vocational technical school, or private training institution. For example, an estimated 2.5 million people of the 8 million receiving services under WIA between June 2009 and June 2010 received occupational training. In an effort to increase accountability and ensure that training is linked to the labor market, the reimbursement of providers for training under WIA is tied to a series of achievement benchmarks—enrollment, delivery of training, job placement in positions paying a certain amount over minimum wage, and retention in this employment over 30-, 60-, and 120-day periods. These provisions were instituted to align the incentives of trainers with the interests of their clients in attaining economic mobility, and with the interests of the public sector in deploying limited training dollars wisely. However, compliance with reporting requirements is so time-consuming—and the amount and timing of reimbursements so unpredictable—that many providers do not find it worth their while to accept WIA vouchers. Training that consistently leads to earnings gains tends to cost significantly more than a training voucher will buy;

WIA vouchers cover only a fraction of the per-participant cost at the high-performing sector-based program Per Scholas, for example (Leavitt 2011).

Workforce Investment Boards, the county and municipal bodies that typically administer One-Stop Centers, play research and policy roles and may sponsor special programs that meet particular cities' or counties' labor market needs and challenges. Many Workforce Boards have leveraged local funding allocations with federal demonstration grants and philanthropic funding. Overall, however, even the system's advocates agree that the current configuration of services under the Workforce Investment Act could perform more effectively the task of promoting economic self-sufficiency among individuals who are not made labor market ready by the education system (Stone and Worgs 2004; Osterman 2007).

The tortuous evolution of federal "second chance" workforce policies from the 1940s forward (of which WIA represents the current instantiation) has been well described elsewhere by political economists and historians (Mucciaroni 1990; Weir 1992; Giloth 2004). We highlight here some themes of that literature that shed light on the crisis in which the system currently finds itself. First, workforce training policy (originally called "manpower planning") has been pursued separately, at federal, state, and local levels, from education and literacy policy, and from efforts to manage and direct economic growth. Training policy and institutions also have been functionally bifurcated from policies and institutions governing collective bargaining. Second, workforce programs have been means-tested and targeted at the poor, structured (in spite of efforts to involve private employers on advisory boards) more as a social service for the disadvantaged then as a response to employer needs.[6] Third (and relatedly), over the past two decades, poverty policy has shifted drastically away from human capital development and income support and toward work itself. This trend was embodied in and effectuated by the dramatic expansion of the Earned Income Tax Credit in 1993, and then by the passage of the Clinton Administration's welfare reform legislation, the Personal Responsibility and Work Opportunity Reconciliation Act of 1997 (PRWORA). PRWORA block-granted public assistance to the states but kept the federal government involved in welfare policy by (1) mandating that states place time limits on cash benefits, (2) offering funding for services such as childcare to support labor market entry, and (3) requiring that transition into the workforce for former beneficiaries become a central goal for city and state human services agencies (Lower-Basch and Greenberg 2008).

The drive to address poverty and welfare dependency by incentivizing working-age adults to work (and providing supports for their entry in to the workforce) rather than by using government funds to invest in their human capital up front has a strong basis in evaluation research. Beginning with Abt Associates' national Job Training Partnership Act evaluation in 1995—one of the first studies to use a randomized experimental design to gauge the effect of a program intervention—rigorously designed studies routinely showed only modest earnings gains for individuals participating in training programs when compared with control groups who received only job search assistance. Programs to retrain displaced workers whose skill sets (in manufacturing, for example) had become mismatched to labor demand produced particularly disappointing results (see Heckman, LaLonde, and Smith 1999). Recognizing that "to date, local workforce systems largely fail to satisfy the needs and aspirations of both jobseekers/workers and businesses" (Giloth 2004: 15), many in the workforce field have put tireless effort into making these systems more effective at poverty alleviation, for example by advocating that they feature the kinds of long-term, sector-based training programs that have demonstrated success at raising earnings (see below). However, given the substantial difference in cost between training and "work first" interventions, many legislators and policy administrators have seen little reason to continue allocating resources to training for disadvantaged adults and youth and displaced workers. Respected economists have argued that "second chance" programs for adults are simply not a good investment, and that attention and funding should go toward intervening in early childhood and at the primary school level (see Carneiro and Heckman 2003).

A countervailing interpretation of the evidence on second chance employment training programs recently has begun to emerge. This interpretation focuses on earnings gains observed in a recent non-experimental evaluation of WIA, including an estimated marginal benefit of $400 in earnings each quarter for recipients of training (Heinrich, Meuser, and Troske 2008). Scholars also are challenging the assumption of previous studies that earnings and employment outcomes for participants constitute the sole relevant measures of success, suggesting that economic productivity benefits and avoided social welfare spending should be factored into evaluations of workforce training, much as they figure into evaluations of programs like Head Start and preschool (King 2008; King and Heinrich 2010). Despite rebuttals of the "received wisdom" about second chance workforce training,

however, the prospects for it as a significant component of social policy remain bleak. By 2003, only 40 percent of Workforce Investment Act dollars
spent by local governments were going to training vouchers (GAO 2005),
meaning that the majority of services being delivered under the second
chance workforce development system were short term and oriented toward
placement in jobs. Moreover, following a slow decline that began in the early
2000s, funding for the Workforce Investment Act and other programs for
working-age adults has recently fallen precipitously (see Carnevale 2010;
King and Heinrich 2010). An original fiscal year (FY) 2011 budget that
amounted to about $4 billion was cut by several hundred million dollars in
the FY 2011 continuing resolution passed in April 2011, and the 2012 budget
process promises to "radically transform the federal role in investing in the
skills of the U.S. workforce" (National Skills Coalition 2011). Congress may
well decide in the course of the FY 2012 budget process to significantly scale
back many elements of the WIA system, particularly those related to training (Title I programs).

Whether justified by the empirical evidence or not, the "work first" approach now dominates policy for individuals left behind by the K–12 education system. Work is seen as an opportunity to gain experience, to develop
skills, and to contribute to the economy. However, as more studies of welfare
leavers and displaced workers become available, it is also apparent that it is
uncommon in the current political economy for low-skilled adults to emerge
from poverty through work alone. A cohort of low earners followed by Andersson, Holzer, and Lane during six years of strong economic growth from
1996 to 2001 did experience transition to higher earning status, but only 27
percent of the sample consistently raised their incomes enough to rise above
the poverty line for a family of four (Andersson, Holzer, and Lane 2005).
Theodos and Bednarzik examined a low-income cohort from 1995 to 2001,
using Panel Study of Income Dynamics data, and found two distinct "earners" groups, one of which gained earnings over the period due to work experience, and a "sizable minority of individuals who fail to realize earnings
advancement even while remaining employed" (2006, 45). The Theodos/Bed-
narzik cohort also included a group of individuals who were not job holders
(earners) in 1995; 80 percent of these remained unemployed throughout the
subsequent six years.

Part of the explanation for lack of mobility among earners is clearly the
disproportionately low amount of employer-provided training offered on
the job to less skilled workers (Osterman 2007). According to one study,

low-skilled workers require up to 1,000 hours of basic education and training to achieve economic mobility (Carnevale and Reich 2000 as cited by Giloth 2004). Additionally, across the board, fewer working-age people are participating in the labor force. Economics writer David Leonhardt recently pointed out that a fifth of working-aged American men are currently out of the labor force, down from only about 5 percent in the 1950s (Leonhardt 2011).

In sum, although the evidence on the success of government-funded training is ambiguous, it is far from clear that the "work first" approach now pervasive in anti-poverty policy is capable of improving the economic status of those individuals who emerge from K–12 schooling without the tools to attach to the labor market. Urban adults with the most serious barriers to employment, if they choose to seek help from the workforce system, engage with institutions that embody decades of conflict about the purpose, instruments, beneficiaries, and fundamental value of public sector workforce training— institutions that could potentially offer pathways to family-sustaining work, but that do so only in exceptional circumstances. Those attempting to reform what is left of this fragmented system are contending with barriers that include unstable and dysfunctional local governance regimes, mistrust from employers and job-seekers, and deeply inadequate resources (Carnevale 2010; Giloth 2004; Stone and Worgs 2004). New strategies are clearly needed.

Local and Metropolitan Economic Development Policy and the Sector Partnership Model

Just as federal workforce training policy has traditionally been separate from national economic policy, the same is true at the municipal and metropolitan levels. One often cited reason for the limited effectiveness of the public workforce development system is its disconnection from urban and regional economic development strategies. Local and metropolitan economic development policy consists of efforts to enhance the competitiveness of locales for business activity; local officials' twin motivations are revenue with which to operate the public sector and jobs for their constituents.[7] Concrete steps to address fiscal stress and un- and underemployment include financial incentives to attract business, tax abatements, and targeted infrastructure investments. Other tools (sometimes called "new wave" economic development

policies) include support and training for entrepreneurs, business incuba-
tors, venture capital, and technical assistance to small and medium-sized
enterprises. Most communities that undertake economic development programs, however, devote a significant portion of their attention and resources
to tax and infrastructure policies, often coming under fire for subsidizing
industrial location without critically examining either the fiscal implications or the labor market effects of the subsidy packages extended (see Fisher
2007; Schweke 2007; Weber 2007).

In recent years, as economic development practitioners have begun recognizing the vital role of human capital in economic growth, explicitly
labor-centered regional development strategy has expanded (Markusen
2008). One vehicle for human capital-centered regional development is the
sector initiative or industry partnership, under which economic development agencies, employers, industry associations, and providers of education
and training collaborate to build and enhance labor "pipelines" in strategically important industries and occupations.[8] Common industries for sector
programs include health care, biotechnology, and advanced manufacturing.
While governments have mounted sector initiatives in forty states and the
District of Columbia, the State of Pennsylvania's Department of Labor and
Industry has one of the most active industry partnership programs, having
served more than 6,000 employers and reached tens of thousands of (largely
incumbent) workers with training and skills upgrading (National Skills Coalition 2009). In 2006, the U.S. Department of Labor conferred a federal
imprimatur on sector partnerships at a metropolitan level with its Workforce Innovation in Regional Development (WIRED) Initiative, granting
$325 million to thirty-nine metropolitan regions for strategic human capital
partnerships. A central goal of WIRED was to help each region build a more
competitive workforce or "talent pipeline" that would drive innovation in a
sector or sectors (see Wolf-Powers 2012).

There is a subtle distinction (though not a necessary contradiction) between (1) sector initiatives aimed primarily at training incumbent workers
or students in postsecondary programs with the goal of making a region's
businesses more competitive and (2) initiatives aimed at creating pathways
into the workforce for the disadvantaged individuals discussed at the start
of this chapter. One example illustrating this distinction is the Biotech Human Capital Project, an initiative sponsored in the Delaware Valley Region
from 2006 to 2009 by an intermediary called the Life Science Career Alliance.

The project engaged area community colleges to design a curriculum for entry-level technical employees in bio-research and bio-manufacturing, leading to a certificate in two frequently used laboratory procedures, cell culture and fermentation. While program sponsors had originally envisioned that this certificate could work as a stand-alone credential, obtained in a short period by disadvantaged workers who would then be eligible for entry-level jobs, all but one of the participating community colleges chose to integrate the curriculum into their two-year associate's degree programs in biotechnology. It was clear in retrospect that a talent pipeline conceived of as preparing today's (post-high school) students for tomorrow's jobs led directly through a two-year degree program. While promising, this model will not reach students who have failed in (and been failed by) secondary schools and whose chances of attaining postsecondary degrees (as opposed to shorter-term credentials) are small (see Wolf-Powers 2012).

Other sector initiatives have the express purpose of helping people without postsecondary degrees gain enough industry-specific occupational skills to increase their earnings. These efforts rely on strong and direct ties to the demand side of the labor market, on intensive "wraparound" case management and follow-up services for participants who require them, and on workplace literacy and numeracy as fundamental areas of instruction. They target "middle-skilled" occupations in which an industry-recognized credential, such as a practical nursing license or a computer technology certification (such as A+), is both valid and valuable in the labor market (see Holzer and Lerman 2007). For example, Per Scholas, a Bronx-based program founded in 1995, trains between 400 and 500 low-income adults and youth per year in information technology skills, and achieved an 85 percent graduation rate and an 80 percent placement rate in 2010, primarily in entry-level IT administrator jobs with annual salaries of $30,000–$45,000.[9] Per Scholas' success relies on contextualized learning, a recognized industry certification process including customer service accreditation, internship opportunities during training, and active programs for "alumni" who wish to continue their education or obtain additional credentials (Chapple 2006; Leavitt 2011; Maguire et al. 2010). Brooklyn Networks, run under the auspices of an established neighborhood-based housing development and social services organization, is similarly structured to provide entrée to blue- and gray-collar jobs in telecommunications data cabling. This program, which like Per Scholas offers industry-certified training, depends on its strong connections with large companies like Time Warner Cable as well as with small contractors whose clients hire them to outfit offices with wire-line and wireless data communications equipment (see Wolf-Powers 2005).

Evidence strongly suggests that sector-based programs are effective. A random assignment study published by Public/Private Ventures in 2010 evaluated Per Scholas and two other model sector programs—the Wisconsin Regional Training Partnership in Milwaukee, and Jewish Vocational Service in Boston—and found that, compared with a control group, participants in these programs[10] had higher earnings, were more likely to be consistently working, were more likely to work in jobs with higher wages, and were more likely to work in jobs with benefits (Maguire et al. 2010). In Philadelphia, the Job Opportunity Investment Network (JOIN), which supports a number of sector and industry partnership initiatives,[11] is conducting a return on investment study of these programs that relies on direct and contingent estimation of costs and benefits for both businesses and worker participants. Examples of business benefits include reduced hiring and training costs, increased government grants, and increased profit attributable to enhanced worker productivity, while the benefits to workers are increased compensation and enhanced skills. Preliminary results indicate highly positive returns to both business and worker participants in JOIN's sector initiatives, although businesses capture the most value from short-term training and general participation in partnerships, while workers gain more when training is longer term and leads to promotion (Green and Back 2011). Community colleges are also important actors in sectoral training programs. North Carolina's acclaimed BioWork program, run through thirteen community colleges, is designed to create opportunities for non-college-educated workers in the "new economy" industry of bio-pharmaceutical manufacturing. A recent study found that students at BioWork colleges that had strong relationships with employers and offered "integrated intermediary services" in addition to training (such as structured exchanges with company representatives, internships, and active, sector-specific job placement) were more likely than students from BioWork colleges with weaker employer relationships to receive offers from pharmaceutical and bio-processing manufacturing employers (Lowe, Goldstein, and Donegan 2011).

The initiatives that the founders of the "sector strategies" movement began in the early 1990s have improved substantially with adjustment and experimentation over the past two decades. Sectoral employment initiatives attract the most talented and creative administrators and program managers entering the workforce field today. They have gained an increasingly strong reputation for effectiveness when compared to standard short-term training in the public workforce system. Particularly when labor markets are tight, they have also contributed to economic development goals, raising productivity and lowering firms' turnover and training costs. These initiatives acknowledge the consensus that the equivalent of a secondary education, plus some postsecondary occupational training, is a gating condition both for household economic well-being and for household contribution to a healthy metropolitan economy. Although the sector programs often involve secondary schools or community colleges as partners, they also acknowledge the need for pathways through the education system that are non-traditional, and that culminate in certifications rather than formal degrees (Green and Back 2011; Lowe, Goldstein, and Donegan 2011; Maguire et al. 2010; National Network of Sector Partners 2011).

Notably, the development and refinement of sector programs over the past two decades has been driven almost entirely by private philanthropies: the Ford Foundation, the Annie E. Casey Foundation, the Knight Foundation, the Hitachi Foundation, and other national and local funders. The vast majority of successful sector-based initiatives operate apart from the public workforce system, finding it impossible to fit their activities into that system's often inflexible template. As noted above, participants in Workforce Investment Act programs sometimes access training vouchers that they can apply to programs of their choice, but many providers find the compliance process prohibitive and choose not to participate, particularly given the low level of resources available (Leavitt 2011). Sector initiatives are also only tenuously linked to secondary school curricula in most cases; as Carnevale aptly puts it, "school to work has been supplanted by school to college" (2010: 6).

The limited effectiveness of the public workforce development system is a result of its disconnection both from formal educational pathways and from urban and regional economic development strategies. Sector initiatives present an opportunity to affirmatively bridge that disconnection. In an urban and metropolitan policy context, it is difficult to achieve the same level of mobilization around effective workforce development that cities apply in the economic development arena, because the benefits of workforce development accrue over the long term and do not provide obvious opportunities to powerful stakeholders in the way that infrastructure investments, real estate development subsidies, and traditional tax incentives do (see Giloth 2004: 18). However, human capital-centered responses to the problems of poverty, inequality, and underutilized urban and metropolitan assets have become a matter of increasing public interest and awareness. The current moment—when the so-called "educational slow-down" seems to be of increasing concern to economic policymakers all along the political spectrum— may offer an occasion for renewed mobilization.

Aligning Workforce Policy with Economic Development Policy

Other contributors to this volume discuss other important pieces of this puzzle, including how to connect expanded access to postsecondary training more directly to high schools through school-to-career initiatives (Nancy Hoffman), and how to improve outcomes at the postsecondary institutions that economically vulnerable students are most likely to attend (Thomas Bailey and Clive R. Belfield; William G. Tierney). We propose two policies that would transform the second chance workforce system and link it more directly with urban and metropolitan economic development practices. We also propose a shift in local economic development policy that would orient it more directly toward the development of human capital.

Convert Second Chance Workforce Development into a Truly Joint Effort Between Federal and State Labor and Education Departments

While there has been a gradual but dramatic reorientation toward education policy as the nation's primary employment-related policy, this shift has yet to be institutionalized. The Obama Administration moved affirmatively in this direction in its FY 2011 budget with the Workforce Innovation Fund, an initiative to spur collaborations between state-level adult literacy, postsecondary education access, and occupational training efforts through the use of cross-program waivers and other mechanisms (Rahman and Muro 2010). Given the centrality of postsecondary learning to employment, and the fact that mainstream education institutions serve disadvantaged adults' needs particularly poorly, the shift embodied in the Workforce Innovation Fund is timely and important; continued administrative differentiation among services concerned with job readiness, basic verbal and mathematical skills, workplace literacy, and occupational training serves no one. If work-force development professionals are brave enough to turn their backs on the sinking ship that is WIA Title I and embrace an entirely new paradigm, the result could be new and repaired connections between education and em-ployment that would help reduce poverty and strengthen urban and metro-politan economies.

Like many of the current administration's innovative social policies, however, the extreme fiscal timidity of the labor-education harmonization idea imperils its chances of achieving change. Reconciliation legislation for FY 2011 cut the fund's size from $261 million to $125 million, with $380 million proposed for 2012—amounts profoundly inappropriate to the scale of the problem. In a few states, collaborations between workforce systems, education systems, and welfare-to-work systems housed in human services agencies are undertaking bolder experiments in this regard. Examples of this collaboration—in Washington, Oregon, Kentucky, and Arkansas—can lead the way for other states (Center for an Urban Future 2011).

Make Sector-Based Initiatives Central to the Postsecondary Education and Training Proposition

As described above, evidence suggests that public and philanthropic invest-ments in sector-based occupational training programs are paying notable dividends for disadvantaged workers and for employers. Sector programs honor adults' need for pathways through the education system that are non-traditional in nature and that can culminate in certifications rather than formal degrees. They engage employers directly and intensively, provide ex-tensive support services, including literacy and numeracy training, and as noted above, prioritize "middle-skill" jobs for which industry-recognized credentials translate into family-supporting earnings. However, these pro-grams reach a miniscule proportion of all potential beneficiaries. No esti-mate of the number of people served annually by sector-based initiatives exists, but it is surely less than 1 percent of the "11 million low-income, dis-located or imprisoned adults with an immediate ability to benefit" from adult education and training (Carnevale 2010: 9).

The philanthropic actors whose resources drove the sector strategies movement at its outset were acting on the hypothesis that by raising skill lev-els, productivity, and industry-specific preparation on the supply side of the

labor market, and by working closely with employers, labor market intermediaries could help non-college-bound individuals increase their chances of
escaping poverty. Provisionally, at least, this hypothesis has proven valid. A
comprehensive policy to improve postsecondary educational opportunities
for this population can draw directly on these successes.

Use Economic Development Incentives to Maximize
the Hysteresis Effect of Workforce Investment

We now move from policies that explicitly target human capital to an adaptation strategy for traditional economic development policy. Traditional
economic development incentive policies are frequent targets of criticism.
Detractors claim that any increases in demand for local labor or increases in
the wage that result from these policies will quickly be canceled out by in-
migration and by rising prices. They argue as well that economic development is a "zero sum game" because it shifts jobs around from place to place
rather than creating new wealth, and that the tax expenditures associated
with development incentives have deleterious local fiscal effects. Economic
development incentives are thus inefficient, and their benefits accrue to
owners of land and capital and do not reach un- and underemployed populations (Fisher 2007).

Some scholars have countered, however, that traditional economic development incentives can lead to positive economic impacts, especially in communities that have high unemployment (Bartik 1991, 2007). The theoretical
basis for this conclusion is that people in places with high unemployment
have lower reservation wages (meaning that they need less inducement to
trade off leisure for labor) and thus place a higher value on the earnings from
any job they may obtain. An empirical analysis by Bartik (1991) showed that
for a 1 percent increase in unemployment in an area, people reduce their
reservation wage between 1.2 and 1.6 percent. The local "value of a job" in a
high-unemployment area will be significantly higher than in a low-
unemployment area. If economic development incentive policies help move
jobs to these areas, the policies create value. In other words, attracting jobs to
places with high unemployment increases national "labor-producer surplus."

In addition to gains in labor-producer surplus, according to Bartik, traditional economic development policies, if they induce job growth, have
long-run labor market effects. This conclusion is based on data indicating

that shocks that affect the employment growth rate in a region, even temporarily, permanently affect employment and earnings levels through a "hysteresis" phenomenon (1991: 11). Economic theory predicts a rapid return to equilibrium in the wake of demand shocks, implying that an increase in local job growth has essentially no effect on long-run employment or earnings. However, Bartik found, using a model estimated from data on unemployment, wage rates, prices, and worker characteristics for twenty-five large metropolitan areas, that employment growth increased labor force participation rates and raised real earnings; earnings growth resulted not from increases in the real wage rate but from upgrades in occupational status, and from the acquisition of skills and employability by unemployed workers who obtained jobs in the short run. Significantly, Bartik found that real income growth in the wake of demand shocks is greatest for low-income groups, for Blacks and for less educated workers—even accounting for a regressive distribution of benefits from the increased property values induced by growth. This suggests that if economic development incentives induce investment that would not otherwise have occurred in a local labor market, they can have a positive effect on growth and a progressive impact on the income distribution.[12]

In addition to constituting a strong argument for traditional industrial attraction policies, the credibility of the hysteresis argument also provides a rationale for policies centered on the development of human capital. The logic is as follows: if economic development by traditional means can increase overall welfare and help low-income individuals in high-unemployment cities, then what if the shocks catalyzed by industrial attraction activity were accompanied by concerted local efforts to improve educational attainment and preparation for work? Under this rubric, officials offering subsidies to a firm to locate in their city would actively accompany location incentives with incentives to create on-the-job learning opportunities for incumbent workers, and to focus more resources on employing, training, and promoting entry-level workers. As noted above, low-earning workers receive very little of the incumbent worker training offered by private firms to their employees; a policy linked to a financial incentive (for example, a workforce development participation clause in a tax abatement agreement) could change this in a particular case, yielding benefits for a locality's low-paid and unemployed workers. Workforce development intermediaries have been shown to help direct businesses toward a more even distribution of workforce training opportunities (Lowe 2007).

Business participation in workforce development via incentive agree-ments could take several forms. Businesses might chose to work with local educational and training intermediaries to "order" training services for their incumbent and/or entry level employees. Or they might offer in-house training in cooperation with local workforce investment boards. Workforce development participation may not create many additional cost demands on businesses, and could actually work to target already existing training funds. Economic development officials in local and state government also need to be more selective about the types of firms they attract and grow by means of incentives. Firms with mid-level job positions that are likely to be filled by unemployed and underemployed people from the surrounding re-gion have a larger positive welfare effect than firms that create higher-paying jobs more likely to be filled by in-migrants (see Persky, Felsenstein, and Carlson 2004).

How could we evaluate localities' efforts to apply human capital strate-gies within traditional economic development practice? One way would be to measure changes over time in various measures of the "human capital

Table 10.2. Measures of Human Capital

	Pre-Workforce	Transition	Workforce	Source
Basic Learning Stocks				
Reading proficiency scores	+	+	+	NCES
Math proficiency scores	+	+	+	NCES
High school graduation rate	+	+		Census
Grade school attainment (literacy proxy)		−	−	NCES/Census
Complex Learning Stocks				
Percent college educated		+	+	Census
Percent post secondary		+	+	Census
Doctorate/professional production		+	+	Census
Median years of education		+	+	Census
Grade school attainment (literacy proxy)		−	−	NCES/Census

+ = positive indicator
− = negatve indicator
Source: Framework adapted from Lehnen and McGregor 1994.

stocks" in a city or metro region. The table below proposes a set of such measures. "Complex learning" stocks, which include indicators such as proportion of college graduates in the population, speak to the ability of an area to be economically competitive in the near term. The "basic learning" measure indicates levels of literacy and skill as measured in a region's school-age population. This metric is roughly predictive of a region's future competitiveness, an indication of what is in store as young learners mature and enter postsecondary education and the labor force.[13] Using the basic and/or complex human capital stocks of a region (or changes in these) as dependent variables in an equation, researchers might attempt to isolate the effect of policy on changes in those stocks.

Conclusion

Urban and regional economists have shown that a skilled labor force is a key source of place-based competitive advantage. The evidence is so compelling that policymakers are now routinely urged to accord human capital a stature equal to that of physical capital in their conceptualization of growth. Cities with relatively low endowments of human capital are unlikely to have healthy growth going forward if they do not make strategic investments in secondary and postsecondary education for their residents. Yet subsidies to capital and real estate ventures continue to dominate economic development practice, while education and training interventions play a marginal role.

This chapter proposes several ways to draw labor market institutions (specifically, those serving adults whose K–12 education has not prepared them well for the labor market) further into the center of ongoing conversations about place-based competitive advantage and regional equity. First, analyzing the current "state of play" in adult vocational training and basic literacy policy as funded under the Workforce Investment Act, the chapter suggests that "second chance" workforce development should become a truly joint effort between departments of education and labor at both the federal and the state levels. Employment and training for adults that is divorced from basic education and pathways to postsecondary credentialization is no longer a credible strategy—if indeed it ever was. Second, the chapter recommends the widespread adoption by the public sector of the kinds of sector-based initiatives largely funded heretofore with philanthropic dollars. These initiatives have proven successful in helping disadvantaged adults navigate postsecondary pathways that, while culminating in certifications rather than formal degrees, nevertheless have a strong track record in promoting economic mobility and success. Finally, we argue that since job growth in high-unemployment areas generates a hysteresis effect, permanently elevating a region's employment and labor force participation rates and growing workers' long-term earnings, investment in workforce preparation (either by private firms or in the public sector), is a key complement to traditional economic development incentives. Whether provided by the public sector or required of firms in exchange for considerations such as tax abatements, training for frontline workers can amplify the expected hysteresis effect of local economic development.

If political mobilization around these proposals begins tomorrow, it will occur in an extremely hostile budget environment. Current policy, in the form of the Obama Administration's Workforce Innovation Fund initiative, offers the states grants to better align their education and labor force policies, and shrewd states and localities can implement economic development incentives more effectively without necessarily spending more money than before. But in order to be more widely adopted and better supported by the federal government in the future, policies that align education, economic development, and workforce development must show that they do a better job than the status quo policy at creating real changes in social welfare in cities and metropolitan regions. Researchers will need to develop and apply evaluation methodologies that test the efficacy of these proposed interventions and guide policymakers accordingly.

CHAPTER 11

Creating Effective Education and Workforce Policies for Metropolitan Labor Markets in the United States

Harry J. Holzer

How well do our education policies prepare America's youth for the labor market? What challenges limit our success, and what opportunities do we have for improvement? Can public policy play a greater role in encouraging more success? Many chapters in this volume have addressed these issues already. In this chapter, I provide my own summary of what we know on these issues, incorporating but also complementing many of the perspectives provided by the other authors.

In addition, I consider these questions as they apply to the unique characteristics of metropolitan areas in the United States. Most labor markets are metropolitan in nature, with workers commuting across center cities and suburban municipalities to jobs wherever they are located. In most metro areas, jobs (especially those paying higher wages) and different groups of residents are distributed unevenly; White and minority residents and those with higher and lower incomes are often quite highly segregated from each other residentially. These characteristics of metro areas should be taken into account as we consider what kinds of education and workforce policies and reforms to implement.

Accordingly, this chapter begins with a brief overview of the future U.S. labor market, including a review of trends in the demand for labor. In particular, I consider demand for both middle- and high-skill jobs, where the former are defined as those requiring some postsecondary education or training (broadly defined) beyond a high school diploma but less than a bachelor's degree, and the latter are defined as those requiring a bachelor's degree or higher. I then review the challenges limiting so many young Americans as they prepare for the labor market, as well as what we know about programs and policies that might improve observed outcomes.

Finally, I review the characteristics of U.S. metropolitan areas that exacerbate the challenges we face—especially the uneven distribution of people and jobs within and across those areas. I argue that residential segregation and the patterns of job location we observe in these areas worsen outcomes for disadvantaged populations, in terms of both education and employment. Given these patterns and consequences, I consider how education and workforce policies can be adapted to the metropolitan context in the United States. The chapter closes with some recommendations for advancing a strong education and workforce agenda in metropolitan America.

For What Jobs Should We Prepare Workers? The Future of the U.S. Labor Market

Are well-paying jobs generally disappearing from America, as some critics (such as Dobbs 2004) have alleged? Not really. In previous work (Holzer et al. 2011), I have shown that high-quality jobs continued to grow strongly in numbers and compensation during the 1990s and into the 2000s.[1]

But well-paying jobs now require a higher range of worker skills than in the past. Indeed, the kinds of jobs that are disappearing are those that pay well for workers with very few cognitive skills or educational credentials beyond high school; manufacturing jobs for unskilled workers in particular are disappearing. Instead well-paying jobs now appear in a range of sectors—including construction, health care, professional services, and even retail trade—that require stronger analytical or communication skills as well as postsecondary education or training of some kind. These good jobs are increasingly being filled by more highly skilled workers than in earlier years.[2]

Another issue that frequently appears in the literature involves the extent to which the labor market in the United States is becoming "polarized" between a growing high-skill, high-wage sector and a growing low-skill, low-wage sector, with a rapidly shrinking middle. David Autor (2010) presents evidence on growing polarization, and his work has led commentators and journalists to describe the future U.S. labor market as an "hourglass" or a "dumbbell," with lots of low-wage service sector jobs and lots of high-wage jobs for those with college and graduate degrees, but few well-paying jobs in the middle for those without such degrees. Autor attributes such developments to the replacement of routine task performance in middle-paying jobs by computer technology, whereas both higher- and lower-skill jobs require either analytical or communication tasks that are not routine and thus not easily done by computers.

But, as I have also previously argued (Holzer 2010), the polarization argument has been vastly overblown. Autor is correct that some categories of middle-wage jobs, especially those for production and clerical workers, have shrunk since 1980. But this has not occurred more generally. Other broad occupational categories that are frequently considered middle-skill or middle-wage—such as technicians, sales, construction, installation/repair of mechanical systems, and some service categories—have seen growing employment and/or relative wages over time, indicating positive shifts in employer demand toward these fields.[3] Educational or training requirements have grown in many of these categories, with most of the better-paying jobs now requiring at least some postsecondary education or training.

Indeed, projections suggest that most jobs over the next decade will require some education or training beyond high school (Holzer and Lerman 2007; Carnevale, this volume). Yet at least half of American youth continue to leave school with only a high school diploma. While labor markets ultimately equilibrate, with most jobs filled, the imbalance between the demand for and supply of postsecondary education and training over time tends to widen the earnings gaps between those who have education and training and those who do not (Goldin and Katz 2008), thus leading to growing inequality overall.[4] As Baby Boomers begin to retire in greater numbers in the coming years and are replaced in the workforce by immigrants, "replacement demand" will further widen gaps between the demand for and supply of skills at both the middle and high ends of the labor market, contributing to a further widening of the gaps in pay between those with and those without the relevant skills.[5]

Challenges That Limit Our Ability to Prepare Young Adults with the Needed Skills

Why does the United States seem to have such difficulty generating enough workers with the skills needed to fill middle- and high-skill jobs without widening inequality?

Many factors contribute to our national "skills gaps." As is now well known, achievement gaps between lower-income Americans and those from middle- and upper-income families, and between Whites and minorities, open up very early in life (Fryer and Levitt 2004; Magnuson and Waldfogel 2008). Children from disadvantaged groups enter kindergarten already well behind their peers, and then they fall even further behind during their first several years of schooling. If anything, the gaps between income groups are likely widening as overall income inequality has grown more pronounced over time (Reardon 2010). Only modest progress has been made on closing the racial gap.

These gaps limit the ability of many youth to complete a high school diploma or to pursue any kind of postsecondary education or training, even of a more technical nature. These difficulties are further compounded by the fact that career and technical education (CTE) in the United States has not been developed to its fullest capacity. CTE has been plagued by legitimate concerns over tracking and a frequent disconnect between CTE and the labor market, and as a result, interest in CTE has fallen dramatically—in spite of the fact that there is evidence of quite positive impacts of CTE on short-term and medium-term earnings here and abroad, and perhaps on high school graduation rates as well (Silverberg et al. 2004; Ryan 2001). As Nancy Hoffman (this volume) concludes, much more could clearly be done to improve both the academic quality and labor market linkages of CTE.

For those who choose to pursue postsecondary education, a number of major challenges exist beyond just poor academic training in the K–12 years (Haskins, Holzer, and Lerman 2009). Rapid increases in the financial costs of higher education (outside of community colleges and the weakest public four-year institutions), in addition to capital market failures that constrain the liquidity of households, limit the access of lower- to middle-income households to public flagship universities as well as to elite private colleges and universities. Resource constraints at the non-flagship public colleges and universities increasingly limit opportunities there for many students (Bound and Turner 2008). In addition, many young people—including those with strong basic skills—lack information about the academic requirements for college study and do not adequately prepare in high school, and many seem relatively uninformed about financial aid options and other opportunities. The pressures of generating income and caring for children, especially among single parents, make college attendance and completion difficult as well.

Finally, our education and workforce systems are largely disconnected from employers and from each other, making transitions between these institutional worlds unnecessarily difficult. For instance, the U.S. Department of Labor runs over 3,000 One-Stop Career Centers around the country, which provide a range of employment services and some limited training to workers.[6] But this program, funded under the Workforce Investment Act (WIA), is much too small and under-resourced to have major impacts on the overall labor market.[7] (See Laura Wolf-Powers and Stuart Andreason's chapter in this volume for further discussion of this program.) Two- and four-year colleges often provide fairly little in the way of career counseling and job placement services, and students choose courses and concentrations with very little information on labor market conditions in their chosen fields (Jacobson and Mokher 2009). Even when college students know what fields (like health technology or nursing) provide strong demand and strong earnings, they often find limited course offerings and oversubscribed classes. At the same time, colleges and universities that receive the same per capita subsidies from their states regardless of what students study have few incentives to shift resources into areas of high demand, especially if the costs of equipment and instruction in these areas are high. And employers are frequently disconnected from both educational and labor market institutions, and are often unwilling to invest their own resources in training (especially for non-professional and non-managerial employees) for a variety of reasons.[8]

As a result of all of these factors, secondary and postsecondary student success rates as well as labor market outcomes in the United States are often discouraging. High school dropout rates, by the best estimates available (Heckman and Lafontaine 2007), remain close to 25 percent.[9] While attendance at postsecondary institutions has risen in recent years, completion rates of any kind of credential have not improved much. Completion rates are also highly correlated with the status and costs of the institutions themselves, even controlling for the characteristics of the students who attend them. Thus, completion rates are quite high at the elite private and public postsecondary institutions but much lower at low-cost public schools, and are quite low at most community colleges (Bailey et al. 2005). Since at least some of the return to education seems to be a "sheepskin effect"—or the value that comes with obtaining a diploma, as distinct from the return to time spent or courses completed—those who drop out of college enjoy fairly little return for their often substantial investments.

Even among those who complete degrees or certificates, the variance in earnings is extremely high (see also Carnevale, this volume). On average, those with associate's degrees earn more than those with certificates but considerably less than those with bachelor's degrees (Bailey and Belfield, this volume). But in some technical areas, earnings for those receiving certificates are higher than for many kinds of associate's degrees and even some four-year degrees, while the marginal returns for less-prepared students might be lower than the average returns we observe. All of this suggests that some students would be better off if steered to certain kinds of certificate programs, but such counseling is rarely available.

Of course, for those who do not complete any postsecondary education or training program, employment rates for the first several years are quite limited, and their earnings overall will stagnate for the longer term. Many such youth "disconnect" from the labor market as well as from school (Edelman, Holzer, and Offner 2006). This is especially true for men. Indeed, labor force participation rates have been declining for many years among less-educated men, while their participation in higher education lags behind that of young women (Jacob 2002). Especially among African American men, declining rates of labor force activity have been accompanied by very high rates of incarceration and non-custodial fatherhood (Holzer, Offner, and Sorensen 2005).

Can We Do Better?

Despite these challenges in our educational institutions and the disappointing education and labor market outcomes they generate, opportunities exist for improving the educational preparation Americans receive and their ability to fill well-paying jobs.

First, we are producing a growing body of rigorous evidence on "what works" at improving these outcomes, especially for the disadvantaged. Starting with secondary schools and their students, research shows that "Small Schools of Choice" in New York City generated significant increases in student achievement and high school graduation rates (Bloom et al. 2010), while the National Guard Challenge program has led to large increases in the attainment of high school diplomas or GEDs for those who had already dropped out (Millenky, Bloom, and Dillon 2010).

As Nancy Hoffman (this volume) writes, research findings also demonstrate the potential of high-quality CTE to improve educational attainment as well as labor market earnings, especially among those not bound for college. In rigorous evaluations, the career academies—technical schools within broader high schools that target specific economic sectors for which students receive training and part-time employment in addition to their other academic classes—generated large increases in earnings, especially for at-risk young men, which persisted for at least eight years after high school (Kemple 2008). At least early on in the program, high school dropout rates were reduced as well.[10] Analyses of other efforts, such as tech-prep and apprenticeship training more broadly, reinforce the notion that high-quality CTE can have quite positive effects on educational and earnings outcomes (Lerman 2007).

At the postsecondary level, the Opening Doors demonstration has shown that a variety of approaches—including learning communities, mandatory counseling sessions, and merit-based financial aid—can increase course completion and credit attainment among low-income students in community college (Brock 2010). While the track record of developmental or remedial classes in community colleges is not very positive in general, programs that integrate remedial and occupational training, like I-BEST in the state of Washington, hold the promise of improving student performance and course completion rates.[11]

As for using education and training to improve labor market outcomes of the disadvantaged, the track record of training funded by the Workforce Investment Act is relatively strong, given the very small amounts invested (Heinrich and King 2010). But, as Laura Wolf-Powers and Stuart Andreason (this volume) observe, much bigger average impacts have been generated by sectoral training programs, in which an intermediary works with employers in a particular sector to generate training for jobs in that sector plus support services for the disadvantaged (Osterman 2007; Maguire et al. 2010; Roder and Elliott 2011). Interestingly, completion rates and labor market success after completion appear to be somewhat higher at private proprietary schools than at community colleges (Rosenbaum, Deil-Amen, and Person 2006), at least partly because they provide much stricter student guidance on course-taking and much stronger linkages to the labor market through job placement activities and counseling.[12]

For displaced as opposed to disadvantaged workers, the best evidence on education and training comes from Jacobson, Lalonde, and Sullivan (2005), who find quite sizable returns in more technical fields and/or those facing strong labor market demand. For incumbent workers, somewhat less rigorous evidence strongly suggests that state-level tax credits raise the amount of such training, and provide cost-effective returns to the less-educated frontline employees who get such training (Holzer et al. 1993; Hollenbeck 2008). Finally, for low-income youth, we have some recent evidence from the Youth Opportunities program at the U.S. Department of Labor, which provided grants to thirty-six low-income neighborhoods to generate comprehensive education and employment programs for youth. Evaluations of the program showed that resources targeted at neighborhoods could be used to generate systemic efforts that lead to improvements in both school enrollment and employment and earnings (DIR 2008).

Of course, much remains to be learned about effective education and training for future American workers, and the need for continued experimentation and evaluation is great. Nevertheless, some patterns of what is effective at improving skills and earnings can be inferred from these results. In general, some combination of the following seems to work:

- having students obtain some kind of occupational training or certification at either the secondary or postsecondary level;
- actively steering students toward, and linking them with, employers who provide well-paying jobs in high-demand sectors, especially guided by labor market data; and
- providing students with a range of effective supports and services (such as child care and transportation, mandatory counseling, performance-linked financial aid, or stipends) while they are training and even after employment has begun.

Frequently, an effective intermediary is needed to bring together the students (or workers), training providers, and employers, as well as the supports needed for student success.

Some caveats should also be mentioned here, in terms of what kinds of education and training should be provided, and to whom. For instance, it is important that the training provided be at least somewhat portable when individuals ultimately change jobs and industries, and especially when future labor market demands shift (toward new goods and services or new modes of producing them). The training provided should therefore not be too narrowly tailored, and should provide a range of more general skills as well as skills that are more narrowly occupational or sectoral. Employers must also be encouraged and assisted in retraining incumbent or newly hired workers whose general skills are largely appropriate but who now require some newer or more specific skills to meet new production needs.[13]

In addition, there have been legitimate concerns historically over whether low-income and minority children get "tracked" away from routes to college when they are placed into vocational education. To maximize educational opportunities for all young people, any efforts to strengthen CTE approaches must incorporate strong academics and keep open (or even encourage) postsecondary options for those students, as the Career Academies have clearly done.[14] Finally, we must also recognize that high-quality CTE, sectoral training, and the like do not target those students or workers with the worst basic skill deficits, but instead focus on those who are capable of reading at least at the ninth-grade level and can handle some community college-level work. For those not capable of mastering this level of classroom instruction, other options might be more appropriate. These could include transitional jobs to encourage more successful participation in the labor market, plus a range of additional incentives and supports to reward and help with that participation (Bloom and Butler 2007).

To improve our knowledge base regarding what works in preparing students for the workplace and to encourage and support more innovative activities, the U.S. Department of Labor and major foundations have both awarded a range of competitive grants to community colleges, community-based organizations, localities, and states in the past few years (Holzer and Nightingale 2009).[15] These grants not only seek to develop innovative approaches to curricula and support services that would raise completion rates at community colleges. They also seek to improve the linkages between educational institutions and the labor market, often trying to generate state-level systems (as Bradlow and colleagues, this volume, discuss) that merge education, workforce development, and economic development, while relying on the use of administrative data on labor market trends to guide these developments. We anticipate that we will learn more about what works in this area over the next several years from all of this innovative activity and from rigorous evaluation of these efforts.

The Geographic Context: U.S. Metropolitan Areas

The vast majority of Americans now live in metropolitan areas, including both central cities and suburbs. Furthermore, most labor markets are metropolitan in nature, with workers commuting between city centers and suburban municipalities as they travel to work and back home each day.

Most workers and their families make choices about where to live and where to work, and also about how much time they are willing to spend commuting between those two locations; but these choices are constrained by the relative costs of living in different areas and, for minorities, by housing discrimination. Employers also choose where to locate their businesses based on a variety of factors, such as costs and the kinds of customers and employees to whom they want to be most accessible.

The result is that different demographic groups and jobs are distributed quite unevenly within and across metropolitan areas. Residential populations are segregated by race/ethnicity as well as income, and jobs are distributed unevenly as well. While declining somewhat in recent decades, such segregation remains very high among Blacks and fairly high among Latinos, especially new immigrants (Raphael and Stoll 2005, 2010; Frey 2010).[16]

Residential populations for all major groups and jobs have also been decentralizing in recent years, with greater growth in suburban areas than in central cities. But even within the suburbs, residential segregation and uneven job distributions persist. Holzer and Stoll (2007) have documented that minority populations are growing most rapidly in suburbs with lower average incomes while jobs are growing more rapidly in those with higher incomes. Furthermore, Andersson, Holzer, and Lane (2005) have shown that not only the quantity of jobs but also their quality is uneven, with the best (highest-wage) jobs locating either downtown or in the higher-income suburban areas where they are most accessible to workers with the highest levels of skill (as well as Whites).

This pattern of unevenness in the locations of populations and jobs within metropolitan areas appears to have important effects on the outcomes observed for different groups. In particular, minority and lower-income groups experience two kinds of adverse consequences as a result of

metropolitan segregation and decentralization: (1) worse employment outcomes, due to "spatial mismatch" between their places of residence and
work;[17] and (2) worse educational and personal outcomes, caused by "neighborhood" effects and other forms of uneven access to good schools and other
kinds of resources.[18]

To be most effective, then, any policies designed to improve the preparation of American students for the workforce should take into account the
unevenness of opportunity in metropolitan America and strive to counter
its negative effects on both education and employment. But how might these
policies be adapted to fit our metropolitan areas and to maximize opportunities for minority and/or low-income residents there?

Policies designed to address metropolitan issues and effects are frequently categorized into those that

- improve the mobility of inner-city and/or minority residents to
  suburban areas of mixed races and incomes;
- develop housing, schools, and/or businesses in inner-city or predominantly low-income areas; or
- improve the access of inner-city/low-income residents to schools
  or jobs throughout the metro area (Boustan and Margo 2008; Pastor and Turner 2010).

Efforts to move residents of inner-city or low-income areas to more suburban or mixed-income communities usually include provision of reloca-
tion services and supports to those with Section 8 housing vouchers, as in
the Moving to Opportunity (MTO) demonstration project.[19] Those seeking
to improve the supply of low-income housing in those areas (as opposed to
the demand by residents for that housing) include tax credits for low-income
housing or "inclusionary zoning" arrangements. Efforts to develop low-
income neighborhoods economically include enterprise or empowerment
zones and "New Market" tax credits; most studies have generally found these
to be somewhat ineffective in generating new jobs per dollar spent, especially
for zone residents, though there are a few exceptions.[20] Attempts to improve
the quality of low-income housing in these neighborhoods include the Clinton Administration's Hope VI project to disperse low-income housing and to
create mixed-income housing developments (Popkin and Cunningham
2009), as well as the Choice Neighborhoods grants of the Obama Administration. And efforts to improve the quality of local schools can take a variety

of forms, including the higher accountability and standards approaches emphasized in Washington, D.C. (under Chancellor Michelle Rhee), New York City (under Superintendent Joel Klein), and elsewhere, as well as the best known charter school models, like the Harlem Children's Zone in New York or the KIPP schools.[21]

Finally, the mixed strategies designed to improve the access of inner-city or minority residents to opportunities throughout the metropolitan area might include vouchers and other models of "school choice," like the Washington, D.C. Opportunity Scholarship program (Wolf et al. 2010), as well as efforts designed to improve transportation to suburban jobs, like Bridges to Work (BtW).[22] In a somewhat related vein, metropolitan development strategies aimed at improving opportunities for inner-city residents in suburban economic development projects or limiting sprawl have been developed as well (Pastor and Turner 2010).[23]

Within this range of possible approaches, what might be done to improve the educational preparation of inner-city residents, and those of low-income areas more generally, for metropolitan jobs? Perhaps the most straightforward idea is simply to bring the most promising and proven workforce preparation strategies described above to the schools that serve disadvantaged or minority students within metro areas, and especially to improve their links to employers and the labor market, while also providing supports and services to improve completion rates there. Among the best ways to do this might be the expansion of career academies, apprenticeships, and other high-quality CTE efforts at the relevant secondary schools (along with appropriate postsecondary options), and expanding academic support services, career counseling, and other labor market placement efforts at community colleges attended by large numbers of minority and low-income workers. Of course, these schools might actually be the ones located in low-income or minority neighborhoods, as well as those that are quite accessible to these populations because of a school choice program. Efforts to build youth-serving systems that encompass both education and employment options, like the systems recently created in the Youth Opportunity cities and in other cities, are other ways of accomplishing these goals.[24]

More broadly, there might be ways of building on these latter efforts to create more effective metropolitan-wide education and workforce systems that would give residents of low-income neighborhoods better access to both education opportunities and jobs throughout the entire area. For instance, special technical assistance might be made available to One-Stop Centers in urban areas or career counselors at urban community colleges to improve their contacts with suburban employers. Federal or state workforce boards might encourage local WIBs that have different jurisdictions within the metropolitan area (such as those organized on county lines) to partner more closely in their workforce development activities.

Of course, how to do any of the above effectively is not clearly known at the moment. Yet we have some idea of what the critical ingredients might be in developing these services and building more effective metropolitan-wide systems. For instance, having good data about metropolitan job market opportunities available to all, regardless of where in the metro area they are located, would be an essential first step. Good data are now increasingly available through outlets such as the Local Employment Dynamics (LED) partnership between state labor market information agencies and the U.S. Census Bureau, which provides data on quarterly employment growth, as well as the online Job Central listing of current job vacancies operated by the National Association of State Workforce Agencies (NASWA) and DirectEmployers.[25]

As we noted earlier, listing vacant jobs or rates of employment growth alone will be insufficient to improve job market preparation and access without effective labor market *intermediaries* to read these data and communicate their findings to students and workers. These intermediaries, such as those who have operated the successful sectoral workforce programs described above, can provide a range of services to residents of low-income areas to improve their access to training and jobs wherever the latter are located in the metro area. For instance, the intermediaries can locate employers with job openings and develop effective training strategies to match low-income residents with those employers and with education or training providers. They can help overcome spatial geographic gaps by providing child care and transportation options, and even by effectively communicating to employers the potential of job candidates who might not otherwise appeal to them.[26]

For existing One-Stop Centers or community colleges, technical assistance and incentives might encourage them to cast wider nets, in terms of placing more workers with employers throughout the metro areas. In particular, state assistance to local colleges might be at least partly based on the extent to which they serve low-income individuals or residents of low-income areas, or how successfully they place these students in jobs. Such incentives would not (and should not) specifically need to target suburban jobs, but instead should be designed to encourage placements of graduates in good jobs wherever they are located. Of course, the development of such incentives (and performance measures more broadly) must be done with great care, so as not to generate undue "creaming" of the populations served, or to undercut existing academic standards for performance before credentials are awarded and trainees are placed into jobs.

Furthermore, federal and state governments might also encourage the formation of explicit metropolitan area-wide education and labor market institutions, such as educational agencies or workforce boards, that would bring together those that now exist separately at the county level. On the other hand, divorcing such institutions from the municipal boundaries that define most such jurisdictions might limit their effectiveness, as has sometimes been the case with various municipal planning organizations (MPOs).[27]

Moving Ahead

Whatever specific strategies are chosen to better link disadvantaged urban residents with education and job opportunities, there are a number of general ways forward to encourage such progress. For instance, the upcoming reauthorizations of the Elementary and Secondary Education Act (ESEA), the Workforce Investment Act (WIA) and perhaps the Perkins Act could be used as opportunities to improve educational certifications and links to the labor market, especially along these metropolitan-wide grounds. Special provisions could be included in these new bills to strengthen labor market linkages and support services at education and workforce institutions, and to create more effective metropolitan-wide practices and systems along the lines suggested above.

These legislative vehicles, or more broadly, the relevant federal agencies, could continue to use competitive grants to spur innovation and success. As noted earlier, the federal Departments of Education and Labor (plus several major foundations) have recently used a range of these grants to encourage such activity in community colleges and workforce boards, and more could be done along these lines. Specifically, such grants could be used explicitly to encourage system-building by state or metropolitan authorities, and to ensure that educational and employment opportunities throughout the metropolitan areas are available and accessible to minorities and low-income residents, wherever in those areas they happen to reside.

However we proceed, the goals of improving the educational preparation of all workers residing in metropolitan areas for the jobs available there, along the lines we have described above, should be among our top domestic policy priorities in the years ahead.

Conclusion

Laura W. Perna

Education is clearly critical to the economic status and well-being of individuals and our nation (Baum, Ma, and Payea 2010). In this volume, the chapters by Anthony Carnevale and colleagues as well as Thomas Bailey and Clive Belfield demonstrate that, on average, students have higher earnings when they complete additional levels of education, although the premium varies by major field. Bailey and Belfield also illustrate that the increase in earnings associated with higher levels of education is greater for individuals living in metropolitan than in non-metropolitan areas. While several authors acknowledge the many ways that society in general benefits from higher levels of education, the chapters in this volume also point to the particular benefits of increased educational attainment to metropolitan America.

In light of the well-documented benefits of higher levels of educational attainment, however, the chapters in this volume also articulate the need to do more to align the educational qualifications of workers with the knowledge demands of jobs, especially in our nation's metropolitan areas. Despite the presence of numerous colleges and universities, metropolitan areas are home to many individuals who have low levels of educational attainment. These individuals typically experience high rates of unemployment, have low incomes, and are disproportionately from racial/ethnic minority groups (Baum, Ma, and Payea 2010). Moreover, as Harry Holzer points out, average measures of educational attainment and employment often mask the disparity within a metropolitan area, particularly with regard to the availability of high-quality jobs and the extent to which residential segregation limits access of traditionally under-served populations to these high-quality jobs.

In addition, as Carnevale and his colleagues argue in their chapter, the projected increase in the education requirements of new jobs underscores the growing need to improve the alignment of educational programs with the knowledge and skills required by employers.

This volume offers useful insights into how to better achieve this goal. Together, the chapters in this volume inform understanding of the measurement and definition of the learning required by employers, the roles and contributions to workforce readiness of different educational sectors and providers, and the institutional practices and public policies that promote the educational preparation of today's students for tomorrow's jobs. Drawing from the chapters in this volume, this final chapter identifies recommendations for institutional leaders and public policymakers. The chapter also offers recommendations for future research that will further enhance knowledge of the institutional practices and public policies that most effectively promote the connection between education and employment in metropolitan America.

Implications for Institutional Leaders and Public Policymakers

As several authors of chapters in this volume note (Alan Ruby; Thomas Bailey and Clive Belfield), efforts to reform education to better address workforce needs are not new. Moreover, efforts to reform education and improve workforce readiness have historically been, and will continue to be, challenged by many forces. One challenge is that both the types of jobs available and the skills required to perform the available jobs are continually changing. As Ruby, Carnevale, Smith, and Strohl, and Bailey and Belfield describe, these changes have occurred in response to structural changes in the economy including the decline in the manufacturing industry and growth in the service industry, as well as changes in the organization of work, labor market specialization, and technology. In addition, reform efforts have been, and will continue to be, further challenged by constraints on the public financial resources available to support change.

Reform efforts are also limited by the legacy of past failures. As several authors observe (Bridget O'Connor; Nancy Hoffman), many in the United States are skeptical about the value of new "career and technical education" programs because of the poor performance of previous vocational education programs. These traditional programs have a "history of doing the right things badly or just doing the wrong things," as well as tracking disproportionate shares of low-income students and racial/ethnic minorities into low-wage jobs (see Bridget O'Connor's chapter). Along the same lines, Nancy Hoffman stresses the progress that is required to produce a system of career and technical education in the United States that effectively prepares youth for "productive employment."

While acknowledging the challenges, together the chapters in this volume also point to several programs that hold promise for improving the alignment between education and work and better preparing today's students for tomorrow's jobs. Several chapters note that research shows positive outcomes to be associated with well-designed programs that intentionally connect and integrate vocational training into academic courses (a.k.a. pathways programs, career pathways, or work-based learning initiatives) (Barghaus et al.; Richburg-Hayes, Armijo, and Merrill; O'Connor; Holzer). Such programs include career academies; Washington State's Integrated Basic Education and Skills Training (I-BEST) program; Youth Corps, Job Corps, and ChalleNGe programs; and the U.S. Department of Labor's Youth Opportunities Program. Suggesting the possibility of improving career and technical education in the United States, Hoffman notes that vocational education training systems in some other nations more effectively connect education and employment, and outlines the characteristics of these systems that may contribute to positive outcomes.

Stressing the utility of "multiple pathways," Ronald Ferguson recommends that formal connections between education and employment should begin when students are in the fifth grade, and continue through and beyond high school into postsecondary education. Ferguson also emphasizes the utility of involving multiple stakeholders (such as families, schools, churches, colleges, military, and employers) and identifies ten "strategic threads" for developing and sustaining multiple pathways programs.

Focusing on the workforce readiness of adult students, Laura Wolf-Powers and Stuart Andreason describe the potential of industry partnerships or sectoral initiatives. Representing collaborations involving employers and educational institutions (such as community colleges), as well as others (economic development agencies, industry associations), these initiatives are designed to prepare students for employment in targeted industries and occupations.

Beyond their specific program suggestions, together the chapters in this volume also lead to seven other recommendations for institutional leaders and public policymakers interested in improving the readiness and preparation of today's students for tomorrow's jobs in metropolitan America:

1. Provide a range of high-quality educational opportunities that recognize that not all individuals will earn college degrees.
2. Develop mechanisms that enable students to choose to participate in different education and career pathways without "tracking" them into specific options.
3. Ensure that all individuals have the information and knowledge required to choose the most appropriate education and career pathways.
4. Recognize that both generic and specific skills are required for jobs and careers in metropolitan America.
5. Develop mechanisms that support meaningful collaboration between education providers and employers.
6. Provide the supports and structures required to ensure that students successfully complete the educational programs that they enter.
7. Use public policy to encourage and support improved linkages between education and employment.

Provide a Range of High-Quality Educational Opportunities That Recognize That Not All Individuals Will Earn College Degrees

While the question of what the "right" amount of education is has been the subject of much debate, several chapter authors (Alan Ruby; Bridget O'Connor; Nancy Hoffman; Ronald Ferguson; Harry Holzer) acknowledge the reality that not everyone will earn a college degree. More completely debating the question of whether the United States should strive for "college for all," as advocated by the National Commission on the High School Senior Year (2001) and others, is beyond the scope of this book. What is clear from this volume, however, is the need for structures that recognize that, given the changing nature of the economy and demands of future jobs, all individuals must continue to learn beyond high school. Thus, the more important issues may be (1) What amounts of different kinds of learning, including relative amounts of formal postsecondary education versus specific job or workplace training, do students require? and (2) How should these types of learning be obtained?

One strength of our nation's educational system is the diversity of educational options and potential pathways that are available, especially in our nation's metropolitan areas. The related challenge is to ensure that all options and pathways are high quality, and can equip students with the education, knowledge, and skills required by employers.

The chapters in this volume suggest the roles that educational providers across the P–20 educational pipeline can play in promoting college and career readiness. Ferguson stresses the importance of beginning to integrate career and academic education during elementary school. O'Connor and Hoffman focus on the potential benefits of career and technical education programs for high school students. Hoffman, Bailey and Belfield, and Wolf-Powers and Andreason focus on the utility of initiatives targeting working adult students and students who are underprepared for postsecondary education by their high schools. At the postsecondary level, four-year colleges and universities (Carnevale, Smith, and Strohl), community colleges (Hoffman; Bailey and Belfield), and for-profit institutions (Tierney) all offer programs and degrees that are ultimately designed to prepare students for employment. Attention to all sectors, including for-profit postsecondary educational institutions, is essential if we are to ensure that today's workers have the educational preparation required for tomorrow's jobs.

Develop Mechanisms That Enable Individuals to Choose to Participate in Different Education and Career Pathways without the Use of "Tracking"

Recognizing that a traditional bachelor's degree program is not the best option for everyone, the chapters in this volume underscore the need for educational leaders and administrators as well as public policymakers to consider the best ways to enable individuals to pursue different education and career pathways, without resorting to tracking or some other mechanism that restricts potential educational options based on some set of predetermined characteristics. Institutional leaders and public policymakers must carefully consider such questions as, Who gets access to what amounts and forms of education and training? Who makes decisions about who gets to access what? How is information about various education and training opportunities best provided to various groups of students?

As several chapter authors note (Hoffman; Carnevale, Smith, and Strohl; Holzer), attention to the issue of tracking is especially important with regard to career and technical education programs. The reality of prior vocational educational programs is that low-income students and racial/ethnic minorities were disproportionately tracked into these programs, and these programs had poor outcomes for participating students. This legacy creates skepticism about the possible benefits of new career training and education programs, and concerns that such programs will again become a mechanism for channeling low-income students and racial/ethnic minorities onto a path that yields relatively few education or career-related benefits.

Along the same lines, educational leaders and public policymakers should also be vigilant about mechanisms that may funnel students into for-profit postsecondary educational institutions and other postsecondary educational programs that may produce only limited short- and long-term benefits for participants. For-profit colleges and universities enroll disproportionate shares of Blacks and Hispanics as well as students from low-income families (Baum, Ma, and Payea 2010). At the same time, for-profit postsecondary education institutions are plagued by low completion rates, as well as high rates of student borrowing and student loan default (Baum and Steele 2010; Knapp, Kelly-Reid, and Ginder 2011). For example, only 27 percent of students who enrolled in a four-year for-profit institution for the first time on a full-time basis in 2001 earned a bachelor's degree within six years, compared with 55 percent of their counterparts who entered public four-year institutions and 65 percent of those who entered private not-for-profit four-year institutions (Knapp, Kelly-Reid, and Ginder 2011). More than three-fourths of first-time, full-time students attending four-year for-profit institutions received federal student loans (81 percent) in 2008–9, compared with only 46 percent of those attending public four-year institutions and 59 percent of those attending private four-year not-for-profit institutions (Knapp, Kelly-Reid, and Ginder 2011). More than half (53 percent) of students who received bachelor's degrees from for-profit institutions in 2007–8 had a cumulative total debt of $30,500 or more, compared with only 24 percent of those receiving bachelor's degrees from private not-for-profit four-year institutions and 12 percent of those receiving bachelor's degrees from public four-year institutions (Baum and Steele 2010). The federal student loan default rate is considerably higher for students who attended for-profit institutions than for those who attended public or private colleges and universities (15 percent versus 7.2 percent and 4.6 percent in 2009, U.S. Department of Education 2011).

Thus, as William Tierney describes in his chapter, more attention must be paid to understanding the admissions and other practices of for-profit colleges and universities, as well as the other forces that contribute to the tendency of these institutions to enroll students from groups that are historically underrepresented in higher education. More information is also required to understand the short- and long-term education, career, and social status outcomes for students who receive their education from for-profit postsecondary institutions as well as other types of providers.

Ensure That All Students Have the Information and Knowledge Required to Choose the Most Appropriate Education and Career Pathways

One approach to reducing tracking of students with certain characteristics into specific educational pathways may be to ensure that all students and their families have the information required to make informed decisions at each step in the educational pipeline. As Harry Holzer and other chapter authors note, improved career and college counseling could help students better understand the academic requirements for future education and jobs, and help students make the "right" decisions about their education and career pathways. Yet current structures do not ensure the availability of accurate, complete, and relevant information for all students. Along the same lines, Alan Ruby observes the challenges of conveying information to students and educators about the skills, knowledge, and educational credentials that employers require.

Available data and research consistently indicate that educational providers at all levels can do more to ensure that students and their families have accurate and complete information to make informed decisions about their educational pathways. Although knowledge of college prices and financial aid is an established predictor of numerous college-related outcomes, research documents the low levels of knowledge that most students have about these matters (Perna and Steele 2011). Research also illustrates the ways that high school counselors shape students' high school aspirations, educational plans, readiness for college, and knowledge of college and financial aid (McDonough 1997, 2005a, 2005b; Perna et al. 2008). Moreover, high school counselors may be an especially important source of information when parents do not have the knowledge, prior direct experience, or other resources required to adequately guide their children through college-related processes (Furstenberg et al. 1999; McDonough 1997; Tierney and Auerbach 2005). Yet the availability of college counseling varies across high schools, not only in terms of actual student-to-counselor ratios, but also in terms of time devoted to college counseling, relationships between school counselors and college admissions staff, and types of counseling services offered, as well as the availability of other school structures to support college counseling, such as a school's mission and norms regarding college-going, and the degree of college-preparatory curricular focus (McDonough 1997; Perna and Thomas 2009). Other forces limit the extent to which high school counselors offer college counseling, including the need for counselors to focus on crisis intervention counseling, developmental counseling, scheduling, test administration, and discipline (McDonough 2005a, 2005b; NACAC 2006; Perna et al. 2008; Venezia and Kirst 2005).

Recognize That Both Generic and Specific Skills Are Required for Jobs and Careers in Metropolitan America

As the authors in this volume explicitly and implicitly recognize, commonly asked questions with regard to the role of educational institutions in preparing students for work include: What should be the relative emphasis on "general" versus "specific" (or "academic" versus "occupational") education and training? and How should the provision of these different types of skills vary across education providers?

Together the chapters shed light on several dimensions of these questions. First, attention to these questions may obscure the reality, as suggested by several of the chapters in this volume (Barghaus et al.; Bailey and Belfield; Hoffman), that all students are in fact learning to get a job at some point in time. Second, answering these questions is complicated by the variations in job preparation that appear to be associated with different major fields within any particular degree level, as demonstrated in the chapter by Bailey and Belfield and the chapter by Carnevale, Smith, and Strohl. These variations raise additional questions about the relevance of the general skills versus specific skills dichotomy. Moreover, other trends, including the frequency with which individuals change jobs over their careers (as described by Ruby) and the shifting requirements of employers (as described by Holzer) suggest the importance of other dimensions of what students learn, including the extent to which students receive education, training, and learning that is durable.

The competency-based approach to defining readiness for work that Alan Ruby offers may be particularly helpful in identifying the skills that students need. Ruby recommends that educational programs be designed to develop the competencies or sets of skills that reflect the "actions, activities, and tasks that individuals and teams undertake in workplaces and in other social settings."

Develop Mechanisms That Support Meaningful Collaboration between Education Providers and Employers

Another theme across the chapters in this volume is the potential value of engaging employers in the development of education and training programs. Ferguson argues for stronger connections between schools and employers, recommending that employers work with schools to integrate career education into academic programming throughout the educational pipeline. Holzer observes the need to intentionally guide students toward, and provide linkages to, "well-paying jobs in high-demand sectors."

At the same time, other authors observe that employers are typically not involved in designing career and technical education programs. Hoffman notes that this situation is in contrast to the ways that vocational training systems in other nations "provide a structure, guidance, and incentives for young people to connect to appropriate employers" and integrate into their educational programs opportunities for students to learn about occupational issues, situations, and challenges. Along the same lines, O'Connor concludes that effective work-based learning initiatives engage employers, thereby providing not only information about particular occupations and workforce needs but also providing additional adults (beyond the teacher) who can promote and encourage students' academic and career progress.

Providing meaningful involvement with and connections to employers may be particularly important to education and workforce outcomes for urban youth (O'Connor). As Ferguson discusses, many urban youth, particularly those with lower levels of academic achievement, have few connections to the world of work and postsecondary education.

Provide the Supports and Structures Required to Ensure That Students Successfully Complete the Educational Programs That They Enter

In addition to promoting the opportunity to choose from multiple meaningful pathways, institutional leaders and public policymakers must also ensure that students have the ability to persist to completion of the selected educational program or degree. Too many students fail to complete the educational programs that they enter, be it a high school diploma, postsecondary certificate program, or associate's or bachelor's degree. Moreover, completion rates are lower for urban youth, students from low-income families, and African Americans and Hispanics than for others. While the introduction to this volume describes the low high school completion rates, especially for youth in the nation's cities, other data document the low completion rates of postsecondary educational programs. For instance, only slightly more than half (56 percent) of students who first enrolled full-time in a four-year college or university in 2003 completed a bachelor's degree within six years. Bachelor's degree completion rates were considerably lower for Blacks (38 percent) and Hispanics (46 percent) than for Whites (59 percent) (Knapp, Kelly-Reid, and Ginder 2011). Only a third (32 percent) of students who first enrolled full-time in a two-year college or university in 2006 completed an associate's degree within three years (Knapp, Kelly-Reid, and Ginder 2011).

Carnevale and his coauthors note the potential benefits of for-profit postsecondary education institutions to students, given the connections that these providers typically make between education and training. Yet the likelihood of realizing an increase in earnings from an occupational certificate or degree program depends at least in part on whether the student completes the program (Bailey and Belfield), and completion rates are even lower for students who attend for-profit rather than not-for-profit higher education institutions (Knapp, Kelly-Reid, and Ginder 2011). The earnings premium associated with occupational certificate and degree programs may also be limited by structures that restrict the ability of students to transfer credits from these programs into degree-granting programs (Bailey and Belfield). Supporting students through the completion of their educational programs is especially important in the case of those who are utilizing loans to finance the educational costs. As data presented earlier in this conclusion suggest, the debt burden of many students attending for-profit institutions can have important consequences for students' future financial well-being. The burden of student loan debt is even greater if the student fails to complete the program and secure a job that produces the expected earnings premium (Gladieux and Perna 2005).

The types of supports required to promote students' persistence to program and degree completion will likely vary across institutions. In his chapter, Holzer points to the potential value of services that address students' needs for child care and transportation, academic and/or personal counseling, and student financial assistance. Other resources offer recommendations for promoting educational attainment for low-income college students (Kezar 2011) and college students who work while enrolled (Perna 2010).

Use Public Policy to Encourage and Support Improved Linkages between Education and Employment

Together the chapters in this book also suggest the utility of strategically using public policy mechanisms to promote connections between education and employment. At the local level, Wolf-Powers and Andreason note that, ideally, sectoral initiatives will be part of broader urban and regional development strategies. They also recommend that government entities provide incentives to support the development of workforce training efforts, particularly those emphasizing improved workforce readiness for low-income and unemployed individuals.

Holzer points to the need to focus available resources, including technical assistance, on initiatives designed to improve the connections between education and employment among those who are now least well-served in our nation's urban areas, namely those from low-income families, racial/ethnic minority students, and students who are underprepared academically.

Other chapters urge institutional and public policymakers to support federal and state legislation that encourages and supports improved linkages between education and employment. As Hoffman observes, unlike other nations the United States lacks "special youth policies that view younger generations as important to support, protect, and engage with as an investment in future prosperity." As Holzer notes in his chapter, mechanisms to facilitate these linkages could be included in several federal acts, including the Elementary and Secondary Education Act (ESEA) and the Workforce Investment Act (WIA). In addition, federal and state agencies should be encouraged to fund grant competitions that encourage innovation and experimentation in the types of programs and approaches that best promote connections between education and employment (Holzer).

Implications for Future Research

The chapters in this volume improve knowledge in several fundamental areas, including the measurement and definition of the learning that is required by employers; the roles and contributions to workforce readiness of various education providers; and the types of institutional practices and public policies that promote the educational preparation of today's workers for tomorrow's jobs. Yet, as observed by several chapter authors, more research is also required. In particular, this volume underscores the value of future research that further examines

1. How are workforce readiness skills and outcomes best defined and measured?, and
2. What programs and policies are most effective in improving connections between education and work?

Definition and Measurement of Workforce Readiness Skills and Outcomes

Several chapters note that much existing research is limited by the absence of consensus on the definition of readiness for work, the skills required to be ready for work, and the outcomes that characterize "a successful workforce readiness program" (Barghaus et al.). As a result, key questions remain, including how to measure whether students have the competencies required for employment (Ruby). Other recent reports document the challenges associated with assessing the match between the skills that employers require and the skills that employees possess (ACT 2011). For example, surveys asking employers to identify gaps between the skills required for available jobs and the skills possessed by available workers typically (a) reflect not actual gaps but perceptions of the gaps, (b) are restricted to the opinions of the individual completing the questionnaire, and (c) focus on recent graduates rather than incumbent workers (ACT 2011). Using educational attainment as a measure of skill level provides limited insights into the skills required for "middle-skill" jobs (ACT 2011). ACT offers an alternative approach, comparing the occupational profiles of more than 18,000 jobs (that is, the demand for skills) with results from WorkKeys assessments of workers in three areas: Reading for Information, Locating Information, and Applied Mathematics (the supply of skills). The analyses reveal substantial national skills gaps in "manufacturing, healthcare, construction, and energy-related target occupations that require a middle or high level of education completion" (p. 19), and suggest the utility of similar analyses examining the skills gaps at the state, regional, and local levels.

Future research should also consider a range of outcomes to understand the effects of efforts to improve workforce readiness. Although much existing research emphasizes earnings as the most relevant outcome, the chapters in this volume remind us that other (especially non-economic) outcomes also have value (Bailey and Belfield; Carnevale, Smith, and Strohl). O'Connor implies these multiple outcomes in her proposed framework for assessing work-based learning initiatives. This framework considers five categories of outcomes: "student satisfaction with programs (reaction); the actual learning that takes place (learning); the application of what was learned outside of the classroom (behavior); graduation rates (organizational impact); and . . . earning power upon completion (labor market outcomes)."

Additional research is also required to better understand both the short- and long-term outcomes of different workforce readiness initiatives and approaches. Some research suggests that the probability of employment does not vary over the life cycle for individuals participating in vocational rather than general education programs in the United States and other nations that lack a strong vocational education system (Hanushek, Woessman, and Zhang 2011). In contrast, in countries with extensive vocational education programs (for example, direct apprenticeships with industry), individuals with vocational education realize employment benefits relative to individuals with general education early in the life cycle but this advantage declines over time. Specifically, individuals with vocational education are more likely than those with general education to be employed up to age fifty, but this relative benefit declines as the individual continues to age. Additional analyses show that this pattern reflects the fact that in more vocationally oriented countries, individuals with general education have a greater tendency to acquire career-related training as adults than those with vocational education (Hanushek, Woessman, and Zhang 2011). This study has many strengths, as it uses an extensive dataset that contains detailed information for individuals in eighteen countries, employs statistical procedures that control for the self-selection of individuals into different educational programs, and controls for relevant characteristics of individuals and countries. Yet the findings also point to the need for future research, as the analyses are limited to men and use a very basic approach to categorizing educational programs as vocational rather than general.

Most Effective Institutional Practices and Public Policies

The chapters in this volume highlight several programs that have been shown by research to have promise for improving students' readiness for work. Nonetheless, additional research is required to further understand the best practices and approaches for connecting education to work, especially for students in metropolitan America. Future research should be designed to improve understanding of how and whether specific dimensions of particular programs work (Ruby; Barghaus et al.; Richburg-Hayes, Armijo, and Merrill). Such research should include attention to how the effectiveness of various approaches to improving workforce readiness varies across educational providers (high schools, community colleges, for-profit postsecondary institutions, four-year colleges and universities) and different types of curricular programs (such as short-term certificate programs and occupational two-year degree programs) (Tierney).

As recommended in several chapters (Barghaus et al.; Richburg-Hayes, Armijo, and Merrill) knowledge of the programs and practices that best improve workforce readiness could be enhanced in at least three ways. First, future research should incorporate quasi-experimental research designs to better establish the extent to which a program or practice causes improved student outcomes. Although the use of rigorous experimental designs such as randomized controlled trials, to study these practices is generally not possible, quasi-experimental designs offer a feasible and potentially fruitful alternative for establishing causal relationships.

Second, building on the recommendation by Barghaus et al., researchers should encourage the inclusion of relevant measures of workforce readiness in emerging statewide longitudinal data systems. Researchers should then utilize these data for future studies that examine the connections between multiple types of educational experiences and employment.

Third, as Richburg-Hayes and her colleagues note, simply knowing whether a particular intervention "works" or not is not sufficient. Future research should focus on developing greater understanding of how and why a particular intervention does or does not achieve expected outcomes. Such research should also include attention to how and why a particular program works "on average" across participating students, as well as for students from certain subgroups, especially groups who have historically experienced lower educational and career outcomes.

Summary

Educational providers at all levels can and must do more to better prepare today's students for tomorrow's jobs, especially in metropolitan America. Despite the many forces that have challenged past reform efforts and that will challenge efforts into the future, the need to act now is underscored by the projected increased demand for more-educated workers (Carnevale, Smith, and Strohl 2010). The chapters in this volume offer critical insights for practitioners, policymakers, and researchers seeking to productively address this problem.

NOTES

Introduction

1. Urban centers are one part of a larger metropolitan area. Most metropolitan areas have one urban center (e.g., Las Vegas, Nevada), although some metropolitan areas have multiple urban centers (e.g., Dallas, Fort Worth, and Arlington, Texas are within the same metropolitan area but each is among the nation's fifty largest cities) (Swanson 2008).

2. The Cumulative Promotion Index measures high school graduation as a process occurring over time rather than a single event, considering grade-to-grade promotions from 9 to 10, 10 to 11, and 11 to 12, and receipt of a diploma.

Chapter 4. Improving Career and Technical Education in the United States

1. The OECD study of transitions from school to work is based on 2005–7 data, so it predates the fiscal crisis. The situation for the United States is more precarious now as confirmed by the statistics about rising youth unemployment even for young people with bachelor's degrees. See Godofsky, Jessica, Cliff Zukin, and Carl Van Horn 2011: 120.

2. "MDC Degrees, Certificates Pay Off for Graduates," *Miami Dade College Forum* 15(2) (April 2011). Graduates of the Florida College System (FCS) colleges, including Miami Dade College's degree and certificate programs, earn higher salaries than graduates of the State University System (SUS) and Florida independent (private) colleges and universities (ICUF), according to data provided by Florida Employment Training Placement Information Program (FETPIP). The study shows that 2008–9 graduates with two-year Associate in Science degrees from Miami Dade College and the Florida College System (FCS) earned $10,357 more, and graduates of four-year bachelor's degree programs earned $6,758 more, on average, than baccalaureate graduates of the State University System.

In addition, MDC and FCS baccalaureate and A.S. graduates earned about $1,000 to $4,600 more than baccalaureate graduates of the private colleges and universities. With average costs for MDC programs less than half of the cost of comparable programs in the State University System and about a tenth of the cost of the private colleges, MDC and FCS students get more for a much smaller investment in their education.

These data attest to the value of these programs in preparing students for high-demand, high-paying careers in a wide variety of industries. A few of these fields and jobs include

- business—accounting technology and business administration;
- creative—computer design technology and radio and television broadcasting;
- education—Exceptional Student Education, secondary math and science, and early childhood education;
- health care—nursing, physician assistants, and specialized medical technicians;
- high tech—networking service technician, Microsoft database administration, and computer-aided drafting and design; and
- public safety—corrections, fire-fighting, and emergency medical services

3. For the most recent data on early colleges and a variety of community college initiatives at Jobs for the Future, see http://www.JFF.org. For the Learn and Earn Early Colleges, see the North Carolina New Schools Project and http://newschoolsproject.org/.

Chapter 5. Postsecondary Education and Economic Opportunity

1. This chapter will focus on a more general need for educated workers; however, the ideas discussed herein apply to metropolitan areas as much as to the rest of the country.

2. This is even more true in urban areas where the minority-White performance gaps on standardized tests—an outcome that is very highly correlated with socioeconomic status—cascades into missed educational opportunities and contributes to the intergenerational persistence of poverty.

3. In a separate analysis of the demand for certificates we find that postsecondary certificates requiring at least one year of study add market value and comprise an increasing share of the education landscape—close to 8 percent of all education attainment.

4. This is true for industries that require relatively more education as well as industries that require relatively less.

5. We use median and not average because the average can be skewed by outliers or extreme values.

6. The discounted cost of the degree here attempts to calculate the added burden of repayment in the future as part of the cost of the degree. Usually, an interest rate is attached to the principal and valued at today's prices.

7. At the following interest rates for money invested today, the present value (PV) of an additional $1 million forty years into the future is: $675,000 (1 percent), $453,000 (2 percent), $307,000 (3 percent).

8. Tuition and fees, $9,000 per year; books, $1,500 per year; trips and extra costs, $1,500 per year. Rent and food are excluded from these calculations since these are costs that one incurs regardless of whether one is attending college or working.

9. Salary forgone should also be considered at the high school median earnings potential for four years. We have excluded this from the immediate analysis, given the relatively high unemployment rates for recent young high school graduates—irrespective of the state of the economy. We can, however, assume an average annual wage of $23,000 as income forgone for a college education.

10. Many critics have pointed out that the unemployment rate for recent college graduates is much higher than the rate for graduates as a whole. This is to be expected—they typically have no labor market experience. However, comparing the unemployment rate of recent college graduates, which was about 9 percent last year, with the overall unemployment rate of 9 percent presents a skewed picture of the benefits of college. It is more appropriate to compare the unemployment rate for recent college graduates with the unemployment rate of recent high school graduates—whose unemployment rate was about 35 percent last year, much higher than 9 percent for recent college graduates.

11. By "required," we mean paid the applicants a significant premium for having a college degree.

12. Prime age is defined as ages twenty-five to fifty-four.

13. This argument is fully developed in Goldin and Katz 2008.

14. Our projections assume we were producing enough postsecondary graduates in the base year and only measure unmet demand going forward, when in fact other evidence suggests otherwise (see Goldin and Katz 2008, and Carnevale and Rose 2011).

15. We have adopted a standardized definition of a sustainable wage if its level of earnings exceeds the median. This definition will depend on the state in question and its associated cost of living. For the nation, that value is about $35,000.

16. More and more the phrase "non-traditional student," defined loosely as anyone over the age of twenty-six who is not in school full-time pursuing a major, is becoming irrelevant, as larger shares of the college-going population are over twenty-six, first- or second-generation Americans, first-generation college-goers, minorities, parents, working learners, or a combination of the above.

17. Granted, problems are highlighted by recent rulemaking that requires for-profits to justify many of their programs' value in the marketplace, particularly as it pertains to repaying federal debt.

Chapter 6. Community College Occupational Degrees

1. The argument that modern workplaces require general skills such as time management, working in teams, evaluating data, understanding technological systems, and others was popularized in the 1990s by the Secretary of the U.S. Department of Education's Commission on Achieving Necessary Skills (SCANS) (1991). For contemporary examples of this perspective, see Fischer 2011 and Schneider 2011.

2. These calculations do not include noncredit education.

3. We emphasize that these proportions are out of the total career education provision of these institutions.

4. Using Unemployment Insurance (UI) data from Kentucky in the 2000s, Jepsen, Troske, and Coomes (2009) found the highest gains in vocational subjects (for similar results for Florida, see Jacobson and Mokher 2009). Earlier data show a similar pattern (Grubb 1997). That said, other studies have reported mixed results by subject (Gill and Leigh 2003; Jaeger and Page 1996); and Marcotte (2010) found no difference between returns to academic and vocational credits, but attributed it to the fact that many students accumulate both sets of credits.

5. Jacobson and Mokher (2009) reported basic wage differentials for vocational certificates in Florida. These too show positive gains from completing a vocational certificate.

6. This has been a dominant theme in community college research for a half a century (Clark 1960).

7. The diversion effect is even stronger for certificates: far fewer vocational courses transfer to other institutions, compared with liberal arts courses; and vocational course transfer equivalencies are negotiated in a more idiosyncratic manner.

8. Many community college students never complete any award. For example, in the first decade of this century, within six years of entering community college, only 34.5 percent of the cohort will have obtained a credential (Bailey 2011: Table 2, BPS2004-2010 data). Given these low completion rates, the high certificate completion rates have attracted the attention of analysts and policymakers who believe that the spread of certificates represents a strategy to increase overall completions.

9. A third perspective—that of dividing jobs by their routine and cognitive requirements (Autor, Levy, and Murnane 2003)—is also insufficiently prescriptive. Occupational credentials are offered for all classifications with the possible exception of routine manual jobs (such as typing). As examples, a routine cognitive job is a machinist; a routine manual job is a firefighter; a non-routine interactive job is a teacher; and non-routine analytical job is an architect. Each of these jobs requires some occupational credential independent of a general college education.

10. In fact, the CEA report (2009: Figure 6) predicts employment growth over the period up to 2016 to be 16 percent for associate degrees and vocational awards, compared with 15 percent for bachelor's degrees (and 8 percent for medium/short-term training).

11. In recent work, Scott-Clayton and Weiss (2011) compared occupational credentials earned at technical colleges versus credentials from comprehensive community colleges in Washington state. Technical colleges did have significantly higher certificate completion rates than comprehensive community colleges. But the most interesting finding of the paper was the difficulty in finding similar students in the two institutions. Thus comparisons among institutions must take account of the degree type, the substance of the program, and the goals and characteristics of the students.

12. For example, it may depend on the proportion of high school graduates or college graduates within the metropolitan area (Abel et al. 2010).

13. Our goal is not to identify the true causal effect of education on earnings but to examine differentials within education levels and between metro/non-metro residents. See Belfield and Bailey 2011 for a discussion of the extent to which the Mincerian function approximates to a causal effect of education on earnings.

14. The SIPP is somewhat limited in personal characteristics and labor market history, which restricts the number of covariates that we can include.

15. We perform a similar exercise for B.A. degree holders (details available from the authors).

Chapter 8. Strengthening the Education and Workforce Connection

1. As previous chapters have noted, random assignment is the gold standard methodology for evaluation. While other research approaches can provide compelling evidence and may be more suitable for certain questions, we limit our review to the causal and quasi-experimental evidence on career pathways and other interventions with similar components to isolate the effect of the intervention on outcomes while confidently removing alternative explanations. For example, unless students are randomly assigned to participate in a program, it may be possible for participants to be more (or less) motivated than a matched comparison group. Since there are a reasonable number of experimental and quasi-experimental studies available, the contribution of this chapter is to summarize the findings across a diverse body of work.

2. Results are summarized only if findings meet conventional levels of statistical significance (generally p-values < 0.10).

3. While a comparison group was employed in the analysis, the matching procedures may have failed to adequately control for the factors that affected selection into the career academies group.

4. An evaluation of Youth Build using a random assignment design is planned to start in 2011.

5. For example, propensity score matching techniques assume (1) unconfoundedness (also known as the conditional independence assumption), or that systematic differences in outcomes between treated and comparison individuals with the same values for covariates are attributable to treatment; (2) common support, or that persons

with the same characteristic values have a positive probability of being both partici- pants and nonparticipants (together 1 and 2 imply strong ignorability); (3) uncon- foundedness given the propensity score, which implies that all biases resulting from observable components can be removed through conditioning on the propensity score. In addition, causal inference requires the stable unit treatment value assumption, which implies that individual program participation decisions and potential outcomes are unrelated to the treatment status of others. In practice, unconfoundedness and common support are often violated.

6. The primary research assumption implies the researcher has access to the staff involved and the environment in which the intervention operates. In other words, the researcher is involved in the collection of primary data. In contrast, secondary re- search implies the analysis of post-program administrative or survey data that have been previously collected, often for other sets of analyses.

7. The Carnegie Foundation for the Advancement of Teaching is a leading propo- nent of incorporating driver diagrams into program development work in the educa- tion field as part of their initiative to support networked improvement communities. See Bryk, Gomez, and Grunow 2010.

8. Special thanks to Timothy Rudd of MDRC for suggesting the consideration of costs at the start of the design phase.

9. While random assignment provides causal impacts of the intervention on the mediator, it does not provide an estimate of the causal relationship between the me- diator and the outcome. That is, only the relationships between the intervention and the outcome and the intervention and the mediator are causal. Nonexperimental techniques are needed to analyze the relationship between the mediator and the out- come. Nonetheless, understanding whether the intervention affects the mediators can help shed light on whether the mediators are reasonable and, if so, help researchers refine future interventions and evaluation designs.

10. Figure is adapted from Bloom, Weiss, and Hill 2011 with contributions from the research team of the Performance-Based Scholarship Demonstration (Reshma Patel, Alissa Gardenhire, and Katherine Morriss).

11. This is the same as the "relative strength" terminology used in Cordray and Pion 2006.

12. That is, an intent-to-treat analysis yields a causal estimate of the program eli- gibility even if program group members do not receive the treatment as assigned (Shadish, Cook, and Campbell 2002: 320).

13. Hulleman and Cordray (2009: 90) refer to the difference between planned ser- vices and offered services as "infidelity."

14. These concepts are related to two different impact estimators in a random as- signment framework. The intent-to-treat (ITT) estimator answers the question: What is the average effect of the offered treatment (independent of who received it)? The lo- cal average treatment effect (LATE) estimator answers the question: What is the aver- age effect of the treatment for those induced by randomization to receive it? The

treatment contrast is what is accounted for during an ITT analysis. The realized treatment contrast is accounted for when calculating the LATE, which accounts for the receipt of services by the control group. For more background on the different impact estimators, see Gennetian et al. 2005.

15. Hulleman and Cordray (2009) refer to this difference as achieved relative strength.

Chapter 9. Conceiving Regional Pathways to Prosperity Systems

I would like to thank my colleagues Robert Schwartz and William Symonds for helpful conversations. The ideas expressed in this chapter have evolved over the period that we have worked together on the Pathways to Prosperity project. Of course, neither Schwartz nor Symonds is responsible for any flaws in what I have written here. I would also like to thank the students who formed a discussion group and gathered background materials for this project. Led by Andrew Volkert, that group included John Peirce, Reynaldo Faustino, Jared Joyner, William Johnston, Thomas Santel, and Tyler S. Thigpen. Finally, Charlotte Krontiris and Robert Hanna provided helpful editorial support.

1. This recommendation is modeled after a program developed by Patricia Spence of Boston, called "They made it, so can I." Adults visit fifth-grade classrooms to tell their life stories.

2. Additional information at http://www.connectedcalifornia.org/alliance.

3. Personal communication.

4. See Jencks and Phillips 1998.

5. See Ferguson 2008, and the website of the Achievement Gap Initiative at Harvard University: http://www.agi.harvard.edu.

Chapter 10. Aligning Secondary and Postsecondary Credentialization
with Economic Development Strategy

1. Many adult earners in the city are of course part of two-earner families or have fewer than three dependents, suggesting that this statistic overstates the proportion of working Philadelphians whose households are in poverty.

2. Research suggests that regional growth in jobs and income is correlated with economically healthy and growing central cities (Voith 1998; Hill and Brennan 2005).

3. WIA replaced the Job Training Partnership Act of 1982, which in turn replaced the Comprehensive Employment and Training Act (1973) and the Manpower Development and Training Act (1963).

4. In the twelve-month period ending in June 2010, 8 million people received WIA Title I services. Title I services are equated with WIA in the minds of most policy-makers.

5. The Obama Administration has recently begun to create incentives for harmonization between labor and education funding through Workforce Innovation Fund initiatives, some recently enacted and others proposed for the future.

6. Indeed, private labor exchange mechanisms appear to function well for all but the most undesirable of jobs, solidifying the reputation of public operations as effective only in connecting people who are low-skilled to positions that are low-paid.

7. The goals of local economic development officials are not perfectly aligned with those of more politically detached observers. As Malizia and Feser succinctly put it, the creation of jobs and of tax base is not necessarily the same as the creation of wealth: "jobs/tax base creation may erode, not generate, wealth . . . [according to a neo-classical theory] more consumption produced by less labor and fewer government services benefits the community, while more employment or tax revenues without more consumption imposes unnecessary costs" (1999: 14). Practitioners, however, tend to elide this distinction, and as discussed below, some research suggests that job growth prompted by local incentivization of investment can produce long-run social benefits, in part due to a "hysteresis" effect that will be discussed elsewhere in this chapter (Bartik 1991, 2007).

8. "Successful sector partnerships leverage partner resources to address both short- and long-term human capital needs of a particular sector, including by analyzing current labor markets and identifying barriers to employment within the industry; developing cross-firm skill standards, curricula, and training programs; and developing occupational career ladders to ensure workers of all skill levels can advance within the industry" (National Skills Coalition 2009: 1).

9. An experimental study conducted by Public/Private Ventures found that Per Scholas "participants earned significantly more than control group counterparts—$4,663—in the second year of the study" (Maguire et al. 2010).

10. Of a total of 1,014 people participating in the control and experimental groups, 7 percent had less than high school attainment, 22 percent had a GED, 53 percent had a high school degree, and 18 percent had more than a high school degree.

11. The nine initiatives undergoing evaluation in JOIN's return on investment study include the West Philadelphia Apprenticeship Program (a project designed to link residents of Philadelphia's University City with training and employment as nursing and surgical assistants, laboratory technicians, and veterinary technicians), the health care-focused SEIU Local 1199 Training and Education Fund, a horticulture training program for formerly incarcerated individuals (Roots to Re-Entry), and several partnerships with local manufacturers.

12. This positive outcome depends on several conditions that certainly do not obtain in every instance in which a locality is extending economic development assistance. First, the "but for" condition must be met: job growth must not have occurred "but for" the public sector incentive. Second, the benefits of the incentive with respect to growth in income and labor force participation must outweigh associated fiscal costs. As Bartik notes, "net benefits of economic development policies are most likely to be positive in

areas of high unemployment and for programs that have large effects on business location, expansion and start–up decisions per dollar of government spending" (1991: 14).

13. Of course, high rates of inter-regional labor force mobility imply that today's basic human capital stocks are not identical to those of a region's future working population.

Chapter 11. Creating Effective Education and Workforce Policies for Metropolitan Labor Markets in the United States

1. This book uses micro longitudinal data on both workers and firms to separately measure trends in the qualities of workers and the jobs they hold. The data are from the Longitudinal Employer Household Dynamics (LEHD) project at the U.S. Census Bureau, which are based on the universe of state Unemployment Insurance earnings records linked to other Census data. Because the data are longitudinal for both firms and workers, it has been possible to calculate employer and worker "fixed effects," which represent the components of each that contribute to the observed pay of workers in any given job, thus allowing us to measure the quality of each separately. This book uses data for twelve states over the period 1992–2003 to investigate trends in job quality and in the nature of the job-worker matching process, among other issues.

2. For instance, there is a growing correlation between worker and employer fixed effects in jobs over time, which seems to indicate a closer match over time between good workers and good jobs. The most dramatic shifts observed were within manufacturing jobs, which not only shrank dramatically in number but were increasingly filled by highly skilled workers over time.

3. For instance, the broad occupational categories that are usually considered middle-skill or middle-wage have shrunk in terms of the percentages of the workforce that they account for, but only by about one-sixth (from 64 to 53 percent of all employment) since 1979, while the frequency of more complex task performance in these occupations has grown. Returns to those who gain community college degrees or certificates have also grown over time, in contrast to what we might expect if the middle of the job market were really disappearing. More details are available from the author.

4. Of course, inequality in the labor market has grown for other reasons as well, such as weakening of the labor market institutions that protect low-wage workers (Card and Dinardo 2007).

5. Since immigrants are more heavily concentrated than natives at both the top and bottom of the educational distributions, their tendency to replace retiring Baby Boomers in the labor market might exacerbate gaps between demand and supply in the middle-skill jobs as well as those at the top. See Aspen Institute 2002 as well as Holzer and Lerman 2007. For a more skeptical view on replacement demand see Freeman 2007.

6. As Laura Wolf-Powers and Stuart Andreason (this volume) also point out, these services include "core" services that help prospective workers find vacant jobs; "intensive" services such as testing to identify worker aptitudes and career counseling; as well as training paid for by vouchers (known as Individual Training Accounts, or ITAs). Workers can also sign up for other Department of Labor programs for which they might qualify, including Unemployment Insurance and Trade Adjustment Assistance, at such offices.

7. Funding for employment services under Title I of the Workforce Investment Act has fallen by as much as 90 percent since peaking around 1980 (Holzer 2009). Such funding, at under $3 billion per year in a $15 trillion economy (as of fiscal year [FY] 2012), now constitutes the smallest fraction of Gross Domestic Product spent on such services of any major industrial economy.

8. It is well-known among economists that employers will hesitate to invest their own resources in general training (as opposed to firm-specific) because trainees might soon leave and eliminate the employers' potential returns; thus, they are unlikely to make the investment unless they can deduct the training costs somehow from worker wages. Other causes of limited investments by firms in their workers might include imperfect information about worker skills and training approaches, as well as capital market imperfections.

9. Heckman's estimates are somewhere in between those of Mishel and Roy (2006), based on survey data, and those of Swanson (2004) based on school administrative records.

10. High school dropout rates were reduced early on for those in the treatment group relative to the control group. Eventually high school graduation rates roughly equalized across the two groups, but at quite high levels, indicating perhaps that the control groups were managing to get some additional services and supports as well to raise their own graduation rates.

11. Jenkins, Ziedenberg, and Kienzl (2009) have used propensity score matching estimates to show that I-BEST participants have better educational outcomes, in terms of courses passed and credits received, than similar students who do not participate.

12. The chapters by William G. Tierney and by Thomas Bailey and Clive R. Belfield (this volume) also make these points.

13. See, for instance, Uchitelle 2009 for evidence on employer complaints about a welder shortage at the trough of the Great Depression. While tens of thousands of welders were unemployed nationally, many employers were looking for welders with very particular skills and saw no way to generate such skilled welders on their own.

14. Career academy students routinely take many academic courses outside of those aimed at training for specific occupations in the relevant sectors. The tendency of academy enrollees to attend postsecondary institutions was just as high as among the control group, indicating that the academy students were not being tracked away from college.

15. The competitive grants by DOL include the Trade Adjustment Assistance Community College and Career Training (TAACCCT) and Pathways Out of Poverty grants, as well as some earlier ones from the Bush Administration. Foundation-supported programs include the National Fund for Workforce Solutions, Achieving the Dream, Breaking Through, and Shifting Gears; all are described in Holzer and Nightingale 2009.

16. Trends in residential segregation over time are measured by the "dissimilarity index" for pairs of race/ethnic groups, computed across census tracts within metropolitan areas. Until 2000 these were computed only with micro data from the Decennial Census of Population, though some more recent estimates are possible in off-census years with data from the American Community Surveys.

17. The best-known reviews of the literature on "spatial mismatch" include Holzer 1991, Kain 1992, and Ihlanfeldt and Sjoquist 1998. The most rigorous evidence can be found in Weinberg 2000, while the most recent trends in the locations of workers' residences and their jobs are discussed in Raphael and Stoll 2005.

18. The strongest and most rigorous evidence of negative impacts of racial segregation on education and other outcomes can be found in Cutler and Glaeser 1997, while evidence of how school segregation negatively affects student outcomes appears in Hanushek and Rivkin 2008. The quality of the evidence on neighborhood effects, popularized by William J. Wilson 1987, has been more controversial. Recent evidence suggesting the continuing deleterious effects of concentrated residential poverty on personal outcomes appears in Sampson and Sharkey 2008 and in Shonkoff and Phillips 2000.

19. See Briggs, Popkin, and Goering 2010 for a summary of what was learned from MTO research. Researchers found that those receiving MTO treatments enjoyed better health and emotional outcomes but no higher employment or earnings than did those receiving only Section 8 vouchers; and, among their children, girls experienced some schooling and behavioral improvements but boys generally did not. Services were provided only for one year, and many families eventually moved back to their earlier neighborhoods. See Quigley and Raphael 2008 for some interpretation and criticism of the MTO design.

20. The most recent study to find little effect is Kolko and Neumark 2009, while Ham, Imrohoroglu, and Swenson 2009 do find stronger effects on employment outcomes.

21. See Fryer and Dobbie 2009 as well as Whitehurst and Croft 2010 on the effects of the Harlem Children Zone; as well as Angrist et al. 2010 on KIPP schools and Hoxby and Murarka 2009 on charter schools in New York more broadly.

22. See Ravitch 2010 for a critique of vouchers and other forms of student choice. BtW also proved largely ineffective at increasing employment and earnings among inner-city residents.

23. These include the "sustainable communities" initiative of the Obama Administration and "smart growth" projects to limit suburban sprawl.

24. See Decision Information Resources 2008; Harris 2006; Martin and Halperin 2006; and a description of the Philadelphia Youth Network at http://www.pyninc.org/.

25. The LED data are drawn from the LEHD program, and appear on the Census Bureau website for detailed industries and demographic groups on a quarterly basis at the county level. The job vacancies data represent a recent update of America's Job Bank, begun by the U.S. Department of Labor in the late 1990s but recently discontinued.

26. Since "statistical discrimination" by employers often limits the willingness of suburban employers to hire inner-city and/or minority residents, efforts by intermediaries to limit such discrimination by providing more candidate-specific information to employers might be quite effective. See Holzer 2003. Temporary help agencies can also play this role, and there is at least some evidence that these agencies can play a positive role in linking workers to well-paying jobs that the workers might not find on their own (Andersson, Holzer, and Lane 2005).

27. For more information on these MPOs and the challenges they face see Pastor and Turner 2010.

REFERENCES

Abel, J. R. and Gabe, T. M. 2010. Human capital and economic activity in urban America. Staff Report 332. New York: FRB of New York.

ACT. 2011. A better measure of skills gaps: Utilizing ACT skill profile and assessment data for strategic skill research. Accessed October 18, 2011, http://www.act.org /research/policymakers/pdf/abettermeasure.pdf.

Agrawal, A., J. L. Alssid, K. Bird, M. Goldberg, S. Hess, J. Jacobs, D. Jenkins, G. Joseph, R. Kazis, S. King- Simms, N. Laprade, S. Long, M. Maduro, J. Petty, K. McClenney, P. McKeehan, J. McKenney, I. Mendoza, A. Meyer, M. Pfeiffer, N. Poppe, J. Rubin, D. Snyder, J. Taylor, and L. Warford. 2007. *Career Pathways as a Systemic Framework: Rethinking Education for Student Success in College and Careers.* Phoenix, Ariz.: League for Innovation in the Community College.

Alfonso, Mariana. 2006. The impact of community college attendance on baccalaureate attainment. *Research in Higher Education* 47(8): 873–903.

Andersson, Fredrik, Harry J. Holzer, and Julia Lane. 2005. *Moving Up or Moving On? Who Advances in the Low-wage Labor Market.* New York: Russell Sage Foundation.

Angrist, Joshua, Susan Dynarski, Thomas Kane, Parag Pathak, and Christopher Walters. 2010. Inputs and impacts in charter schools: KIPP Lynn. *American Economic Association Papers and Proceedings* 100(2): 239–43.

Arum, Richard, and Josipa Roksa. 2011. *Academically Adrift: Limited Learning on College Campuses.* Chicago: University of Chicago Press.

Aspen Institute. 2002. *Growing Together or Growing Apart?* Boulder, Colo.: Domestic Strategies Group.

Association for Career and Technical Education. 2010. Fact sheet: Research demonstrates the value of career and technical education. Accessed December 17, 2010, http://www.acteonline.org/content.aspx?id=9452.

Autor, David H. 2010. *The Polarization of the U.S. Labor Market.* Washington, D.C.: Center for American Progress.

Autor, David H., and David Dorn. 2009. *Inequality and Specialization: The Growth of Low-Skill Service Jobs in the United States.* Cambridge, Mass.: Massachusetts Institute of Technology. (Mimeo.)

Autor, David H., Frank Levy, and Richard J. Murnane. 2003. The skill content of recent technological change: An empirical explanation. *Quarterly Journal of Economics* 118(4): 1279–333.

Bailey, Thomas R. 2009. Challenge and opportunity: Rethinking the role and function of developmental education in community college. *New Directions for Community Colleges* 145: 11–30.

Bailey, Thomas R. 2011. Can community colleges achieve ambitious graduation goals? Paper presented at the American Enterprise Institute, Washington, D.C. http://www.aei.org/docLib/Can%20Community%20Colleges%20Achieve%20Ambitious%20Graduation%20Goals%20by%20Thomas%20Bailey.pdf.

Bailey, Thomas R., Katherine L. Hughes, and David T. Moore. 2004. *Working Knowledge: Work-Based Learning and Education Reform*. New York and London: RoutledgeFalmer.

Bailey, Thomas R., Dong W. Jeong, and Sung-Woo Cho. 2010. Referral, enrollment, and completion in developmental education sequences in community colleges. *Economics of Education Review* 29(2): 255–70.

Bailey, Thomas R., Gregory S. Kienzl, and D. E. Marcotte. 2004. The returns to a subbaccalaureate education: The effects of schooling, credentials, and program of study on economic outcomes. Monograph. New York: Community College Research Center, Columbia University.

Bailey, Thomas R., and Donna Merritt, 1997. *School-to-Work for the College-Bound*. Washington, D.C.: National Center for Research in Vocational Education.

Bailey, Thomas R., D. Timothy Leinbach, and Davis Jenkins. 2005. Graduation rates, student goals, and measuring community college effectiveness. New York: Community College Research Center, Columbia University.

Balfanz, Robert. 2011. *Building a Grad Nation 2010–2011 Annual Update*. http://www.every1graduates.org/.

Baring-Gould, William S. and Ceil Baring-Gould. 1962. *The Annotated Mother Goose*. New York: Potter.

Bartik, Timothy. 1991. *Who Benefits from State and Local Economic Development Policies?* Kalamazoo, Mich.: W. E. Upjohn Institute for Employment Research.

Bartik, Timothy. 2007. Solving the problems of economic development incentives. In *Reining in the Competition for Capital*, ed. A. Markusen. Kalamazoo, Mich.: W. E. Upjohn Institute for Employment Research.

Baum, Sandy, and Jennifer Ma. 2010. *Trends in College Pricing 2010*. Trends in Higher Education Series. Washington, D.C.: The College Board. http://trends.collegeboard.org/.

Baum, Sandy, Jennifer Ma, and Kathleen Payea. 2010. *Education Pays 2010*. Washington, D.C.: The College Board. Accessed June 1, 2011, http://trends.collegeboard.org/downloads/Education_Pays_2010.pdf.

Baum, Sandy, and Patricia Steele. 2010. *Who Borrows Most? Bachelor's Degree Recipients with High Levels of Student Debt*. New York: College Board Advocacy and

Policy Center Trends in Higher Education Series. http://advocacy.collegeboard
.org/sites/default/files/Trends-Who-Borrows-Most-Brief.pdf.

Belfield, Clive R., and Thomas R, Bailey. 2011. The benefits of attending community
college: A review of the evidence. *Community College Review* 39(1): 46–68.

Belfield, Clive R., and Henry M. Levin, eds. 2007. *The Price We Pay: The Economic and
Social Consequences of Inadequate Education*. Washington, D.C.: Brookings Institution Press.

Bennett, Daniel, Adam Lucchesi, and Richard Vedder. 2010. *For-Profit Higher Education: Growth, Innovation and Regulation*. Washington, D.C.: Center for College
Affordability and Productivity. http://www.centerforcollegeaffordability.org/up
loads/ForProfit_HigherEd.pdf.

Bennett, Neville, Elisabeth Dunne, and Clive Carré. 1999. Patterns of core and generic
skill provision in higher education. *Higher Education* 37: 71–93.

Bill and Melinda Gates Foundation. 2009. *Postsecondary Success*. Accessed April 17,
2011, http://www.completionbydesign.org/sites/default/files/postsecondary-
education-success-plan-brochure.pdf.

Bloom, Dan, and David Butler. 2007. Overcoming employment barriers: Strategies to
help the "hard to employ." In *Reshaping the American Workforce in a Changing
Economy*, ed. H. Holzer and D. Nightingale. Washington, D.C.: Urban Institute
Press.

Bloom, Howard S. 1995. Minimum detectable effects: A simple way to report the statistical power of experimental designs. *Evaluation Review* 19(5): 547–56.

Bloom, Howard S., Charles Michalopoulos, Carolyn Hill, and Ying Lei. 2002. Can
nonexperimental comparison group methods match the findings from a random
assignment evaluation of mandatory welfare-to-work programs? MDRC Working
Papers on Research Methodology. New York: MDRC.

Bloom, Howard S., Michael Weiss, and Carolyn Hill. 2011. On frameworks for studying variation in the implementation and impacts of interventions. Working Paper.
New York: MDRC.

Bloom, Howard S., Saskia Levy Thompson, and Rebecca Unterman with Corinne
Herlihy and Colin Payne. 2010. *Transforming the High School Experience: How
New York City's New Small Schools Are Boosting Student Achievement and Gradu-
ation Rates*. New York: MDRC.

Bornstein, David. 2011. Training youths in the ways of the workplace. *New York
Times*, March 24, 2011. Accessed March 24, 2011, http://opinionator.blogs.nytimes
.com/author/david-bornstein/page/2/?scp=3andsq=training+youths+in+the
+ways+of+the+workplaceandst=cse.

Boruch, Robert F. 1997. *Randomized Experiments for Planning and Evaluation: A
Practical Guide*. Thousand Oaks, Calif.: Sage.

Bottoms, Gene. 2008. Promote more powerful learning. *Techniques* 83(8): 16–22.

Bound, John, and Sarah Turner. 2008. Cohort crowding: How resources affect colle-
giate attainment. *Journal of Public Economics* 91(2): 877–99.

Boustan, Leah, and Robert Margo. 2008. Job decentralization and residential location. NBER Working Paper. Cambridge, Mass.: National Bureau of Economic Research.

Bozick, Robert. 2009. Job opportunities, economic resources, and the postsecondary destinations of American youth. *Demography* 46(3): 493–512.

Bridges to Opportunity. 2008. *Bridges to Opportunity for Underprepared Adults: A State Policy Guide for Community College Leaders.* Accessed June 19, 2011, http://www.communitycollegecentral.org/BridgesStatePolicyGuide.pdf.

Briggs, Xavier, Susan Popkin, and John Goering. 2010. *Moving to Opportunity: The Story of an American Experiment to Fight Ghetto Poverty.* Oxford: Oxford University Press.

Brock, Thomas. 2010. Young adults and higher education: Barriers and breakthroughs to success. *Future of Children* 20(1): 109–33.

Brookings Institution Metropolitan Policy Program. 2010. *The State of Metropolitan America: On the Front Lines of Demographic Transformation.* Washington, D.C.: Author. Accessed June 1, 2011, http://www.brookings.edu/~/media/Files/Programs/Metro/state_of_metro_america/metro_america_report.pdf.

Brown, Phillip, Hugh Lauder, and D. N. Ashton. 2010. *The Global Auction: The Broken Promises of Education, Jobs, and Incomes.* New York: Oxford University Press.

Bryk, Anthony, Louis Gomez, and Alicia Grunow. 2010. *Getting Ideas into Action: Building Improvement Communities in Education.* Accessed June 19, 2011, http://www.carnegiefoundation.org/sites/default/files/bryk-gomez_building-nics-education.pdf.

Burd, Stephen. 2009. The subprime student loan racket. *Washington Monthly,* November/December. http://www.washingtonmonthly.com/features/2009/0911.burd.html.

Burd, Stephen. 2010. How much evidence of career college abuses do they need? *Higher Ed Watch: A Blog from New America's Higher Education Initiative,* November 18, 2010. http://higheredwatch.newamerica.net/blogposts/2010/how_much_evidence_of_career_college_abuses_do_they_need-40281.

Bureau of Labor Statistics. 2009a. Table 27: Civilian labor force participation rates, employment-population ratios, and unemployment rates, by sex, age, race, Hispanic or Latino ethnicity, and marital status. Washington, D.C.: U.S. Department of Labor. Accessed June 1, 2011, http://www.bls.gov/opub/gp/pdf/gp09_27.pdf.

Bureau of Labor Statistics. 2009b. Table 28: Selected metropolitan areas, metropolitan divisions, and cities: Civilian labor force participation rates, employment-population ratios, and unemployment rates for the noninstitutional population 25 years and over, by educational attainment. Washington, D.C.: U.S. Department of Labor. Accessed June 1, 2011, http://www.bls.gov/opub/gp/pdf/gp09_28.pdf.

Burghardt, John, Peter Schochet, Sheena McConnell, Terry Johnson, R. Mark Gritz, Steven Glazerman, John Homrighausen, and Russell Jackson. 2001. *Does Job Corps Work?* Princeton, N.J.: Mathematica Policy Research.

Business Higher Education Round Table (B-HERT). 2002. Enhancing the learning and employability of graduates: The role of generic skills. http://www.bhert.com /publications/position-papers/B-HERTPositionPaper09.pdf.

Business Higher Education Roundtable (B-HERT). 1992. *Educating for Excellence: A Survey*. Camberwell, Australia: Author.

Business Roundtable. 2009. *Getting Ahead, Staying Ahead: Helping America's Workforce Succeed in the 21st Century*. Washington, D.C.: Springboard Project.

Business-Higher Education Forum. 2011. Aligning education and workforce to foster economic development. Proceedings from *Cities for Success: A BHEF Leadership Summit*. Washington, D.C.: Author. Accessed June 2, 2011, http://www.bhef.com /publications/documents/Cities_For_Success_Proceedings.pdf.

Caliendo, Marco, and Sabine Kopeinig. 2008. Some practical guidance for the implementation of propensity score matching. *Journal of Economic Surveys* 22(1): 31–72.

California Community Colleges Chancellor's Office. June 15, 2011. California community colleges Chancellor Jack Scott glad system avoided further budget cuts; says deferrals still cause for concern. (Press release.) Sacramento, Calif: http:// californiacommunitycolleges.cccco.edu/Portals/0/DocDownloads/PressReleases /JUN2011/DemocraticBudgetProposal2011-12Passed_FINAL_6-15-11.pdf.

Card, David, and Jonathan Dinardo. 2007. The impact of technological change on low-wage workers: A review. In *Working and Poor: How Economic and Policy Changes Are Affecting Low-wage Workers*, ed. R. Blank, S. Danziger and R. Schoeni. New York: Russell Sage Foundation.

Cardosa, Ana Rute, Miguel Portela, Carla Sá, and Fernando Alexandre. 2006. Demand for higher education programs: The impact of the Bologna process. IZA discussion paper 2532. Bonn, Germany: Institute for the Study of Labor.

Carneiro, Pedro, and James J. Heckman. 2003. Human capital policy. In *Inequality in America: What Role for Human Capital Policies?* ed. James J. Heckman, Alan B. Krueger, and Benjamin M. Friedman. Cambridge, Mass.: MIT Press.

Carnevale, Anthony P. 1991. *America and the New Economy: How New Competitive Standards Are Radically Changing American Workplaces*. San Francisco: Jossey Bass.

Carnevale, Anthony P. 2010. Postsecondary education and training as we know it is not enough: Why we need to leaven postsecondary strategy with more attention to employment policy, social policy, and career and technical education in high school. Paper prepared for the Georgetown University and Urban Institute Conference on Reducing Poverty and Economic Distress after ARRA, Washington, D.C.

Carnevale, Anthony P., and Kathleen Reich. 2000. *A Piece of the Puzzle: States Can Use Education to Make Work Pay for Welfare Recipients*. Princeton, N.J.: Educational Testing Service.

Carnevale, Anthony P., and Stephen J. Rose. 2001. Low earners: Who are they? Do they have a way out? In *Low Wage Workers in the New Economy*, ed. Richard Kazis and Marc Miller. Washington, D.C.: Urban Institute Press.

Carnevale, Anthony P., and Stephen J. Rose. 2011. *The Undereducated American.* Washington, D.C.: Georgetown University Center on Education and the Workforce. http://cew.georgetown.edu/undereducated.

Carnevale, Anthony P., Stephen J. Rose, and Ban Cheah. 2011. *The College Payoff: Education, Occupation, Lifetime Earnings.* Washington, D.C.: Georgetown University Center on Education and the Workforce. http://cew.georgetown.edu/collegepayoff.

Carnevale, Anthony P., Nicole Smith, and Jeff Strohl. 2010. *Help Wanted: Projections of Jobs and Education Requirements Through 2018.* Washington, D.C.: Georgetown University Center on Education and the Workforce.

Carnevale, Anthony P., and Jeff Strohl. 2010. How increasing college access is increasing inequality, and what to do about it. In *Rewarding the Strivers: Helping Low Income Students Succeed in College,* ed. Richard Kahlenberg. New York: Century Foundation.

Carnevale, Anthony P., Jeff Strohl, and Michelle Melton. 2011. *What's It Worth? The Economic Value of College Majors.* Washington, D.C.: Georgetown University Center on Education and the Workforce.

Carson, John. 2001. Defining and selecting competencies: Historical reflections on the case of IQ. In *Defining and Selecting Key Competencies,* ed. D. S. Rychen and L. Salganik. Seattle: Hogrefe and Huber.

Casner-Lotto, Jill, Elyse Rosenblum, and Mary Wright. 2009. *The Ill-Prepared U.S. Workforce: Exploring the Challenges of Employer-Provided Workforce Readiness Training.* New York: Conference Board, Corporate Voices, American Society for Training and Development, and Society for Human Resource Management.

Cave, George, Hans Bos, Fred Doolittle, and Cyril Toussaint. 1993. *JOBSTART: Final Report on a Program for School Dropouts.* New York: MDRC.

Center for an Urban Future. 2011. *Pathway to Prosperity.* February 2011. Accessed April 17, 2011, http://www.nycfuture.org/images_pdfs/pdfs/PathwaytoProsperity.pdf.

Center for Collaborative Learning. 2010. College access and success in Philadelphia, Part II: College enrollment activity. Presentation to the John S. and James L. Knight Foundation, October 29, 2010. Accessed June 1, 2011, http://www.knightfoundation.org/dotAsset/375819.pdf.

Chapple, Karen. 2006. *Moving beyond the Divide: Workforce Development and Upward Mobility in Information Technology.* Berkeley, Calif.: PolicyLink. Accessed April 17, 2011, http://www.policylink.org/atf/cf/&{97c6d565-bb43-406d-a6d5-eca3bbf35af0}/MOVINGBEYONDTHEDIVIDE_FINAL.PDF.

Cheah, Y. M. 1996. Beyond functional literacy: A new curriculum in Singapore schools. *Journal of Adolescent and Adult Literacy* 40(3): 218–20.

Cheeseman Day, Jennifer, and Eric C. Newburger. 2002. *The Big Payoff: Educational Attainment and Synthetic Estimates of Work-Life Earning.* Current Population Reports. Washington, D.C.: U.S. Census Bureau. http://www.census.gov/prod/2002pubs/p23-210.pdf.

Clark, B. R. 1960. The "cooling out" function in higher education. *American Journal of Sociology* 65(6): 569–76.

Coatsworth, John. 2004. Globalization, growth and welfare in history. In *Globalization: Culture and Education in the New Millennium*, ed. M. M. Suarez-Orozco and D. B. Hilliard. Berkeley: University of California Press.

Cohen, John, and Dan Balz. 2011. Poll: Whites without college degrees especially pessimistic about economy. *Washington Post*, February 22, 2011. http://www .washingtonpost.com/wp-dyn/content/article/2011/02/22/AR2011022200005. html?nav=emailpage.

College Board. 2010. *Trends in College Pricing 2010*. Washington, D.C.: Author. Accessed June 3, 2011, http://advocacy.collegeboard.org/sites/default/files/2010_Trends _College_Pricing_Final_Web.pdf.

Committee on Community-Level Programs for Youth, National Research Council and Institute of Medicine. 2002. *Community Programs to Promote Youth Development*. Edited by Jacquelynne S. Eccles and Jennifer Appleton Gootman. Washington, D.C.: National Academies Press.

Community Research Partners. 2008. *Ohio Stackable Certificates: Models for Success*. Columbus, Ohio: Author. http://www.communityresearchpartners.org/uploads /publications/Ohio_Stackable_Certificates_Models_for_Success.pdf.

Conference Board. 2008. *New Graduates' Workforce Readiness: Report R-1413-08-RR*. New York: Author.

ConnectEd. N.d. *Linked Learning Fact Sheet*. ConnectEd: The California Center for College and Career. Accessed June 30, 2011, http://www.connectedcalifornia.org /pathways/index.php.

Cordray, David, and Georgine Pion. 2006. Treatment strength and integrity: Models and methods. In *Strengthening Research Methodology: Psychological Measurement and Evaluation*, ed. R. R. Bootzin and P. E. McKnight. Washington, D.C.: American Psychological Association.

Corporation for National and Community Service. 2011. *WorkAdvance: A Sector-Focused Advancement Initiative for Low-Wage Working Adults*. Accessed June 19, 2011, http://www.nyc.gov/html/ceo/downloads/pdf/workadvance_march_2011 .pdf.

Cota, Adam, Kartik Jayaram, and Martha C. A. Laboissière. 2011. Boosting productivity in U.S. higher education. *McKinsey Quarterly* (April): 1–8.

Council of Economic Advisers (CEA). 2009. *Preparing the Workers of Today for the Jobs of Tomorrow*. Washington, D.C.: Executive Office of the President. http:// www.whitehouse.gov/assets/documents/Jobs_of_the_Future.pdf.

Council on Competitiveness. 2008. *Thrive: The Skills Imperative*. http://www.compete .org/publications/detail/472/thrive/.

Cutler, David, and Edward Glaeser. 1997. Are ghettoes good or bad? *Quarterly Journal of Economics* 112(3): 827–75.

Danson, Mike. 2005. Old industrial regions and employability. *Urban Studies* 42(2): 285–300.

Davis, Greg. 2011. "Completion by design": Bill Gates on the Community College Horizon. *Perspective* 42(2): 7.

Deardorff, David K. 2006. Identification and assessment of intercultural competence as a student outcome of internationalization. *Journal of Studies in International Education* 10(3): 241–66.

Decision Information Resources (DIR). 2008. *Evaluation of Youth Opportunity Grant.* Houston, Tex.: Author.

Dewey, John. 1916. *Democracy and Education: An Introduction to the Philosophy of Education.* New York: Macmillan.

Dobbs, Lou. 2004. *Exporting America: Why Corporate Greed Is Shipping American Jobs Overseas.* New York: Warner Business Books.

Eaton, Judith. 1997. The evolution of access policy: 1965–1990. In *Public Policy in Higher Education,* ed. L. F. Goodchild, C. D. Lovell, E. R. Hines, and J. I. Gill. Needham Heights, Mass.: Pearson Custom Publishing.

Eck, Alan. 1993. Job-related education and training: Their impact on earnings. *Monthly Labor Review* 116(10): 21–38. http://www.bls.gov/opub/mlr/1993/10/contents.htm.

Edelman, Peter, Harry J. Holzer, and Paul Offner. 2006. *Reconnecting Disadvantaged Young Men.* Washington, D.C.: Urban Institute.

Fantuzzo, John, Dennis Culhane, Heather R. Rouse, R. Bloom, and A. Roig. 2006. The Kids Integrated Data System (KIDS). Invited presentation for the Assistant Secretary of Planning and Evaluation, Department of Education. Washington, D.C.: U.S. Department of Education.

Farrington, Camille A., and Margaret H. Small. 2008. *A New Model of Student Assessment for the 21st Century.* Washington, D.C.: American Youth Policy Forum.

Fein, David. 2009. *Innovative Strategies for Increasing Self-Sufficiency (ISIS) Project: Stakeholder Views from Early Outreach.* Bethesda, Md.: Abt Associates, Inc.

Ferguson, Ronald F. 2008. *Toward Excellence with Equity: An Emerging Vision for Closing the Achievement Gap.* Cambridge, Mass.: Harvard Education Press.

Fischer, Karin. 2011. Crisis of confidence threatens colleges. *Chronicle of Higher Education,* May 15, 2011. http://chronicle.com.

Fischer, Martin, and Waldemar Bauer. 2002. Competing approaches towards work process orientation in German curriculum development. *European Journal of Vocational Training* 40: 142.

Fish, Stanley. What did Watson the computer do? *New York Times,* February 21, 2011. Accessed March 1, 2011, http://opinionator.blogs.nytimes.com/2011/02/21/what-did-watson-the-computer-do/?scp=3andsq=stanley%20fish%20watsonandst=cse.

Fisher, Peter. 2007. The fiscal consequences of competition for capital. In *Reining in the Competition for Capital,* ed. A. Markusen. Kalamazoo, Mich.: W. E. Upjohn Institute for Employment Research.

Flack, Michael J. 1976. Results and effects of study abroad. *Annals of the American Academy of Political and Social Science* 424(1): 107–17.

Floud, R. 2006. The Bologna Process. *Change* 38(4): 8–15.

Flynn, Gillian. 1995. Give today's kids a taste of work—and you'll get better employees tomorrow. *Personnel Journal, Survival Guide for Recruitment Supplement*: 19–22.

Frechtling, Joy. 2007. *Logic Modeling Methods in Program Evaluation*. San Francisco: John Wiley and Sons.

Freeman Butts, Robert. 1955. *Assumptions Underlying Australian Education*. Campberwell: Australian Council for Education Research.

Freeman, Richard. 2007. Is a great labor shortage coming? Replacement demand in a global labor market. In *Reshaping the American Workforce in a Changing Economy*, ed. H. Holzer and D. Nightingale. Washington, D.C.: Urban Institute Press.

Frey, William. 2010. *Census Data: Blacks and Hispanics Take Different Segregation Paths*. Washington, D.C.: Brookings Institution.

Fryer, Roland, and Steven Levitt. 2004. Understanding the black-white test score gap in the first two years of schooling. *Review of Economics and Statistics* 86(2): 447–64.

Fryer, Roland, and Will Dobbie. 2009. Are high quality schools enough to close the achievement gap? Evidence from a social experiment in Harlem. National Bureau of Economic Research Working Paper 15473. Cambridge, Mass.: National Bureau of Economic Research.

Furstenberg, Frank F., Thomas D. Cook, Jacquelynn Eccles, Glen H. Elder, and Arnold Sameroff. 1999. *Managing to Make It: Urban Families and Adolescent Success*. Chicago: University of Chicago Press.

Gallagher, Jason. 2011. Pennsylvania education budget cuts have wide consequences. *Yahoo!News*, March 15, 2011. Accessed June 3, 2011, http://news.yahoo.com/s/ac /20110315/tr_ac/8068682_pennsylvania_education_budget_cuts_have_wide_ consequences.

GAO. *See* U.S. Government Accountability Office.

Gardner, Howard. 2004. How education changes: Consideration of history, science and values. In *Globalization: Culture and Education in the New Millennium*, ed. M. M. Suarez-Orozco and D. B. Hilliard. Berkeley: University of California Press.

Gennetian, Lisa, Pamela Morris, Johannes Bos, and Howard Bloom. 2005. Constructing instrumental variables from experimental data to explore how treatments produce effects. In *Learning More from Social Experiments: Evolving Analytic Approaches*, ed. Howard Bloom. New York: Russell Sage Foundation.

Gilbreth, Frank, and Lillian Gilbreth. 1919. *The Fatigue Study*. London: Routledge.

Gill, Andrew M., and Duane E. Leigh. 2003. Do the returns to community colleges differ between academic and vocational programs? *Journal of Human Resources* 38(1): 134–55.

Giloth, Robert. 2004. The "Local" in Workforce Development Politics. In *Workforce Development Politics: Civic Capacity and Performance*, ed. R. Giloth. Philadelphia: Temple University Press.

Gladieux, Lawrence, and Laura W. Perna. 2005. *Borrowers Who Drop Out: A Ne-glected Aspect of the College Student Loan Trend.* San Jose, Calif.: National Center for Public Policy and Higher Education.

Glaeser, Edward L. 2005. Re-inventing Boston 1630–2003. *Journal of Economic Geography* 5(2): 119–53.

Glaeser, Edward L., and Albert Saiz. 2003. *The Rise of the Skilled City.* NBER Working Paper 10191. Cambridge, Mass.: National Bureau of Economic Research.

Glaeser, Edward L., and Jesse M. Shapiro. 2001. *City Growth and the 2000 Census: Which Places Grew, and Why.* Washington, D.C.: Brookings Institution Center on Urban and Metropolitan Policy.

Godofsky, Jessica, Cliff Zukin, and Carl Van Horn. 2011. *Unfulfilled Expectations: Recent College Graduates Struggle in a Troubled Economy.* New Brunswick, N.J.: John J. Heldrich Center for Workforce Development, Edward J. Bloustein School of Planning and Public Policy, Rutgers University.

Goldin, Claudia, and Lawrence F. Katz. 2008. *The Race between Education and Technology.* Cambridge, Mass.: Harvard University Press.

Goldstein, Dana. 2011. Should all kids go to college? *The Nation* July 4–11, 2011. http://www.thenation.com/article/161463/should-all-kids-go-college.

Gonczi, Andrew. 2003. Teaching and learning of the key competencies. In *Definition and Selection of Key Competencies,* ed. D. S. Rychen, L. Salganik, and M. E. McLaughlin. Neuchatel: Swiss Federal Statistical Office.

Gottlieb, Paul D., and Michael Fogarty. 2003. Educational attainment and metropolitan growth. *Economic Development Quarterly* 17(4): 325–36.

Green, S, and E. Back. 2011. Job opportunity investment network return on investment model review. Presented to students in CPLN 624, Metropolitan Labor Markets and Workforce Development, University of Pennsylvania, April 15, 2011.

Grubb, W. Norton. 1997. The returns to education in the sub-baccalaureate labor market, 1984–1990. *Economics of Education Review* 16(3): 231–45.

Hagerty, James R. 2011. Pennsylvania budget cuts hit education. *Wall Street Journal.* March 9, 2011. Accessed June 3, 2011, http://online.wsj.com/article/SB1000142405 2748704758904576188633406924322.html.

Ham, John, Ayse Imrohoroglu, and Charles Swenson. 2009. *Government Programs Can Improve Local Labor Markets: Evidence from State Enterprise Zones, Federal Empowerment Zones and Federal Enterprise Zones.* Working paper. https://msbfile03.usc.edu/digitalmeasures/cswenson/intellcont/Government%20Programs%20Can%20Improve%20Local%20Labor%20Markets-1.pdf.

Hanushek, Eric A., Ludger Woessman, and Lei Zhang. 2011. *General Education, Vocational Education, Labor-Market Outcomes over the Life-Cycle.* NBER Working Paper 17504. Cambridge, Mass.: National Bureau of Economic Research. http://www.nber.org/tmp/81478-w17504.pdf .

Hanushek, Eric, and Steven Rivkin. 2008. *Harming the Best: How Schools Affect the Black-White Achievement Gap.* NBER Working Paper 14211. Cambridge, Mass.: National Bureau of Economic Research.

Harris, Linda. 2006. *Learning from the Youth Opportunity Experience.* Washington, D.C.: Center on Law and Social Policy.

Haskins, Ron, Harry J. Holzer, and Robert Lerman. 2009. *Promoting Economic Mobility by Increasing Access to Postsecondary Education.* Washington, D.C.: Economic Mobility Project, Pew Charitable Trusts.

Hawkins, David, and Amanda Modar. 2011. Career college group's lawsuit shows an industry defiantly unwilling to own up to its abuses. *Higher Ed Watch: A Blog from New America's Higher Education Initiative,* April 14, 2011. http://highered watch.newamerica.net/blogposts/2011/career_college_groups_lawsuit_shows_an_industry_unwilling_to_own_up_to_its_abuses-485.

Heckman, James, Robert LaLonde, and Jeffrey Smith. 1999. The economics and econometrics of active labor market programs. In *The Handbook of Labor Economics,* ed. O. Ashenfelter and D. Card. Amsterdam: North Holland.

Heckman, James, and Paul Lafontaine. 2007. *Trends and Facts in the American High School Graduation Rate.* NBER Working Paper 13670. Cambridge, Mass.: National Bureau of Economic Research.

Heinrich, C. J., P. R. Meuser, and K. R. Troske. 2008. *Workforce Investment Act Non-Experimental Net Impact Evaluation: Final Report.* Columbia, Md.: Impaq International. December.

Heinrich, Carolyn, and Christopher King. 2010. *How Effective Are Workforce Development Programs? Implications for U.S. Workforce Policies in 2010 and Beyond.* Austin: University of Texas at Austin.

Hentschke, Guilbert C., Vicente M. Lechuga, and William G. Tierney, eds. 2010. *For-Profit Colleges and Universities: Their Markets, Regulation, Performance, and Place in Higher Education.* Sterling, Va.: Stylus.

Hentschke, Guilbert C., and William G. Tierney. Forthcoming. *Barbarians at the Schoolhouse Gates: Education in an Entrepreneurial World.* Cambridge, Mass.: Harvard University Press.

Hess, Frederick M., and Whitney Downs. 2011. Partnership is a two-way street: What it takes for business to help drive school reform. Washington, D.C.: Institute for a Competitive Workforce, U.S. Chamber of Commerce. http://icw.uschamber.com/event/partnership-two-way-street-what-it-takes-business-help-drive-school-reform.

Hill, Edward W., and John Brennan. 2005. America's central cities and the location of work: Can cities compete with their suburbs? *Journal of the American Planning Association* 71(4): 411–32.

Hoachlander, Gary. 2008. Bringing industry to the classroom. *Educational Leadership* 65(8): 22.

Hollenbeck, Kevin. 2008. *Is There a Role for Public Support in Incumbent Worker On-the-Job Training?* Kalamazoo Mich.: W. E. Upjohn Institute for Employment Research.

Holzer, Harry J. 1991. The spatial mismatch hypothesis: What has the evidence shown? *Urban Studies* 28(1): 105–22.

Holzer, Harry J. 2003. Employment barriers facing ex-offenders. Presented at the Reentry Roundtable, Urban Institute, May 2003.

Holzer, Harry J. 2009. Workforce development as an antipoverty strategy: What do we know? What should we do? In *Changing Poverty, Changing Policies,* ed. M. Cancian and S. Danziger. New York: Russell Sage Foundation.

Holzer, Harry J. 2010. *Is the Middle of the U.S. Job Market Really Disappearing? Comments on the Polarization Hypothesis.* Washington, D.C.: Center for American Progress.

Holzer, Harry J., and Demetra Nightingale. 2009. *Strong Students, Strong Workers: Models for Student Success through Workforce Development and Community College Partnerships.* Washington, D.C.: Center for American Progress.

Holzer, Harry J., and Michael Stoll. 2007. *Where Workers Go, Do Jobs Follow? Metropolitan Labor Markets in the U.S., 1990-2000.* Washington, D.C.: Brookings Institution. http://www.brookings.edu/~/media/Files/rc/reports/2007/1231_cities_holzer/1231_cities_holzer.pdf.

Holzer, Harry J., and Robert Lerman. 2007. *America's Forgotten Middle-Skill Jobs: Education and Training Requirements for the Next Decade and Beyond.* Washington, D.C.: Workforce Alliance.

Holzer, Harry J., Julia Lane, David Rosenblum, and Fredrik Andersson. 2011. *Where Are All the Good Jobs Going?* New York: Russell Sage Foundation.

Holzer, Harry J., Paul Offner, and Elaine Sorensen. 2005. Declining employment among young black men: The role of incarceration and child support. *Journal of Policy Analysis and Management.* 24(2): 329-50.

Holzer, Harry J., Richard Block, Marcus Cheatam, and Jack Knott. 1993. Are training subsidies for firms effective? The Michigan experience. *Industrial and Labor Relations Review* 46(4): 625–36.

Hoxby, Caroline and Sonali Murarka. 2009. *Charter Schools in New York City: Who Enrolls and How They Affect Student Success.* NBER Working Paper 14852. Cambridge, Mass.: National Bureau of Economic Research.

Horn, Michael B. 2011. *Beyond Good and Evil: Understanding the Role of For-Profits in Education through the Theories of Disruptive Innovation.* Washington, D.C.: American Enterprise Institute. http://www.aei.org/docLib/Enterprise-Issue-1.pdf.

Hughes, Katherine, and Melinda Karp. 2006. Strengthening transitions by encouraging career pathways: A look at state policies and practices. CCRC Brief no. 30. New York: Community College Research Center, Columbia University.

Hull, Dan. 2005. *Career Pathways: Education with a Purpose.* Waco, Tex.: Center for Occupational Research and Development.

Hulleman, Chris, and David Cordray. 2009. Moving from the lab to the field: The role of fidelity and achieved relative intervention strength. *Journal of Research on Educational Effectiveness* 2: 88–110.

Ihlanfeldt, Keith, and David Sjoquist. 1998. The spatial mismatch hypothesis: A review of recent evidence and their implications for welfare reform. *Housing Policy Debate* 9(4): 849–92.

Institute for a Competitive Workforce and National Career Pathways Network. 2009. *Thriving in Challenging Times: Connecting Education to Economic Development through Career Pathways.* Accessed June 19, 2011, http://www.cord.org/uploaded files/Thriving_in_Challenging_Times(web).pdf.

Institute of Education Sciences (IES). 2008. *What Works Clearinghouse: Procedures and Standards Handbook* (Version 2.0). http://ies.ed.gov/ncee/wwc/pdf/wwc_procedures_v2_standards_handbook.pdf.

Institute of Education Sciences (IES). 2009. *Statewide Longitudinal Data Systems Features.* http://nces.ed.gov/programs/slds/pdf/features_summary.pdf.

Institute of International Education. 2009. *The Value of International Education to U.S. Business and Industry Leaders: Key Findings from a Survey of CEOs.* New York: Author.

Jacob, Brian. 2002. Where the boys aren't: Non-cognitive skills, the return to school, and the gender gap in higher education. *Economics of Education Review* 21(6): 589–98.

Jacobson, Louis. 2011. *Improving Community College Outcome Measures Using Florida Longitudinal Academic and Earnings Data.* Monograph. http://www.workforceatm .org/sections/pdf/2011/JacobsonImprovingCommunityCollegeOutcomeMea sures.pdf?CFID=1250396andCFTOKEN=66544230.

Jacobson, Louis, Robert J. LaLonde, and Daniel Sullivan. 2005. The impact of community college retraining on older displaced workers: Should we teach old dogs new tricks? *Industrial and Labor Relations Review* 583(3): 398–416.

Jacobson, Louis, and Christina Mokher. 2009. *Pathways to Boosting the Earnings of Low-Income Students by Increasing Their Educational Attainment.* Arlington, Va.: The Hudson Institute and CNA.

Jaeger, David A., and Marianne E. Page. 1996. Degrees matter: New evidence on sheepskin effects in the returns to education. *Review of Economics and Statistics* 784(4): 733–40.

Jarvis, Peter. 2006. *Towards a Comprehensive Theory of Human Learning.* London: Routledge.

Jastrzab, JoAnn, Julie Masker, John Blomquist, and Larry Orr. 1996. *Impacts of Service: Final Report on the Evaluation of American Conservation and Youth Service Corps.* Cambridge, Mass.: Abt Associates.

Jencks, Christopher, and Meredith Phillips. 1998. *The Black-White Test Score Gap.* Washington, D.C.: Brookings Press.

Jenkins, Davis. 2006. *Career Pathways: Aligning Public Resources to Support Individual and Regional Economic Advancement in the Knowledge Economy.* New York: Workforce Strategy Center.

Jenkins, Davis. 2011. Get with the program: Accelerating community college students' entry into and completion of programs of study. CCRC Working Paper 32. New York: Community College Research Center, Columbia University.

Jenkins, Davis, Matthew Zeidenberg, and Gregory Kienzl. 2009. *Building Bridges to Postsecondary Training for Low-Skilled Adults: Outcomes of Washington State's I-BEST Program.* New York: Community College Research Center, Columbia University.

Jepsen, Christopher, Kenneth Troske, and Paul Coomes. 2009. *The Labor-Market Returns to Community College Degrees, Diplomas, and Certificates.* Discussion Paper Series 2009-8. Lexington: University of Kentucky Center for Poverty Research.

Jez, Su Jin. 2011. The role of for-profit colleges in increasing completions in California. Presentation at the annual conference of the Association for Education Finance and Policy. Seattle, Wash., March 24–26, 2011.

Jobs for Youth Review. 2011. Paris: OECD Publishing.

Jones, Dennis, and Patrick Kelly. 2007. *The Emerging Policy Triangle: Economic Development, Workforce Development and Education.* Boulder, Colo.: Western Interstate Commission for Higher Education. http://www.wiche.edu/info/publications/EmergingPolicyTriangle.pdf.

Johnson, Hans. June 2009. *Educating California: Choices for the Future.* San Francisco: Public Policy Institute of California. http://www.ppic.org/content/pubs/report/R_609HJR.pdf.

Johnson, Hans. January 2011. *California Workforce: Planning for a Better Future.* San Francisco: Public Policy Institute of California. http://www.ppic.org/content/pubs/report/R_111HJ2R.pdf.

Johnson, Hans, and Ria Sengupta. April 2009. *Closing the Gap: Meeting California's Need for College Graduates.* San Francisco: Public Policy Institute of California. http://www.ppic.org/content/pubs/report/R_409HJR.pdf.

Kain, John F. 1992. The Spatial Mismatch Hypothesis: Three Decades Later. *Housing Policy Debate* 3(2): 371-459.

Kalleberg, Arne L. 2009. Precarious work, insecure workers: Employment relations in transition. *American Sociological Review* 74(1): 1–22.

Kania, John, and Mark Kramer. 2011. Collective impact. *Stanford Social Innovation Review,* Winter 9(1). http://www.ssireview.org/articles/entry/collective_impact.

Kelly, Patrick. J., and Julie Strawn. June 2011. *Not Just Kid Stuff Anymore: The Economic Imperative for More Adults to Complete College.* Boulder, Colo.: Center for Law and Social Policy (CLASP) and the National Center for Higher Education Management Systems (NCHEMS). http://www.nchems.org/pubs/docs/NotKidStuffAnymoreAdultStudentProfile-1.pdf.

Kemple, James. 2008. *Career Academies: Long-Term Impacts on Earnings, Educational Attainment and the Transition to Adulthood*. New York: MDRC.

Kemple, James, and Judith Scott-Clayton. 2004. *Career Academies: Impacts on Labor Market Outcomes and Educational Attainment*. New York: MDRC.

Kemple, James, and Jason Snipes. 2000. *Career Academies: Impacts on Students' Engagement and Performance in High School*. New York: MDRC.

Kemple, James, and Cynthia J. Willner. 2008. *Career Academies: Long Term Impacts on Labor Market Outcomes, Educational Attainment, and Transitions to Adulthood*. New York: MDRC. Accessed May 31, 2011, http://www.mdrc.org/publications/482.

Kezar, Adrianna. 2011. *Recognizing Social Class and Serving Low-Income Students in Higher Education: Institutional Policies, Practices, and Culture*. New York: Routledge.

King, Christopher T. 2008. *Does Workforce Development Work?* White paper prepared for the workforce narrative project. Austin, Tex.: Ray Marshall Center for the Study of Human Resources, Lyndon B. Johnson School of Public Affairs, University of Texas, Austin.

King, Christopher T., and Heinrich, Carolyn J. 2010. How effective are workforce development programs? Implications for U.S. workforce policies in 2010 and beyond. Presentation prepared for the Symposium Celebrating the Ray Marshall Center's 40th Anniversary, October 19, 2010.

Kirkpatrick, Donald L. 1994. *Evaluating Training Programs*. San Francisco: Berrett-Koehler.

Kleiner, Morris M., and Alan B. Krueger. 2010. The prevalence and effects of occupational licensing. *British Journal of Industrial Relations* 48(4): 676–87.

Kliebard, Herbert M. 2004. *The Struggle for the American Curriculum, 1893–1958*. 3rd ed. New York: RoutledgeFalmer.

Klor de Alva, Jorge, and Mark Schneider. May 2011. *Who Wins, Who Pays? The Economic Returns and Costs of a Bachelors Degree*. Washington, D.C.: Nexus Research and Policy Center and American Institutes for Research. http://www.air.org/files/WhoWins_bookmarked_050411.pdf.

Knapp, Laura G., J. E. Kelly-Reid, and S. A. Ginder. 2011. *Enrollment in Postsecondary Institutions, Fall 2009; Graduation Rates, 2003 and 2006 Cohorts; and Financial Statistics, Fiscal Year 2009, First Look*. NCES-2011-320. Washington, D.C.: National Center for Education Statistics.

Kolko, Jed, and David Neumark. 2009. Do some Enterprise Zones create jobs? NBER Working Paper 15206. Cambridge, Mass.: National Bureau of Economic Research.

Konkola, Riitta, Tettru Tuomi-Grohn, Piro Lambert, and Sten Ludvigsen. 2007. Promoting learning and transfer between school and workplace. *Journal of Education and Work* 20: 122–228.

Krahn, Harvey, Graham S. Lowe, and Wolfgang Lehmann. 2002. Acquisition of employability skills by high school students. *Canadian Public Policy / Analyse de Politiques* 28(2): 275–96.

Kresl, Peter K., and Earl H. Fry. 2005. *The Urban Response to Internationalization.* Cheltenham, UK: Edward Elgar Publishers.

Kroch, Eugene A., and Kriss Sjoblom. 1994. Schooling as human capital or a signal: Some evidence. *Journal of Human Resources* 29(1): 156–80.

Krueger, Alan B. 1993. How computers have changed the wage structure: Evidence from microdata, 1984–89. *Quarterly Journal of Economics* 108(1): 33–60. http://econpapers.repec.org/article/tprqjecon/v_3a108_3ay_3a1993_3ai_3a1_3ap_3a33 -60.htm.

Lacey, Alan T., and Benjamin Wright. 2010. *Occupational Employment Projections to 2018.* Bureau of Labor Statistics, Employment Outlook: 2008-18, December 22. Washington, D.C.: BLS.

Langley, Gerald, Ronald Moen, Kevin Nolan, Thomas Nolan, Clifford Norman, and Lloyd Provost. 2009. *The Improvement Guide: A Practical Approach to Enhancing Organizational Performance.* San Francisco: Jossey-Bass.

Larson, E. A., and J. A. Vanderift. 1998. *Seventh Grade Students' Perceptions of Career Awareness and Exploration Activities in Arizona Schools: Two-Year Trends.* Tempe: Arizona State University Morrison Institute for Public Policy.

Leavitt, J. 2011. Job training that works: Findings from the field. Presentation to students in CPLN 624, Metropolitan Labor Markets and Workforce Development, University of Pennsylvania. February 11, 2011.

Leef, George C. September 2006. *The Overselling of Higher Education.* Raleigh, N.C.: John William Pope Center for Higher Education Policy. http://www.johnlocke .org/acrobat/pope_articles/the_overselling_of_higher_education_report.pdf.

Lehnen, Robert G., and Eugene McGregor. 1994. Human capital report cards for American states. *Policy Sciences* 27(1): 19–35.

Leonhardt, David. 2011. Men, unemployment, and disability. *Economix Blog, New York Times* April 11, 2011. Accessed May 12, 2011, http://economix.blogs.nytimes .com/2011/04/08/men-unemployment-and-disability/.

Lerman, Robert. 2007. Career-focused training for youth. In *Reshaping the American Workforce in a Changing Economy,* ed. H. Hölzer and D. Nightingale. Washington D.C.: Urban Institute Press.

Levin, Henry M. 1994. Education and workplace needs. *Theory into Practice* 33(2): 132–35.

Lewin, Tamar. 2010. Scrutiny takes toll on for-profit college company. *New York Times,* November 9. Accessed March 7, 2012, http://www.nytimes.com/2010/11 /10/education/10kaplan.html?_r=1&sq=for-profit%20education%20security %20guard&st=nyt&scp=1&pagewanted=all.

Lin, Jeffrey. 2009. Technological adaptation, cities and new work. Working Paper 09-17, July 28. Federal Reserve Bank of Philadelphia.

London, Rebecca A., and Oded Gurantz. 2010. Data infrastructure and secondary to postsecondary tracking. *Journal of Education for Students Placed at Risk* 15: 186–99.

Long, Bridget. 2007. Financial aid and older workers: Supporting the nontraditional student. Draft manuscript prepared for *Strategies for Improving the Economic Mobility of Workers* Conference, Federal Reserve Bank of Chicago.

Lowe, Nichola J. 2007. Job creation and the knowledge economy: Lessons from North Carolina's life science manufacturing initiative. *Economic Development Quarterly* 21(4): 339–53.

Lowe, Nichola J., Harvey Goldstein, and Mary Donegan. 2011. Patchwork intermediation: Challenges and opportunities for regionally coordinated workforce development. *Economic Development Quarterly* 25(2): 158–71.

Lower-Basch, Elizabeth, and Mark H. Greenberg. 2008. Single mothers in the era of welfare reform. In *The Gloves-Off Economy: Workplace Standards at the Bottom of the American Labor Market*, ed. A. Bernhardt, H. Boushey, L. Dresser, and C. Tilly. Champaign-Urbana, Ill.: Labor and Employment Relations Association.

Lumina Foundation. 2009. *Goal 2025: Lumina Foundation's Strategic Plan*. Indianapolis, Ind.: Author. Accessed April 17, 2011, http://www.luminafoundation.org /goal_2025/Lumina_Strategic_Plan.pdf.

Lumina Foundation. 2011. *Lumina Foundation Awards Three Degree Profile Grants: Testing a New Framework for Learning*. Indianapolis, Ind.: Author. Accessed June 3, 2011, http://www.luminafoundation.org/newsroom/news_releases/2011-05-12 -degree_profile_grants.html.

Lumina Foundation. N.d. *Lumina's Big Goal: To Increase the Proportion of Americans with High-Quality Degrees and Credentials to 60 Percent by the Year 2025*. Indianapolis, Ind.: Author. Accessed October 4, 2011, http://www.luminafoundation .org/goal_2025/goal2.html.

Magnuson, Katherine, and Jane Waldfogel. 2008. *Steady Gains and Stalled Progress*. New York: Russell Sage Foundation.

Maguire, Sheila, Joshua Freely, Carol Clymer, and Maureen Conway. 2009. *Job Training That Works: Findings from the Sectoral Employment Impact Study*. Philadelphia: Public/Private Ventures.

Maguire, Sheila, Joshua Freely, Carol Clymer, Maureen Conway, and Deena Schwartz. 2010. *Tuning in to Local Labor Markets: Findings from the Sectoral Employment Study*. Philadelphia: Public/Private Ventures.

Malizia, Emil, and Edward Feser. 1999. *Understanding Local Economic Development*. New Brunswick, N.J.: Center for Urban Policy Research.

Manpower Demonstration Research Corporation (MDRC). Career academies project: Linking education and careers. Accessed May 31, 2011, http://www.mdrc.org /project_29_1.html.

Marcotte, Dave E. 2010. The earnings effect of education at community college. *Contemporary Economic Policy* 28(1): 36–51.

Marcotte, Dave E., Thomas Bailey, Carey Borkoski, and Gregory S. Kienzl. 2005. The returns of a community college education: Evidence from the National Education Longitudinal Survey. *Educational Evaluation and Policy Analysis* 272(2): 157–75.

Markusen, Ann. 2008. Human versus physical capital: Government's role in regional development. In *Public Policy for Regional Development*, ed. J. Martinez-Vazquez and F. Vaillancourt. London: Routledge.

Markusen, Ann, and Greg Schrock. 2008. Placing labor center-stage in industrial city revitalization. In *Retooling for Growth: Building a 21ˢᵗ Century Economy in America's Older Industrial Areas*, ed. Richard McGahey and Jennifer S. Vey. Washington, D.C.: Brookings Press.

Martin, Nancy, and Samuel Halperin. 2006. *Whatever It Takes: How Twelve Communities Are Reconnecting Out of School Youth*. Washington, D.C.: American Youth Policy Forum.

Massachusetts Workforce Investment Board (MWIB). 2010. *Preparing Youth for Work and Learning in the 21ˢᵗ Century Economy*. Commonwealth of Massachusetts. http://www.mass.gov/Elwd/docs/mwib/2010_youth_report.pdf.

Maxwell, Nan, and Victor Rubin. 2001. *Career Academy Programs in California: Outcomes and Implementation*. Berkeley: University of California, California Policy Research Center.

McDonough, Patricia M. 1997. *Choosing Colleges: How Social Class and Schools Structure Opportunity*. Albany: State University of New York Press.

McDonough, Patricia M. 2005a. Counseling and college counseling in America's high schools. In *State of College Admission*, ed. D. A. Hawkins and J. Lautz. Washington, D.C.: National Association for College Admission Counseling.

McDonough, Patricia M. 2005b. Counseling matters: Knowledge, assistance, and organizational commitment in college preparation. In *Preparing for College: Nine Elements of Effective Outreach*, ed. W. G. Tierney, Z. B. Corwin, and J. E. Colyar. Albany: State University of New York Press.

McNeal, Ralph B., Jr. 2011. Labor market effects on dropping out of high school: Variations by gender, race, and employment status. *Youth and Society* 1(43): 305–32.

MDC degrees, certificates pay off for graduates. *Miami Dade College Forum*, April 2011, 15(2).

Millenky, Megan, Dan Bloom, and Colleen Dillon. 2010. *Interim Results from a Random Assignment Evaluation of the National Guard Youth ChalleNGe Program*. New York: MDRC.

Minnesota Budget Project. June 2010. 2010 legislative session closes with many opportunities lost. St. Paul, Minn.: Author. Accessed October 4, 2011, http://www.mnbudgetproject.org/research-analysis/minnesota-budget/proposals-budget-outcomes/2010-Legislative-Session-Summary.pdf.

Mishel, Lawrence, Jared Bernstein, and Sylvia Allegretto. 2007. *The State of Working America, 2006/2007*. Ithaca, N.Y.: Cornell University Press.

Mishel, Lawrence, and Joydeep Roy. 2006. *Rethinking High School Graduation Rates and Trends*. Washington, D.C.: Economic Policy Institute.

Mucciaroni, Gary. 1990. *The Political Failure of Employment Policy 1945–1982*. Pittsburgh, Pa.: University of Pittsburgh Press.

National Assessment of Educational Progress (NAEP). Washington, D.C.: National Center for Education Statistics. http://nces.ed.gov/nationsreportcard.

National Academy Foundation. 2010. Statistics and research. Accessed December 20, 2010, http://naf.org/statistics-and-research.

National Association for College Admissions Counselors (NACAC). 2006. *State of College Admission, 2006.* Washington, D.C.: Author

National Association of State Budget Officers. 2010. *Fall 2010 Fiscal Survey of States.* Washington, D.C.: Author.

National Center for Education Statistics (NCES). 2011a. *The Condition of Education 2011.* Washington, D.C.: U.S. Department of Education. Accessed June 2, 2011, http://nces.ed.gov/pubs2011/2011033_1.pdf.

National Center for Education Statistics (NCES). 2011b. *The Digest of Education Statistics.* Washington, D.C.: U.S. Department of Education. Accessed June 2, 2011, http://nces.ed.gov/pubs2011/2011015_3a.pdf.

National Center for Education Statistics (NCES). N.d. Career/technical education (CTE) statistics. http://nces.ed.gov/surveys/ctes/tables/index.asp.

National Center for Education Statistics (NCES). 2008. *Career and Technical Education in the United States: 1990 to 2005. Statistical Analysis Report.* Washington, D.C.: U.S. Department of Education. http://*nces.ed.gov/pubs2008/2008035* *.pdf.*

National Commission on Excellence in Education. 1983. *A Nation at Risk.* Washington, D.C.: GPO.

National Commission on the High School Senior Year. 2001. *Raising Our Sights: No High School Senior Left Behind.* Princeton: Woodrow Wilson National Fellowship Foundation. Accessed June 2, 2001, http://www.woodrow.org/images/pdf/policy /raising_our_sights.pdf.

National Governors Association. 2011. *Degrees for What Jobs?* http://www.nga.org/ Files/pdf/1103DEGREESJOBS.PDF.

National Network of Sector Partners. 2011. *What Is a Sector Initiative? An Introduction for Sector Initiative Leaders, Policy-Makers, and Other Partners.* Insight Center for Community Economic Development. Accessed May 1, 2011, http://www .insightcced.org/index.php?page=what-is-sector-initiative.

National Skills Coalition. 2009. *Sector Partnerships: Frequently Asked Questions.* October 2009. http://www.nationalskillscoalition.org/federal-policies/sector-partnerships/sectors-documents/nsc_sectorpartnerships_factsheet_2009-10.pdf.

National Skills Coalition. 2011. *House Fiscal Year 2012 Budget Resolution Impact on Workforce Development Programs.* Accessed May 12, 2011, http://www.national skillscoalition.org/federal-policies/federal-funding/federal-funding-documents /nsc_fy2012_housebudgetresolution_2011-04.pdf.

Neild, Ruth C. 2009. Falling off the track during the transition to high school: What we know and what can be done. *Future of Children* 19: 53–76.

No Child Left Behind Act of 2001, Pub. L. No. 17- 110, § 1001, 115 Stat. 1426. 2002.

Nocera, Joe. 2011. The limits of school reform. *New York Times,* April 25, 2011. Accessed May 17, 2011, http://www.nytimes.com/2011/04/26/opinion/26nocera .html?_r=1andref=education.

Norris, Emily M., and Joan Gillespie. 2009. How study abroad shapes global careers: Evidence from the United States. *Journal of Studies in International Education* 13(3): 382–97.

O'Connor, Bridget N. 2002. Work-based learning initiatives, anticipated benefits, and stakeholder involvement: A survey of state school administrators. *NABTE Review* 29: 47–51.

O'Connor, Bridget N., and Lisa S. Ponti. 2008. Economics and school-to-work. In *21ˢᵗ Century Education: A Reference Handbook*, ed. Thomas L. Good. Los Angeles: Sage.

Obama, Barack. 2009. Address to a joint session of Congress (February 24, 2009). Washington, D.C.: Author.

Offenstein, Jeremy, Colleen Moore, and Nancy Shulock. 2009. *Pathways to Success: Lessons from the Literature on Career and Technical Education.* Sacramento, Calif.: Institute for Higher Education Leadership and Policy.

Olson, Amy. M., and Darrell Sabers. 2008. Standardized tests. In *21ˢᵗ Century Education: A Reference Handbook*, ed. Thomas L. Good. Los Angeles: Sage.

Opie, Iona, and Peter Opie. 1952. *The Oxford Dictionary of Nursery Rhymes,* 2ⁿᵈ ed. Oxford: Oxford University Press.

Opper, S. 1991. A competitive edge for women? *Oxford Review of Education* 17(1): 45–64.

Organisation for Economic Co-operation and Development (OECD). 2009. *Tertiary Level Educational Attainment for Age Group 25–64: As a Percentage of the Population of that Age Group.* Last updated November 19, 2009. doi: 10.1787/20755120-table3.

Organisation for Economic Co-operation and Development (OECD). 2010a. *Tertiary Education Entry Rates: First Time Entrants as a Percentage of the Population in the Corresponding Age Group.* Last updated June 14, 2010. doi: 10.1787/20755120-table2.

Organisation for Economic Co-operation and Development (OECD). 2010b. *Tertiary Education Graduation Rates: Percentage of Graduates to the Population at the Typical age of Graduation.* Last updated June 14, 2010. doi: 10.1787/20755120-table1.

Ornstein, Allan C., and Francis P. Hunkins. 2009. *Curriculum: Foundations, Principles, and Issues,* 5ᵗʰ ed. New York: Pearson.

Orozco, Edith A. 2010. A comparison of career technical education—16 career pathway high school participants with non participants on academic achievement, school engagement, and development of technical skills. Unpublished doctoral dissertation, University of Texas at El Paso.

Osterman, Paul. 2007. Employment and training policies: New directions for less-skilled adults. In *Reshaping the American Workforce in a Changing Economy,* ed. H. Holzer and D. Nightingale. Washington, D.C.: Urban Institute Press.

Paige, R. M., G. W. Fry, E. M. Stallman, J. Josic, and J. E. Jon. 2009. Study abroad for global engagement: The long term impact of mobility experiences. *Intercultural Education* 20 (October): 29-44.

Partington, Geoffrey. 1987. The concept of progress in educational thought: Instrumental theories considered. *Oxford Review of Education* 13(2): 141-49.

Partnership for 21st Century Skills. 2009. *The MILE Guide: Milestones for Improving Learning and Education.* Washington, D.C.: Author. Accessed June 3, 2011, http://p21.org/documents/MILE_Guide_091101.pdf.

Pastor, Manuel, and Marjorie Turner. 2010. *Reducing Poverty and Economic Distress after ARRA: Potential Roles for Place-Conscious Strategies.* Washington, D.C.: Urban Institute.

Pearson, Donna, Jennifer Sawyer, Travis Park, Laura Santamaria, Elizabeth van der Mandele, Barrett Keene, and Marissa Taylor. 2010. *Capitalizing on Context: Curriculum Integration in Career and Technical Education.* Louisville, Ky.: National Research Center for Career and Technical Education.

Peikes, Deborah, Lorenzo Moreno, and Sean Orzol. 2008. Propensity score matching: A note of caution for evaluators of social programs. *American Statistician* 62(3): 222–31.

Pell Institute for the Study of Opportunity in Higher Education. May 2011. *Developing 20/20 Vision on the 2020 Degree Attainment Goal: The Threat of Income-Based Inequality in Education.* Washington, D.C.: Author.

Perlin, Ross. 2011. Unpaid interns, complicit colleges. *New York Times*, April 2, 2011.

Perna, Laura W. 2010. *Understanding the Working College Student: New Research and Its Implications for Policy and Practice.* Herndon, Va.: Stylus.

Perna, Laura W., and Patricia Steele. 2011. The role of context in understanding the contributions of financial aid to college opportunity. *Teachers College Record* 113: 895–933.

Perna, Laura W., and Scott L. Thomas. 2009. Barriers to college opportunity: The unintended consequences of state-mandated tests. *Educational Policy* 23(3): 451–79.

Perna, Laura W., Heather Rowan-Kenyon, Scott L. Thomas, Angela Bell, Robert Anderson, and Chunyan Li. 2008. The role of college counseling in shaping college opportunity: Variations across high schools. *Review of Higher Education* 31: 131–60.

Persky, Joseph, David Felsenstein, and Virginia Carlson. 2004. *Does "Trickle Down" Work? Economic Development Strategies and Job Chains in Local Labor Markets.* Kalamazoo, Mich.: W. E. Upjohn Institute.

Philadelphia Workforce Investment Board. 2007. *A Tale of Two Cities.* Philadelphia: Author.

Philadelphia Workforce Investment Board. 2009. *Help Wanted: Knowledge Workers Needed.* Philadelphia: Author.

Popkin, Susan, and Mary Cunningham. 2009. *Has HOPE VI Transformed Residents' Lives?* Washington, D.C.: Urban Institute.

Porter, J. A., and. F. Bradwick. 1996. School-to-work preparedness: Integrating tax clinics into the business curriculum. *Tax Advisor* 27(8): 503–6.

Quaglia Institute. 2010. *My Voice National Student Report 2010*. Accessed April 14, 2011, http://qisa.org/publications/docs/MyVoice6-12StudentNationalReport2010 -Final.pdf.

Quigley, John, and Steven Raphael. 2008. *Neighborhoods, Economic Self-Sufficiency, and the* MTO *Program*. Brookings-Wharton Papers on Urban Affairs. Washington, D.C.: Brookings Institution.

Quint, Janet. 2006. *Meeting Five Critical Challenges of High School Reform: Lessons from Research on Three Reform Models*. New York: MDRC.

Quintini, Glenda. 2009. *Going Separate Ways? School-to-Work Transitions in the United States and Europe*. Paris: OECD.

Raelin, Joe. January 30, 2011. Personal communications to author.

Rahman, Sarah, and Mark Muro. 2010. Budget 2011: Joined up government. *The Avenue* (blog, *The New Republic*), February 12, 2010. http://www.tnr.com/blog/the -avenue/budget-2011-joined-government-0.

Raphael, Steven, and Michael Stoll. 2005. *Modest Progress: The Narrowing Spatial Mismatch between Blacks and Jobs in the 1990s*. Washington, D.C.: Brookings Institution.

Raphael, Steven, and Michael Stoll. 2010. *Job Sprawl and the Suburbanization of Poverty*. Washington, D.C.: Brookings Institution.

Ravitch, Diane. 2010. *The Death and Life of the Great American School System*. New York: Basic Books.

Ray, Carol A, and Rosalyn A. Mickelson. 1990. Business leaders and the politics of school reform. In *Education Politics for the New Century,* ed. M. Goertz and D. E. Mitchell. Politics of Education Association Yearbook. Bristol, UK: Falmer Press.

Reardon, Sean. 2010. The widening academic achievement gap between the rich and the poor: New evidence and possible explanations. Working paper, Stanford University.

Reynolds, C. Lockwood, and Stephen DesJardins. 2009. The use of matching methods in higher education research: Answering whether attendance at a 2-year institution results in differences in educational attainment. *Higher Education: Handbook of Theory and Research* 24: 47–104.

Rhoder, Carol, and Joyce N. French. 1999. School-to-work: Making specific connections. *Phi Delta Kappan* 80(9): 534–41.

Richardson, Richard, and Louis Bender. 1986. Students in urban settings: Achieving the baccalaureate degree. *Association for the Study of Higher Education*. http:// www.ericdigests.org/pre-926/urban.htm.

Roder, Anne, and Mark Elliott. 2011. *A Promising Start: Year Up's Initial Impacts on Low-Income Young Adults' Careers*. New York: Economic Mobility Corporation.

Rose, Mike. 2011. Untangling the post-secondary debate. *Education Week*, June 11, 2011.

Rosenbaum, James, and Ann E. Person. 2006. Educational outcomes of labor market linking and job placement for students at public and private two-year colleges. *Economics of Education Review* 25: 412–29.

Rosenbaum, James, Regina Deil-Amen, and Ann E. Person. 2006. *After Admission: From College Access to College Success.* New York: Russell Sage Foundation.

Rosenbaum, Paul R. 2010. *Design of Observational Studies.* New York: Springer.

Rossi, Peter, Mark W. Lipsey, and Howard E. Freeman. 2004. *Evaluation: A Systematic Approach.* 7th ed. Thousand Oaks, Calif.: Sage.

Rothstein, Jesse M. 2004. College performance predictions and the SAT. *Journal of Econometrics* 121(1–2, July–August): 297–317. http://gsppi.berkeley.edu/faculty/jrothstein/published/sat_may03_updated.pdf.

Ruch, Richard S. 2001. *Higher Ed, Inc.: The Rise of the For-Profit University.* Baltimore: Johns Hopkins University Press.

Ryan, Paul. 2001. The school-to-work transition: A cross-national perspective. *Journal of Economic Literature* 39(1): 34–92.

Rychen, Dominique S. 2004. Key competencies for all: An overarching conceptual frame of reference. In *Developing Key Competencies in Education,* ed. D. S. Rychen and A. Tiana. Paris: International Bureau of Education, UNESCO.

Ryken, Amy. E. 2004. The holding power of internships: Analyzing retention in a school-to-career program. *Community College Enterprise* 10(2): 37–46.

Sampson, Robert, and Patrick Sharkey. 2008. Neighborhood selection and the social reproduction of concentrated racial inequality. *Demography* 45(1): 1–29.

Scarpetta, Stefano, Anne Sonnet, and Thomas Manfredi. 2010. Rising youth unemployment during the crisis: How to prevent negative long-term consequences on a generation? OECD Social, Employment and Migration Papers 106.

Schneider, Carol G. May 1, 2011. "Degrees for what jobs?" Wrong questions, wrong answers. *Chronicle of Higher Education.* http://chronicle.com/article/Degrees-for-What-Jobs-Wrong/127328/.

Schochet, Peter, Sheena McConnell, and John Burghardt. 2003. *National Job Corps Study: Findings Using Administrative Earnings Records Data.* Princeton, N.J.: Mathematica Policy Research.

Schone, P. 2009. New technologies, new work practices and the age structure of the workers. *Journal of Population Economics* 22(3): 803–26.

Schweke, William. 2007. Do better job creation subsidies hold real promise for business incentive reformers? In *Reining in the Competition for Capital,* ed. A. Markusen. Kalamazoo, Mich.: W. E. Upjohn Institute for Employment Research.

Scott-Clayton, Judith. 2011. The shapeless river: Does a lack of structure inhibit students' progress at community colleges? CCRC Working Paper 25, Assessment of Evidence Series. New York: Community College Research Center, Columbia University. http://ccrc.tc.columbia.edu/Publication.asp?uid=839.

Scott-Clayton, J and M.J. Weiss. 2011. Institutional variation in credential completion: Evidence from Washington State community and technical colleges. CCRC

Working Paper 33. New York: Community College Research Center, Teachers College.

Sechrest, L., S. West, M. Philips, R. Redner, and W. Yeaton. 1979. Some neglected problems in evaluation research: Strength and integrity of treatments. In *Evaluation Studies Review Annual* 4, ed. L. Sechrest, S. West, M. Phillips, R. Redner, and W. Yeaton. Beverly Hills, Calif.: Sage.

Select Greater Philadelphia. 2011. Education in greater Philadelphia. Accessed May 31, 2011, http://www.selectgreaterphiladelphia.com/data/education.cfm.

Shadish, William, Thomas Cook, and Donald Campbell. 2002. *Experimental and Quasi-Experimental Designs for Generalized Causal Inference.* Boston: Houghton Mifflin.

Shaw, Angela. 2011. The value of work experience in outcomes for students: An investigation into the importance of work experience in the lives of undergraduates and postgraduate job seekers. Paper presented at the American Educational Research Association Meeting, April 2011, New Orleans, La.

Shaw, Jane S. 2010. Education: A bad public good? *Independent Review* 15(2): 241–56.

Shonkoff, Jack, and Deborah Phillips. 2000. *From Neurons to Neighborhoods: The Science of Early Childhood Development.* Washington, D.C.: National Academies Press.

Shorr, Lori. May 25, 2011. Presentation at the Preparing Today's Students for Tomorrow's Jobs in Metropolitan America Conference. Philadelphia.

Shulock, Nancy, Jeremy Offenstein, and Colleen Moore. 2011. *The Road Less Traveled: Realizing the Potential of Career Technical Education in the California Community Colleges.* Sacramento, Calif.: Institute for Higher Education Leadership and Policy.

Silverberg, Marsha, Elizabeth Warner, Michael Fong, and David Goodwin. 2004. *National Assessment of Vocational Education: Final Report to Congress.* Washington, D.C.: U.S. Department of Education.

SIPP. 2008. Survey of Income and Program Participation. U.S. Census: Washington, D.C. http://www.census.gov/sipp/overview.html.

Skinner, Rebecca, and Richard N. Apling. 2006. The Carl D. Perkins Vocational and Technical Education Act of 1998: Background and implementation. CRS Report for Congress. Received through the CRS Web, updated July 21, 2006 CRS 3.

Slaughter, Sheila, and Gary Rhoades. 2004. *Academic Capitalism and the New Economy: Markets, State, and Higher Education.* Baltimore: Johns Hopkins University Press.

Society for Human Resource Management. 2008. Workforce readiness and the new essential skills. *Workplace Visions, No. 2.* Alexandria, Va.: Author. Accessed June 2, 2011, http://www.shrm.org/Research/Articles/Articles/Documents/08-0175WV _FINAL.pdf.

Southern Regional Education Board. 2009. Measuring technical and academic achievement. Atlanta, Ga.: Author. http://publications.sreb.org/2009/09V01CTExamReport _2009.pdf.

Sparks, Sarah D. 2011. Statistics shed light on costs and benefits of career paths. *Education Week, Diplomas Count*, June 9 (June special issue).

Steele, Claude, and Joshua Aronson. 1995. Stereotype threat and the intellectual test performance of African Americans. *Journal of Personality and Social Psychology* 69(5): 797–811.

Stefanakis, Evangeline H. 2002. *Multiple Intelligences and Portfolios: A Window into the Learner's Mind*. Portsmouth, N.H.: Heinemann.

Stone, Clarence, and Donn Worgs. Poverty and the workforce challenge. In *Workforce Development Politics: Civic Capacity and Performance*, ed. R. Giloth. Philadelphia: Temple University Press.

Swanson, Christopher B. 2008. Cities in crisis: A special analytic report on high school graduation. Editorial Projects in Education Research Center. Accessed May 19, 2011, http://www.edweek.org/media/citiesincrisis040108.pdf.

Swanson, Christopher. 2004. *Who Graduates? Who Doesn't? A Statistical Portrait of Public High School Graduation, Class of 2001*. Washington, D.C.: Urban Institute.

Symonds, William C., Robert B. Schwartz, and Ronald Ferguson. 2011. *Pathways to Prosperity—Meeting the Challenge of Preparing Young Americans for the 21st Century*. Report issued by the Pathways to Prosperity Project. Cambridge, Mass.: Harvard Graduate School of Education.

Theobald, Paul. 1996. The new vocationalism in rural locales. Paper presented at the Annual Meeting of the American Educational Studies Association, Montreal, Quebec, Canada.

Theodos, Brett, and Robert Bednarzik. 2006. Earnings mobility and low wage workers in the United States. *Monthly Labor Review* 129 (July, 6): 34–47.

Thresher, B. Alden. 1989. *College Admissions and the Public Interest*. New York: College Board.

Tienda, Marta, and Sigal Alon. 2007. Diversity and the demographic dividend: Achieving educational equity in an aging white society. In *The Price We Pay: Economic and Social Consequences of Inadequate Education*, ed. C. R. Belfield and H. M. Levin. Washington, D.C.: Brookings Institution Press.

Tierney, William G., and Susan Auerbach. 2005. Toward developing an untapped resource: The role of families in college preparation. In *Preparing for College: Nine Elements of Effective Outreach*, ed. W. G. Tierney, Z. Corwin, and J. E. Colyar. Albany: State University of New York Press.

Tierney, William G., and Guilbert C. Hentschke. 2007. *New Players, Different Game: Understanding the Rise of For-Profit Colleges and Universities*. Baltimore: Johns Hopkins University Press.

Tierney, William G., and Guilbert C. Hentschke. 2011. *Making It Happen: Increasing College Access in California Higher Education: The Role of Private Postsecondary Providers*. La Jolla, Calif.: National University System Institute for Policy Research.

Tierney, William G., and Guilbert C. Hentschke. Forthcoming. *Barbarians at the Gates: Schools, Colleges and Universities in an Entrepreneurial World.* Cambridge, Mass.: Harvard University Press.

Tierney, William G., Guilbert C. Hentschke, and Giselle Ragusa. 2011. For-profit universities and "the public good": Oxymoron or shining example. Paper presented at the annual meeting for the American Educational Research Association, New Orleans, La., April 8–12, 2011.

Tremmel, Robert. 2006. Changing the way we think in English education: A conversation in the universal barbershop. *English Education* 39(1): 10–45.

Turkheimer, Eric, Andreana Haley, Mary Waldron, Brian D'Onofrio, and Irving I. Gottesman. 2003. Socioeconomic status modifies heritability of IQ in young children. *Psychological Science* 14: 623–28. http://people.virginia.edu/~ent3c/papers2/Articles%20for%20Online%20CV/(38)%20Turkheimer%20et%20al%20(2003).pdf.

Tyack, David. 1974. *The One Best System: A History of American Urban Education.* Cambridge, Mass.: Harvard University Press.

U.S. Bureau of Labor Statistics. 2010. *Number of Jobs Held, Labor Market Activity, and Earnings Growth amongst the Youngest Baby Boomers.* USDL-10-1243, September 10, 2010. Washington, D.C.: U.S. Bureau of Labor Statistics.

U.S. Census Bureau. Current Population Survey, microdata 1980 and March, 2010. Accessed March 15, 2011, http://www.census.gov/cps/data/.

U.S. Census Bureau. 2011. FILES: 2005–2009 American Community Survey. Washington, D.C.

U.S. Department of Education. 2011. Postsecondary and Labor Force Transitions Among Public High School Career and Technical Education Participants. NCES 2011-234. Accessed May 31, 2011, http://nces.ed.gov/pubs2011/2011234.pdf.

U.S. Department of Education. 2010. National Center for Education Statistics, The Condition of Education, 2010. NCES 2010-027. Washington, D.C.: Author.

U.S. Department of Education. 2011. Default rates rise for federal student loans. September 12. (Press release.) Accessed October 14, 2011, http://www.ed.gov/news/press-releases/default-rates-rise-federal-student-loans.

U.S. Department of Labor. 1991. *What Work Requires of Schools: A SCANS Report for America 2000.* Washington, D.C.: Author.

U.S. Department of Labor. 1992. *Learning a Living: A SCANS Report for America 2000.* Washington, D.C.: Author.

U.S. Government Accountability Office (GAO). 2005. *Workforce Investment Act: Substantial Funds Are Used for Training, but Little Is Known Nationally about Training Outcomes.* GAO-05-650. Washington, D.C.: GAO. Accessed May 31, 2011, http://www.gao.gov/new.items/d05650.pdf.

U.S. Government Accountability Office (GAO). 2010. *For-Profit Colleges: Undercover Testing Finds Colleges Encouraged Fraud and Engaged in Deceptive and Questionable Marketing Practices.* GAO-10-948T. Washington, D.C.: Author.

Uchitelle, Louis. 2009. Despite recession, high demand for skilled labor. *New York Times*, June 24, 2009.

University of Cincinnati. 2006. President Launches "Strive" Educational Partnership. August 18. (Press release.) www.uc.edu/News/NR.aspx?ID=4258.

Vande Berg, Michael. 2007. Intervening in the learning of U.S. students abroad. *Journal of Studies in International Education* 11(3/4): 392–99.

Venezia, Andrea, and Michael W. Kirst. 2005. Inequitable opportunities: How current education systems and policies undermine the chances for student persistence and success in college. *Educational Policy* 19: 293–307.

Viggiano, Anna M. 2009. A study of secondary teachers' implementation of an electronic portfolio initiative. Unpublished doctoral dissertation, University of Hawai'i at Manoa.

Voith, Richard. 1998. Do suburbs need cities? *Journal of Regional Science* 38(3): 445–64.

Wachen, John, Davis Jenkins, and Michelle Van Noy. 2010. *How I-BEST Works: Findings from a Field Study of Washington State's Integrated Basic Education and Skills Training Program*. New York: Community College Research Center, Columbia University. http://ccrc.tc.columbia.edu/Publication.asp?UID=806.

Walker, Thomas J. 1995. *Work-Based Mentor Training for Pennsylvania's School-to-Work System: Final Report*. Harrisburg: Pennsylvania State Department of Education.

Warford, Laurance, ed. 2006. *Pathways to Student Success: Case Studies from The College and Career Transitions Initiative*. Phoenix, Ariz.: League for Innovation in the Community College.

Weber, Rachel. 2007. Negotiating the ideal deal: Which local governments have the most bargaining leverage? In *Reining in the Competition for Capital*, ed. A. Markusen. Kalamazoo, Mich.: W. E. Upjohn Institute for Employment Research.

Weinberg, Bruce. 2000. Black residential centralization and the spatial mismatch hypothesis. *Journal of Urban Economics* 48(1): 110–34.

Weinert, Franz E. 2001. Concept of competence: A conceptual clarification. In *Defining and Selecting Key Competencies,* ed. D. S. Rychen and L. Salganik. Seattle: Hogrefe and Huber.

Weir, Margaret. 1992. *Politics and Jobs: The Boundaries of Employment Policy in the United States*. Princeton, N.J.: Princeton University Press.

Weisbrod, Burton A., Jeffrey P. Ballou, and Evelyn D. Asch. 2008. *Mission and Money: Understanding the University*. Cambridge: Cambridge University Press.

Wheeler, Christopher H. 2004. Cities, skills, and inequality. Working Paper 2004-020A. St. Louis, Mo.: Federal Reserve Bank of St. Louis. http://research.stlouisfed.org/wp/2004/2004-020.pdf.

Whitehurst, Russ, and Michelle Croft. 2010. *The Harlem Children's Zone, Promise Neighborhoods, and the Broader, Bolder Approach to Education*. Washington, D.C.: Brookings Institution.

Willis, Paul. 1977. *Learning to Labor: How Working Class Boys Get Working Class Jobs.* Farmborough, England: Saxon House.

Wilson, William J. 1987. *The Truly Disadvantaged.* Chicago: University of Chicago Press.

Wolf-Powers, Laura. 2004. Building a workforce infrastructure. In *Moving People, Goods and Information in the 21ˢᵗ Century: The Cutting-Edge Infrastructures of Networked Cities,* ed. R. Hanley. New York: Routledge.

Wolf-Powers, Laura. 2005. Beyond the first job: Career-ladder initiatives in telecommunications and related information technology industries. In *Communities and Workforce Development,* ed. Edwin Melendez. Kalamazoo, Mich.: W. E. Upjohn Institute.

Wolf-Powers, Laura. 2012. Human capital-centered regionalism in economic development: A case of analytics outpacing institutions? *Urban Studies.* Prepublished March 28, 2012. doi: 10.1177/0042098012440123.

Wolf, Patrick, Babette Gutmann, Michael Puma, Brian Kisida, Lou Rizzo, Nada Eissa, and Matthew Carr. 2010. *Evaluation of the DC Opportunity Scholarship Program: Final Report.* Washington, D.C.: U.S. Department of Education.

Xu, Zeyu, Jane Hannaway, and Colin Taylor. 2007. Making a difference? The effect of Teach for America on student performance in high school. Working Paper 17. Washington, D.C.: Urban Institute. http://www.urban.org/publications/411642.html.

Yates, Julie A. 2005. The transition from school to work: Education and work opportunities. *Monthly Labor Review* 128(2): 21–32.

Zeidenberg, Matthew, Sung Woo Cho, and Davis Jenkins. 2010. Washington State's Integrated Basic Education and Skills Training Program (I-BEST): New evidence of effectiveness. CCRC Working Paper 20. New York: Community College Research Center, Columbia University. http://ccrc.tc.columbia.edu/Publication.asp?UID=805.

Zumeta, William. 2010. Does the U.S. need more college graduates to remain a world class economic power? Paper prepared for National Discussion and Debate Series, Miller Center of Public Affairs, University of Virginia.

CONTRIBUTORS

Stuart Andreason is a doctoral student in the Department of City and Regional Planning in the School of Design at the University of Pennsylvania. His research interests are community and economic development, urban revitalization, and workforce development. Previously he served as the Executive Director of the Orange Downtown Alliance, in Orange, Virginia.

Michael Armijo is an Institute of Education Sciences Pre-Doctoral Fellow and Ph.D. student at the University of Pennsylvania Graduate School of Education. His research interests include college completion, public policy, and the transition from high school to college.

Thomas Bailey is the George and Abby O'Neill Professor of Economics and Education at Teachers College, Columbia University. He is also Director of the Community College Research Center (CCRC) and of two National Centers, the National Center for Postsecondary Research (NCPR), established in 2006, and the Center for Analysis of Postsecondary Education and Employment (CAPSEE), established in 2011. In June 2010, U.S. Secretary of Education Arne Duncan appointed him chairperson of the Committee on Measures of Student Success, which developed recommendations for community colleges to comply with completion rate disclosure requirements under the Higher Education Opportunity Act.

Katherine M. Barghaus is an Institute of Education Sciences (IES) Pre-Doctoral Fellow and Ph.D. candidate in quantitative methods at the University of Pennsylvania Graduate School of Education. Her main research interests include measurement, early childhood education, educational entrepreneurship, and gender and education.

Clive R. Belfield is Associate Professor of Economics, Queens College, City University of New York. His most recent book is *The Price We Pay: The Costs of Inadequate Education.*

Eric T. Bradlow is Vice-Dean and Director, Wharton Doctoral Programs, the K. P. Chao Professor, Professor of Marketing, Statistics and Education, and Codirector of the Wharton Customer Analytics Initiative, The Wharton School of the University of Pennsylvania. He is a fellow of the University of Pennsylvania, the American Statistical Association, the American Education Research Association, and the Wharton Risk Center, and a Senior Fellow of the Leonard Davis Institute for Health Economics.

Anthony P. Carnevale is Director of the Georgetown University Center on Education and the Workforce. He recently authored the report *Help Wanted: Projections of Jobs and Education Requirements Through 2018.* Between 1996 and 2006, Dr. Carnevale served as Vice President for Public Leadership at the Educational Testing Service (ETS). He has served on commissions under multiple U.S. presidents and been a senior staff member in both houses of the U.S. Congress.

Ronald F. Ferguson is Senior Lecturer in Education and Public Policy at the Harvard Graduate School of Education and the Harvard Kennedy School and an economist and Senior Research Associate at the Malcolm Wiener Center for Social Policy. His most recent book is *Toward Excellence with Equity: An Emerging Vision for Closing the Achievement Gap.* He is the creator of the Tripod Project for School Improvement, the faculty Co-chair and Director of the Achievement Gap Initiative at Harvard University, and the faculty Codirector of the Pathways to Prosperity project at the Harvard Graduate School of Education.

Nancy Hoffman is a Vice President and Senior Advisor at Jobs for the Future (JFF) and consults for the education policy unit of the Organization for Economic Cooperation and Development (OECD). She and Joel Vargas (with Andrea Venezia and Marc Miller) recently published the edited volume *Minding the Gap: Why Integrating High School with College Makes Sense and How to Do It.* She serves on the Massachusetts Board of Higher Education and the board of the Feminist Press.

Harry J. Holzer is a Professor of Public Policy at Georgetown University and an Institute Fellow at the Urban Institute in Washington, D.C. He is a Senior Affiliate of the National Poverty Center at the University of Michigan, a Research Affiliate of the Institute for Research on Poverty at the University of Wisconsin-Madison, and a Nonresident Senior Fellow with the Brookings Metropolitan Policy Program.

Jennifer McMaken is an Institute for Education Sciences (IES) Pre-Doctoral Fellow and Ph.D. student at the University of Pennsylvania. Her primary research includes design and analysis of an IES-funded center on learning and cognition and a mixed-methods study of the effects of teacher induction practices. Previously, she taught English in Japan and worked as a researcher at Public/Private Ventures.

Lisa Merrill is an Institute of Education Sciences (IES) Pre-Doctoral Fellow and Ph.D. student in education policy at the University of Pennsylvania. She is interested in organizational theory, knowledge management, the politics of education policy, and mixed-methods research. Previously she taught eighth-grade math in Brooklyn, New York, where she served as her school's union chapter leader and worked with local politicians and interest groups to improve the New York City schools.

Bridget N. O'Connor is Professor of Higher Education and Business Education at the Steinhardt School of Culture, Education, and Human Development at New York University. She is a co-editor of *The Sage Handbook of Workplace Learning* and co-author of two college-level textbooks: *End-user Information Systems: Implementing Individual and Group Technologies* and *Learning at Work*.

Laura W. Perna is Professor at the Graduate School of Education at the University of Pennsylvania. She is currently serving as Project Director for the IES-Sponsored Pre-Doctoral Training Program in Interdisciplinary Methods for Field-Based Research in Education at the University of Pennsylvania and Vice President of the Postsecondary Education Division of the American Education Research Association. She recently published the edited volume *Understanding the Working College Student: New Research and Its Implications for Policy and Practice*.

Lashawn Richburg-Hayes is Deputy Director, Young Adults and Postsecondary Education Policy Area at MDRC. Her current research focuses on measuring effects of new forms of financial aid, non-experimental methods of data analysis, and applications of behavioral economics to social policy for low-income individuals.

Samuel H. Rikoon is an Institute of Education Sciences (IES) Pre-Doctoral Fellow and Ph.D. candidate in quantitative methods at the University of Pennsylvania Graduate School of Education. His current work focuses on the psychometric analysis of early childhood learning behaviors and the development of these behaviors across the transition from prekindergarten to school.

Alan Ruby is an independent education policy consultant and Senior Lecturer in the Graduate School of Education at the University of Pennsylvania. He is currently adviser to the President of Kazakhstan's administration on the creation of a network of twenty schools for gifted and talented mathematics and science students and an internationally recognized university. He also consults to the World Bank on benchmarking education systems and on student and labor mobility in the Middle East and North Africa.

Nicole Smith is a Research Professor and Senior Economist at the Georgetown University Center on Education and the Workforce, where she leads the Center's econometric and methodological work. She has developed a framework for restructuring long-term occupational and educational projections, which forms the underlying methodology for a report that projects education demand for occupations in the U.S. economy through 2020.

Jeff Strohl is the Director of Research at the Georgetown University Center on Education and the Workforce, where he continues his long involvement in the analysis of education and labor market outcomes and policy. He leads the Center's research investigating the supply and demand of education and how education enhances career opportunities for today's workforce.

William G. Tierney is Director of the Pullias Center for Higher Education, University Professor and Wilbur-Kieffer Professor of Higher Education at the Rossier School of Education at the University of Southern California. He served as President of the Association for the Study of Higher Education and currently is President of the American Educational Research Association. He recently received funding to build an interactive game that will help low-income youth learn how to apply for college. He has written (with Guilbert Hentschke) *New Players, Different Game: Understanding the Rise of For-Profit Higher Education.*

Laura Wolf-Powers is Assistant Professor in the graduate City and Regional Planning program in the School of Design, University of Pennsylvania. Her work has been published in *Journal of the American Planning Association, Journal of Planning Education and Research, Economic Development Quarterly,* and several edited books on economic and workforce development. She received the School of Design's G. Holmes Perkins Award for Distinguished Teaching in 2011.

INDEX

Page numbers in italics represent tables and figures.

Abt Associates, 231

ACT (2011), 271–72

Adorno, Theodor W., 118

after-school job placements, *60*

Alfonso, Mariana, 131

Alignment Nashville, 210–11, 212–13, 218

American Association of University Professors, 162

American Federation of Teachers (AFT), 149

American Recovery and Reinvestment Act (2009), 9

ANCOVA approach, 46

Andersson, Fredrik, 232, 254

Andreason, Stuart, 14, 27, 224–44, 251, 262, 264, 270, 284n6. *See also* urban economic development strategies

Annie E. Casey Foundation, 237

Apollo Group, 164

apprenticeships, 21, *60*, 89

Armijo, Michael, 13, 177–202. *See also* career pathways programs (future research strategies)

Arum, Richard, 122

associate's degrees. *See* community college occupational degrees

Association for Career and Technical Education, 69–70

Association of American Colleges and Universities, 162

Autor, David, 247

Baby Boomers and the labor market, 247, 283n5

Bailey, Thomas R., 12–13, 59, 80, 121–48, 131, 260, 261, 264, 267. *See also* community college occupational degrees

Baltimore, Maryland, 5, 7, 225

Barghaus, Katherine M., 11, 37–56, 274. *See also* workforce readiness (assessing and measuring)

Bartik, Timothy, 240–41, 282n12

Bednarzik, Robert, 232

Belfield, Clive R., 12–13, 80, 121–48, 260, 261, 264, 267. *See also* community college occupational degrees

Bennett, Neville, 40–42, 45

Biotech Human Capital Project (Delaware Valley Region initiative), 234–35

BioWork program (North Carolina community colleges), 236

Bloom, Dan, *182*

Bobbitt, John Franklin, 23

Borkoski, Carey, 131

Bradlow, Eric T., 11, 37–56. *See also* workforce readiness (assessing and measuring)

Bridges to Work (BtW), 256

Brookings Institution, 3

Brooklyn Networks, 235–36

Burghardt, John, *182*

Bush administration (George W. Bush), 164

Business-Higher Education Forum (2011), 2

Business Higher Education Round Table (B-HERT 2002), 42–45

Business Roundtable Commission, 2

California: for-profit colleges and universities (FPCUs), 154–57, 158–59, 160, 164; percentage of civilians participating in workforce by level of education, *154*; studies projecting shortfalls in educated

California (continued)
  workers, 155–57, *156*; workforce
  projections for various education levels
  (in 2025), *155*
California State University systems, 159
California Workforce Advisory Board, *156*
Campbell, Donald, 190
career academies, 59–61, *60*, 70, 71, 81,
  88–89, 180–85, *181*, 251, 253, 262, 284n14;
  "Alignment Nashville," 210–11, 212–13,
  217–18; and high school dropout rates, 70,
  251, 284n10
career and technical education (CTE), 12,
  57–72, 75–92, 248; building blocks
  characterizing best practices today,
  91–92; certification and licensure
  requirements for completion, 89; community colleges, 81, 82–84, 91; debates about
  tracking, 85–86, 117, 248, 265; demands
  of the new "knowledge economy," 75–76;
  and employers, 91; employment and
  earnings gains from participation in,
  81–82; high schools, 79–82; and
  indicators of youth status in the labor
  market, 12, 76–79; internships, 59, *60*, 81,
  87–88; measurements of learning, 63–66;
  and national education policy, 84–87;
  and national philanthropies, 90, 237;
  persistent challenges faced, 81–82, 83–84,
  248; political obstacles to developing, 117;
  promising practices and initiatives,
  58–61, *60*, 88–90; and socioeconomics/
  social justice issues, 86; students' reasons
  for taking CTE coursework, 49; and
  traditional vocational education, 57–58,
  71, 80, 85–86, 88; and vocational
  education and training (VET) systems,
  75, 76, 78, 79, 272–73; work-based
  learning, 57–72, 87–88. *See also*
  community college occupational degrees;
  work-based learning (WBL) initiatives
career education initiatives, *60*
career fairs, *60*
career pathways programs: and "academics
  in action," 39; career academies, 59–61,
  70, 71, 81, 88–89, 180–85, 210–11, 217–18,
  251, 253, 262, 284n14; comparing
  traditional education outcomes with
  Pathway Educational (PE) methods,
  45–47, 49; defining, 178–79; Job Corps,

182, 185–87, 262; JOBSTART, *182*, 186,
  187; "multiple pathways" approaches, 14,
  47–48, 53, 262; National Guard Youth
  ChalleNGe, *182*, 185–87, 251, 262; new
  initiatives in formative stages, 188–89;
  Sectoral Employment Impact study, *184*,
  187–88; and shortcomings of current
  workforce training, 177–78, 249–50;
  Washington State's I-BEST, 90, *183*, 185,
  251, 262; and workforce readiness, 39,
  45–49, 53; Youth Build, 186; Youth Corps,
  184, 185–86, 262. *See also* career pathways
  programs (future research strategies);
  Pathways to Prosperity programs
career pathways programs (future research
  strategies), 13, 39, 45–49, 53, 124, 145,
  177–202; causal interpretations, 189–90;
  and driver diagrams, 191–92, *192*, 201,
  280n7; evaluation design ideas/tools to
  further increase knowledge of, 189–99;
  and implementation fidelity, 196–97;
  intended intervention strength and
  planned treatment contrast, 194–96; the
  intervention, 13, 191–92; logic models
  illustrating theory of change underlying
  interventions, 192–94, *193*, 201; mechanisms believed to generate outcomes, 13,
  192–94; methodology issues, 189–90,
  280n6, 280n9; offered strength tool/
  protocol, 197–99, *198*, 201; program
  implementation, 196–99; quasi-
  experimental methods (propensity
  score matching techniques), 190,
  279n5; randomized controlled trials
  (RCTs), 48–50, 189–90; realized strength
  tool/protocol, 199, *200*, 201, 280n14;
  strength tools or protocols, 194–96,
  195, 197–99, 201; summary of evidence,
  179–89, *181–84*, 279n1
Carnegie Foundation for the Advancement
  of Teaching, 280n7
Carnevale, Anthony P., 1, 5, 12, 29–30, 83,
  93–120, 135, 177–78, 203, 237, 260, 261,
  264, 267, 269. *See also* postsecondary
  education and economic opportunity
Carré, Clive, 40–42, 45
Cave, George, *182*
Center for Economic Opportunity, 188
certificates. *See* vocational certificates
charter schools, 256

Chertavian, Gerald, 67
Cho, Sung Woo, *183*
Choice Neighborhoods grants, 255
Cigarran, Tom, 210
cities. *See* metropolitan labor markets; urban economic development strategies
City University of New York (CUNY), 89
Classification of Instructional Programs (CIP), 126
Clinton administration: Hope VI project, 255; welfare reform legislation, 230
college admissions process: Bush administration and "safe harbors" (loopholes), 164; federal guidelines and legislation monitoring, 163–64; for-profit colleges and universities, 163–65, 169–70; and low-income students, 94–95
College and Career Transitions Initiative, 179
The College Board, 94–95, 167
"college for all" idea, 13–14, 85, 204, 223, 263
Colorado for-profit colleges and universities (FPCUs), 164
Committee on Community-Level Programs for Youth (2002), 205–6
Common Core State Standards, 55
community college occupational degrees (associate's degrees and certificates), 12–13, 82–84, 121–48; analysis using 2008 SIPP data, 13, 123, 137–44; certificate programs, 83–84, 103, 126–36, 138–40, 276n3; credentials conferred/awarded, 83–84, 126–30, *127–30*; demand-side issues, 134–35; demography issues, 137, 142; and dichotomy between occupational and academic education, 122, 123–26, 144; diversion effect of, 133, 278n7; earnings (returns), 130–44, *131*, *139*, *141–43*, 145, *147*, *148*; earnings by field of study, 140–42, *141–43*; and general labor market issues, 134–37; graduation rates/completion rates, 83–84, 132–34, 136, 250, 269–70, 278n8; high-demand fields and issue of prerequisites, 83; lessons for policy from the evidence, 144–45; methodological/conceptual issues in estimating the benefits of career education, 132–34; metropolitan issues, 136–37, 142–44; and skills, behaviors, and cognitive requirements expected for an occupation, 135,

278n9; so-called sheepskin effect, 133–34, 250; supply-side issues, 135–36; trend in associate's degrees, bachelor's degrees, and certificates, 126–27. *See also* community colleges; postsecondary education and economic opportunity
community colleges: academic education and career-focused education, 123–30, 144; compared to for-profit colleges and universities, 150–51; CTE in, 81, 82–84, 91; earnings (returns) to community college courses, 130–37, *131*, 145, 278nn4–5; and the Great Recession, 122, 146–47; identifying the "typical" student, 132–33; incentives to place students in jobs, 257–58; popularity of, 85; and remediation, 83, 126; and sectoral training programs, 236; "terminal" programs trend (late 1990s), 124. *See also* community college occupational degrees
competency-based education, 11, 19–36, 268; apparent simplicity of, 25; criticisms of, 25; defining "competence" and capabilities, 22–23, 25–26; and the demand for job skills, 27–32, 268; generic quality of competencies, 11, 26–27; history of, 23–26; and personal reflections on childhood in rural Australia, 20–21; and policy debates in general education (1970s and 1980s), 24–25; public policy and the school-to-work transition, 21–27, 35–36; and "scientific" curriculum designers, 23–24, 34, 35; scope and sequence curricula, 23–24; and study abroad, 11, 32–34; what we know/need to know about the school-to-work transition, 35–36; why additional schooling increases income, 28–29
"Completion by Design" initiative, 149
completion rates, 178, 249–50, 269–70; community college occupational degrees and certificates, 83–84, 132–34, 136, 250, 269–70, 278n8; determining the generic skills necessary for degree completion, 44–45; for-profit colleges and universities, 136, 149, 158, 170, 265, 269–70, 279n11; provision of supports and structures to ensure successful completion, 269–70; and racial/ethnic minorities, 269

ConnectEd: The California Center for
  College and Career, 212, 216–17; ToolKit,
  216–17
Cook, Thomas, 190
cooperative education initiatives, *60*
Corbett, Tom, 9
Corporation for National and Community
  Service, 188–89
Council of Economic Advisers (CEA), 135,
  278n10
counseling, career, 266–67; and admissions,
  165; and career pathways programs, 186,
  207; and CTE programs, 92, 256; and
  for-profit colleges, 172
Cristo Rey, 89
CTE. *See* career and technical education
Cumulative Promotion Index (CPI), 7,
  275n2
Cyra/Com (Tucson-based organization), 68

Danson, Mike, 28
Davis, Greg, 149
D.C. Opportunity Scholarship program, 256
debt burdens and loan default rates, 149,
  165–68, 171–72, 265–66, 270
Degrees for What Jobs? (National Governors
  Association), 1–2
Deil-Amen, Regina, 136
Detroit, Michigan: educational attainment
  and unemployment rates, 4–5; high
  school graduate rates, 7, 255
Dewey, John, 63, 86, 125
Dillon, Colleen, *182*
DirectEmployers, 257
Downs, Whitney, 217–18
Dunne, Elisabeth, 40–42, 45

Early College High Schools (ECHS), 90
Earned Income Tax Credit (1993), 230
earnings. *See* postsecondary education and
  economic opportunity
Economic Mobility Corporation (EMC),
  70–71
Editorial Projects in Education Research
  Center, 7
educational providers' roles in preparing
  students for work. *See* career and
  technical education; career pathways
  programs; community college occupational degrees; for-profit colleges and

universities; postsecondary education
  and economic opportunity
Elementary and Secondary Education Act
  (ESEA), 258, 271
employers: comments on types of training
  for workforce entrants, 68; developing
  mechanisms that support collaboration
  with education providers, 268–69;
  disjunction between students' perceptions of skills and preferences of, 34;
  employer-provided training programs,
  103, *104*, 284n8; engaging in community
  college CTE programs, 91; reluctance to
  invest in training, 249, 284n8; Year Up
  program linking community colleges
  and, 67–68, 70–71, 89
employment initiatives and work-based
  learning (WBL) initiatives (high school
  level), *60*
Europe. *See* Organization for Economic
  Cooperation and Development (OECD)
  countries
European Economy Community, 28
European Higher Education Zone, 28

Farrington, Camille A., 204
Federal Reserve Bank of Philadelphia, 227
Ferguson, Ronald F., 13–14, 117, 203–23,
  262, 264, 268–69. *See also* Pathways to
  Prosperity programs
Feser, Edward, 282n7
Fish, Stanley, 58
Florida College System (FCS) colleges,
  275n2
Florida data on earnings for degree holders,
  83, 275n2
Florida's independent colleges and
  universities (ICUF), 275n2
Florida State University System (SUS), 83,
  275n2
Ford Foundation: Bridges to Opportunity
  Initiative, 179; Manpower Demonstration
  Research Corporation (MDRC), 70; and
  sector partnership programs, 237
for-profit colleges and universities (FPCUs),
  13, 117, 149–74, 265–66; accreditation,
  161–62; admissions criteria, 163–65,
  169–70; advertising, 160–61, 164;
  awarding of certificates, 160; California
  case, 154–60, 164; completion rates and

completion agendas, 136, 149, 158, 170, 265, 269–70, 279n11; criticisms of, 149–50, 152, 162–69; curriculum designers and teaching, 161; debt burdens and loan default rates, 149, 165–68, 171–72, 265–66, 270; differences from traditional colleges and universities (TCUs), 160–67; enrollment increases, 160; faculty and administration, 161; and gainful employment, 168–69, 172; governance structures, 162, 172–73; learning outcomes, 161; low-income and "at-risk" students, 8–9, 117, 160, 166; and national efforts calling for college access and attainment, 157–58; and non-profit community colleges, 150–51; "nontraditional students," 117, 159–60, 166, 277n16; and Obama administration, 149, 156, 157; and projected state shortfalls in educated workers, 155–57, 156; regulatory frameworks, 162, 172–73; and remediation, 171; setting the stage for 2020–25, 151–59; and U.S. tertiary education participation indicators and rankings among OECD nations, 157, 158; what we need to know (six topics for a research agenda), 169–73; and workforce projections for various education levels, 155

Gates Foundation, 70, 149, 157
Georgetown Center on Education and the Workforce, 107–8, 155, 156
Goldin, Claudia, 31–32, 121, 224
Goldstein, Dana, 86
graduation rates (high school): urban centers, 7, 275nn1–2; urban schools, 7; and work-based learning (WBL) initiatives, 69–70. See also completion rates; high school dropout rates
grants, federal, 253, 258–59, 271
Great Recession, 4, 9, 93, 98–100, 100, 105–6, 122, 146–47, 177

Harkin, Tom, 162
Harlem Children's Zone, 256
Harvard Graduate School of Education, Pathways to Prosperity report (2011), 86–87, 204–5, 220
Hawkins, David, 164–65

Head Start, 231
Heldrich Center, 85
Help Wanted: Projections of Jobs and Education Requirements through 2018 (Carnevale, Smith, and Strohl), 1
Hess, Frederick M., 217–18
Higher Education Act, 161–62, 163, 168
high school dropout rates, 77–78, 249; and career academies, 70, 251, 284n10; and enrollment in CTE courses, 49; and household income (1970/2007), 96–97, 97; U.S. rates/OECD rates, 78
high schools: CTE programs and courses, 79–82; work-based learning (WBL) initiatives, 57–72. See also vocational education, traditional; work-based learning (WBL) initiatives
High Schools That Work (HSTW), 88–89
Hitachi Foundation, 237
Hoachlander, Gary, 47–49
Hoffman, Nancy, 12, 75–92, 248, 251, 261–62, 264, 268, 270–71. See also career and technical education
Holzer, Harry J., 14, 27, 232, 245–60, 266, 268, 270–71. See also metropolitan labor markets
Hope VI project, 255
Hughes, Katherine L., 59
human capital theory, 28–29, 108

I-BEST (Integrated Basic Education and Skills Training), 90, 183, 185, 251, 262
immigrants and the labor market, 247, 283n5
Ingram, Orrin, 210
Innovative Strategies for Increasing Self-Sufficiency (ISIS) project (U.S. Department of Health and Human Services), 188
Institute of Educational Sciences (IES), 51–52
institutional practice and public policy: implications for future research, 271–74; recommendations for institutional leaders and public policymakers, 260–74. See also career pathways programs (future research strategies); metropolitan labor markets; Pathways to Prosperity programs; urban economic development strategies and school-to-work policies

Integrated Postsecondary Data System (IPEDS), 132

internships (paid/non-paid), 59, *60*, 81, 87–88

ISIS (Innovative Strategies for Increasing Self-Sufficiency) project, 188

Jacobson, Louis, 132, 252

Jarvis, Peter, 63

Jastrzab, JoAnn, *184*

Jefferson, Thomas, 203

Jenkins, Davis, *183*

Jewish Vocational Service (Boston), 236

Job Central, 257

Job Corps, *182*, 185–87, 262

Job Opportunity Investment Network (JOIN) (Philadelphia), 236, 282n11

JOBSTART, *182*, 186, 187

Job Training Partnership Act evaluation (1995), 231

Kania, John, 217, 219

Katz, Lawrence F., 31–32, 121, 224

Kemple, James, *181*

Kienzl, Gregory S., 131, *183*

KIPP schools, 256

Kirkpatrick, Donald, 61

Klein, Joel, 256

Kleiner, Morris M., 134

Knight Foundation, 237

Konkola, Riitta, 65

Krahn, Harvey, 34

Kramer, Mark, 217, 219

Krueger, Alan B., 134

Lacey, Alan T., 29

LaLonde, Robert J., 132, 252

Lane, Julia, 232, 254

Learn and Earn schools (North Carolina), 90

Learning a Living (1992 Department of Labor report), 24

learning outcomes and work-based learning initiatives, 63–66; definitions of learning, 63; portfolio development, 65–66; standardized testing, 63–65

Learning to Labor (Willis), 36

Leef, George, 153–54

Lehmann, Wolfgang, 34

Leonhardt, David, 233

Levin, Henry M., 29, 31

Life Science Career Alliance, 234–35

Lin, Jeffrey, 227

Linked Learning Alliance, 212

Linked Learning program, 88, 89, 212, 215, 216

Lipset, Seymour Martin, 118

Local Employment Dynamics (LED) data, 286n25

Lowe, Graham S., 34

low-income housing, 255

low-income young people: bachelor's degree attainment rates, 8; debt burdens, 166; and for-profit colleges and universities, 8–9, 117, 160, 166; internships (paid/unpaid), 87–88; and merit-based opportunity, 94; Pathways to Prosperity programs, 14, 206, 223; rates of postsecondary enrollment, 8–9; and selective college admissions process, 94–95; and shortcomings of educational system and workforce training, 178; unfair access to postsecondary education, 94–95, 276n2

Lumina Foundation, 10, 153, *156*, 157

Maguire, Sheila, *184*

Malizia, Emil, 282n7

Manpower Demonstration Research Corporation (MDRC), 70, 88

Marcotte, Dave E., 131

Marxian analyses of higher education, 153

Massachusetts Workforce Investment Board (MWIB), *Preparing Youth for Work and Learning in the 21st Century Economy* (2010), 215

Maxwell, Nan, *181*, 185

Mayor's Fund to Advance NYC, 188

McConnell, Sheena, *182*

McMaken, Jennifer, 11, 37–56. *See also* workforce readiness (assessing and measuring)

mentoring programs, *60*, 67–68, 70–71, 89

Merchant, Kathy, 221

Merrill, Lisa, 13, 177–202. *See also* career pathways programs (future research strategies)

metropolitan labor markets, 2–10, 14–15, 245–59; availability of higher educational opportunities, 7–8; challenges that limit preparation of young adults, 248–50; creating effective education and workforce policies for, 14–15, 245–59;

educational attainment and per capita income in U.S. cities, 225–27, *227*; educational attainment and poor metropolitan competitiveness, 224–28; educational attainment and poverty measures in U.S. cities, 225, *226*; federal grants to encourage system-building, 253, 258–59, 271; formation of area-wide education and labor market institutions, 258; high school graduation rates, 7, 275nn1–2; legislative vehicles to link residents with education and job opportunities, 258, 270–71; mismatches between educational attainment and educational requirements of jobs, 2–6, *3*, 260–61, 271–72; necessity of having good data about job market and opportunities, 257; necessity of having labor market intermediaries, 257, 286n26; and non-economic benefits of educational attainment, 5–6; overview/future of the U.S. labor market, 246–47, 283nn2–5; policies designed to address metropolitan issues and effects, 255–57; recommendations, 258–59; residential segregation and uneven job distribution, 254–55; "skilled anchors" metro areas, 3–4; unemployment rates, 4–5; urban economic development strategies, 224–44, 282n7; what is effective at improving skills and earnings, 252–53; workforce preparation for inner-city residents, 256–57. *See also* urban economic development strategies and school-to-work policies

Metropolitan Nashville Public Schools (MNPS), 210–11

Millenky, Megan, *182*

Million Voice Project, 62

Minnesota state reductions in higher education budget, 159

Modar, Amanda, 164–65

Moore, David T., 59

Mortenson, Tom, 8

Moving to Opportunity (MTO) demonstration projects, 255, 285n19

Nashville Chamber of Commerce, 210, 217–18

National Academy Foundation (NAF), 70

National Alliance of Business, 24

National and Community Service Act (1990), 186

National Assessment of Educational Progress (NAEP), 40

National Association of College Admission Counseling (NACAC), 165

National Association of State Budget Officers, 9

National Association of State Workforce Agencies (NASWA), 257

National Career Pathways Network, 179

National Center for Education Statistics (NCES), 69, 132

National Commission on Excellence in Education, 24

National Commission on the High School Senior Year (2001), 263

National Council of Teachers of English in the United States, 24

National Education Longitudinal Study, 49

National Governors Association, 1–2

National Guard Youth ChalleNGe, *182*, 185–86, 187, 251, 262

National Job Corps Study, 186

National Research Center for Career and Vocational Education (NRCCVE), 64–65

A Nation at Risk (1983), 24

"NEET" (neither job seekers nor in education or training), 77

New York Times, 168

No Child Left Behind (NCLB), 40

"non-traditional students," 117, 159–60, 166, 277n16

nursing degrees (A.D.N./B.S.N.), 145

Obama administration, 5–6; Choice Neighborhoods grants, 255; community college "Completion by Design" initiative, 149; and for-profit colleges and universities, 149, *156*, 157; studies projecting shortfalls in California's educated workers, *156*; Workforce Innovation Fund, 238–39, 244, 282n5

O'Connor, Bridget N., 11–12, 57–72, 87, 261–62, 264, 268, 272. *See also* work-based learning (WBL) initiatives

Office of Planning, Research and Evaluation in the Administration for Children and Families (U.S. Department of Health and Human Services), 188

Ohio Board of Regents, 188
Ohio Department of Education, 188
One-Stop Centers, 229, 230, 249, 257
Opening Doors, 251
Oregon State Legislature study of small
    learning communities and school
    dropout rates, 70
Organization for Economic Cooperation
    and Development (OECD) countries:
    approaches to competency-based
    education, 25; comparing U.S. tertiary
    education participation indicators and
    rankings among, 157, *158*; indicators of
    youth status in the labor market, 12,
    77, 78; PISA assessment of academic
    achievement, 78; secondary education
    completion rates, 78; youth unemploy-
    ment rates, 77
Orozco, Edith Aimee, "A Comparison of
    Career Technical Education" (2010),
    45–47, 49

Partnership for 21st Century Skills, 10
Pathways to Prosperity programs, 13–14,
    203–23; accountability, 218; clear themes
    that provide focus, 213–15; commitments
    to low-income, minorities, and underpre-
    pared young people, 14, 206, 223;
    community involvement and resources,
    221–22; data-driven decision making and
    transparency, 219–20; "engines," 212–13,
    222; grade-level timeline for a sequence
    of experiences, 206–7, 262; instigators,
    211–12, 222; institutionalized data
    gathering, 219; key elements of a regional
    pathways system, 207–9, *208*; leadership,
    210–11, 222; organizational structures,
    217–18; as part of a larger social
    movement, 206; and the *Pathways to
    Prosperity* report, 86–87, 204–5; and
    private sector, 205–9, 212–13, 222–23; and
    problems with the "college for all" idea,
    204, 223; and public sector systems,
    207–9; social contract defining public/
    private sector roles and responsibilities,
    205–9, 222–23; streamlined and coherent
    "curriculum," 216–17; support from
    businesses and associated intermediaries,
    208–9; system developers, 208; system
    regulators and monitors, 208; ten

strategic threads for developing, 209–22,
    262; and the underdeveloped school-to-
    career pathway system, 203–4, 222.
    See also career pathways programs
Pathways to Prosperity report (Symonds,
    Schwartz, and Ferguson), 86–87, 204–5,
    220
Pearson Foundation, 62
Pell Institute for the Study of Opportunity
    in Education (2011 report), 8
PENCIL (Nashville business organization),
    218
Pennsylvania's Department of Labor, 234
Pennsylvania Self-Sufficiency Standard, 225
Perkins Act, 258
Perna, Laura W., 1–15, 27, 91, 260–74
Per Scholas, 230, 235–36, 282n9
Person, Ann E., 136
Personal Responsibility and Work
    Opportunity Reconciliation Act
    (PRWORA), 230
Philadelphia, Pennsylvania: college
    enrollment and completion rates, 8;
    colleges and universities, 8; educational
    attainment and poverty rates, 225,
    226, 281n1; educational attainment vs.
    educational requirements of jobs, 2–3, *3*;
    Job Opportunity Investment Network
    (JOIN), 236, 282n11
Philadelphia Workforce Investment Board,
    225
philanthropies and career preparation
    programs, 90, 237
postsecondary education and economic
    opportunity, 5, 12, 93–120; calculating
    the present value of degrees and
    hypothetical cost-benefit analysis, 98,
    276n6, 277n7; consensus view of link
    between, 93–96; distribution of jobs by
    education level, *101*; distribution of
    postsecondary programs, 103, *104*;
    earnings, 5, 12, 96–101, 110–12, 114, 115,
    130–44; earnings by college major/field of
    study, 115, *116*, 140–42, *141*, *142*, *143*;
    earnings by education level within
    occupations, *114*; earnings overlap by
    degree level, 110–11, *111*; economic costs
    of attending college, 98–99, 277nn8–9;
    employer-provided training programs,
    103, *104*; failure to produce postsecondary

degrees at steady rate, 106–8; increasing demand for postsecondary education, *101*, 101–2; the knowledge economy and democratization of higher education, 115–17; lifetime earnings from college, 98–101, *99*, 119; majors matter, 115, *116*; middle-class earnings, 5, 96–97, *97*, 119; occupation matters, 112–15, *114*; relative wages/annual salaries by education level, 108–9, *109*; and skill-biased technological change, 105; STEM occupations, 90, 95, 113–15, *114*; supply/demand for skilled workers relative to 1970 conditions, *107*; technology skills driving demand, 95–96, 103–6, 119; and unemployment rates, 4–5, 99–100, *100*, 277n10; unfair access to education for low-income students, 94–95, 276n2; the "wage premium," 107, 108–9. *See also* community college occupational degrees

Preparing Youth for Work and Learning in the 21st Century Economy (Massachusetts Workforce Investment Board, 2010), 215

private sector and pathways programs: as powerful "engines," 212–13, 222; social contract that defines roles and responsibilities, 205–9, 222–23; as system developers, 208

profit-making institutions in higher education. *See* for-profit colleges and universities

Project Lead the Way, 88

Public Policy Institute of California, 154, *156*

Public/Private Ventures, 236, 282n9

Quaglia Institute, 62

racial/ethnic minorities: completion rates, 269; educational attainment by, 8–9, 157, 269; impact of career pathways programs for, 186; mismatches of educational qualifications and educational requirements of jobs, 6; pathways programs and commitments to, 14, 206, 223; shortcomings of current workforce training, 178; urban populations, 6

remediation: and community colleges, 83, 126; and for-profit colleges and universities, 171; and vocational certificates, 126

residential segregation and uneven job distribution, 254–55

Rhee, Michelle, 256

Richburg-Hayes, Lashawn, 13, 177–202, 274. *See also* career pathways programs (future research strategies)

Rikoon, Samuel H., 11, 37–56. *See also* workforce readiness (assessing and measuring)

Roksa, Josipa, 122

Rose, Mike, 86–87

Rosenbaum, James, 136

Rubin, Victor, *181*, 185

Ruby, Alan, 11, 19–36, 261, 266, 268. *See also* competency-based education

Schochet, Peter, *182*

Schone, P., 31–32

school vouchers and "school choice," 256

scientific management and "scientific" curriculum designers, 23–24, 34, 35

second chance workforce system. *See* urban economic development strategies and school-to-work policies

Secretary of the U.S. Department of Education's Commission on Achieving Necessary Skills (SCANS), 278n1

Sectoral Employment Impact study (a career pathways program), *184*, 187–88

sector partnership model, 233–40, 251, 262, 282n8; community college programs, 236; examples, 234–37; and philanthropies, 237

Select Greater Philadelphia, 8

Shadish, William, 190

Shaw, Jane, 153–54

sheepskin effect, 133–34, 250

"signaling," 28–29

SIPP (Survey of Income and Program Participation) data on returns to occupational programs (2008), 13, 123, 137–44

skill-biased technological change, 105

skills, 2, 37–49, 52–54, 267–68; challenges that limit ability to prepare young adults, 248–50; core skill acquisition/generic skill acquisition, 40–41; defining generic skills, 42–43; generic skills and specific skills, 11, 26–27, 38–45, 267–68; generic skills necessary for key levels of

skills (continued)
  educational attainment, 44–45; high
  school work-based learning and skill
  development initiatives, *60*; measurement
  of generic skills, 41–44; technology,
  31–32, 95–96, 103–6, 119, 121–22; urban
  economic development strategies and
  training for low-skilled workers, 232–33;
  what shapes the demand for, 27–32; and
  workforce readiness, 37–49, 52–54,
  271–73. *See also* competency-based
  education; workforce readiness (assessing
  and measuring)
Small, Margaret H., 204
Small Learning Communities (SLC)
  program, U.S. Department of Education,
  210
Small Schools of Choice (New York City),
  250–51
Smith, Nicole, 1, 5, 12, 29–30, 83, 93–120,
  135, 261, 264, 267. *See also* postsecondary
  education and economic opportunity
Snipes, Jason, *181*
Society for Human Resource Management, 2
Southern Regional Education Board, 88–89,
  188
Springboard Project, 2
The State of Metropolitan America,
  Brookings Institution's 2010 report, 3–4
state reductions in higher education
  budgets, 9, 159
Statewide Longitudinal Data Systems
  (SLDS), 51–52, 53; using data from (for
  tracking students' progress/eventual
  engagement in workforce), 51–52, 53,
  54, 55
Stoll, Michael, 254
Strive (Cincinnati and northern Kentucky),
  211–14, 217, 218, 219, 221; and Student
  Success Networks (SSNs), 217
Strohl, Jeff, 1, 5, 12, 29–30, 83, 93–120, 135,
  261, 264, 267. *See also* postsecondary
  education and economic opportunity
student loans, grants, and financial aid,
  166–67, 171–72, 265–66, 270
study abroad, economic value of, 11, 32–34
Sullivan, Daniel, 132, 252

Taylor, Frederick Winslow, 23
Teach for America, 124–25

technology jobs, 103–6
technology skills, 31–32, 95–96, 103–6, 119,
  121–22
Theobald, Paul, 61
Theodos, Brett, 232
Thresher, Alden, 94–95
Tierney, William G., 8–9, 13, 85, 117,
  149–74, 264, 266. *See also* for-profit
  colleges and universities
tracking: and backlash against traditional
  vocational education, 57–58, 262; CTE
  and debates about, 85–86, 117, 248,
  265; development of mechanisms for
  participation in different education and
  career pathways without use of, 264–65;
  and secondary school organization in
  Australia of 1950s and early 1960s, 21
Turkheimer, Eric, 95

unemployment rates: for college graduates,
  by education level, 4–5, 99–100, *100*,
  277n10; for young adults and people of
  color, 4–5, 76–77, 88; youth in U.S. and
  OECD countries, 76–77, 88
University of California, 159
University of Cincinnati, 211
University of Phoenix, 164, 168
urban economic development strategies
  and school-to-work policies, 14, 224–44;
  aligning workforce policy with economic
  development policy, 238–43; converting
  second chance workforce development
  into joint effort between federal/state
  labor and education departments,
  238–39; government-funded second
  chance employment training and
  placement system for adults, 228–33,
  238–40; local and metropolitan economic
  development policy, 233–38, 282n7;
  making sector-based initiatives central,
  239–40; measures of human capital, *242*;
  Obama's Workforce Innovation Fund
  initiative, 238–39, 244, 282n5; sector
  partnership model, 233–40, 251, 262,
  282n8; shifting local economic development policy toward development of
  human capital, 240–43; training for
  low-skilled workers, 232–33; using
  economic incentives to maximize the
  hysteresis effect of workforce investment,

240–43, 282n12; and workforce investment programs under WIA rubric, 228–32, 237, 249, 251, 284n6. *See also* metropolitan labor markets

U.S. Bureau of Labor Statistics (BLS) projections, 29–30

U.S. Census Bureau: and Local Employment Dynamics (LED) data, 286n25; Longitudinal Employer Household Dynamics (LEHD) project, 283n1, 286n25; study of average lifetime earnings of a bachelor's degree holder (2002), 98

U.S. Department of Education: and for-profit colleges and universities (FCPUs), 162; Office of Vocational and Adult Education and WIA Title II, 228; rules regarding definition of gainful employment (for use by for-profit institutions), 168; Small Learning Communities (SLC) program, 210

U.S. Department of Health and Human Services, Innovative Strategies for Increasing Self-Sufficiency (ISIS) project, 188

U.S. Department of Labor: competitive grants to organizations linking education and labor market, 253, 258, 285n15; Employment and Training Administration and WIA Title I, 228; *Learning a Living* (1992 report), 24; Workforce Innovation in Regional Development (WIRED) Initiative, 234; Youth Opportunities program, 252, 256, 262

U.S. Government Accountability Office (GAO), 168

Vande Berg, Michael, 32–33

Vedder, Richard, 153–54

vocational certificates, 83–84, 103, 126–36, 138–40, 276n3; and associate's degrees, 133–34; completion rates, 83–84, 132–34, 136, 269–70, 278n8; conferred, 128–30, *130*; diversion effect of, 133, 278n7; and earnings (returns), 131–32, 138–40, *139*, *142*, *148*, 269, 278n5; flexibility and issue of value/quality of, 135–36; and for-profit colleges and universities (FPCUs), 160; popularity, 126; and remediation, 126. *See also* community college occupational degrees

vocational education, traditional, 57–58, 71, 80–81, 85–86, 88; CTE programs and vocational technical schools/centers, 81; and dichotomy between occupational and academic education, 123–24; and tracking into low-wage jobs, 57–58, 262; and vocational education and training (VET) systems, 76, 78, 79, 272–73. *See also* career and technical education

vocational education and training (VET) systems, 76, 78, 79, 272–73

Wagner-Peyser Act (1933), 228

Washington, D.C.'s Opportunity Scholarship program, 256

Washington State Board for Community and Technical Colleges' Integrated Basic Education and Skills Training (I-BEST), 90, *183*, 185, 251, 262

WBL. *See* work-based learning (WBL) initiatives

welfare reform legislation, 230

Westrich, Keith, 214–15

Willis, Paul, 36

Wisconsin Regional Training Partnership, 236

Wolf-Powers, Laura, 14, 27, 224–44, 251, 262, 264, 270, 284n6. *See also* urban economic development strategies and school-to-work policies

WorkAdvance, 188–89

work-based learning (WBL) initiatives (high school level), 57–72, 87–88; career awareness initiatives, *60*; employment (paid) initiatives, *60*; how school districts implement initiatives, 61; impact of (five domains), 61–71, 272; impact on behavior (outside the classroom), 66–69; initiatives, 58–61, *60*; labor market outcomes (earning power upon completion), 70–71; and learning (the actual learning taking place), 63–66; organizational results (graduation rates), 69–70; and problems with a one-size-fits-all curriculum, 58; reaction (students' satisfaction with programs), 62; similarities of successful programs, 72; skill development initiatives, *60*; socioeconomic status and students' school success, 57; and traditional vocational education, 57–58,

work-based learning (WBL) initiatives
(high school level) (continued)
71, 88; work-like experiences (non-paid),
60. See also career and technical
education
Workforce Innovation Fund, 238–39, 244,
282n5
Workforce Innovation in Regional
Development (WIRED) Initiative, 234
Workforce Investment Act of 1998 (WIA)
and workforce training programs,
228–32, 237, 249, 251, 258, 271, 281nn3–4;
"One-Stop Centers," 229, 230, 249, 257;
Title I (job development and training
programs), 228–30, 239, 284n7; Title II
(adult basic education and literacy
programs), 228; Title III (state-based
labor exchange services), 228; Title IV
(money to states for vocational rehabilitation of people with disabilities), 228;
Workforce Investment Boards, 230
workforce readiness (assessing and
measuring), 11, 37–56, 271–73; Bennett,
Dunne, and Carré (1999), 40–42, 45;
best practices for acquiring, 39, 45–49;
Business Higher Education Round Table
(B-HERT 2002), 42–45; curriculum
design to enhance, 52–53; data from the
Institute of Educational Sciences (IES)
and Statewide Longitudinal Data Systems
(SLDS), 51–52, 53, 54, 55; data wish list
(addressing the knowledge gaps), 49–54;
defining meaning of, 11, 38, 40–45,
271–73; determining the outcomes and
measures that indicate, 39–40, 53–54,
272–73; dual nature of "readiness," 38;
Hoachlander (2008), 47–49; and
improved measurement of lifelong
outcomes, 55–56; key issues, 38–40;

Orozco's comparison of traditional
education outcomes with Pathway
Educational (PE) methods, 45–47, 49; and
pathways programs, 39, 45–49, 53; to
"prepare and make ready," 37; recommendations for research, 54, 271–74; review of
four recent articles, 40–49; studying the
impact of readiness on outcomes, 39–40,
45–49, 272–73. *See also* competency-
based education
workforce readiness, defining success in,
271–73. *See also* competency-based
education; work-based learning (WBL);
workforce readiness (assessing and
measuring)
WorkKeys assessments, 272
Work Self-Efficacy Inventory (WS-Ei),
66–67
Wright, Benjamin, 29

Year Up, 67–68, 70–71, 89
Youth Build, 186
Youth Corps, *184*, 185–86, 262
Youth Opportunities program, 252, 256, 262
youth status in the labor market, 76–79;
academic achievement, 78; and characteristics shared by countries that are doing
better to support young people, 78–79;
high school dropout rates, 77–78, 249;
left-behind youth, 77; "NEET" (neither
job seekers nor in education or training),
77; poorly integrated new entrants, 77;
transition from school to labor market,
77, 275n1; unemployment rates, 4–5,
76–77, 88. *See also* low-income young
people

Zeidenberg, Matthew, *183*
Zimpher, Nancy L., 211

ACKNOWLEDGMENTS

This volume would not have been possible without the assistance and support of a number of organizations and individuals. Earlier versions of the chapters in this volume were first presented at a conference entitled "Preparing Today's Students for Tomorrow's Jobs: The Practice, Policy, and Research Issues," held at the University of Pennsylvania, May 25–26, 2011. This conference was sponsored by the University of Pennsylvania's Pre-Doctoral Training Program in Interdisciplinary Methods for Field-Based Research in Education, with funding from the U.S. Department of Education's Institute for Education Sciences (IES). Penn's Graduate School of Education (GSE) and Institute for Urban Research (IUR) collaborated in the organization of the conference.

Several individuals within each of these groups played particularly noteworthy roles. Laura Kitson, the administrative coordinator of the Pre-Doctoral Training Program at the time, invested essential attention into every logistical detail of the conference. Henry May, Senior Research Investigator at the Consortium for Policy Research in Education (CPRE) at Penn and Director of Research and Methodological Training for the IES-funded Pre-Doctoral Training Program, assisted with the conceptualization of the "research-reflection" chapters in the volume. Joni Finney, Practice Professor at GSE, assisted with the identification of potential chapter authors. Robert Zemsky, Professor at GSE and Chair of The Learning Alliance, provided useful feedback on an early conceptualization of the project. Tom Kecskemethy, former Assistant Dean at GSE, led efforts to communicate information about the conference. Andrew Porter, Dean and George and Diane Weiss Professor of Education at GSE, has provided critical support of the IES-funded Predoctoral Training Program in general and of this effort in particular. Rebecca Maynard, the original project director for the Predoctoral Training Program, gave me the opportunity to serve as the current project director while she is on leave to serve as Commissioner of the National Center for Education Evaluation and Regional Assistance, and put in place many of the pieces of the conference that led to this subsequent volume.

Susan Wachter, Codirector of Penn's Institute for Urban Research, was a terrific collaborator on the conference and offered many useful recommendations about potential chapter authors. Other IUR staff, particularly Amy Montgomery and Jon Stover, were particularly integral to the success of the conference. Finally, Cara Griffin from IUR provided invaluable assistance with the production of this volume. She not only provided a keen editorial eye to earlier drafts of this manuscript but also effectively kept the publication process on our aggressive schedule. I very much appreciate the assistance of all of these individuals.

Laura W. Perna